Lucy Aikin, Philip Hemery Le Breton

Memoirs, Miscellanies and Letters of the late Lucy Aikin

Including those addressed to the Rev. Dr. Channing 1826 to 1842

Lucy Aikin, Philip Hemery Le Breton

Memoirs, Miscellanies and Letters of the late Lucy Aikin
Including those addressed to the Rev. Dr. Channing 1826 to 1842

ISBN/EAN: 9783337136239

Printed in Europe, USA, Canada, Australia, Japan

Cover: Foto ©ninafisch / pixelio.de

More available books at **www.hansebooks.com**

MEMOIRS, MISCELLANIES

AND LETTERS

OF THE LATE

LUCY AIKIN:

INCLUDING

THOSE ADDRESSED TO THE REV. DR. CHANNING FROM 1826 TO 1842.

EDITED BY

PHILIP HEMERY LE BRETON

OF THE INNER TEMPLE.

LONDON:
LONGMAN, GREEN, LONGMAN, ROBERTS, & GREEN.
1864.

PREFACE.

The following pages comprise unpublished Essays and Memoirs written by the late Miss Aikin, and also some of her Letters : by far the larger part of these are addressed to the late Rev. Dr. Channing, with whom she corresponded for nearly twenty years. It is believed that, besides the value which belongs to these letters from their leading topics, the literature and politics of a stirring period interspersed with anecdotes of the writer's distinguished contemporaries, a peculiar interest will be found in many of them at the present crisis in the history of the United States.

A Memoir of Miss Aikin is added. Her inmost thoughts, convictions, and matured opinions on all important subjects, are so completely disclosed in her own writings in this volume as to render it unnecessary to present more than a brief record of the incidents of her life.

London: *October* 1864.

CONTENTS.

	PAGE
Memoir of Miss Aikin	ix
Memoir of Miss Benger	1
Recollections of Joanna Baillie	7
Old Times: a Dialogue	11
How Character is formed	21
On the Spirit of Aristocracy	29
Example and Precept	39
Envy and Pity	47
Sorrow and Anger	49
Doubt	51
Motives	54
Frankness	56
Tempters	57
Popular Fallacies	58
Words upon Words	61

LETTERS.

To Mrs. Aikin	81
,, Mrs. Barbauld	82
,, Dr. Aikin	85
,, Mrs. Barbauld	88
,, Mrs. Aikin	89
,, Dr. Aikin	93
,, Mr. Edmund Aikin	96
,, Dr. and Mrs. Aikin	115
,, Mr. E. Aikin	117
,, Her Niece	119

		PAGE
To Mrs. Taylor	. . . .	124
,, Mr. Taylor	. . . .	136
,, Mrs. Taylor	. . . . . .	138
,, Mrs. Mallet	. . . . .	149
,, Mr. and Mrs. Mallet	. . . . . .	150
,, Mr. Mallet	. . . . .	152
,, Mrs. Mallet	. . . . . .	153
,, Mr. and Mrs. Mallet	. . . . . .	157
,, Mr. Mallet	. . . .	160
,, Mr. and Mrs. Mallet	. . .	167
,, Mr. Mallet	. . . . .	169
,, Mr. and Mrs. Mallet	. . .	173
,, Jerom Murch, Esq.	. . . . .	175
,, The Rev. Dr. Channing	. . .	180

MEMOIR.

LUCY AIKIN was the daughter of John Aikin, M.D. She was born at Warrington, where her parents then resided, on November 6, 1781. Her mother was Martha, daughter of Arthur Jennings, Esq., of Harlington, in the county of Bedford, who was her husband's first cousin. Miss Aikin's grandfather, the Rev. John Aikin, D.D., had been first Classical and afterwards (as successor to Dr. John Taylor, the learned author of the 'Hebrew Concordance') Divinity tutor in the Academy established at Warrington in 1757. Through the marriages of both her father and grandfather with members of the Jennings family, Miss Aikin was descended from Sir Francis Wingate, of Harlington, who married the Lady Ann Annesley, daughter of the first Earl of Anglesey. Perhaps no provincial town in the kingdom, certainly none of its size, possessed so refined and cultivated a society as Warrington, when it was the seat of the Academy.* Miss Aikin, however, was too young

---

* An interesting account of Warrington Academy and its worthies has been written by Dr. Kendrick of that town, and scattered notices of most of the alumni of that institution will be found in the 'Monthly Repository.'

to benefit by it, as she was only three years old when her father removed to Yarmouth, where he practised medicine for several years. She has written of herself:—
'The earliest event which dwells in my recollection was a journey. In those days it was indeed an event. I had just completed my third year, when my father decided on a removal from Warrington to Yarmouth, in Norfolk. My grandmother, her maid, my little brother, and myself, were packed in a post-chaise; my father accompanied us on horseback. It was Christmas week, the snow deep on the ground; the whole distance was two hundred and forty miles across the country, and we were six days in accomplishing it. The last night we arrived at my aunt's, Mrs. Barbauld's, house at Palgrave, where my grandmother remained behind; she died in a few days of the cold and fatigue of the journey.'

Miss Aikin has also left the following reminiscences of her early days: 'As my father removed from Warrington when I was only three years old, and although I still retain some distinct recollections of it, and of persons whom I knew there, I am not able clearly to trace any part of my after character to impressions stamped on my mind at this early period. One circumstance, however, rests strongly on my memory. My father's mother, who lived in the house with us, made some attempts to teach me to read; the extraordinary precocity of my aunt and of my eldest brother had perhaps rendered her unreasonable in her expectations of progress; she called me "Little Dunce;" the reproach sank deep, and its effect was certainly unfavourable; it did not rouse me to further exertion, for I had already done my utmost, and it filled me with a sense of incurable deficiency. How soon may the tender spirit of a child be broken, and its faculties permanently dulled by such treatment!

'I was in little danger, however, from this source. My grandmother died on our journey from Lancashire, and I had small discouragement to encounter from other quarters. If slow at my book, I was quick, almost to a wonder, with my tongue; it was the report, long after, of a lady who visited in our house at Warrington, that my voice was always heard in it, and that my papa never checked me, because he was so fond of me.'

Although Lucy Aikin may not have been as precocious as her aunt, Mrs. Barbauld, who could read with ease before she was twenty months old, it is certain that she did not long deserve the reproach of being a 'little dunce.' Her father thus writes of her: 'Lucy has not been well lately, and I should be sorry to have verified in her the saying, "So wise, so young, do not live long." I must anticipate her mother in telling one story of her sense. We were talking of Cadmus, and I was saying I was not certain whether he lived before or after the Trojan war; when this chit of six years old decided the matter, by observing that she had heard her brother Edmund read in Pope's "Homer" about a son of Cadmus fighting against the Trojans.'

The next event which left a lasting impression on her mind was meeting her father's friend, John Howard, and of this she began to write to a friend shortly before her decease: 'Several months ago you asked me whether I had not seen Mr. Howard, the patriarch of English philanthropists; I answered that I had, and that, eight years' child as I was, I retained the most distinct recollections of his person, his manners, and his interesting conversations with us children, to whom he was ever full of kindness. Once recalled to recollections thus faithfully cherished during the whole of a long life, it began to dawn upon my perception that the world had not yet learned all, or nearly all, that it ought and would be glad to know of that ever-memorable man; that I myself must be now nearly, if not quite, the last survivor of those who had beheld him with living eye, and that I could still dictate at least, to those better able to hold the pen, some few anecdotes which the true lovers of virtuous fame would not willingly let die.'

This intention was, however, never fulfilled. The letters of her father and aunt contain some mention of the great philanthropist, and tend to explain the cause of the unfounded imputation cast upon that good man of ill-treating his son, as no doubt any restraint placed upon him was occasioned by the unfortunate condition of his mind, and also refute the statement that the insanity of young Howard was the result of his early dissipation—it is clear that it was an hereditary disease. Dr. Aikin thus wrote in 1783: 'Mr. Howard was with us last week, and it gave us great pleasure to see him in good health, and full of his usual activity; though it is evident that the thought of his son continually comes across him and checks his flow of spirits. Mrs. Jennings has written to show that there was a strain of insanity in Mr. Howard's family.'

Mrs. Barbauld wrote in 1787 to Dr. Aikin, who was

then engaged in writing a notice of Mr. Howard—'I suppose you know that young Howard is quite disordered. The first time he showed any evident symptoms of madness was at Mr. Whitbread's; Miss Whitbread was making tea, and he sat by his uncle Leeds. "Pray," says he, "is it possible to mix a quantity of arsenic sufficient to kill a man in a dish of tea?" "I suppose it may," replied Mr. Leeds. Upon this he started up, threw his dish of tea upon the floor, and said Miss W. had attempted to poison him.'

On another occasion Mrs. Barbauld wrote—'My dear brother, you must write the character of Mr. Howard: that you are taking care of the fair fame of your friend, and rescuing his memory from the scandalous imputation thrown on it in the Magazine, I rejoice. I was thinking to write to exhort you to do this when I heard that he had left you his papers.'

On reaching Yarmouth, Dr. Aikin at once entered on the active discharge of his profession. His daughter thus describes her early experience of her new residence: 'The arrival of a new physician, already a writer of some distinction, of polished and unaffected manners, and endowed with powers and with tact which rendered his conversation attractive and acceptable to all, was an event of no small importance in the town of Yarmouth. His speedy popularity was reflected upon all the members of his family, and upon none more strongly than on the little rosy, laughing, chattering girl of three years old. I was soon in danger of being totally spoiled with flattery; nothing indeed could have saved me but the good sense, the firmness, the parental affection well understood of my excellent mother. She taught me what flattery was, and strongly warned me against being led away by it.

'The lesson was doubly painful; it showed me that those who knew me best were aware that I was far from deserving the praises lavished upon me by strangers, and it gave me the impression that these most agreeable strangers were guilty of the horrible offence of telling fibs. I bore the shock pretty well, however, and was the better for the warning. Still my little heart *would* beat with triumph when the Rev. Dr. Cooper * withstood, I know not how long, the impatient summonses of three grown ladies to the quadrille table with the answer, "I had rather talk with this child." To confess the whole truth, I have still a kind of tenderness for the first man that ever flattered me.

'One circumstance, wholly overlooked in its moral bearings even by parents vigilant as mine, tended to produce in me a settled conviction of my own superiority to those around me, which I feel to have been permanently injurious. This was the constant attention paid to preserving my speech free from the vulgar and ungrammatical dialect of the place. My own language and pronunciation, I was taught, were right; those of the children my companions were, of course, *very wrong*, and I indulged in a truly Pharisaical spirit of self-satisfaction in the comparison. Could it have been foreseen that I was finally to leave Norfolk at so early an age, it might have been better to pass over a few provincialisms, caught from playfellows or servants, than to call forth such sentiments; but after all, is not this *the* difficulty which meets us at every turn in moral as well as intellectual training, to

* The rector of Yarmouth, father of the eminent surgeon Sir Astley Cooper, Bart.

teach the young and ardent spirit, full of the love of excellence, and sanguine in its hopes and anticipations of its own proficiency, to look with due indulgence on the defects of others? To be "only of itself a judge severe" is the last perfection of a pure and noble spirit. Candour, the virtue of the wise, is little to be looked for in youth.

'At the age of six, I was sent for one quarter to a day-school, while my mother, my able and indefatigable instructress, was visiting her relations in London. Many new, and some durable impressions were made upon me here. I soon discovered that I was far beyond my schoolfellows of the same age. Lessons which occupied them half the morning I would learn in a few minutes, and my reading was incomparably better—a new ground of self-conceit! I likewise found myself indulged and flattered exorbitantly by my governess; but without then understanding her selfish views in this conduct, I had a kind of instinctive distrust of her, mingled with a sense of contempt, which effectually preserved me from her seductions. One day I had, I know not how, so offended her, that she inflicted on me a very slight box on the ear. "That did not hurt," cried I. This was thought saucy, and brought me a second box, which I had the wit to receive in silence. My speech was not sauciness, however; but only an ill-timed display of the stoical fortitude which I had been taught to pride myself in practising on all occasions. This experiment, by showing me that I was understood neither by my governess nor by the other children, who all laughed at me, caused me to wrap myself up more closely in my shell of self-importance.

'A different lesson was stamped upon me thus. My

governess, with much whining, sighing, and casting up of her eyes, made known to the young ladies that a poor girl, her niece, who had sometimes been admitted to say her lessons with them, had actually been seen, such was the distress of her family, walking without shoes and stockings; and she invited them to make a small collection for her benefit. "I have no money," cried I, "except my *pretty sixpence*" (a newly-coined one.) "And I am sure," my governess replied, with an odious twinkling of her eye, "that you will have the greatest delight in giving your pretty sixpence to poor Mary Wright." I stood aghast, never having contemplated the bare possibility of either spending or giving away a *pretty* sixpence, but there was no help; I was compelled to produce the precious piece, praised for my amiable alacrity, and sent back to my place bursting with indignation. I felt myself diddled, and from that day to this I have hated collectors of subscriptions—those strainers of the qualities of mercy. Let such as desire to awaken in children the virtue of charity, consider a little how far the nature of the distress is level to their comprehension, the object one likely to awaken their sympathy, the sacrifice such as may reasonably be required of them, and, above all, let their own motives be free from all suspicion; for even childhood will suspect when its anger has been excited. Young as I was, I remember thinking that my governess should have given shoes to her own niece herself, instead of begging from us. Some time after I was taken to visit a poor family who were going to make their dinner on a single turnip. How eagerly did I cast my little store, to the last half penny, into the mother's lap! But then I saw the distress, and no one prompted my bounty.

'The utmost vigilance will not always preserve an innocent child from contact with those who are corrupted. I met with one whose precocious wickedness still surprises me—it did me no harm, however; I felt only disgust and horror. She was fortunately detected in shameful falsehoods, and our acquaintance dropped. One memorable day, my brother George, several years older, seized and devoured half of a tart destined for the supper of us two little ones. Fired at the injury, I ran with the fragment into the presence of papa and mamma, and denounced the offender in most emphatic terms. "You should be willing to give your brother part of your tart," said my mother. "But he did not ask us," I replied—"he took it;" and I still think that the distinction was just, and that his action ought to have brought him, and not me, the reprimand. But how many fold was I compensated when my father, who had listened with great attention to my harangue, exclaimed, "Why Lucy, you are quite eloquent!" O! never-to-be-forgotten praise! Had I been a boy, it might have made me an orator; as it was, it incited me to exert to the utmost, by tongue and by pen, all the power of words I possessed or could ever acquire—I had learned where my strength lay.

'There are none among the impressions of my childhood which I recollect with such unmingled satisfaction as the strong love of nature awakened in me with the first dawnings of sensibility. In our long snowy journey out of Lancashire, nothing so stimulated my imagination as the long lines of blue hills which arose from time to time in the distant horizon. My lot was cast among the plains, and I never again beheld this appearance till I revisited

Lancashire at the age of nineteen, and I then hailed it with the rapture of a lost delight recovered.

'My first view of the ocean from Yarmouth jetty filled my little bosom with sentiments too big for utterance, and the sea was my never-failing source of wonder and delight during all the years that I dwelt beside its murmurs. The land indeed had few charms at this spot to attract the eye or move the fancy—a flat, barren, sandy down, extending to the beech, was our daily walk; but so much the keener was my delight when we accompanied my father in his professional drives through the shady lanes of rural villages on the Suffolk side. He was an admirable observer of nature—not a plant, not a bird, not a wild animal, escaped him; he knew them all, and taught his children to know and love them too.

'This interest was inexpressibly exalted by Mrs. Barbauld's prose hymns, which were taught me, I know not how soon. Her "Early Lessons" had prepared the way, for in them too there dwells the spirit of poetry; but the hymns gave me the idea of something bright and glorious, hung on high above my present reach, but not above my aspirations. They gave me first the sentiment of sublimity, and of the Author of all that is sublime. They taught me piety.'

From this period we possess no other auto-biographical notes, but what may be gathered from Miss Aikin's letters.

Dr. Aikin resided in Yarmouth until 1792, and then settled with his family in London, where he successfully practised as a physician until his failing health compelled him to abandon his profession in the year 1797. He then removed to Stoke Newington, and devoted the remainder of his life to literature. Of the many elaborate, elegant, and useful works which he published, none has had so wide a circulation as the 'Evenings at Home,' written by him in conjunction with his gifted sister, Anna Letitia Barbauld. It still keeps its place in the juvenile library, notwithstanding the profusion of books which have since been written for the purpose of rendering knowledge attractive to the young. Miss Aikin lived with her parents at Stoke Newington till the death of her father, in December 1822. He had carefully cultivated the talent which she had early displayed, and her literary attainments far exceeded those which at that period usually fell to the lot of her sex. The best French and Italian authors were familiar to her, and she read the Latin classics with facility. Up to the last few weeks of her life she retained her relish for the literature of which in her earlier days she had been a diligent and delighted student.

Her father's studies were chiefly historical and biographical, and this naturally guided the course of his daughter's reading. Her first efforts in writing were in the way of translation. The English version of the 'Adventures of Rolando,' so long popular with the young, was from her pen. She was an author from her seventeenth year; many articles in reviews and magazines, and in the 'Annual Register,' were hers. In 1819 she produced her first historical work, 'Memoirs of the Court of Queen Elizabeth.' The subject was happily chosen—a female reign was fitly illustrated by a female pen. The plan comprehended the private life of the queen, and the domestic history of the period; biographies and anecdotes of the principal families who formed her brilliant court, and notices of the manner, opinions, and literature of the age. The author had prepared herself for the work by careful research into the ample materials which the memoirs and letters of that time furnish; they were skilfully condensed and combined, so as to afford an animated picture of England in a reign which Englishmen have always contemplated with pride. Two similar works on the reign of James I. and Charles I. followed. Miss Aikin published biographical memoirs of her father and of his sister, Mrs. Barbauld. Both may be regarded as works of filial piety; for her aunt shared with her father in the reverence and affection with which she regarded the union of virtue and talent. The cast of her own mind fitted her better for sympathising with the strong practical sense, the liberal views, and the literary diligence of her father, than with the sensibility and poetical elegance of her aunt. Her own principal poetical works, 'Epistles on Women,' is a specimen of that moral and didactic poetry of which Pope had given the model—terse and compact in language, and smooth in versification, but not aiming at the higher qualities of imagination or invention. The smaller poetical pieces, some of which appeared in the 'Athenæum' edited by her father, are marked by elegance and fancy. She addressed a consolatory poem to Montgomery, who had been deeply wounded by the ridicule thrown upon his 'Wanderer of Switzerland.' The death of the Rev. Gilbert Wakefield called forth a poetical tribute from her pen, in which justice is rendered to his uncompromising integrity and public spirit. His daughter was her most intimate friend, and afterwards became the

wife of her brother, the 'Charles' of Mrs. Barbauld's
'Early Lessons.' Miss Aikin had also, in 1814, published
a work of fiction, 'Lorimer; a Tale,' the incidents of
which have been appropriated, without acknowledgement,
by a popular modern writer of novels.

Her life at Stoke Newington was passed in great quietness. In addition to tending her invalid father, her chief occupation was in writing and study; of literary society at this period she had little. The regularity of her life was occasionally diversified by visits to friends at Norwich and elsewhere. At this city she had the great advantage of an intimate acquaintance with the family of Mr. and Mrs. John Taylor, both of them accomplished and congenial. To the latter are addressed some letters, which will be found in this collection. With their children, distinguished in various ways, she continued on intimate terms. Seldom have so many of one family attained distinction: Mr. John Taylor, the eldest son, was the eminent mining engineer and geologist; Richard and Arthur both distinguished antiquaries; Edward, the Gresham Professor of Music, was a scientific musician—his lectures were very able and interesting, and remarkable for the beauty of their style. Mrs. Austin's admirable translation of Ranke's 'History of the Popes,' and her original works, are well known and appreciated. For Mr. William Taylor of Norwich, no relation, however, of Mr. John Taylor, she had a great admiration. A discriminating notice of him will be found in a letter to Mr. Murch of Bath. William Taylor's very original work on 'English Synonyms' deserves to be more widely known than it is. Subsequent writers on the same subject have largely made use of its contents, and generally without any acknowledgement of their obligations.

Of the visit Miss Aikin paid to Edinburgh in the winter of 1812, she makes mention in a letter—'The appearance and situation of the town fully equalled all my expectations; but with respect to literary conversation, I certainly was a little disappointed. The fashion of making large parties is now so prevalent there, that I scarcely ever saw a small one, and what "feast of reason" or "flow of soul" can be enjoyed where a hundred people are standing huddled together in a large room, where Italian trills are faintly heard above the general buzz? It is true that when this crowd is at length arranged round four or five supper tables, if you are fortunate in your neighbours, you have the prospect of a very pleasant hour, and fortunate I often was. The dinner parties that I attended were seldom brilliant; at table each one talks to his next neighbour, and it rarely happened that I had ever seen mine before. A total stranger, as I was, cannot expect to taste the pleasures of society, of which intimacy and confidence form so important a part, in their full perfection—the Scotch character, too, which is grave and cautious, is unfavourable to the pleasures of slight acquaintance. But on the whole the people please me; they are kind, hospitable, ingenious and well informed, and I have gained from my expedition a store of instruction and amusement which was well worth the pains of the journey. Of their eminent men in science and letters (all of whom I saw except Scott and Dugald Stewart) Playfair delighted me by far the most. His simplicity, his benignant courtesy, his deference for others, his modesty, his extensive knowledge, and the genius and sensibility he is always unconsciously betraying, are quite enchanting and surprisingly *piquants*. Dr. Brown is my second favourite: after getting over the unfavourable impression of his pert manner and habitual smile, I was pleased with his great acuteness, his imagination, and his goodness of heart; nature meant him for a grave character, and if he would subdue his unfortunate ambition to appear a wit, he would be much more pleasing. But Jeffrey!—after having won from him a handsome letter of apology, of course I did not object to being introduced to him; and it would indeed have been a pity not to have seen the most amusing man, one of the few amusing men, of Edinburgh. He has vivacity, fluency, rapidity of manner—rare qualities in a Scotchman. He gesticulates like a Frenchman, and *dashes* in conversation like an Irishman—hit or miss. He coins new words, applies old ones grotesquely, disdains nothing for the sake of effect, and altogether gives the idea of *a very clever fellow*, rather than of a first-rate wit or a great genius. I saw Mrs. Hamilton often by her own fire-side, which she was unable to quit; she was very kind to me, and I had great pleasure in her conversation; her good sense, her cheerfulness, her knowledge of the world, and her great kindness of heart, make her a delightful companion. Her prejudices indeed are strong, but that did not signify to me, who never sought to conquer them. Of other ladies, such as were naturally Scotch, for the most part pleased me better than those who were affectedly English. An old Scotch gentlewoman, with her native dignity, her acute observation of life and manners, and her cordial hospitality, is a fine creature, by whom I am at once interested and instructed; but from a fine Edinburgh Miss, drawling out in a hoarse whisper a jargon neither Scotch nor English—affecting ease without an idea of elegance, and dressing her coarse features in assumed languishment, to attract the attention of any man who can offer her an establishment—Good Lord deliver us! You will not imagine that all the young ladies I met with were the odious creatures I have described; there were certainly some who possessed, like Miss Edgeworth's Belinda, "delicacy of mind and dignity of manners;" but the female fortune-hunters, who form a large body there, deserve all I have said and much more.'

Miss Aikin resided at Stoke Newington until her father's decease in 1822. His increasing infirmities required her constant care, and during this period she had but few opportunities of enjoying the literary society which at a later date fell to her share. She thus describes her every-day life in a letter to her friend Mr. Holland of Knutsford—'Our little home is now in all its glory; the garden is full of flowers and fruit as it can hold. Arthur (her brother) is with us at present, and he and my mother almost live in it. Shall I give you an account of our different manners of spending the day? Whoever is down first in the morning, turns into the garden and rambles about till I summon to breakfast. As soon as that is over, my father sits down to biography in his study; my mother and Arthur begin their operations in the garden, where she often stays, gathering fruit and vegetables, cutting off dead flowers, &c., most of the morning; he, after a while, retires to his room upstairs, to write for the "Encyclopædia." I step to the butcher's to order dinner, after which I shut myself up in my little closet, where I stay till dinner time; after dinner my father and mother play backgammon, Arthur and I walk in the garden for some time, and then return to our studies, while my father and mother nap or read; after tea we walk or sit down to our business till candle-light, when we meet with books, and work in the study; after supper we play whist for some time, I read Virgil to my father, and at eleven we march off to bed.'

Mrs. Aikin shortly after her husband's death removed with her daughter to Hampstead, and died there in 1830. During her residence here in 1827, Miss Aikin made a visit to Cambridge, of which she gave the following account to her correspondent, Mr. Holland:—'I am very little addicted to journies myself; but lately an irresistible temptation was thrown in my way, and I indulged myself in the pleasantest thing possible—a jaunt to Cambridge, which I had never seen, planned by Mr. Whishaw and Professor Smyth, and in which our very agreeable neighbours, Mr. and Mrs. Mallet (he is a son of Mallet du Pan, and Secretary to the Audit Board, and she a charming woman) partook. Mr. Whishaw took her and me down in his carriage, and a very amiable young Romilly on the box; Mr. Mallet went down by coach. We left on the Thursday and returned on the Sunday. The professor gave us two grand dinners, and assembled several of the brightest stars of the university to meet us; among the rest the Bishop of Lincoln, certainly one of the most admirable persons I have seen—mild, polished, perfectly unassuming; but firm and consistent in liberal views and principles, and acute and full of talent. We had also Mr. Sedgwick,

Woodwardian Professor, and the great mathematician Whewell. These two are intimate friends, and a good deal alike in their cast of mind and manners; that is to say, they are very clever and able men of that kind of which Mr. Brougham is the great exemplar—men of wonderful energy and activity of mind, profound in one or two branches of knowledge, and ignorant of none, whose conversation teems with allusions drawn from the most various and distant sources, illustrating bright and original ideas of their own—men to whom it is a delight, but not a relaxation, to listen—whose thoughts flow almost too rapidly for language to overtake them—whose ideas come crowding and jostling like a throng in a narrow gate. In Mr. Brougham, the experience of the world and the habit of applying his eloquence to practical points in law and politics, on which it is his business to talk down to very ordinary capacities, has moderated the exuberance which reigns unchecked in the discourse of these academics; but if any force of circumstances could have tied him down to a college life, he would have been such as one of these. It pleased me to observe how completely in these instances the spirit of the nineteenth century has mastered the spirit of monkery and the middle ages in which our universities were founded; but the forms are still kept up, more than the forms in some things.'

Miss Aikin's only literary publication during her residence in Hampstead was the 'Memoirs of Addison,' which appeared in 1843; she continued to reside in the same village until the following year, when after a short sojourn in London, in the house of her nephew Mr. C. A. Aikin, she became an inmate of the family of Mr. P. H. Le Breton and his wife, her niece, the daughter of her brother Charles—for the first six years at Wimbledon, and during the last twelve years of her life at Hampstead. To this place she was ever much attached, and her return to it gave her much pleasure—many dear relatives and friends lived there. The vicinity of Hampstead to the metropolis afforded at the same time the opportunity of intercourse with a more varied society. She enjoyed with keen relish, and thoroughly appreciated, the company of literary men, and of the eminent politicians and lawyers, with whom she delighted to discuss questions of interest. With almost every distinguished writer of this period she was acquainted, and of many of them notices will be found in her correspondence.

One who knew her well* has truly said of her—'that she possessed in a remarkable degree the art of conversation, an art which seems in some danger of being lost in the crowds which fashion brings together. It was not, however, an art cultivated for display. Whether in intercourse with a single friend in a small circle, or an assemblage of persons of intellectual attainments equal to her own, there was the same flow of anecdote, quotation and allusion, furnished by a most retentive memory, and enlivened by wit and humour.'

For nearly twenty years Miss Aikin kept up a correspondence with the Rev. Dr. Channing, of Boston in the United States on all the interesting topics of the times. To the last she retained her memory and her faculties.

After a few days' illness, from an attack of influenza, she died on the 29th of January 1864, in the 83rd year of her age. Her grave in the old churchyard of Hampstead

* The Rev. John Kenrick, of York.

is next to that of her beloved and honoured friend, Joanna Baillie, with whom during a large portion of life she had been in constant intercourse. In her loss one of the links of the chain which binds us to the last century is broken. For solid acquirements, brilliant talent, sound judgement, and high and noble principles, it will be difficult to find one more worthy to be held in remembrance.

MISCELLANIES

BY THE LATE

LUCY AIKIN.

MEMOIR OF MISS BENGER.

ELIZABETH OGILVY BENGER, whose life affords an interesting example of female genius struggling into day through obstacles which might well have daunted even the bolder energies of manly enterprise, was born in the city of Wells, in February 1778. She was an only child—a circumstance which her affectionate heart always led her to regard as a misfortune. Her father, somewhat late in life, was impelled by an adventurous disposition to give up commerce and enter the navy, and ultimately became a purser. In consequence of this change, he removed his family to Chatham when his daughter was four years of age; and, with the exception of about two years' residence at Portsmouth, Chatham or Rochester was her abode till the year 1797. An ardour for knowledge, a passion for literary distinction, disclosed itself with the first dawnings of reason, and never left her. Her connections were not literary; and her sex, no less than her situation, debarred her from the most effective means of mental cultivation. She has been heard to relate, that in the tormenting want of books which she suffered during her childhood, it was one of her resources to plant herself at the window of the only bookseller's shop in the place, to read the open pages of the new publications there displayed, and to return again, day after day, to examine whether, by good fortune, a leaf of any of them might have been turned over. But the bent of her mind was so decided, that a judicious friend prevailed upon her mother at length to indulge it; and at twelve years of age she received instruction in the Latin language. At thirteen she wrote a poem of considerable length, called 'The Female Geniad,' in which, imperfect as it necessarily was, strong traces of literary genius were discerned. With the sanction of her father it appeared in print, dedicated to Lady de Crespigny, to whom she was introduced by her uncle, Sir David Ogilvy, and from whom she afterwards received many kind and flattering attentions.

Her father contemplated her literary progress with delight and with pride; and on his appointment to the lucrative situation of purser on board Admiral Lord Keith's own ship, it was his first care to direct that no expense should be spared in procuring instruction for his daughter in every branch of knowledge which it might be her wish to acquire; but the death of this indulgent parent in the East Indies, within a year afterwards, blighted the fair prospect now opening upon her. Cares and difficulties succeeded; the widow and the orphan, destitute of effectual protection in the prosecution of their just claims, became the victims of fraud and rapacity, and a very slender provision was all that could be secured from the wreck of their hopes and fortunes. In the course of the following year, 1797, they removed to the neighbourhood of Devizes, where, together with the society of affectionate friends and kind relations, Miss Benger also enjoyed free access to a well-stored library.

But that intense longing for the society of the eminent and the excellent, which always distinguished her, could only be gratified, as she was sensible, in London; and thither, about the beginning of 1800, her mother was induced to remove. Here, partly through the favour of Lady de Crespigny, partly by means of her early intimates, Miss Jane and Miss Anna Maria Porter, but principally through the zealous friendship of Miss Sarah Wesley, who had already discovered her in her retirement, she almost immediately found herself ushered into society where her merit was fully appreciated and warmly fostered. The late Dr. George Gregory, well known in the literary world, and his admirable wife, a lady equally distinguished by talents and virtues, were soon amongst the firmest and most affectionate of her friends. By them she was gratified with an introduction to Mrs. Elizabeth Hamilton, of whom she afterwards gave so interesting a memoir; to the author of 'Pleasures of Hope;' to Mrs. Barbauld, and to the late Dr. Aikin, with the different members of whose family, but especially with her who now inscribes, with an aching heart, this slender record of her genius and virtues, she contracted an affectionate intimacy, never interrupted through a period of more than twenty years, and only severed at length by the stroke which all things mortal must obey. Another, and a most valuable connection, which she afterwards formed, was with the family of R. Smirke, Esq. R. A., in whose accomplished daughter she found an assiduous and faithful friend, whose offices of love followed her without remission to the last. Mrs. Inchbald, Mrs. Joanna Baillie, the excellent Mrs. Weddell, and many other names distinguished in literature or in society, might be added to the list of those who delighted in her conversation and took an interest in her happiness. Her circle of acquaintance extended with her fame and with the knowledge of her excellent qualities; and she was often enabled to assemble as guests at her humble tea-table, names whose celebrity would have insured attention in the proudest saloons of the metropolis.

Early in her literary career, Miss Benger had been induced to fix her hopes of fame on the drama, for which her genius appeared in many respects well adapted; but after ample experience of the anxieties, delays, and disappointments which in this age sicken the heart of almost every candidate for celebrity in this department, she tried her powers in other attempts, and produced, first, her poem on the 'Abolition of the Slave Trade,' and afterwards two novels, published anonymously. Many passages in the poem are replete with sentiment and imagination, and there are lines of great harmony and beauty; but a suggested subject is unfavourable to inspiration, and the piece would have borne condensation with advantage. Of the novels, 'Marian,' the first and the best, did not obtain the attention which it deserved, and which the name of the author would probably have secured it. The style is eloquent and striking; the characters have often the air of well-drawn portraits; the situations are sometimes highly interesting, and with many passages of pathos, there are several of genuine humour; the principal failure is in the plot, which, in itself improbable, is neither naturally nor perspicuously unfolded. The same general character applies to 'Valsinore, or the Heart and the Fancy;' but of this piece the story is equally faulty and the interest less highly wrought. No judicious person, however, could peruse either work without perceiving that the artist was superior to the work; that the excellences were such as genius only could reach, the deficiencies what a more accurate and comprehensive knowledge of the laws of composition, or a more patient application of the labour of correcti n, might without difficulty have supplied. No one, in fact, was more sensible than herself that she had not yet attained the power of doing justice in the execution to the first conceptions of her fancy; and finding herself in many respects unfavourably circumstanced for acquiring that mastery in literary skill, she prudently turned her attention from fictitious narrative to biography and criticism—rising in her later works to the department of history. Between the years 1814 and 1825, she gave to the world, in rapid succession, 'Remarks on Madame de Staël's Germany;' 'Memoir of Mrs. Hamilton;' 'Memoirs of John Tobin' (author of the 'Honeymoon'); 'Notices of Klopstock and his Friends,' prefixed to a translation of their 'Letters' from the German; and the 'Life of Anne Boleyn,' and 'Memoirs of Mary Queen of Scots, and of the Queen of Bohemia.' Most of these works obtained deserved popularity; and she would probably have added to her reputation by her projected 'Memoirs of Henry IV. of France,' had life and health been lent her for their completion.

But to those who knew her and enjoyed her friendship, her writings, pleasing and beautiful as they are, were the smallest part of her merit and her attraction. Endowed with the warmest and most grateful of human hearts, she united to the utmost delicacy and nobleness of sentiment, active benevolence, which knew no limit but the furthest extent of her ability, and a boundless enthusiasm for the good and fair, wherever she discovered them. Her lively imagination, and the flow of eloquence which it inspired, aided by one of the most melodious of voices, lent an inexpressible charm to her conversation; which was heightened by an intuitive discernment of character, rare in itself, and still more so in combination with such fertility of fancy and ardency of feeling. As a companion, whether for the graver or the gayer hour, she had indeed few equals; and her constant forgetfulness of self, and unfailing sympathy for others, rendered her the general friend, and favourite, and confidante, of persons of both sexes, all classes, and all ages. Many would have concurred in judgment with Madame de Staël, when she pronounced Miss Benger the most interesting woman she had seen during her visit to England.

With so much to admire and love she had everything to esteem. Of envy and jealousy there was not a trace in her composition; her probity, veracity, and honour, derived, as she gratefully acknowledged, from the early precepts of an assiduous and most respectable mother, were perfect. Though not less free from pride than from vanity, her sense of independence was such, that no one could fix upon her the slightest obligation capable of lowering her in any eyes; and her generous propensity to seek those most who needed her offices of friendship, rendered her, in the intercourses of society, much oftener the obliger than the party obliged. No one was more scrupulously just to the characters and performances of others, no one more candid, no one more deserving of every kind of reliance.

It is gratifying to reflect to how many hearts her unassisted merit found its way. Few persons have been more widely or deeply deplored in their sphere of acquaintance; but even those who knew and loved her best, could not but confess that their regrets were purely selfish. To her the pains of sensibility seemed to be dealt in even fuller measure than its joys; her childhood and early youth were consumed in a solitude of mind, and under a sense of the contrariety between her genius and her fate, which had rendered them sad and full of bitterness; her maturer years were tried by cares, privations, and disappointments, and not seldom by unfeeling slights or thankless neglect. The irritability of her constitution, aggravated by inquietude of mind, had rendered her life one long disease. Old age, which she neither wished nor expected to attain, might have found her solitary and ill provided—now she has taken 'the wings of the dove, to flee away and be at rest.'

A short but painful illness terminated her career on January 9, 1827.

RECOLLECTIONS OF JOANNA BAILLIE.

It has been my privilege to have had more or less of personal acquaintance with almost every literary woman of celebrity who adorned English society from the latter years of the last century nearly to the present time, and there was scarcely one of the number in whose society I did not find much to interest me; but of all these, excepting of course Mrs. Barbauld from the comparison, Joanna Baillie made by far the deepest impression upon me. Her genius was surpassing, her character the most endearing and exalted.

I was a young girl when I first met her at Mrs. Barbauld's, to whom she had become known through her residence at Hampstead, her attendance on Mr. B.'s ministry, and her connection with the Denman family. Her genius had shrouded itself under so thick a veil of silent reserve, that its existence seems scarcely to have been even suspected beyond the domestic circle, when the 'Plays on the Passions' burst on the world. The dedication to Dr. Baillie gave a hint in what quarter the author was to be sought; but the person chiefly suspected was the accomplished widow of his uncle John Hunter. Of Joanna no one dreamt on the occasion. She and her sister—I well remember the scene—arrived on a morning call at Mrs. Barbauld's; my aunt immediately introduced the topic of the anonymous tragedies, and gave utterance to her admiration with that generous delight in the manifestation of kindred genius, which distinguished her. But not even the sudden delight of such praise, so given, could seduce our Scottish damsel into self-betrayal. The faithful sister rushed forward, as we afterwards recollected, to bear the brunt, while the unsuspected author lay snug in the asylum of her taciturnity. Repression of all emotions, even the gentlest, and those most honourable to human nature, seems to have been indeed the constant lesson of her Presbyterian home. Her sister once told me that their father was an excellent parent: when she had once been bitten by a dog thought to be mad, he had sucked the wound, at the hazard, as was supposed, of his own life —but that he had never given her a kiss. Joanna spoke to me once of her yearning to be caressed when a child. She would sometimes venture, she said, to clasp her little arms about her mother's knees, who would seem to chide her—'but I know she liked it.' Be that as it may, the first thing which drew upon Joanna the admiring notice of Hampstead society, was the devoted assiduity of her attention to her mother, then blind as well as aged, whom she attended day and night. But this task of duty came at length to its natural termination, and the secret of her authorship having been permitted to transpire, she was no longer privileged to sit in the shade, shuffling off upon others her own fair share in the expenses of conversation. Latterly, her discourse flowed freely, and it had too much of her own nature in it not to be ever welcome and delightful; but of all the writers, I might almost say the readers, I have ever known, she spoke the least of books. In fact she never loved them; it was not from them, but from real life, and from the aspects of rural nature, that her imagination drew the materials in which it worked, and it had been the penance of her youth to be drawn away from these to her studies. 'I could not read well,' she once said to me, 'till nine years old!' 'O Joanna,' cried her sister, 'not till eleven!' 'I made my father melancholy breakfasts,' she continued, 'for I used to say my lesson to him then, and I always cried over it. And yet they used to say, "this girl is not stupid neither; she is handy at her needle, and understands common matters well enough." I rambled over the heaths and plashed in the brook most of the day.'

At school, by her sister's report, she was the ringleader in all pranks and frolics, and used to entertain her companions with an endless string of stories of her own invention. She was also addicted to clambering on the roof of the house, to act over her scenes alone and in secret. At the time of her birth, and during all her girlhood, her father, who afterwards became Divinity Professor in the University of Glasgow, was the minister of a rural parish in the neighbourhood, and his children ran about with those of his humble parishioners, barefoot like the rest. It was even a sacrifice to her to give up the practice. In summer she would confess her longing to pad in the grass, free from the incumbrance of hose and shoes; and I have known her throw away some eloquence in vain endeavours to prevail upon prejudiced English parents to allow their children to partake in so *healthful* an indulgence.

She had, in fact, a full share of the national predilections for which the Scotch are remarkable. But her large benevolence of nature purified this sentiment in her from the spirit of boasting and the gross unfairness which are its usual concomitants. It appeared practicable in her to love Scotch things and persons more, without loving the English less. Yet in many respects she never Anglicised in the least degree. Whether she and her sister actually took pains to keep up their native dialect, I know not, but it is certain that on their revisiting Glasgow twenty or thirty years after they had first quitted it, their friends were surprised to find them speaking with a broader accent than themselves, by whom the English pronunciation had long been anxiously cultivated as a genteel accomplishment. If, however, any stranger, on the strength of these her primitive notions and Scottish provincialisms, had expected to detect in her the slightest deficiency in good manners or social refinement, he would speedily have found his error. Joanna Baillie was an innate gentlewoman, and over the meekness of her disposition and the simplicity of her demeanour, there presided a genuine dignity, capable of repelling arrogance, and striking unworthiness with 'blank awe.' Her reserve had much of caution, but nothing of cowardice; she had perfect self-possession, and courage sufficient to say and do whatever in her high moral sense she judged right, regardless of any one's opinion. But such was her indulgence, and the truly Christian humility of her spirit, that practically she was only too tolerant of impertinence and intrusions. She was the only person I have ever known, towards whom fifty years of close acquaintance, while they continually deepened my affection, wore away nothing of my reverence.

So little was she fitted or disposed for intellectual display, that it was seldom that her genius shone out with its full lustre in conversation; but I have seen her powerful eye kindle with all a poet's fire, while her language rose for a few moments to the full height of some 'great argument.' Her deep knowledge of the human heart, also, would at times break loose from the habitual cautiousness, and I have then thought that if she were not the most candid and benevolent, she would be one of the most formidable of observers. Nothing escaped her, and there was much humour in her quiet touches. The acuteness and originality of her mind displayed itself most in her off-hand remarks. Now and then, when I have been on my way to relate to her something new, which I thought might amuse or interest her, I have said to myself, 'What will be her comment? No—that I cannot anticipate, but I am sure that it will be the best thing said on the occasion.' And such it never failed to prove.

No one would ever have taken her for a married woman. An innocent and maiden grace still hovered over her to the end of her old age. It was one of her peculiar charms, and often brought to my mind the line addressed to the vowed Isabella in 'Measure for Measure'—'I hold you for a thing enskied and saintly.' If there were ever human creature 'pure in the last recesses of the soul,' it was surely this meek, this pious, this noble-minded and nobly gifted woman, who, after attaining her ninetieth year, carried with her to the grave the love, the reverence, the regrets, of all who had ever enjoyed the privilege of her society.

OLD TIMES.

A DIALOGUE.

MRS. HARFORD. SOPHIA.

Sophia. I have often read and heard, grandmamma, that elderly people always give the preference to past days over the present, but I think I have observed the contrary in you. 'These are glorious times,' you sometimes say; 'they are continually improving something.' One might suppose that every age made improvements; but perhaps there may have been more, or greater ones, within your memory than in former periods, or is it only, my dear grandmamma, that you are more inclined than other people to be pleased with the present, whatever it may be?

Mrs. Harford. I should be very willing, my dear, to accept the compliment of your last supposition if I honestly could. To be particularly disposed to be pleased with the present, would be no small merit at the age of eighty; but there have, as I think, been unusually rapid advances made in most things since the accession of George III., which is about the time that my distinct recollections begin. I take the pleasure which I suppose almost all people do in looking back to the days of my youth, but if I were to give you an account of the kind of life I then had, I am pretty sure you would not think it one to be envied.

S. I wish you would give me such an account, madam. I should like very much to be able to make comparisons between these times and those.

Mrs. H. To do that fairly you must take as much as possible the same class and place and condition. My recollections are chiefly of London; my father being, as you may have heard, in a great wholesale and retail business in one of the best streets of the city. He was the younger son of a country gentleman, poor, but of good family, and having an education better than common stood high in his class. Being a weakly infant, unable to bear the closeness of London, I was therefore sent out to nurse with an elder sister at Islington, then a rural village; for in those days, till a man in trade became wealthy and took a younger partner, he always lived at his shop; he had usually apprentices living in his house, and his wife, who, besides attending to domestic affairs, assisted him behind the counter or in the counting-house, was much too important a person in the family to be spared to go into the country with every child whose health might happen to require it. Thus we early lost the caresses of a mother. Nor was there any very extraordinary attention paid to us by our nurse; she treated us, however, pretty much like her own children, and like them we scrambled through. Domestic instruction was out of the question with parents so fully occupied; governesses were then unknown, except, perhaps, in some families of very high rank. And after quitting our nurse, my sister and I were quickly sent off to a London boarding school.

S. And what were you taught there?

Mrs. H. Our worthy governess chiefly professed, in her own words, 'to bring up young women in the fear of God, and in neatness;' but some few other branches of knowledge were also taught, or at least attempted. We had a French teacher, with whom we read a little of Gil Blas— an odd school-book for girls, but it supplied us with a considerable number of familiar phrases, which we patched together as well as we could to make up the school jargon which we were compelled to use under the name of French. We read a little English, learned a little arithmetic, and to write. Some were taught the Italian hand, a long narrow delicate character, slowly traced with a crowquill, and appropriated to women; others the round hand which succeeded it, and which, I will take the liberty to remark, was at least more legible than the running scribble of modern young ladies. That we were all made expert with our needles you may be sure, for at that time plain work was a woman's chief employment, and fine works were her principal amusement.

S. But you learned music and drawing without doubt?

Mrs. H. They were not so much as thought of for us. I think there were in my time about four or five of the richest and most fashionable of our young ladies who took a few lessons on the spinet, and about as many more who learned a very little drawing, in very bad taste; but the parents of the rest of us would have thought it not only extravagance, but presumption, to give such showy and expensive accomplishments to girls destined for good housewives. We all learned to dance, however, both minuets and country dances, and I well remember that before our grand annual exhibition at the master's ball, such of us as nature had not favoured with the high forehead, then esteemed a beauty, were obliged to submit to the application of a strip of pitch plaister round the edges of the hair, by means of which it was torn up by the roots.

S. Ah, how barbarous!

Mrs. H. We had other penances to undergo, unknown to the damsels of these happier days. There were backboards, iron collars, stocks for the feet, and a frightful kind of neck swing, in which we were suspended every morning whilst one of the teachers was lacing our stays; all which contrivances were intended and imagined to improve the figure and the air. Nothing was thought so awkward and vulgar as anything approaching to a stoop. 'Hold up your head! hold up your head, miss!' was the constant cry. I wonder any of us kept our health: we had very little exercise of any kind, were tightlaced in very stiff stays, not sufficiently warmed in winter, and both coarsely and sparely fed. The only advantage we enjoyed above modern young ladies—but this is perhaps an important one—was in not having our faculties overstrained by too many lessons in too great a variety of pursuits. I was released from my school at about fourteen, and glad enough, I assure you. By this time my father had become a man of considerable property. He had quitted the house of business for Bloomsbury Square, then accounted a very genteel situation, and set up his carriage. He had purchased a small estate about forty miles from London, and we divided the year between town and country, but I do not think you would much have relished our way of life in either.

S. Pray describe it to me.

Mrs. H. In the first place, the journey from one to the other was not performed quite with modern ease and rapidity. Although we travelled with post horses, we generally found it necessary to sleep on the road;—we always did so, at least, when we went to keep our Christmas in the country. Finchley Common, which lay in our way, was a tract over which nobody then ventured to travel in the dusk; and even at noonday the appearance of a horseman-traveller caused us some palpitations. The by-roads were formidably bad, and even the great north road was crossed in four or five places by streams, over which there were no bridges, and which, in times of flood, it was somewhat dangerous to pass. In one place we had to pass close under a gibbet on which the body of a murderer was hung in chains. When at length we were arrived, the Christmas logs hardly sufficed tolerably to warm the windy old mansion with its rattling casements and floors scantily carpeted. Neighbours we had very few, and the annual dinner or tea visits which we paid were formal and dull. We had but a small assortment of books of any kind, and no new ones.

S. How did you contrive to fill up your time?

Mrs. H. Oh, there was no great difficulty in that. Besides, our own sewing included a vast deal of laborious flourishing upon cambric, gauze, and catgut; we had all the shirts to make for my father and the boys; we had all the pastry and sweets to make, besides a good deal of exercise in potting, pickling, preserving, and wine-making. At washing times we were required to assist in hanging out the linen, folding, clear-starching, and ironing; we——

S. My dear grandmamma, is it possible that young ladies were put to all this drudgery? You might as well have been cooks or laundry-maids.

Mrs. H. We did not think so, I assure you. As these acts were then regarded as an essential part of female education, and as all our neighbours spent their time in the same occupations, we never regarded these things as hardships. Still it was a life of little variety, or what in modern phrase is called excitement. I confess I should have liked at least to make the tour of the county, but excursions of this kind were not much the fashion. We did, however, sometimes pay visits to relations at a distance, which we enjoyed with a zest only known, I believe, to those whose pleasures come but seldom; and a county assembly was an event to be reckoned upon for weeks and talked over for months. The chief alloy of our social enjoyments was the stiff and really barbarous ceremonial which then accompanied all the common actions of life. From the retired life that they led, and the awe and subjection in which they were kept by their elders, damsels had then a degree of bashfulness, or awkwardness if you please, of which it is my private opinion that the accomplished young ladies of these days cannot even form an idea. Imagine, then, what it was, in the midst of a formal dinner, after calling for beer and receiving it from the servant in a cup or glass, by the bye, which had previously served half the company——

S. Ah, filthy!

Mrs. H. It was so. After this, I say, think what it was to go round the company, crying out with an audible voice, 'Mrs. A., your health; Dr. B., your good health,' and so on—each person as you proceeded laying down his knife and fork to be ready to acknowledge the compliment!

S. Dreadful indeed!

Mrs. H. I have often sat almost choking with thirst, but quite unable to summon courage for the operation of drinking. I remember once seeing an awkward girl surprised by the approach of a health as she was in the act of picking the leg bone of a fowl with her teeth—another graceful practice of that day—who suddenly dropped both her hands and sat quite still with the bone across her mouth.

S. Ha! ha! like a death's head with cross bones in the border to a bill of mortality!

Mrs. H. It was even worse when we came to the wine after dinner or supper; it was then not sufficient to drink healths: a young lady would often be required, in spite of blushes and entreaties, to give as a toast either the name of a single gentleman or a sentiment.

S. How tormenting! but what kind of sentiments?

Mrs. H. Perhaps some such flat affair as this: 'May the single be married, and the married happy.' But I ramble—these old recollections carry me away. I was going to describe to you our town life. We were here exempted from a part of our household business, and a few more diversions fell in our way—such as a good play, or now and then a concert, or a visit to Ranelagh or Vauxhall. But the ordinary style of visiting was dull enough. Morning calls were not much the fashion, but after what would now be called a very early dinner, the custom was to drive to the house of some acquaintance and sit perhaps half an hour, then to another, and another, contriving to reach by tea-time some lady whose visiting day it was. With her you perhaps found some half-dozen people assembled, and either a pool or a rubber was made up, or the visit was spent sitting in a formal circle, where, as Cowper says,—

> 'Yes, ma'am,' and 'No, ma'am,' uttered softly, show
> Every five minutes how the minutes go.

Well-bred ease was then rare indeed; in fact it was scarcely known except in very high life; the middle classes might be said to be mere beginners in the arts of social entertainment. Great improvements have since been made in this way. At this time the fashion of frequenting watering-places, which has both good and evil in it, was but just introduced. Few frequented them except upon the plea at least of health. We went one season to Bath, for my father's gout. It was very shortly after the publication of 'Anstey's Bath Guide,' and you have only to treat yourself with the perusal of that witty and entertaining piece to gain a very good notion of the manners and customs of the place at that time.

S. I have read it, and it seemed to me like an account of some foreign country—everything is since so changed. The fashions of dress appear to have been signally barbarous in taste.

Mrs. H. The powdered and frizzled wigs worn by young ladies were bad enough, certainly. In other points I know not that the present times have any great advantage. As far as I can compare things, it seems to me that dress was rather more costly, in proportion to other expenses, then than at present, owing no doubt to the improvement of our manufactures by the invention of the steam-engine and machinery. But we had much fewer changes of apparel. The choice of a best gown was really only second in importance to the choice of a husband; it was not every year that we bought a new one.

S. What, not one new dress in a year!

Mrs. H. Not a best dress. Young women in our station of life would buy one year a rich silk gown and petticoat, called a suit of clothes, which would cost five pounds or more, and the next year they would content themselves with a slighter one, less trimmed and without a petticoat of the same, which was called a night-gown.

S. What a very ugly name for a dress!

Mrs. H. Yes, that name, and still more the custom which I remember amongst ladies of fashion, of receiving their company in an apartment adorned in other respect like a drawing-room, but bearing the name of a dressing-room, and set out with a showy toilet, at which the lady sometimes appeared actually under the hands of the hairdresser, were certainly relics of the gross manners and slatternly customs of the French court, first brought here under Charles II. But every age and country has some practices which, to the rest of the world, appear indecorums. We, for instance, never thought of shaking hands with any gentleman; and the modern custom of lounging upon sofas would have shocked us much in my young time. We had then no sofas.

S. No! How did you exist without them?

Mrs. H. When people were really ill, they went into their own chambers and lay down on the bed. When they were well, they took the trouble to sit upright on their chairs. You know I am even yet no friend to *lolloping*, as I call it.

S. I know, dear grandmamma, that you never practise it. You have no habits of self-indulgence.

Mrs. H. I was brought up in none, and in that respect I do think that former days had the advantage of these. We had much fewer wants, and I have still about me so much of the old school as to think it better in all respects for mind, body, and outward estate, not to wish for luxuries and superfluities than even to possess them. How much better, then, is it than to wish for them and to be unable to procure them—the case of thousands at present! We had neither hearth-rugs nor foot-stools, nor lounging chairs, nor foot-warmers for carriages, and when we entertained a few friends at dinner, it was without silver forks, or napkins, or finger-glasses, or French dishes, or ices. But I cannot think that we were to be pitied on this account. These are all of them things which no one but a spoiled child would wish for, except for the sake of making as genteel an appearance as his neighbours. I do confess, however, that it is very difficult to draw the line between real comforts, or agreeable luxuries, and mere superfluities, and I feel some gratitude to be due to the inventors of Rumford stoves, gas lights, and umbrellas.

S. Is it possible that you had no umbrellas?

Mrs. H. I never possessed one till I married; and it was many years after that before they got into their present universal use.

S. How did you manage to protect yourselves from the rain?

Mrs. H. We had good cloth cloaks, with hoods to them, for very bad weather. When we were caught in a sudden shower with our best bonnets on—coming out of church, for example—I am afraid we were so shocking as to cover them as well as we could with our pocket-handkerchiefs. Nay, I *have* seen the skirt of the gown turned over the head for this purpose. But I do humbly confess the superiority of the umbrella to all these contrivances.

S. You said just now that you never shook hands with gentlemen.

Mrs. H. Never; it would have been thought a strange masculine familiarity.

S. But when you were very glad to see some old friend, how did you receive him?

Mrs. H. In that case, the gentleman would take a salute.

S. And was that less of a favour than shaking hands?

Mrs. H. The lady at least was passive in that case; but now you see girls actually offering their hands to young men. I believe, too, it is held that the ladies are always to speak to gentlemen first at meeting. And now I am tired of telling my old stories, and you, I think, must be tired of hearing them.

S. No, indeed; they interest me very much. But I will not encroach upon your kindness. You will now allow me to give you this soft hassock of my own work to rest your feet upon.

Mrs. H. Well, my dear, I will not refuse to touch modern luxury with the tip of my toe, though I should be very sorry to steep myself in it up to the lips.

HOW CHARACTER IS FORMED.

A DIALOGUE.

> But oars alone can ne'er prevail
> To reach that distant coast;
> The breath of heaven will swell the sail,
> Or all our toil is lost.

Two old schoolfellows, between whom more than twenty years of friendship, cemented by the marriage of one to the sister of the other, had established the most confidential intimacy, had taken advantage of a public holiday, to enjoy the rare indulgence, to men closely occupied in the active business of life, of a long *tête-à-tête* walk. Their conversation, after glancing upon a variety of topics, some general, others personal, settled at length upon a theme of universal interest, and the following dialogue ensued.

A. After all, what is it, do you say, which forms the character?

B. What formed yours?

A. I really cannot say. I never thought about the matter.

B. Will you let me examine you, and cross-examine you too, if I see occasion, since it is my vocation?

A. Examine as much as you please, and I will answer to the best of my knowledge and belief.

B. Temper is a very important feature of character;

can you remember your own ever to have been materially different from what it is, and if so, what changed it?

A. I was excessively passionate when a child, and once in my fury I aimed an unlucky blow at my younger brother, which laid him senseless at my feet. For a few moments I thought myself his murderer; the agony of my terror and remorse I shall never forget. My father confirmed the impression by placing me in solitary confinement for several days. It did me much good. I am still far too irascible, but never since, on any provocation, have I lost all command of myself.

B. That is to say, that your own painful experience of consequences, combined with wholesome discipline, taught you to control your temper, but without changing it.

A. Exactly so. But I never bore malice in my childhood, nor do I now; and I am not envious.

B. No; I can answer for you on both these points. And you were attached to your parents, fond of your brothers and sisters, and willing to give up your own inclinations to theirs.

A. I loved them all dearly, and was usually pretty ready to make sacrifices to those who were not less willing to make them to me.

B. Here we have the influence of sympathy; but did it act equally on all the family?

A. Why, no. There certainly was an exception. If one may speak the truth of him now he is dead and gone, it must be owned that Dick was always a selfish dog, and cunning too. He was the only one amongst us who would tell lies for the sake of gaining little advantages to himself. My parents always made truth-telling the first point with their children; but they could never get a straightforward answer from him if he thought that an equivocation or a falsehood would serve his purpose better.

B. To what do you ascribe this moral obliquity of his?

A. 'All wickedness is weakness,' it has been said, and whether that be absolutely true or not, I have constantly imputed the fatal errors of this unfortunate brother of mine solely to the feebleness of his mental constitution. No moral ideas made a deep or clear impression upon him. Present pain, and present pleasure, were the only things which much affected him; even bitter and often repeated experience could not teach him to weigh the consequences of his actions. I know not what stress you will lay upon the observation, but it is a fact that he was like neither of his parents, nor any one of their children; but bore the strongest resemblance, both in person and manners, to a brother of my mother's, whose character and whose career in life were not less unthinking and unfortunate than his own.

B. I attach great importance to these resemblances; in the same family at least, I have constantly observed that physical and moral likeness go together, and that these inherent qualities, or tendencies, often, as in the case of your brother, render nugatory the most judicious measures of the wisest parents, and even withstand the force of circumstances and the rough discipline of the world. Pray, how did you acquire that ready and skilful use of the pencil which I have admired in you ever since we were first acquainted?

A. Oh, by imitation, no doubt. My father had the talent in a high degree, and was sketching at every leisure moment.

B. And you all inherited or acquired it from him?

A. Not all. William and Sophia had no aptitude whatever for drawing; my father tried in vain to teach them. On the other hand, Sophia alone amongst us had an ear for music, and William, as you know, evinced from childhood a genius for the mathematics, which was certainly no part of his inheritance, but which seemed to be a gift of nature.

B. Who, or what, inspired you with the ardent attachment to civil liberty, which at school caused you many a black eye and bloody nose, and which has not seldom stood in the way of your advancement since?

A. I imbibed the sentiment, almost before I can remember, from my father, who cherished it as the very breath of life. In his early days he had endured both obloquy and loss in the *good old cause*, as he used fondly to call it; and I should have felt myself unworthy to bear his name had I abandoned his principles. I now begin to perceive that it must have been his general influence over me which had the greatest share in the formation of my character, or at all events of my opinions, sentiments, and acquirements.

B. Your habits?

A. His, all his, and my mother's; which were indeed moulded upon his. Everything in our house went as if by clockwork. My parents were never on any occasion to be waited for, and never one moment idle; and the like punctuality and diligence were required of us children. It was not that we had no play—that would have rendered our home and its ways irksome to us; on the contrary, we had rather a large allowance; but the rule was, work when you work, and play when you play; no lounging! To this training I owe more than I can reckon.

B. You may well say so, if it be to this that you are indebted for the best business habits I have seen in any man. But again I ask, did this admirable training produce similar effects on you all?

A. Yes, I think so, more or less. Poor Dick, indeed, could not be made either punctual or industrious. In spite of daily objurgations he would never make his appearance in the morning till breakfast was half over; he was always behindhand with his task, and had to be roused from a recumbent posture, either on the sofa or the lawn, half a dozen times in the day. Sophia, too, was somewhat indolently disposed; but I think that in her this infirmity was connected with deeper sensibility, and a more poetical imagination, than the rest of us were blessed with.

B. You call these blessings?

A. Surely I do. They give to life its *aroma*. Since I have enjoyed the happiness of a union with one whose pre-eminence in these gifts you know so well, I have learnt to value them aright; and I have even discovered that more of both existed in the depths of my own nature than I had ever before been aware of. Among the influences which have contributed to form my tastes, and in good measure my character, I should be ungrateful indeed to forget those of a wife not less the object of my admiration than my tenderness. I know not when the education of a man may be said to be finished, but assuredly mine was in many respects still in its rudiments when I first formed my attachment to your sister.

B. She has had an apt scholar, at any rate. But let us now, in an orderly manner, sum up the results of your testimony. Temper, probably innate and constitutional, controlled by experience, reflection, and discipline, but never changed. The selfish principle successfully combated among a family of children, and domestic affections instilled by the silent force of sympathy. The principle of veracity firmly established among them by parental influence and example; but these means failing with one child, probably from feebleness of intellectual constitution, of which the race had exhibited a previous example. Political sentiments taken up early, and steadily persevered in from filial deference, and regarded as a point of honour. Habits formed by the same influence acting through the established rules of a happy and well-ordered home. Tastes and talents inherited or acquired from a parent by some of the children, not by all; and a decided genius for mathematical science in one child, not traceable to any known source. New qualities brought out, and the formation of character completed, by the influence of a beloved object.

A. And what are your deductions from these facts?

B. In the first place I perceive nothing exceptional in your case. These are the agents by which all human characters are formed, though the proportions in which they exert their influence on individuals, and the nature of that influence, vary exceedingly, according to circumstances, according to the native vigour of the mind, and according to certain peculiarities of disposition which we are unable to account for. Some resist the action of other minds, and even the force of external circumstances, from strength of character, or of will—of which Napoleon was a striking example; others are incapable, from weakness or levity, of any permanent impression.

A. You are far, then, from holding that we come into the world, as some have said, sheets of blank paper, on which our instructors may trace what characters they please.

B. I hold it in one sense—that is, I believe that our ideas are all acquired, not innate; but as to the capacity of receiving and retaining impressions, these blank sheets differ as much as whity-brown from the finest woven post, or that which bears ink the best from mere blotting-paper, on which you can write nothing legibly or distinctly.

A. It has been the theory of some writers, that everything is decided by first impressions; or that it is on the associations formed by apparently trifling and unnoticed circumstances during the first two or three years of life, that the whole future character depends.

B. I have no faith in those occult causes; at most I would only admit their possible agency in the absence of all more obvious and probable explanations of the phenomena. As I said before, I attach great importance to the tendencies or qualities of race. You may indeed call this an occult cause, which no doubt it is, in the same sense as all the laws of nature are occult in respect of man; but no one can doubt the existence of such tendencies, who looks at mankind in the large way, whether with the eyes of the traveller, the historian, or the ethnologist.

A. In what part of our constitution do you hold that these tendencies are most prevalent?

B. It is hard to say. The likeness of an individual, whether of a family or of a people, among themselves, and their unlikeness to others, manifests itself both in the great outlines of character, in disposition, temperament, and capacity, and in particulars often so minute that it would appear ridiculous to mention them. It is the same in the bodily frame, in the mien and carriage, and in little ways and oddities. You may trace family resemblance as often in the shape of the finger nails or the growth of the hair, as in the voice, the outline of the features, or the mould of the form. What are called tricks in children, often spring from this deep root, and it is, therefore, that their correction is often obliged to be given up as hopeless. 'Why,' I once heard an anatomist exclaim to an anxious governess, 'do you take so much pains to make that girl hold up her head? It is all in vain. Look at her mother—mother crab and daughter crab.'

A. Dangerous doctrine! According to this, education has no influence; and to correct anything we see amiss in children is a vain attempt.

B. Not so neither. Though everything is not in our power, much is. There *are* means by which bodily tricks may be overcome. Under the care of the drill-sergeant every recruit learns to hold up his head, at least during exercise; and the most left-handed by nature never persist in carrying the musket wrong. The force of discipline, and the principle of imitation, exert a steady counteracting power over all idiosyncrasies, physical or moral. We have also acknowledged the influence of sympathy, of precept, and of habit. Yet it is very clear that, on the whole, the formation of character has not been subjected to the will and pleasure of man. No one can say, 'I will make my son a distinguished man—a great poet, a great painter, or mathematician,' nor can he say positively, although I hold his power to be greater in the moral part, 'I will make him upright and benevolent.' On the other hand, no father, however wicked or unnatural, could find out a certain method of rendering his boy either stupid or profligate. It must always be with the prudent reservation of that adept who professed that he could make a child immortal, provided he were *a fit subject* for the experiment.

Here the conversation of our two friends was interrupted by the hasty approach of a gentleman of their acquaintance, who, descrying them from his window, came out in haste to meet them, and insisted on taking them in to partake of his abundant and hospitable luncheon—a refreshment which they found very seasonable after so much grave discourse.

ON THE SPIRIT OF ARISTOCRACY.

A DIALOGUE.

ALBERT. SOPHIA.

Albert. I fear I have disturbed some learned debate. I heard the voices of Frank and Harry loud and earnest as I approached, but on my appearance they are gone.

Sophia. And time they were. They would waste the whole day in talking, if I did not now and then hold up my watch to them. But this morning they got upon rather an interesting subject, as I thought, and I should be glad, my dear uncle, to hear your opinion upon it. Frank says there is more of the spirit of aristocracy in England than in any other country of Europe. This Harry denies, but what say you?

A. In the first place I do not pretend, whatever these academic youths may do, to possess sufficient knowledge of every country in Europe to give a proper answer to the question; but perhaps the assertion may, or it may not be true, according to the sense which you attach to terms.

S. How so?

A. That this is not the country in which there is the broadest line of demarcation between patrician and plebeian, *noble* and *roturier*, is evident from our possessing no native words to express exactly this distinction. We have, indeed, lords and commoners, but as the younger children of peers have always been included in the latter class, the nobility have never with us, as in France or Germany, formed a race, or *caste*, who could insult the rest of the nation by the boast of better blood than theirs. In one sense, therefore, the assertion is plainly incorrect.

S. This was Harry's argument. How could it be true,

he said, that aristocracy was so prevalent here, when even the aristocratic part of our constitution was so popularly formed—when so many born plebeians sat and voted among the lords spiritual and temporal? He added, with respect to the nobility here and in the old monarchies of the continent, that it was there a towering palm, shooting up its stately trunk clear from the surrounding underwood, and bearing its whole canopy of leaves and blossoms aloft in air; whilst here, its branches, like those of the banyan, bend ever downwards, and root themselves again in the common earth.

A. Pretty enough; and as much or as little to the purpose as similes commonly are. But in spite of this, if it is meant to assert that this is the country in which people are most uniformly deferential in their manners towards those whom they regard as their superiors, and contemptuous to their inferiors, I am afraid it may be true. We are certainly very great respecters of persons.

S. What can be the reason of it?

A. Several reasons, or rather several causes, may be assigned. In the first place, although we have never, correctly speaking, had patrician families, or a privileged order like the French noblesse, the distinction of ranks has always been very strongly marked among us. You may have read that in old times there was a difference made in gentlemen's houses between those who sat above and those who sat below the salt; and in every baronial hall there were distinct tables for guests of different degrees, who were thus in presence without ever being in company with one another. There were also sumptuary laws by which the use of rich furs, velvet, gold lace, and other expensive materials and fashions of dress, and even of some luxuries of the table, was restricted to persons of a certain rank or fortune. Down to the overthrow of monarchy at the death of Charles I., the ceremonial of the

English court had been almost oriental in its servility, and was viewed with surprise by foreign ambassadors. No one presumed to speak to Queen Elizabeth, but on his knees, and in her days a private gentleman or a knight was expected to stand 'cap in hand' even to a peer. Now, although these appendages of barbarism and the feudal system have long been swept away, I think you will perceive that it may well require ages to wear out the marks left by them on the manners and customs of a people. Down to the present day does not an insignificant young gentlewoman like yourself expect her shoemaker or her milliner to stand in her awful presence while receiving her orders?

S. Why, that is what those kind of people do of course; one never tells them to do it, or thinks about it.

A. Precisely, because there *is* so much in England of the spirit of aristocracy. In America, or in the France of the present day, you would find that such observances are by no means matters of course. There, a common workman would make no scruple of seating himself beside you.

S. How horrid!

A. Yes, 'how horrid!' With English young ladies that silly exclamation, too, is quite of course. You cannot bear the notion of your inferiors forgetting their distance towards you, and yet if you were to call upon a duchess, and she should motion you to a stool at the lower end of the room, you would scarcely be able to find terms strong enough to express your indignation at the arrogance of her behaviour. Is there not a greater distance between you, the daughter of a private gentleman of small fortune, and a duchess, than between you and a respectable milliner?

S. I do not well know what to say to that. In fortune there is, no doubt, and in what one may call consequence, but in another way there seems not to be. It is said, I believe, that a gentleman or a gentlewoman is company for anybody; now I—that is to say, papa is a gentleman, and he sometimes visits noblemen, but a milliner is not a gentlewoman.

A. Speak out at once, child, without affectation, the thing that is in your head, which is this: that when your great neighbours at the castle invite what are called the county families once in the season, you go there with your sister and are received by the duchess as a person of her society; whilst the milliner is never received by you or your sister on that footing.

S. That was what I meant, my dear uncle, but I did not know exactly how to express it.

A. Your claim, then, to a kind of social equality with a duchess is that of a gentlewoman born?

S. Yes.

A. But what if the milliner should turn out to be better gentlewoman of the two? With respect to the one you employ, I happen to know this to be the case. She is the granddaughter of a lord, a poor one indeed, but still a lord.

S. Is it possible?

A. Stranger things are very possible in this world of mutability. Her mother married ill, in every sense of the term, was cast off by her noble father and family, and sank into indigence. She herself married a man of very respectable character, an artist, but he was carried off at an early age and left her with the charge of a young family whom she creditably maintains by the profits of her business. Yet this lady you keep standing at your audience!

S. Oh! but indeed, my dear uncle, I had no idea that she was such a real gentlewoman. I will always make her sit down in future.

A. So far, well. But the disciples of Pythagoras abstained from crushing even a worm, for fear of dispossessing some kindred soul, and I would conjure you by your own gentility to forbear to keep standing *any* milliner or dressmaker you may in future employ, lest you should again be guilty of the horror of failing in respect to the granddaughter of a lord. It is very difficult to know the negative in these cases.

S. You are laughing at me.

A. Oh! by no means. I only suggest the motive most likely to be effectual in persuading you to treat what you call 'those kind of people' like fellow-creatures. But to return to her grace who is so good as to treat you like a fellow-creature. You ascribe this condescension of hers to your gentle birth, but to what, pray, do you ascribe the very marked distinction with which she receives the mistress of Million Hall, as people call it? I dare say you know, for such facts are not easily suffered to fall into oblivion, that she was originally chambermaid at an inn; and to say the truth, she looks it still, with all her blaze of diamonds, and that the enormously rich banker, her husband, began life as a porter in a warehouse. And yet it is more than surmised that this couple are courted by the noble duchess with the hope that their son and heir may be tempted to choose a wife amongst the six lady-daughters who grace her side.

S. Oh no! I cannot believe it.

A. I can, without any difficulty.

S. At least you would surely regard it as a very base sacrifice of dignity to wealth, if any one of those ladies could consent to marry the son of such parents. And were not the old strict rules you have been mentioning of this use at least, that they prevented such *mésalliances,* as the French call them?

A. But they did not prevent them. As long as great

fortunes have been raised by trade in this country—that is, for centuries past—our nobility have consented to take their share in the profit by means of those alliances which shock you so much, and against which, indeed, their own pride revolted even whilst they were driven into them by avarice or necessity. Low birth, therefore, is not of itself sufficient to exclude the rich from the intimate society of the first nobles of the land. But neither does it always exclude those who are poor.

S. No! that seems very strange. What kind of persons at once poor and ignoble do the great associate with?

A. Mr. Burke has ventured to observe that kings are fond of low company, and the same may be said of many of their nobles. First, there is the whole class called led-captains, or toad-eaters, the meanest of the mean, whom, nevertheless, the proudest of the proud habitually admit to their tables and make a part of their familiar society. Above these, the professors of various dexterities, arts, and sciences, take stations determined by the tastes and fancies of the noble owners of those great caravanseras called family seats. In some great mansions, actors, singers, and musicians find a welcome; in others, religious enthusiasts; in some, boxers, jockeys, and cockfighters; artists in others; and in a few, men of science or sound learning. The greater part of these persons are obscurely born and have no other revenue than their wits, yet as a class they may certainly pride themselves on a far greater share of the notice and society of the nobility than your rural gentry, with their formal annual visit to the great man of the neighbourhood, who merely tolerates their incursion in consideration of his office of lord-lieutenant of the county, or in hopes of influencing their votes at an election.

S. But I am certain that many of those whom you mention as so familiar with the great, are persons whom you, uncle, would not like to associate with, and whom I suppose, therefore, that you consider as your inferiors.

A. To be sure, I should not choose to open my humble doors to boxers and cockfighters, to led-captains and toad-eaters, or even to professors of the unknown tongue. I do look down upon all these guests of great houses, and many others.

S. But what is it, after all, on which a person's place in society does depend? The more I think about it the more I am puzzled.

A. That I can easily believe. To be puzzled is usually the first effect of beginning to think in earnest upon a subject, and those who are impatient of this feeling will never come to understand any properly. In the first place, however, what do you mean by the expression 'place in society?' A herald would tell you that a man's place in society is that assigned him in the rules of precedence, by which he marshals a procession; and in fact it is by these rules that people accounted well-bred arrange, at a ball or a dinner-table, such of their guests as happen to be thus entitled to any place at all. A knowledge of them may be attained without difficulty by the meanest capacity.

S. Yes, that I know; but they determine only rank, and it seems to me that what is called consequence is a different thing, and depends upon I know not what.

A. You are right. It is only on a few formal occasions that these rules will now apply; the progress of civilisation has nearly superseded them. In modern society it is perpetually seen and felt that the last in rank may be the first in consequence. For many purposes wealth is power, knowledge is power, popular eloquence is power, genius is power, virtue is power, and from power result influence, consequence, eminence. But these are sources of distinction quite out of the cognisance of the Herald's College.

S. I have sometimes heard it said that a person's place in society is wherever he chooses to put himself, and I begin to think there may be something in it.

A. True! Amongst my powers I forgot assumption, which well deserves to be reckoned for one. You may have seen young ladies lead the dance by that title only.

S. Yes, by mere rudeness and pushing. And I have observed at our county assemblies that the best bred, and sometimes, too, the best born young ladies, would stand back till they were invited to come forward, whilst the vulgar and ill-behaved struggled boldly for the best places, and often gained them.

A. So it will always be, more or less, in the graver competitions of life; and there are circumstances in the present state of society and manners among ourselves which peculiarly favour the bold. Men and women, too, live in more, and consequently more various, society than they used to do. Continental travelling, the resort to watering-places, great routs of parties, and those associations which it has been the fashion to form for such a variety of religious, political, benevolent, scientific, literary, and miscellaneous objects, all tend to enlarge the circle of every one's acquaintance and to mingle different ranks and classes. Amid this 'various bustle of resort,' there is little leisure critically to examine claims of merit or titles of precedence. A new acquaintance is commonly rated partly according to the direct pleasure or advantage, of whatever kind, to be derived from his society, partly according to the value which seems to be set upon him by others, and partly, no doubt, according to that which he appears to set upon himself. This is so well understood that the cold and haughty air, affected by many towards strangers, is often to be regarded rather as an artifice designed to convey an exaggerated impression of the consequence of him who uses it, than an evidence of what is properly called the spirit of aristocracy.

S. Is it not true that the *real* born nobleman or gentleman is distinguished from the new or the counterfeit by the unpretending simplicity and universal courtesy of his behaviour?

A. That is an idea which has been much inculcated by some of our best novel-writers. It is plausible, and probably founded in part on observation. At least it is likely that insolence should be the ordinary badge of an upstart. But pride and ill-nature have often run, too, in the highest blood; kings themselves are not always exempt from the taint. A vulgar mind is very compatible with a noble race; and, generally speaking, it is only by a resolute determination on the part of the many to resist the arrogant assumptions of the few, that the fierce spirit of hereditary aristocracy has ever been, or ever can be, kept in order. But to reply to your question, on what it is that a person's place in society depends. The grounds of social distinction amongst us are three: rank, hereditary or official, including the political power annexed to it;—wealth;—and personal endowments, achievements, or acquirements of every kind. It is obvious that he would be the first man in society who should unite in himself all these kinds of eminence in the highest degree; since he would claim the homage of all, everywhere. But nature and fortune have seldom agreed in lavishing their favours on the same object; and distinction in one kind, without signal deficiency in other respects, is as much as usually falls to the lot of man. Hence it happens—and every sort of pride ought to stand rebuked by the reflection—that scarcely any one is the head of every company which he enters. In one circle he will be estimated by what he has, and in another by what he wants; not to mention that every one, excepting the first in every line, is liable to be mortified by meeting a superior in his own department.

S. Still, a nobleman is noble, a rich man rich, and a man of genius a man of genius in every company.

A. No doubt; but *eminence* is literally nothing but *overtopping,* and therefore must always be relative. Besides this, men do not long pay even outward respect to qualities from which they derive no kind of benefit. You may remember that Lord Halifax in his advice to his daughters, which is full of observation and knowledge of the world, tells them that 'the old housekeeper shall make a better figure in the family' than the lady, if from pride and indolence she neglects to take her proper part in the government and business of it. A nobleman, though of high and ancient lineage, if, either from poverty or avarice, he fails to make returns to the hospitalities he receives, will find more of contempt than honour from his acquaintance; a man even of acknowledged genius, if careless and uncouth in the common intercourses of life, will be valued only by those conversant with his own art or science; and the merely rich man will have to encounter the scorn of 'inferiors not dependent' as often as he presumes upon his single talent. I recollect a person of this kind, who once taking an overbearing tone in argument with an acquaintance beneath him in fortune but above him in sense and powers of reasoning, the other suddenly interrupted him with 'Pray, sir, have you made your will?' 'Yes,' he said, 'I have, but what makes you ask?' 'Have you left me a legacy?' 'No, indeed.' 'Then I see no reason why I should submit my opinion to yours.' On the whole it must be owned that pride and surliness are features much too prominent in our national character; and we shall then, and then only, truly deserve the character of a civilised people, when, our eyes being properly open to the offensiveness of these qualities, a wholesome dread of the general indignation shall restrain all, whatever may be their rank or pretensions, from the airs of contempt and insult by which so many in every company now endeavour to assert their own importance and superiority.

EXAMPLE AND PRECEPT.

A DIALOGUE.

Henry. Since, then, example, as every one knows, is of more force than precept——

Albert. Stop, if you please, or you will reduce me to nonentity; for so far am I from knowing this, that I am firmly convinced of the contrary.

H. Come, come, this is carrying your love of paradox a little too far. You well know this, at least, that ancient and modern philosophers, moralists and divines, are all against you; there is absolutely not a dissenting voice in the matter.

A. No! What says Jeremy Taylor? 'Against a rule no example is a competent warrant, and if the example be according to the rule, it is not the example but the rule that is the measure of our action.' But I care not what or who is against me, provided truth and reason be for me; and I should not despair of even convincing you that in this case they are so, provided your prejudices would allow you to give me a fair hearing.

H. Yes, to be sure, I must always be prejudiced, because I am apt to think with the rest of mankind. But if you choose to try, you shall find that I can give you a fair hearing nevertheless.

A. Very well, I take you at your word. In what cases, or for what purposes, do you hold that example is of more force than precept?

H. In that which was the subject of our discourse, in education, in the moral training of children; and on this head I speak from experience.

A. Indeed! and you forget what happened no longer ago than yesterday?

H. To what do you refer?

A. We had promised, you know, to take your little daughter with us on our water party. When the rain came on and our project was given up, the child cried with the disappointment. 'Fie, fie! Mary,' you exclaimed with an air of triumph, 'you do not see me cry because I cannot go on the water.' 'No, papa,' replied the poor child, very sensibly as I thought, 'but you are a great man, and I am only a poor little girl of six years old.' You were silenced by the retort, as well you might be, and so fell the power of example to the ground. A simple precept against giving way to fretfulness or disappointment, backed by arguments suited to the child's comprehension, might have had some effect—at least it would not have exposed you to an inglorious defeat.

H. Well, I confess that to propose an example open to this kind of objection, is injudicious; mine was an ill-chosen one.

A. Very true. But although the example were ever so fit for the occasion, the person to whom you should modestly propose yourself as a pattern, might still turn round upon you, and ask in the spirit of Maria's taunt to Malvolio, 'Dost thou think, because thou art virtuous, that there shall be no more cakes and ale?' That is, why should your conduct serve as a rule to me?

H. From my own children, at least, I trust I should never have that question to apprehend.

A. I would not be too certain of that. There is a strange propensity in human nature to fly at anything which pretends to set itself up on high, and tear it down if possible. I could mention a case in point. The thing happened to a lady of my acquaintance, who assuredly does not carry the virtue of humility to any excess. 'How awkward you are!' I heard her say to her little girl. '*I* do not hold my head down; *I* do not turn in my toes as I walk; *I* do not lean my elbows on the table.' 'I beg your pardon, mamma,' said the child, who is really a well-behaved little creature, 'but are you not rather fond of praising yourself?' To which no answer was given. On this plan, too, there is sometimes the opposite question to be asked, Why am I *not* to follow your example? which puzzled you not a little when Master Harry made bold to put it to you the other day. It was when we surprised him in the dining-room with a bumper at his lips. 'You drink wine, papa, and why should not I?' Between these opposite dilemmas it would not be wonderful if children should come at last to the conclusion, that papa's example is a rule, or is not a rule, just as he pleases to make it—in short, no rule at all.

H. With such perverse ingenuity as you are kind enough to lend them, they would equally find flaws in any rule or precept which might be given them for their guidance, since there is none without an exception.

A. May be so. But then, at least, their objections, or their cavils, might be brought to the test of fair reasoning, without your finding yourself embarrassed with the *argumentum ad hominem.*

H. Now, at last, I understand the matter! This quarrel of yours against example is but another form of your old jealousy of the interference of authority in matters where you would have reason sole and sovereign judge.

A. I own it; I hold it an unworthy thing as well as a dangerous, to impose upon a child the habit of relying on precedents, and bowing to examples, instead of encouraging him to enquire into the nature of things and the tendencies and results of actions, and thus to form himself on the immutable principles of reason and of duty. Can anything be more to the reproach of the ordinary training of youth than the large fact, which no one can question, that through life the great mass of mankind are constantly governed by a precedent rather than a rule, a rule rather than a reason? Is there, indeed, one man in ten—in a hundred—who will take his stand boldly and independently upon the truth, the sense, the right of a thing, so long as he can catch hold of any broken reed of an example, an analogy, a prejudice, a fancy, an idle superstition, to lean upon? Is there——

H. Gently, gently! now you have mounted your hobby, and as usual he is running away with you, carrying you quite out of the course. Be pleased to recollect, that reason is not the only principle by which it is designed that we should be actuated. We have also imaginations, passions, sympathies, affections, associations, by all of which our opinions and our conduct must and will be influenced, more or less. What wise parent or teacher would not, therefore, be anxious to gain over these mighty powers to the side of virtue? and how can he do this so effectually as by the aid of well-selected examples? You would scarcely, I suppose, banish from the school-room all our biographers with Plutarch at their head.

A. By no means. On the contrary, I set a higher value upon them, because it is *principles* that they teach. The very remoteness of the circumstances, especially in the ancient lives, from all that a youth sees around him, and hence their inapplicability in the way of direct precedent, is in my mind a great recommendation. You will allow it to be by no feeble effort of generalisation, that a boy deduces, from his inward approbation of the refusal of Aristides to sanction a profitable scheme which was not just, a rule for his own guidance in his transactions with his schoolfellows?

H. Your distinction is too fine for me. Is it to living examples only that you object?

A. I have pointed out, as I think, very serious inconveniences attending the practice of setting any person, but especially one's self, before a child as an example. I am sensible, however, that both children and older people often derive great benefit from examples, whether in books or in life, which they find out and apply for themselves, because in this case the mind acts freely, and not under dictation, and the principle or sentiment is adopted, rather than the action itself imitated or repeated. In whatever belongs to physical education, in the manual arts and bodily exercises, example or the principle of imitation is indeed all in all. Such things can scarcely be taught otherwise than by *showing how,* but let us beware of subjecting to its authority those provinces in which reason and conscience ought of right to bear sway. Here, unless you establish principles, you do nothing; for one example or authority may always be neutralised by another.

H. Yet it is constantly held forth as one of the most imperative duties of every man to set a good example in his station; and it is even maintained that a worthy man ought to abstain from many practices not evil in themselves, nor dangerous to his own virtue, rather than give an example which may be hurtful to others.

A. Yes, this is language, or this is a cant which passes current in very many places, as I very well know; and it is likely it should, because it assists grave and weak persons, filling stations which render them more or less conspicuous, to flatter themselves into a very undue opinion of the importance of all that they say or do. But of this I am clear, that the man or woman who sets up for being 'to all an example,' is sure enough of becoming 'to no one a pattern.' For the rest, practices are of three kinds—good, bad, and indifferent; and a man should have much more cogent motives for following the first, and avoiding the second, than the supposed effects of his example on his neighbours; and how his indulging in practices which are indifferent can endanger the virtue of any one, I am unable to conjecture.

H. Card-playing, for instance, and frequenting the theatre, are pastimes which you may reckon indifferent, but should you say that a clergyman was setting up a good example by openly indulging in them?

A. You begin the question by describing them as indifferent. I should say that if a clergyman, or any other man, finds himself the better or the worse for them, to him they are not indifferent. But if it were maintained to be the duty of every *grave* character to abstain totally, for example's sake, from amusements innocent and salutary in moderation, because there may be dissipated persons who will indulge in them to excess, I should venture to reply, that such self-denial is totally thrown away. It is not by *grave* examples that people of this kind regulate their proceedings.

H. But there are positive examples as well as negative ones, and you can scarcely deny the efficacy of these. Is it not, for instance, quite certain and notorious that in a village where the squire and his family are constant in attendance at church, their example will bring the farmers and labourers thither with unfailing punctuality, but that, as soon as these leaders of the people happen to be succeeded by others who are negligent and indifferent on this great point, the clergyman may officiate to bare walls?

A. I like that instance—it shows so clearly the shallowness and servility of such a motive of action. The example of *the family,* or rather the hope of their favour, is sufficient, it seems, to bring all the parish to church, but with so little sense of the purpose for which they go, that on the cause ceasing, the effect ceases also. Thus, between the great people who go to set an example, and the little ones who go to follow one, there might be a full congregation without a single person present who should attend for the love of God, or the good of his own soul! But I take this to be a tale of other times; our present generation of rustics is surely not left in such Egyptian darkness by those whose duty it is to bear to them the light of religion. In morals, the imitative principle will go thus far—it will teach men to 'dwell in decencies,' but for anything higher, or anything deeper, anything that shall render a man worthy to be made himself an example, never let it be trusted. Imitators in virtue, as in letters or in arts, must of course be content to take their place below their models; but this is not all: in many cases it is not even an inferior degree in the same class that they will attain. Change the motive or the rule, and you change the very nature of actions or of qualities. What, in characters of principle and reflection, was patriotism, philanthropy, or piety, is subject to become in their copyists ostentation, cant, hypocrisy. Deeds belong to the first class, words to the second. Even the same act assumes different aspects according to the actor. That very insignificant person—I forget his name—who killed himself to resemble Cato, earned nothing for his pains but the sarcastic remark, that *he* might well have borne to yield to Cæsar, although Cato could not. And let me ask whether you have not experienced a profound disgust when some atrocious malefactor, assuming the person of the holiest martyr, has presumed to announce from the scaffold his solemn forgiveness of all his enemies, intending very particularly, by that designation, the judge, jury, prosecutor, and witnesses, who have all in their several offices contributed to bring him to his deserved punishment?

H. I confess that this has often struck me as a shocking presumption, and indeed as a profanation.

A. Examples, like similes, may serve to give animation and interest to discourse; they may, likewise, be employed to illustrate or explain a maxim or a principle, and, happily chosen, they may kindle emulation; but then they ought not to be set before young people for the nonce, and in short——

H. In short, you are jealous of them. But if good examples do so little service, I hope you will go on to prove that bad ones do as little injury.

A. That does not follow. I believe indeed that their *direct* effect may have been overrated, and that in many cases where young people are said to have been corrupted by them, the contagion might be questioned, and the mischief imputed rather to general causes acting upon numbers at once. *Le feu des jeunes gens prend sans allumer.* But their efficacy in overcoming shame, and putting scruples to flight, cannot be doubted; and as the same persons who set bad examples usually maintain bad principles also, I should dread the influence of evil company fully as much as you could do. I will also freely grant you that precept has no force whatever when it is contradicted by the life of him who utters it, as we naturally give credit to a man's deeds before his words. So that ill example set by persons in any kind of authority involves this great inconvenience, that it deprives them of the power of inculcating good principles with any authority or to any purpose.

H. I am glad you allow as much as this.

A. I can very well afford to do it, and yet stand firmly to my original position, that the practice of setting examples before young people for their imitation, is not so efficacious in forming them to the higher virtues as nourishing their minds with noble precepts, supported by just reasoning and temperate appeals to the affections.

H. Well, I am not convinced as yet, but I admit that it is a matter worth thinking about.

ENVY AND PITY.

'It is better to be envied than pitied.'

Those who adopt this maxim mean no more, it is to be hoped, than that the *causes* of envy, prosperity, or superiority over others in the gifts of nature or fortune, are better than the *causes* of pity, misfortune or some kind of inferiority.

Understood in the obvious import of the words, few sentiments could be more false or more shocking. What! better to be the object of the most malignant than of the gentlest of affections, of a sentiment which degrades rather than one which adorns humanity? It will not bear a thought! As mercy is 'twice blessed,' so is envy twice cursed, in its subject and in its object, and he who is willing to stand within its danger, thinking that his power, his wealth, or his genius, place him above all apprehension of its effects on his fortunes or his reputation, either perceives not, or regards not, its inevitable mischief to his temper and his moral feelings. In speculating on the causes of that hardening of the heart observed in all times as one of the most frequent attendants on great prosperity, the foremost place should doubtless be assigned to the consciousness of being envied.

'He loves not to behold my prosperity,' says the rich man to himself, as he notes the scowl on the brow of his poorer neighbour. 'Nay, so far from that, the very sight of my mansion, my park, my equipage, is odious to him. I never did him the smallest injury, yet it would delight him to hear that calamity, ruin even, had overtaken me; then can I be expected to feel for him, to be touched by his sorrows, to aid him in his objects? You all of you grudge me my success; you watch every occasion to detract from my merits and commendations; you would gladly pull me down, even if it did not raise yourselves.' So murmurs the victorious candidate for the honours of his profession, on reading the eyes of the associates and former equals over whose heads he has just raised himself. 'I despise and I defy your malice, but henceforth be strangers to my bosom, and as much as possible to my sight!' Ask you the cause of that frown which disfigures the brow of innocent beauty? The wearer has just been made to feel that

> The nymph must lose her female friend
> If more admired than she.

And thus it happens that, more sinned against than sinning, the favourites, whether of nature or of fortune, are found so often soured in temper, void of sympathy, little sensible to the pleadings of pity, and reduced to please themselves in nothing but in efforts still to augment that wealth, that dignity, or that celebrity, which has already robbed them of the best and dearest of life's blessings.

But thousands are susceptible of pity for one who is altogether free from the passion of envy; thus he who finds himself, without or even *not* without fault of his own, in circumstances to call forth compassion and appeal for relief, enjoys, very frequently, the satisfaction of viewing his fellow-creatures on the fairest side; pleased with themselves for the exercise of their benevolence, and complacent, therefore, towards him who has called it forth. So far, then, from agreeing in the popular sentiment, we might almost be tempted to say that a pitied adversity is better than an envied prosperity. It is by no means unfrequent to hear a sufferer exclaim that it was almost worth while to have encountered this loss—endured that sickness—sustained that misfortune, for the sake of experiencing so much sympathy and kindness; but when has any one, on coming into possession of a great estate, or attaining any conspicuous success, expressed the sentiment, that the affectionate congratulations of his friends and associates had been the most gratifying circumstance of his good fortune? The spirit of man thirsts for sympathy, even as the hart panteth after the water-brooks. No station, no circumstances, neither the victory car nor the diadem of empire, can justly be called happy which exclude this boon of heaven and summon envy in its place; none miserable which calls it forth in a plenteous and unfailing stream. Lord Bacon in his essay on Envy observes, that 'There is some good yet in public envy, whereas in private there is none; for public envy is as an ostracism, that eclipseth men when they grow too great; and therefore it is a bridle also to keep great ones within bounds.' Politically speaking, the distinction is perhaps just, but moral ends may be served by the former no less than the latter. He who desires to be as little as possible the object of private envy, will equally be kept, or keep himself within bounds. If wealthy he will be generous without ostentation, and above all sympathising; if powerful he will exercise authority not as often, but as seldom, as his duty will permit. If singularly favoured by any of nature's gifts, he will bear his faculties meekly, and cheerfully take delight in bringing forward the just claims of others. By these, if any, acts, while he will preserve his own heart from injury, he may sometimes dilute the venom of this snake in the bosom where it harbours.

SORROW AND ANGER.

THERE are many persons who never can be sorry without being disposed to grow angry. In every calamity, they are certain there must have been blame somewhere, and right or wrong, they must seize upon a scapegoat.

A friend has failed in business; they are full of concern for him and his helpless family—but what? It could scarcely have happened from pure misfortune—some one has been much in fault—want of caution on his own part—an unfeeling creditor—a speculating partner—and amid the storm of indignation aimed at the hypothetical author of the mischief, the sigh of pity for those who suffer by it ceases to be audible.

Is intelligence received of a friend's decease? 'Ah, poor fellow! I am very sorry—so valuable a life—so great a loss! But to think of his putting himself under the care of such a quack! But for that he might have been alive and well. I hope the fellow will be indicted for manslaughter.' Sometimes the blame falls on the dead person himself. 'He was so exceedingly imprudent, walking out in the worst weather without a great coat—and why did he not take advice sooner? There he was, going about just as usual, when everybody who looked at him saw that he ought to have been in his bed. Really if a man will throw away his life, one scarcely knows how to pity him.' Accordingly, he is not pitied.

Why is this? It will scarcely be pretended that the passion of anger is less disturbing to the soul than that gentler emotion of pity, which has always in it some mixture of sweetness. There is indeed somewhat of relief in a change, though it be but from one painful feeling to another; but in this instance the cause seems to lie deeper. A tacit reference to self enters, more or less, into all our sympathetic emotions. It is matter of the most familiar remark, that no misfortunes affect us so much as those which are likely one day to fall to our own lot; and in our anxiety to remove this apprehension from ourselves, we are ever ready to catch hold of some casual or accessory circumstance to which to impute the calamity. 'My friend,' we say, 'was indeed ruined, but it was by negligence, by imprudent trust. I, who am neither imprudent nor negligent, have no such catastrophe to fear. He died, but it was through the ignorance of his physician; I employ one who is skilful.' A little distrust, however, is apt still to intrude upon these consolatory explanations. We fear it may be only a flattering unction that we are laying to our souls, and we endeavour, by our very vehemence, to impose silence on our secret doubts how far it may be well directed.

As, in these cases pity is exchanged for blame, there are others in which, anger being out of the question, it yields to terror. In visitations, or apprehended visitations of a formidable epidemic, all may have observed how little is given to pity for those who have already fallen victims, how much to selfish apprehension.

It is the important duty of candour, of fortitude, and of wisdom, to curb the transports of that weak impatience of the pains of sympathy, and that still weaker dread of similar disaster to ourselves, which in every great or unforeseen calamity, cries out for a victim, as if to appease some angry deity.

DOUBT.

' He well has studied who has learned to doubt.'

A hard saying, and one little flattering to the pride of learning! Is that to be regarded as a valuable and desirable result of study, which leaves behind it nothing but uncertainty and the confession of ignorance? Or is there possibly in this learned doubt something deeper, something more positive even than at first appears?

Several considerations render this probable. The derivation of the word ' dubietas ' from ' duo ' may authorise us, perhaps, to distinguish between doubt in its strict and proper acceptation and mere uncertainty; it seems to express, not total bewilderment, but rather hesitation between two; and in many cases, he who has become aware that the matter under consideration admits of an alternative, or may be reduced to one, already knows much.

Childhood, amid all its ignorance, is unacquainted with doubt. Its simple questions, relating for the most part to outward and familiar facts within the competence of any grown up person, usually receive a ready and decisive answer. Should it even happen, as happen it sometimes will, that the question of an intelligent child has plunged unawares into one of those gulfs, too deep for the plummet of thought, which lie hidden beside every path of human speculation, many expedients are at hand to cover the defeat of parental or preceptorial infallibility. Sometimes a dogmatical assertion will be hazarded where nothing can be known to contradict it. At others, a rebuke for meddling with what does not concern us, will do the business. Best of all, is the discreet reply, 'You are too young at present to understand the subject,' which serves at once to save the credit of the questioned, and to flatter the novice with the expectation that a time will come when all his puzzles shall be solved.

Through these artifices, and others of a similar kind, not seldom practised upon 'children of a larger growth,' we all of us begin by being beguiled in a greater or less degree, into the belief that much more certainty is attainable on every subject than, excepting in the exact sciences, has been in reality accorded to the inquiries of mankind.

'To know how little can be known,' and how much admits of doubt, is the attribute, not of ignorance, not of simplicity, but of sagacity, of experience, and of free inquiry. To confess it, is often one of the most costly efforts of a courageous integrity; for there is no vulgar or disingenuous mind which is not immediately affected with suspicion and anger on any appearance of hesitation, uncertainty or scruple, of which it is either unable to comprehend the grounds, or unwilling to accept the practical consequences. From these causes it has arisen, that in common speech, something sinister attaches to the very words doubt and doubtful.

It might contribute a little to mitigate this prejudice in spirits of a better order, with whom it is often merely the offspring of a vague kind of dread, to draw a clearer distinction than is often done between the intrinsic importance of a truth, and the importance of our knowing or having an opinion upon it.

To remain long in doubt between two different plans of life, or two opposite courses of public or private conduct, is justly to be regarded as the mark of a weak and indolent character, or a cloudy understanding. To halt between two opinions on a question involving the moral character of another, and the conduct which we ought to hold respecting him—one in which doubt takes on the form of suspicion or jealousy—would be intolerable to any one in whom the whole moral and sensitive nature had not become paralysed. There is no man of feeling or of honour, who would not in a similar case exclaim with Othello,

> Think'st thou I'd make a life of jealousy?
> * * * * * * *
> No, to be once in doubt,
> Is once to be resolved.
> I'll see before I doubt, when I doubt, prove.

But, to have come to the conclusion, on any point of history, or on any speculative subject, that it must always remain involved in doubt, whether for want of conclusive evidence in one case, or from the inherent obscurity of the subject in the other, ought never to be made a theme of reproach against any man, nor yet to become a source of disquiet to a firm and rational mind, since no important consequences can by possibility be dependent on questions thus inscrutable.

Let us reassure ourselves in our own insignificance. Nothing renders it necessary that we feeble mortals should strain ourselves with stretching upwards eagerly and vainly, as the drowning catch at straws, after truths hung high above our reach. The nature of deity, the plans of providence, 'fix'd fate, free will, fore-knowledge absolute'—great and eternal as must be the verities involved in these questions—are yet nothing to us, nothing to our duties, nothing to our happiness.

Now, much as it may humble an aspiring mind to find itself compelled to accept of doubts and difficulties as the sole result of its investigations into subjects the vastness of which has tempted only to confound its efforts, ought this effect to be lamented? It, 'feelingly persuades us what we are,' how weak, how open to error, and from what various sources. It inculcates tolerance, the sole effective pacifier of social discords; it schools us into candour, the virtue of the experienced and the wise, and it bows the spirit to that genuine, heartfelt humility, which the dogmatist, of whatever sect or party, in vain lays claim to. Let us then accept it as a thoughtful and a precious saying, that 'he well has studied who has learnt to doubt.'

MOTIVES.

NOTHING more rare than to hear the true motives assigned by any person for any action of his life! Even those who scruple falsehood in any other form, indulge without remorse or without reflection in the habit of assigning plausible reasons in the place of true ones. The boundless curiosity of mankind concerning the actions and the affairs of their neighbours, must bear the chief blame of this pernicious and demoralising practice, 'Ask me no questions and I'll tell you no lies,' is a frequent saying, and one which habitual questioners would do well to take to heart.

For example, I am idly and impertinently curious to know wherefore it is that you propose to change your place of abode. You dislike, or perhaps judge it inexpedient to confess that it is a measure of necessary retrenchment; and therefore in the common phrase you *put it upon* health, the desire to be within nearer reach of friends, or convenient distance from town.

You are apprehensive lest your daughter should form an attachment which you disapprove, and you therefore drop the acquaintance of a particular family; being indiscreetly urged for your reasons, you assign any but the true one.

An intended journey of pleasure is given up, because the family party could not agree among themselves whether to steam up the Rhine, or to make their way through Paris to Geneva. If they have the good sense to keep their domestic squabbles within doors, they will assure inquirers that the unsettled state of the weather, or that of the political aspect of the continent, deterred them from making the excursion. Such cases might perplex a sturdy moralist. It is at least certain that so long as impertinent questioning is not regarded as what it is, a social misdemeanour of the gravest kind, and uniformly repelled with uncompromising sternness, so long will this mean and degrading kind of falsehood prevail, all but universally. A practical inference of some importance is, that in judging a man by the motives which he publicly assigns for his conduct, we are pretty sure to be mistaken. Far more cogent ones may be presumed to lurk behind, and few people act on grounds so frivolous as they pretend to do.

FRANKNESS.

This quality is usually reckoned among the good ones, yet I confess that few characters attract me less, I might almost say repel me more, than one of which it is held forth as the leading feature. Frankness means *freeness*, and a *free* and voluntary declaration of abhorrence of my principles or disapprobation of my conduct may amount to so grave an outrage that self-respect admonishes me to shrink back from the man who may seem capable of such an aggression. Even where extremes like these are scarcely to be apprehended, I find nothing inviting either in the rudeness which disregards giving pain, the malignity which finds a pleasure in it, or the obtuseness which gives pain without perceiving it.

But this is not all; and I have a deeper quarrel with the frank for their impenetrable reserve. There is no paradox in this, though it may at first wear the appearance of one. The rugged nature which is without sympathy for others, is little disposed on any occasion to claim theirs for itself; and where the feelings do not prompt to an opening of the heart, the 'wisdom for a man's self' is always at hand to suggest the safer policy of keeping all close within.

Further, should you venture with the frank man, at the slightest attempt to make an entrance into the penetration of his affairs, or hazard the gentlest criticism on his conduct or behaviour, no man so prompt to take high offence, to tell you that his concerns are none of yours, or that your opinions have no weight with him.

Such is the general case where the frankness is genuine, but it is not seldom assumed, and then serves as a cloak to qualities and designs more dangerous and still more odious.

Shakspeare has sketched the character with his own inimitable touch—

> He can't flatter, he!
> An honest man and plain, he must speak truth,
> An' they will take it so; if not, he's plain.
> These kind of knaves I know, that in this plainness,
> Harbour more craft, and more corrupter ends,
> Than twenty silly ducking observants,
> That stretch their duties nicely.

TEMPTERS.

IMOGEN forgives her husband for the ordeal to which he had exposed her, as a woman all tenderness forgives where she loves. But the reader or the audience cannot forgive him, nor ought they. It is true that the poet has laboured with his master-hand to palliate the abominable wager by all the circumstances of temptation or provocation with which it was possible to surround it; but yet to expose a wife, deliberately and designedly to expose her to a trial of such a nature, must in any imaginable case be reprobated as an offence inexpiable. Similar wagers have been known in real life, and even in our own country, but they are so rare as well as revolting as scarcely to admit of being alluded to, except as the strongest illustration of a principle daily and hourly forgotten or overlooked.

Which of us is guiltless of the crime of exposing others to that temptation into which everyone prays that he may not himself be led? What master, what tutor, what parent even, watches himself on this point as he ought? How much of the vices and crimes of men owe their origin to this neglect?

You, fair and delicate lady, who carelessly throw into an open drawer the copper money which it disgusts you to touch, and which is too heavy for your flimsy pocket, do you reflect that by this practice you are training up your dapper page for the house of correction? drawing on your under-housemaid through habits of petty pilfering to bolder thefts ending in loss of character and utter ruin?

You, sir or madam, who scatter your letters on the library table, or toss them into the elegant card-basket, know you not, that by thus tempting the natural curiosity of youth you are overthrowing in your children the sense of inviolable honour?

You, well meaning but mistaken mother or governess, who in the hope of making yourself mistress of the inmost thoughts of a child, urge it with questions which cannot be truly answered without an effort of courage to which its feeble spirit is unequal—learn that you are thus sowing in that tender bosom ineradicable seeds of artifice and falsehood.

By the wisdom of our laws, the receiver of stolen goods is held more guilty than the thief, because he is in most cases the tempter. He tempts because it is his wicked trade; but how many are there who give occasion to the commission of similar crimes, and incur like, and perhaps equal guilt for want of thought, for the sake of some trifling indulgence to their own convenience or indolence; or for want of that universal sympathy which deserves to be cherished among the most precious dowers of humanity, since it is through this alone that it is given us to feel and understand what things utterly insignificant to ourselves may be irresistible temptations to our weaker or less fortunate fellow-creatures!

POPULAR FALLACIES.

BENTHAM gave to the world a list of fallacies well worth the attention of the politician; and Charles Lamb one of 'popular fallacies' which amused all his readers: and the catalogue might readily be enlarged. For example, 'Silence gives consent.' To a proposal of marriage perhaps: to an assertion, a narrative, or a proposition, decidedly No! To conceive that it does is the cherished fallacy of those members of privileged orders enabled by sufferance to lay down the law in mixed society; of the rich, the great, the celebrated, the dogmatical, the quarrelsome, and those who have the good fortune to be always on the strongest side. That silence dissents would be a safer rule.

A man of consequence, perhaps a noble lord, in the narrative with which he has favoured the company of a late transaction has taken to himself credit which I may well know not to be his due—what then? Shall I disturb the company and possibly make myself a dangerous enemy by interposing to set right a matter which is probably seen in its true light by others besides myself, and which is of no personal importance to any of us?

Shall I disconcert your dealer in hyperbole by exclaiming in the midst of his story, 'Not half so large! not nearly so often! not a tenth of the number!' No, indeed, let those believe him who know no better. I hold my peace;

> Preserve me from the thing I dread and hate,
> A duel in the form of a debate;

therefore, although I differ toto cœlo from the political or the religious system of that furious partisan and loud declaimer, far be it from me to breathe one syllable of contradiction. How, indeed, should I even make myself audible?

It was remarked concerning a late very eminent Scottish writer, that he was fully sensible of the advantages of the laudatory system. If so, he was by no means alone in the perception; it is shared by all true worldlings, and notwithstanding the imputation of censoriousness so largely brought against mankind by divines and moralists, it cannot be doubted that in general society far more is heard of unmerited eulogy than of groundless condemnation. But where do we find the lover of equal-handed justice bold or rash enough to strip from the miserable daw the borrowed plumage in which it has suited the interests or coincided with the prejudices of another to dress him out?

Ignorance beyond all reach of instruction, prepossession which scarcely a miracle could convert, are left to take their own way by the tacit consent of reasonable people; and whoever shall encounter in society a projector, a visionary, a man of one idea, a missionary of parallelograms, or a mesmerist, will do well to leave, and usually does leave, as free a course to him, as to an over-driven ox. From these premises it might be a fair, however startling inference, that the uncontroverted duties of the best society, those to which its silence is universally held by the utterers to give consent,—represent errors rather than truths, violence than candour, prejudice than reason, enthusiasm than wisdom, and cowardice, servility, or self-interest rather than the free judgments of enlightened and independent spirits. But what if some 'sturdy moralist' should arise, and say that it is a duty to protest much oftener than we do, and even at the risk of giving offence and incurring detriment. That bigotry or selfishness should not be permitted to 'bolt their arguments,' while philosophy and independence find 'no tongue to check their pride.' In that supposable case let such a moralist, or such a philanthropist, take courage in the assurance that the hazard would be less, and the charm, both of victory and its reward, far greater than the timid or the indolent suffer themselves to imagine. Such of the hearers as may be already dissentients in their hearts will gladly echo the contradiction or refutation which one man has at length been found courageous enough to utter; others will become his converts; even those who are not gained over to his sentiments will inwardly respect his spirit. By such checks, the bullies, the dictators, and the sycophants who infest society, will be taught to stand in awe of that genuine public opinion which disdains to shroud itself in such an ignominious and little less than fraudulent silence, as is made to pass for unhesitating assent.

WORDS UPON WORDS.

'WHAT is it you read, my lord?' 'Words, words, words!' replies Hamlet, as who should say air, breath, sound, and emptiness. This always offended me. From my youth upwards, I have been a lover of words, a chooser of words, in a slender and superficial manner, a student of words, and instead of acquiescing in such disparagement, reducing them almost to 'airy nothing,' I proclaim myself ready to maintain against all comers that words are things; nay, and things of pith and moment, life and passion. Have we not the right word, the very word, the word of advice, the word in season, the word of comfort, the warning word, the cruel word, and the kind one? And what are these but things? How they fasten themselves on our memory, with a grasp never to be shaken off while life endures! How our associations cling and swarm, and cluster round them! How our hearts beat at the sound with recollected joy, grief, pity, hope, indignation, or gratitude! Things! Nay, I am more inclined to call them persons, in such vivid individuality of feature do they rise before 'the eye of mind.' Have they not also—at least the more distinguished of their race—their pedigrees, their biographies, their private, sometimes their scandalous, histories and anecdotes? Are there not among them ranks and degrees, nobles and commoners, decent people and rabble, natives and aliens, legitimates and illegitimates, pure breeds and mongrels?

A full and true history of words, including only those of our own country, might be made as long, perhaps, too, as full of instruction and entertainment, as a history of England itself. But what Hercules in literature would prove equal to the task? The labour of a life would be lost in it, considering the multitude of collateral branches which it would shoot out, this way and that, upward and downward, into depths, into darkness, out of sight, and beyond all computation of distance.

Hearken to the pregnant hint thrown out as he passes, by the philosophical historian of the 'Decline and Fall.' After observing that 'so sensible were the Romans of the imperfection of valour without skill and practice, that in their language the name of an army was borrowed from the word which signifies exercise,' (*exercitus ab exercitando*); he adds in a note, 'There is room for a very interesting work, which should lay open the connection between the languages and manners of nations.' No doubt, for the field remains as open at the present day as fourscore years ago, when this suggestion was first offered. A curious exemplification of its truth might be drawn from the word itself, which gave occasion to the remark. In none of the modern tongues, formed by the conquering barbarians out of the corruption of the Latin, is this connection between exercise and an assemblage of warriors preserved. The rude boors whose undisciplined bravery had triumphed over the effeminacy of degenerate Rome, were content to call their fighting multitudes *armies*, whether from the instruments of defence and attack which they carried, or from the vigorous limbs which wielded them. The men-at-arms and their followers, who afterwards composed the feudal levies, formed a *host*, and the French chivalry, with their brilliant courage, would have escaped the disastrous defeat of Poictiers had they been formed, by due practice in the discipline of war, into an *exercitus*.

How suggestive, again, is the Latin word *virtus*. Derived from *vir*, it would best be rendered *manliness*, and among the martial barbarians of Rome, its meaning was limited at first to courage in war; but expanding by degrees under the mellowing influences of advancing civilisation, and the schools of Greek philosophy, we hail it at length in the moral writings of Cicero, as the representative of every quality dear and venerable to mankind, or approved by the immortal gods. Transplanted into the languages of Christian Europe, it has retained its comprehensiveness, while its meaning has undergone modifications and improvements, derived from the doctrines of religion. That, in modern Italian, *virtù* should have been employed to signify taste in the objects of fine art, must be accounted an inexplicable caprice of language; for it can scarcely be conceived, that under the most corrupting and degrading influences, technical skill could have become confounded in any minds with moral excellence.

Yet it is by an equally mysterious process that the Italian *valore* and our own word valour, from *valeo*, to be well, has come to stand for that high species of courage, which makes the closest approach to heroism. In the Italian, indeed, it extends to worth and excellence of every kind—to be 'donna valorosa,' a woman of worth, is the highest praise which can be bestowed on a noble-minded lady; and those who occupy the first rank in science or in art, are said to be persons 'di gran valore.' From the same root we have value, and the impurely formed word valuable.

Words bearing a moral or intellectual signification are those whose transformations in their passage from age to age, or language to language, are the most suggestive. Of these, the word *bigot* offers a pregnant example. Camden, to whom English archæology owes a deep debt of gratitude for his protection of her infancy, derives the term from *by* and *God,* and speaks of it as a kind of cant word, invented to stigmatise certain pretenders to devotion, who affected to have the sacred name perpetually on their lips. For the correctness of this etymology no one would now contend, but the explanation sufficiently attests the imputation of insincerity which we at this time attach to the word. In French dictionaries *bigot* and *cagot*, which is said to be only a variation of the term, are interpreted by 'faux devot, hypocrite,' and the name is twice or thrice applied by Molière to Tartuffe himself, 'Bigot,' says Dr. Johnson, 'is a man unreasonably attached to a certain party, prejudiced in favour of certain opinions, a blind zealot;' and his authorities, Watts and Garth, support his definition. Under *bigotry*, however, he quotes this sentence from a letter of Pope's: 'Our silence makes our adversaries think we persist in those *bigotries* which all good and sensible men despise.' Here the poet writing to his friend Mr. Blount, as catholic to catholic, evidently employs the word in its French signification of superstitious observances, *cagotries*. In popular use we strongly attach to the term that accessory idea of malignity against those of differing opinions which is inseparable in all but the most genial natures from ardent zeal—at least for exclusive systems—but contrary to the French, from whom we received it, and in conformity perhaps with our national character, we include in it the notion of sincerity. So completely, indeed, has this become a part of the idea, that the expression, 'a sincere bigot,' has been treated by high authority as a tautology. How far truth will justify us in thus investing with a robe of honour a character so mischievous, odious, and despicable, is a question well worth consideration, but not pertaining to the present argument. It suffices here to hint at the highly authorised conjunction of *Pharisee* and *hypocrite*.

The word *periwig*, whence wig, is a ludicrous corruption of the name of the twisted shell, a periwinkle. In 'Hall's Satires,' the word is written *periwinke*, and seems to have meant a ringlet. Thus, in the accounts delivered of the articles purchased for the court revels in the first year of Edward VI., there are charged 'five coyffs of Venys gold with perukes of here.' From all authorities it may be inferred that wigs were invented rather to decorate the persons of the young and the gay, than to conceal the ravages of time on the heads of their elders; they also appear to have been at first confined to female use. Queen Elizabeth, and other ladies after her example, delighted to adorn themselves in turn with 'seven or eight dressings of other women's hair,' while so 'prime a gallant' of her court as Sir Christopher Hatton, judged it proper, on assuming the dignified character of Lord High Chancellor, to cover his graceful brows with a sober velvet cap 'like unto your honour's,' as Robert Cecil wrote to his venerable father.

In our original penury of words denoting mental powers or qualities, talent was welcomed by our best writers as a useful acquisition. The earliest authority quoted for it in Johnson's Dictionary is Lord Clarendon. Probably he borrowed it from the French, yet his occasional employment of it as synonymous with disposition or inclination, is more conformable to the Italian, in which *un strano talento* is a strange fancy for any object, and to have *mal talento* towards a person is to bear him ill will. Thus his lordship observes that 'the nation generally was without any *ill talent* to the church' &c., but this sense has not prevailed. As the word was undoubtedly formed in allusion to the scripture parable of the talents put to use or buried in a napkin, it ought apparently to mean no more than a gift, or endowment; but this interpretation has not sufficed our ingenious neighbours. The French synonymists, far more metaphysical and less etymological than our own, have exhausted themselves in nice distinctions between talent and genius, and examples formed to exhibit the nature of each. Mackintosh, who, although a great constructor of rhetorical periods, and an eminent *artist of conversation*, was neither a student of the antiquities of the English tongue, nor possessed of the genuine love of words essential to their successful investigation, has treated the subject in a similar spirit. The specimens of his verbal remarks which his biographer has appended to the most delightful of literary journals, are rather elaborate statements of mental facts, than contributions to grammatical or philological science. Thus, he quotes with approval from a French authority, an explanation of talent as 'the union of invention and execution;' but afterwards gives it as his own account of *talents* in the plural, that 'they are the power of executing well a conception either original or adopted,' and that 'they may be possessed in a degree very disproportioned to general power, as habit may strengthen a mind from one sort of exertion far above its general vigour,—a proposition which, correct as it may be, contributes nothing to the illustration of the word. This objection applies, it will be found, more or less to all verbal remarks destitute of a root firmly fixed in the deep soil of etymology.

On the subject of talent, it may be worth while to observe, that the lower regions of our literature are still infested with the mock word *talented*, a verbal without a verb, said to have sprung forth half a century ago, with many other portents of like nature but opposite fortune, from the teeming brain of a 'Wild Irish Girl.' Twenty years have elapsed since Coleridge thus delivered himself respecting it: 'I regret to see that vile and barbarous vocable *talented* stealing out of the newspapers into the leading reviews and most respectable publications of the day. Why not *shillinged, farthinged, ten-penced,* &c. The formation of a participle passive from a noun is a licence that nothing but a very peculiar felicity can excuse. If mere convenience is to justify such attempts upon the idiom, you cannot stop till the language becomes in the proper sense of the word, corrupt.'* Let the perpetrators of such enormities as *industrial, educational,* and *illuminational* lay to heart this warning! But, alas, what care utilitarians for the purity or the grace of our noble tongue? *Talky, talky,* would serve their turn better than Cicero's Latin, or the French of Voltaire.

It is with a kind of simple wonder, sufficiently amusing from such a quarter, that Mackintosh makes the remark that 'in Minshew's "Dictionary of Nine Languages," printed in 1627, there are no such words as *genius* or *talent*. *Wit* is the only word for mental power; and it is rendered in French by *esprit,* and in German by *verstand,* which is understanding.' No doubt; in the age of Minshew it could not be otherwise. The earliest authority given by Johnson for *genius,* in this sense, is Addison, and so far was it from being established in his day, that in the 'Tatler' itself, the word is written after the Italian, *genio.*

Anthony a Wood, a supreme authority in the vulgar tongue, in his 'Athenæ,' published in 1689, often celebrates in his heroes, 'a poetical *geny.*' It should appear that our adoption either from the French or the Italians of this signification of *genius,* must have been connected, either as cause or effect, with the new restriction of the word *wit* to its present peculiar meaning. This meaning is indeed one which it had long borne—as Falstaff says: 'I am both witty myself and the cause that other men are witty,' but in this application it falls far short of being the equivalent of *esprit.* The limitation was evidently not fully drawn in 1647, when Cowley's Poems first appeared,

* Table Talk, ii. 63.

for although in some passages of his 'Ode on Wit,' he may seem to understand the word exactly in the modern sense, the concluding lines are decisive of the contrary:

> If any ask me then
> What thing *right wit* and *height of genius* is,
> I'll only show your lines and say, 'tis this;

implying that the two terms stood for one and the same thing. The notion evidently corresponds with that so ill-explained by Pope in the lines—

> True wit is nature, to advantage drest;
> What oft was thought, but ne'er so well exprest.

where, though it is difficult to conceive what is meant by Nature, the thing described is clearly the opposite of that true wit of which a new and striking thought forms the essence, and indeed no other than what was styled *fine writing*. In the inimitable papers of Addison 'On true and false Wit,' we first find this quality, according to our present idea of it, so delineated as to preclude all misconception, and illustrated by a profusion of the thing itself in its most genuine form. Thus then, it is to Addison we owe both *wit* and *genius*—apt appropriation! But in those idiomatic phrases which are the most enduring part of language, the old sense survives, and we still possess in full vigour 'mother wit,' and 'the wit of man;' we are still 'at our wits end,' and sometimes 'out of our wits.' We have also the proverb, 'an ounce of mother-wit is worth a pound of clergy,' the last word bearing here the sense of *learning*, as in 'benefit of clergy,' a phrase which, already obsolete in law, may in time it is to be hoped become as unintelligible to common readers as the arrogant claims out of which it arose. Such was the scantiness of our vocabulary, that our elder writers sometimes employ the word *wit* to designate the senses as well as the understanding: 'In our last conflict,' says Beatrice, referring to the 'merry war' between herself and Benedick, 'four of his five wits went halting off, and now is the whole man governed with one; so that if he have wit enough to keep himself warm, let him bear it for a difference between himself and his horse.' We have also in Lear 'Bless thy five wits.' It was indeed high time to seek some expedient for increasing our fund of verbal wealth in this direction.

Philologists, since the great discovery in grammar made by Horne Tooke, are unanimously agreed that every word was originally significative and had a sensible idea for its root. For this reason it was that the eminent scholar Gilbert Wakefield, who was employed on the great work of a Greek and English dictionary, at the too early termination of his honourable course, maintained that a good word could have no more than two meanings—a literal and a metaphorical one. Still more rigid on this point was the learned, humorous, and eccentric Dr. Geddes. The most impetuous of disputants, though one of the most kind-hearted of men, he would do battle on a question of etymology as if life and death had hung on the issue; while such was his resolute and systematic opposition to all metaphorical uses of words, that he would declare against employing *understanding* in any other sense than *standing under*. He had other notions on words not less peculiar. Thus, in his version of the Old Testament, magnanimously setting at nought, where system was concerned, all such minor considerations as the influence of custom or the power of association, he was resolute in the substitution of the more graphic term *Skipover* for that of Passover.

But vain are efforts such as these to reduce 'custom of speech to congruity of speech.' 'It is not,' observes Hobbes, 'the universal current of divines and philosophers that giveth words their authority, but the generality of them who acknowledge that they understand them.' Even the unanimous agreement of grammarians and critics, a race proverbial for their differences, would fail to achieve this more than heroic labour. Etymology itself is far from numbering amongst the certain sciences.

The farther research is carried, into whatever language, the more unfathomable become those gulfs of antiquity into which its origins are seen to open. The roots both of the Greek and the German have been traced to the Sanscrit—Sanscrit, of which it cannot even be conjectured how many ages have revolved since it was a living tongue. And had the Sanscrit no parent? Who can answer? What we know certainly in this matter is, that for centuries upon centuries, words have been suffering so much of transformation, disguise and corruption, by accident, error and caprice, learned and unlearned,—by the licences of poets, the figures of orators, the affectations of pedants and coxcombs, the blunders of travellers, and the innovations of colonists—that in numberless instances their radical idea is lost beyond hope of retrieval, and all that can be done is to make use of them like technical terms, standing for some single definite notion to be learned by practice alone.

The most skilful of etymologists must be baffled by at least one class of words, and that no small one; consisting of such as have been adopted from an accidental association, and thus depend for their interpretation not on philological skill but on the knowledge of some particular fact or circumstance. Of these, several curious examples occur. Among the splendid donations showered by our eighth Henry on Wolsey during his lease of favour, was a stately mansion which had come into his possession by the attainder of the obnoxious Empson. It stood a little beyond the boundary wall of London, with gardens stretching down to the river, adorned with a beautiful spring on which a chapel stood, dedicated to St. Bridget. The Emperor Charles V. held his court within its spacious walls during his visit to England, and in it the divorce suit between Henry and Katherine came to a solemn hearing. On the fall of Wolsey it reverted to the crown. Young King Edward, on certain representations made to him of the necessity of the case, liberally granted it to the corporation of London for the purposes of a house of correction, and hence our generic term—a *Bridewell*.

By another odd misappropriation of a name, a group of buildings near Charing Cross, in which the king's hawks with their attendants were anciently lodged, and which was therefore called the Mews, being converted, on the decline of falconry, into a receptacle for the royal carriages and horses, not only retained its old appellation, but has communicated it to all the ranges of coach-houses and stabling in London. Our language possessing no equivalent to the French term *remises*, convenience seized on this, and made it her own. A Repository for horses has surely somewhat of grotesque in the sound.

In the time of James I. a personage made his appearance in London, announcing himself as the bearer of a commission from the Grand Signior, and decorated with the title of a Chiause, which in those days of ignorance was imagined to signify an officer of exalted rank. After preying for a time on the hospitality and generosity of the credulous, the impostor vanished, but he is said to have bequeathed to us, orthography being then of small account, in outlandish words especially, the familiar verb to *chouse*. Ben Jonson thus refers to this person in the 'Alchemist.'

>   What do you think of me,
>   That I am a Chiause?
> FACE.   What's that?
> DAPPER.   The Turk was here,
>   As one would say, 'Do you think I am a Turk?'
> FACE.   Come, noble doctor, pray thee let's prevail;
>   This is the gentleman, and he's no Chiause.
>   *   *   *   *   *   *   *   *   *
>   One that will thank you richly, and he is no Chiause.

Such allusive expressions are the *cross* of translators.

Priestley, in one of his chemical papers had observed in reference to some fact concerning the gases, that 'the experiment of the Black Hole' had proved it. He went soon after to Paris, when his French translator, himself a man of science, thus eagerly accosted him: 'Pray Doctor, what is that Black Hole of yours? I rendered it of course *le trou noir*, but of the meaning I have not the most distant conception.' It is not quite impossible that in the present generation, there may be even English readers unacquainted with the tragical history of the Black Hole of Calcutta, since all things fade sooner or later from memory, if not from record.

In the language of Portugal *marmala* means a quince. It is, therefore, absurd to give the name of *marmalade* to sweetmeat made from oranges or apples, not from quinces. This corruption, however, preserves the memory of the fact that it was from the Portuguese, early culivators of the sugar cane, both in their Oriental and Occidental settlements, that we first learned the art of confectionery. Thus a nearly contemporary describer of the court of Queen Elizabeth says of the ladies who attended on her: 'There is in manner none of them but when they be at home can help to supply the ordinary want of the kitchen with a number of delicate dishes of their own devising, wherein the *Portingale* is their chief counsellor.'*

Sometimes, by the derivation of a word, our thoughts are transported, as at the waving of a wand, from the most familiar objects of modern life down among the depths of primitive barbarism. The ancient Britons transmitted to us our *baskets*, called bascanda by their Roman conquerors; and from the British *crowd*, the elbow, came out jostling crowds, as well as an obsolete kind of fiddle called a *crowd*. From the Anglo-Saxon verb *stellan*, to put or place, probably comes the *still-room* of

---

* Bohun's character of Queen Elizabeth.

our great houses. If it be to the verb *sellan* of the same language, to give or supply, that we owe our *salt-sellars* the orthography ought to preserve the memory of so venerable an origin.

A very slight attention to the meaning of words would preserve us from making infusions—of roses, of sage, or other herbs; and, still more absurd, of beef into *teas*, but such kitchen errors are little worth noting. Far more offensive is the absurd polysyllabic affectation by which all sorts, kinds, and classes, have become *descriptions* of things. This barbarism, which it would be amusing to attempt to translate into any civilised language, smacks strongly of man-millinery, and was probably invented by one of those persuasive orators who declaim to the ladies from behind their counters on muslins, silks and ribbons. Let it return to the shop whence it came.

Polite euphemism, the source of so many moral as well as philological misnomers, has introduced the practice of employing the word *limited* in the sense of small or scanty. Its chief use was to stand as a screen before two things of which no honest man ought to be ashamed—poverty, and school-keeping. *Limited* incomes—as if even the most enormous ones were unlimited—and *limited* numbers of pupils were mincingly prattled of. While this contemptible fashion was still a novelty, a man of learning, wit and spirit, was thus condescendingly addressed on his introduction to a commercial Crœsus of mean mind and silken phrase, 'I believe, Mr. ——, you have a *seminary* for young gentlemen?' 'I keep a boy's school, sir.' 'A limited number, I presume.' 'No, all's fish that comes to my net.'

By imperceptible degrees, to *consider*, has nearly lost in current speech the sense which it bore when we 'considered our ways and applied our hearts unto wisdom.' We now *consider* that song to have been well sung;

consider red hair a misfortune; consider a goose a fine bird (omitting for expedition's sake the *as*, by which this verb was once followed). Thus have we degraded to the mere office of *opining* or believing, one of the highest and gravest words in our language; respectable too in all its derivatives and affinities, such as considerate, considerable, and consideration; excepting only in the memorable phrase 'for a con-sider-ation.' It is also a word for which we have no substitute.

Till very lately it was the exclusive office of grand juries to *ignore*; but whether the present extension of that often very convenient privilege to all classes of Her Majesty's subjects be not a somewhat laudable innovation, may be fit to be *considered*.

The present generation will probably hear with surprise that there may be still living witnesses and partakers of that universal *roar* with which the House of Commons greeted the first utterance within its walls of the strange word *starvation*, proceeding from the lips of no less conspicuous a personage than Mr. Henry Dundas. Partly the grotesque sound of this barbarous hybrid, partly the whimsical notion of a new word for hunger and famine imported from Scotland, so tickled the fancies of honourable members, that the laughter threatened to become inextinguishable as that which shook Olympus at sight of Vulcan in the office of Hebe. Even now, after a denization of half a century, an English classic would assuredly exclude the mongrel with disdain from any work destined to outlast the date of a Blue-Book, or the report of a charitable institution.

A similar occasion of mirth arose in the Lower House, when some statement of numbers made by a member having been disputed, he exclaimed, 'I am certain I am correct, for I noted down the figures at the time with my *keelovine*.' A general stare as well as titter ensued.

Members from the North of England did indeed recognise at once their familiar term for a black lead pencil, but the word not being, it should seem, Scotch, it was condemned without mercy as a provincialism and vulgarism. By some curious enquirer it will here perhaps be asked what may be the ground, or the plea, for this recognised privilege granted to the popular idioms of the northern, above those of the southern banks of the Tweed? Our Caledonian neighbours would not hesitate to answer, that before the union, Scotland had a distinct tongue of her own, which is not to be confounded with mere dialects of the English; also, that Dr. Jamieson, within the present century, published in two goodly quarto volumes, a 'Dictionary of the Scottish language.' To this plea, it is obvious to reply on the English part that, allowing the ancient speech of Scotland for a different language from our own, it must be a manifest corruption to mingle them. But that Dr. Jamieson's work has no claim whatever to its lofty title, is evident on the very face of it, from the care which he takes to assign every word exclusively Scotch, to its native *county*. It is, in fact—what is a great desideratum with ourselves—a collection of provincial dialects, and nothing more. The written language of Scotland, that of her early literature, her court and her aristocracy, has long since merged in that of Great Britain; and the vulgar idioms of Ayrshire or Lothian have assuredly no inherent right to a toleration, in books or in conversation, refused to those of Lancashire or Devon. But the privilege accorded to Scotland in this respect stands on higher ground. It has been won for her by the excellence—not indeed of her graver prose writers, nor yet of her more polished versifiers, from Drummond to Thomson and Beattie, all of whom came as near to the English tongue as they were able—but by her truly national poets, and her novelist of world-wide fame.

Possessed from early times of a national music, the country was rich in ancient ballads and in popular songs, which embodied in the racy idioms of a mother-tongue the traditions of the past, and the fresher inspirations of passion, of fancy, and of humour. In this rustic dialect, imperfectly spelled out, there was found, or fancied, a character of mingled simplicity, tenderness and archness, which happily corresponded with the pastoral style, so long the delight, or pretended delight, of the whole of lettered and polished Europe. By favour of this adaptation it was that Allan Ramsay's partial translation, imitation, or depravation rather, of the most graceful and refined of the Italian *Favole Roschareccie*—the 'Aminta' of Tasso—became popular in England, and even his songs found admirers; an uncouth dialect veiling in some degree their intolerable vulgarity and grossness.

Percy's 'Reliques,' the most popular of poetical collections, and one which effected a signal revolution in literary taste, owed the larger and more interesting portion of its ditties to the bards of the 'North countrie', on which ever side of the border. The repulsiveness of consulting a glossary was surmounted for their sake; and thus the Northumbrian English, and the lowland Scotch, idioms which most nearly approached each other, while their respective speakers continued hereditary foes, became alike familiar to the numerous admirers and the swarm of affected imitators of the ancient ballad.

Burns next arose—a poet always, but twice a poet when he trusted himself with his native Doric, which found favour for his sake, even in Attic ears. The 'Minstrelsy of the Scottish Border' followed; then 'The Lay of the Last Minstrel,' and the rest of that brilliant group of metrical romances struck off with such dazzling rapidity on the same glowing anvil—finally the 'Waverley novels.'

During the Scott mania to which the English public was wrought up by these powerful and repeated efforts, which survived for many years the last and mightiest 'master of the spell,' it was not perceived that we were negligently losing sight of the ancient land-marks of the neighbour tongues; nay, that we were suffering our very bulwarks and fortresses to become Scottish colonies and dependencies, through a process of settlement and occupation not unlike that by which we have seen Texas and other portions of Mexico transmuted into a territory of the United States. Our own people were turning Scotch without knowing it. We began to allow the macaronic of the Edinburgh Review for actual *English*! Instead of acting on behalf of another it was for his *behoof*. Staircases, or pairs of stairs, were totally disused and we were left to ascend by *a stair* as *fully more* convenient. Friends looked *over* the window, and joined each other *on* the street. Forgetful of our honest old idiom '*this here*' and '*that there*' we ceased to perceive any clear difference, however the confusion might perplex us, between this and that, these and those. Inroads and incursions, eruptions and invasions, were all metamorphosed into *raids* and *forays*, and transplanted by writers, too, of no inconsiderable pretensions, into historical narratives of distant times and other countries. A species of anachronism and absurdity scarcely less gross than that committed by Cowper in his translation of Homer, where he repeatedly mentions tapestry by the name of *arras*! In fine, our very instinct of shall and will, should and would, began to waver, and we were left to get out of this sad scrape not as well as we could, but as *we best might*. At length there are encouraging tokens of the decline of this insidious epidemic. No recent cases have been observed, and we might now be beginning to congratulate ourselves on a happy return to vernacular soundness, but for the alarming visitations of another and a far worse contagion—not a brogue, not a dialect; a contraband importation from some province, respectable though obscure, from innocent cottages, or simple rustic farms, where genuine Anglo-Saxon lingers still—but a pestilence drawn forth, reeking and flagrant, from the metropolitan dens of all abomination and corruption, moral and physical, and philological. It is, in short, *slang*, which has dared to intrude itself into common speech, and the literature of *the million*. *Slang*, a term unknown as yet to dictionary or glossary, but which a very high authority has taken the laudable precaution to interpret to the ignorant and the innocent. It is derived, he informs us, from the verb to *sling*, and designates the idiom of those whose career is likely to terminate in *suspension*. What more is to be said!

In the selection of words for the purposes of elegant literature, as in the details of every art which appeals to the imagination or the heart through the sense of the beautiful, association is very nearly all in all. Let a word of the purest origin and most irreproachable connections, once have been compelled to stoop to low company, or base offices, and it *loses caste* once and for ever. Its sentence of perpetual exile from elegant society is like that of the favourite yellow starch from the court of King James, after it had adorned the person of Mrs. Turner, its inventress, at her final public appearance—on the scaffold.

The excellent old critic Puttenham, in his 'Art of Poetry,' shows a fine sense of the seemly and 'decent' in this matter. He severely censures one translator of Virgil for saying 'that Æneas was fain to *trudge* out of Troy, which term better became to be spoken of a beggar, or of a rogue, or of a lackey;' and he blames another, who had called that hero 'by fate a *fugitive*,' and enquired 'What moved Juno to *tug* so great a captain?' a word, 'the most indecent word in this case that could have been devised, since it is derived from the cart, and signifies the draught or pull of the horses.' He reprobates the expression, 'a prince's *pelf*,' 'because pelf means properly the scraps or shreds of tailors or of skinners.'

Robert Southey who, if equalled, was certainly unexcelled among his contemporaries as a master of a pure, correct, and graceful English prose, instances, in one of his excellent letters to William Taylor of Norwich, the verb to *spar* as a word ruined for all better purposes by its application to pugilistic contests. On the other hand, we may be certain that neither his critical nor his moral taste would have sanctioned such a compliance with the *slang* of *sporting men* as could allow public meetings of any greater dignity than a walking match or a steeple chase, to *come off*.

A living language may be viewed as a running commentary on the history of the manners and the pursuits of every passing age, and we are sometimes startled to learn how recent are several of those words which now seem as familiar and necessary to us as our daily bread. What Englishman almost would believe—at least until according to the genius of his nation, as Voltaire said, he had laid and lost a good wager on the point—that the words selfish and selfishness are not to be found in Shakspeare, and were indeed totally unknown to all his contemporaries? Yet such is the unquestionable fact. Bishop Hacket, in his Life of Archbishop Williams, mentions selfish as a Puritanical term; and in a political letter, bearing the earlier date of 1640, the words *selfish* and *drill*, in the sense of exercising soldiers, are ridiculed as newly-invented cant words of the Scotch covenanters. From this parentage it is probable that the first of these which now gives a name to the very cardinal principle on which systems of ethics and metaphysics have been made to turn, was originally nothing more than an abbreviation of *self-seeking*, a well-known term in the religious phraseology of the *godly* of that period, and perhaps not yet disused.

Drill was probably of continental origin, and likely to have been imported by Lesley and his fellow warriors when they returned from fighting the battles of the Protestant hero Gustavus Adolphus, to set their countrymen in array against King Charles and his 'Anglicane episcopacy.'

> Those lazy ages, lost in sleep and ease,
> Such whose supine felicity but makes
> In story charms, in epochas mistakes;
> O'er whom Time gently shakes his wings of down,
> Till with his silent sickle they are mown,

are the golden days of pedantry and affectation, in style and in diction. Every man is then at leisure to study not only, and not so much what he should say, as after what form and figure he shall say it. The satire of Shakspeare indefatigably reproduced in so many shapes and characters, is sufficient proof of this corruption of taste in the 'piping times' of Elizabeth and the first James. By the political storms of the ensuing reign these and all other shining fripperies were swept to dust and oblivion. The pure and simple English of the public papers and parliamentary speeches of the days of King Charles, eloquent and pathetic in its earnestness alone, is still a noble and interesting study for the statesman and the orator. In the court of his successor, language, like manners and public principle, reached their lowest point of declension.

LETTERS.

To Mrs. Aikin.

Stoke Newington: Nov. 1805.

WE do grumble a little, my dear mother, I assure you, at being so long without you; but knowing how very much you are wanted where you are, we think it would be wrong to press your return sooner than the day you mention, against which time I will take care to have all preparations made. Well! what do you all say to this glorious dear-bought victory? Twenty ships for a hero! At this rate I think our enemies would be beggared first. But never was there a more affecting mixture of feelings. Even the hardhearted underwriters assembled at Lloyds to hear the news, could not stand it; when the death of Nelson was proclaimed, they one and all burst into tears. It is thought that the Londoners will put on mourning without any public orders. The illumination of the public offices last night was splendid, but many private streets were not lighted up at all, so much did sorrow prevail over triumph. No windows, it is said, were broken, and some of the mob cried out, 'What, light up because Nelson is killed!' Nobody can, or ought to pity him, however, for what hero ever died a death more glorious? They say that he saw fifteen ships strike before he fell.

My father has been attending Peggy Woods for two or

three days past, and I do not know whether he is quite glad to have her well again; he said she looked so *very* pretty in her night-cap. Just now a man called to enquire if we wanted any pork, saying that he was a person who had lived with Mr. Belsham. I felt the force of the recommendation (Mr. B. always paid great attention to the fatting of his pigs, I know), and finding that it was the size you like, I desired him to bring some to-morrow, when, if I think it nice, I shall get a leg to salt. I thought I should have laughed when I went to speak to the man, but I behaved very prettily. I forgot to tell you that we made a very brilliant figure at the illumination. Thanks to Fanny's love for the tars, we were lighted up sooner than most of our neighbours. The book-meeting was put off on account of the illumination.

I can't think of anything else to say, except that Edmund has made a most beautiful drawing of Mr. Hope's statue gallery, which has delighted him much. I have written four new lines and planned a great many more. The Geography is all printed but the index, which my father has made and pasted, with my help. I have weighed out all the bullace and sugar for preserving, with my own hands. Adieu, my dear mother. My father joins in love &c. with your very affectionate daughter,

L. A.

To Mrs. Barbauld.

Edinburgh: Nov. 1811.

My dear Aunt—It will, I know, give you pleasure to hear immediately from myself of all that I am doing and enjoying in this new and animating scene. You will believe that I find much to gratify both the eye and the mind in the grand situation and picturesque views of this great city—in its ancient remains and its modern improvements. I have climbed the Calton and the Castle Hills; I have wondered at the tower-like houses of the old town, admired the spacious streets and noble squares of the new; moralised in the gloomy apartments where the exiled Bourbons found refuge in the deserted palace of the Stuarts; and shuddered on exploring the dark narrow staircase whence the murderers of Rizzio rushed upon their victim.

As to the society from which I have expected, and still expect, so much, I have not yet quite got into the spirit of it. I cannot expect strangers to give up their mental treasures at sight. The ceremonies of introduction, the questions of routine, how I came, when I came, and how I like Edinburgh, with many more, must first be patiently submitted to. At present, I only seem to have the figures of a magic lantern flitting before my eyes, but the number and the variety afford perpetual amusement. Take the visitors of one morning as a specimen. At breakfast arrives, just imported from the Highlands, a minister of the kirk, of a stern visage and stiff address, who begs a blessing on the meal unasked, and on some mention being made of the Duke of Queensbury, solaces himself greatly with the conviction that he is now roasting. He takes his leave, and enter a fine flourishing colonel; his son has obtained from the Emperor of Russia the appointment of physician to some new baths in Circassia, and he is just giving us an interesting account of his journey from Moscow of 1,800 miles, when he is interrupted by two elegant daughters of Lord Woodhouselee. They give place to a plain Scotch advocate, who gives us a ludicrous account of his distress at a London lodging-house, where nobody could make barley-broth and he was forced to attempt it himself, with indifferent success. Two excellent Miss Hills, who devote themselves to the care of a brother's children, and a London-bred lady, with three dirty dogs, finish the exhibition for that day. My account of these characters has been broken in upon by Lord Buchan, a more complete character than any of them. He desires me to say something very handsome for him to you. Moreover, he has got it into his head that you wrote some verses on Dryburgh Abbey, sitting on the ruins, which he begs to see if they exist; and moreover, again, he has made me promise, and I hope you will not be displeased, to transcribe your lines on the King, for him to send to the Princess Mary. He retains a lively recollection of 'that pretty little winch,' as he calls her, and a still more lively wish to see you again in Scotland. I have seen a good deal of Mrs. Grant,* and she both amuses and wearies me; she talks a vast deal in a low drawling voice, interspersing abundance of parentheses and digressions; but her narratives and remarks display fancy and feeling, and have an interesting air of originality—in short, she is exactly like her letters. With Dr. Brown, Dugald Stewart's successor, I had one evening some pleasant conversation; he is clever and lively, but has an unfortunate flippancy of manner, and laughs whenever he speaks. Dr. Thomson, the chemical, who inquired kindly for Arthur and Charles, pleases me best of all the men I have seen, and his wife, a daughter of Professor Miller, appears to me a most agreeable woman.

Mrs. Hamilton has been so poorly since my arrival that I have seen her but once, but her sister and their visitor, Miss McLean, spent an evening here and made it a very pleasant one. The Highland minister told us that the clan McLeod are offended with Miss Baillie's representation of their ancestor, and that *their poet* has written a long Erse ballad giving a quite different account of the matter. He was himself well acquainted with the traditions about it, and had once been nearly cast away on

---

* Mrs. Grant of Laggan.

the *lady's rock*. The feeling of clanship is still strong, and so much of old manners remain, that I hear of a laird now living who is quite as savage and much less generous than Roderic Dhu.

Pray tell my father that I will write to him very soon—as soon, that is, as I have matter for another letter.

Your grateful and affectionate
L. AIKIN.

To Dr. Aikin.

Edinburgh: Dec. 18, 1811.

And pray have you the conscience to expect that I should remember certain old-fashioned people in the village of Stoke Newington, amidst all the honourable and right honourable society to which I have had the honour of being admitted? Though you would not think magnificently of my last large sheet, I think you must of this, considering the grandeur of the subject. At Lady Apreece's we had a very agreeable and elegant party—a pretty olio of red coats and blue coats—a charming mixture of people of fashion and people of literature. The widow of Professor Dalzell, and Dr. Brown, were those who pleased me best that night. But what were the splendours of that evening to the glories of last Saturday at Mrs. Clavering's! Mr. C. is the elder brother of the noted general C——, his wife is a sister of Mr. Adair the envoy, and both are very highly connected. We calculated on our return that there were more ladies above than below the rank of baronets' daughters, and the gentlemen were mostly of title or high family. I thought their manners very elegant, and saw much graceful dancing, in which, from conscious inferiority, I declined taking a part. 'Tell me what you think of that gentleman's physiognomy,' whispered Mrs. Fletcher, 'and I will tell you a story of him.' He was beyond my ken, so I lost the opportunity of displaying my skill in that certain science, but I got the story. Mr. C——, second son of a gentleman of large estate, is an advocate, and a man admitted in the first circles. Some years ago he went to call one day on Sir Charles Douglas; he was shown into Sir Charles's dressing-room, and when Sir Charles came to him he found Mr. C—— examining his pocket-book, which he had left on the table. 'What are you doing?' cried Douglas. 'I am searching for billets-doux,' returned C——. They were both gay young fellows and very intimate, so the thing passed very well as a joke till the evening, when Douglas, applying to his pocket-book for some bank-notes, found that they had all vanished, to the value of 25*l*. He did not know the numbers, but they were of the Bank of England, which are little in circulation here; his inquisitive friend, he learned, had passed two of that description that very day. Sir Charles did not scruple to report that C—— had picked his pocket. C—— finding himself shunned by his brother advocates, at last learned the cause. He hurried to London and challenged Douglas. Next day a statement appeared in the papers signed by the seconds—very 'honourable men'—stating that both parties had behaved with perfect honour, and had parted without fighting! C—— is received again in society, and the story of the pocket-book remains as it was. Such are the great! and therefore I was not displeased to find myself last night in a humbler set, at the house of Mr. Fergusson, an advocate; where I had some pleasant chat with a son of Professor Miller, also a lawyer, and a very shrewd and intelligent, as well as worthy man, but so grave and abstracted that one can seldom get much out of him. To-night I am to drink tea and play chess with Mrs. Hamilton, and sup at Mrs. Grant's, where I am to meet Jeffrey for the first time. I am now quite habituated to the hours we keep, and never indulge myself in taking breakfast in bed. At half-past eight Mr. Fletcher causes a wakening peal to be rung, which rouses me, and I am often the first in the breakfast-room. Grace, however, is a pretty good riser, and one morning, by way of brag, I gave her a Latin lesson before anybody else made their appearance. You may believe that this same G—— makes a charming pupil. I fain would teach her 'all I know,' and therefore gave her the other day a practical lesson in the art of custard-making, in which Mrs. Fletcher had been lamenting the ignorance of her cook. I never feel the value of the knowledge that you and my dear mother have been at such pains to instil into me so much as when I am among strangers, and find myself capable of improving them in something useful or ornamental. Then, when I meet with any commendations, and people say, 'How did you learn it?' what a proud delight have I in answering—my father taught me this, my mother that—one of my brothers informed me of such a thing—in short, not only the foundation-stone, but every other in the fabric of my mind and manners was laid by an honoured and a loving hand—no mercenary touched it!

As to the weather in this part of the world, I will not pretend to give you my opinion; but that of the natives, which I have carefully collected from various authorities, male and female, is as follows:—That it is much warmer here than in London in the months of November and December—that there is on the whole much less frost and cold here than in London (some 'sturdy moralist,' who keeps a thermometer, told me it was at 4° one day last winter)—that there are never any fogs here (I don't know what it was that hindered me from seeing half way across the street this morning—prejudice, I suppose)—that spring is rather late, owing to the east winds, but that summer is delightful from a refreshing coolness unknown in

England; finally, that the climate is on the whole very dry, and that the Isle of Bute enjoys an air much milder and more favourable to invalids than Madeira. I thankfully acknowledge that they have thick walls and excellent fires here, so that one is warm enough within doors, and that a sedan-chair prevents all risk of cold in coming out at night, yet I find everybody but myself complaining of disorders of the lungs, or of being at least, 'very much *colded.*'

Farewell, my dear father. Ever believe me,
Your grateful and affectionate
L. A.

To Mrs. Barbauld.

Edinburgh: Dec. 25, 1811.

My dear Aunt—For fear of making the frank too heavy, I must not take a whole sheet; but I may here inform you that your correspondent with a long title is the husband of the lady *said* to be the author of 'Self-Control;' but she does not yet avow the work.

Lord Buchan has written some verses on your bonnet, worthy of a person of quality; I will send them by the next opportunity; in the meantime, I hope you can take patience. This Christmas-day is so unlike an English one I scarcely know it. Shops are open, carts rattling along, the usual street cries are heard—in short, it is just like any other day. The only relics of old observances I have witnessed are *waits* playing in the night, and boys dressed up, and called *guisards*, who sing carols from door to door.

I am all impatience for your new poem: what will you call it? Is not Miss Baillie's 'Beacon' a perfect gem, and do you not admire Orra? . . . . In the midst of so much dissipation, expect from me neither ode nor vision; when I am snugly seated at Newington again we shall see, and that will soon be, I hope. This racketing begins to tire me exceedingly, and I have now seen all the sights that I most care for. I wish I could bring you back Grace in my hand; she is a charming creature, full of ardour and enthusiasm, and more unspoiled, more unconscious of her rare endowments, than any young person of talent I ever saw. We read Latin together and discuss fifty topics in a day. I am teaching all the young people chess. Mrs. Hamilton and I have had some stout battles and come off even. Her health is very indifferent, and she never goes out, but she invites me to come to her whenever I have a spare hour, and I find her most agreeable by her own fireside. Dr. Parr says he intends to come and pass a year here, and spend a thousand pounds; but some people doubt whether he is in earnest. I have not been so fortunate as to see Mr. Stewart, but I have several times met with his daughter, who is very pleasing and more cultivated, I think, than any lady I have seen here. The Edinburgh ladies are by no means literary in general. My paper is at an end, and I must hasten to subscribe myself,

Your obliged and affectionate niece,
L. AIKIN.

To Mrs. Aikin.

Edinburgh : Jan. 27, 1812.

My dear Mother—I believe I have been rather longer than usual in thanking you for your kind long letter; the reason was, that I hoped every day to be able to tell you that I had heard of a travelling companion, and fixed the day for my departure. I have not yet, however, heard of a party that entirely pleases me, but I am making diligent enquiries, and hope soon to succeed, for I can have no pleasure in dissipating here, while I think that you may be dull for want of me at home. Do not imagine, however, that I make any kind of sacrifice in returning. I have really had enough of that insipid thing called gaiety. I am tired of seeing faces that I never saw before, nor wish to see again. I am eager to get into the midst of the dear circle at home, and make you all alive with the history of what I have heard and seen. Since I wrote last, I have been at two assemblies, besides dinner-parties, suppers, and musical-parties. I did not think at all of dancing at the assemblies, because few ladies do who are turned five-and-twenty, their amusement is promenading up and down the card-room, holding by the arm of a chaperon or a gentleman, and making remarks on the company. Accordingly, I had refused to dance with Mr. Simpson, but at last the music was so inspiring, and he so pressing, and I knew, too, that he danced so much better than he talked, that I consented; but, to my dismay, we had scarcely joined the set, when the country-dance was changed to reels; however, I do not think they are danced better here than in England, so I took courage, and thought I might pass in the crowd. The second assembly was that annually given in honour of the Queen's birthday; it was really a splendid sight. Lady Buchan presided, sitting on a chair of state, supported by Lady Caithness on one hand, and the Hon. Miss Elphinston on the other. We found seats near her, and saw everybody come up to pay their respects to her ladyship. The assembly-room is a very splendid one, and holds 1,200 people—it was almost full. As everybody is admitted who will pay five shillings, you may imagine that the company is not very select; but though there are many vulgar people, there are none of a worse description, and the spectacle altogether is both gay and amusing. The crowd is too great to allow of many dances, but I went down one with a young Englishman, who danced with so much execution, forcing me to do the same, that I told him we should certainly be taken for Scotch folks.

I conceive that your imagination may have figured me in various situations, but I think it will scarcely have represented me seated at supper between two bishops, and chatting gaily with one of them; yet this was my lot at a large party at Mr. Alison's. They were the Bishops of Meath and Edinburgh—the former is really a very entertaining pleasant man out of the pulpit, whence he has given us two polemical discourses of fifty-five minutes each. . . . What was better, we had delightful Playfair, and lively Brown, who is very acute and original, and improves much upon acquaintance. Mrs. F—— had a warm debate with him on the merit of Miss Baillie's new volume, which she thought he undervalued. Do you think it equal to her former ones? Talking of tragedies reminds me of one on an Icelandic story, by Sir G. Mackenzie, which came out on Wednesday last at this theatre. Scott and Mackenzie wrote prologue and epilogue; Dugald Stewart, Playfair, Alison and Jeffrey, all appeared in the same box, applauding with might and main, and the pit was crammed with friends of the author—notwithstanding all which, the poor tragedy was laughed to death. We were none of us there, but, by all accounts, it must have been an infinitely amusing performance. Sir George is so vain, that nobody pities him, but people are sorry for his wife, who is much liked. By way of contrast to these splendours, I one day took a walk down to Leith, a place as distinct from Edinburgh as if they were fifty miles asunder. The old part of the town is very shabby and very Scotchy, but there are many handsome new houses, and a superb coffee-room and assembly-room is building; there are also new docks on a pretty large scale, on which they are now at work. The view up and down the Firth from the pier-head is truly magnificent; it reminded me of Liverpool, and I snuffed the sea gale, mingled with the odour of pitch and tar, with great delight—to me these 'savours maritime' are 'redolent of joy and youth.' I missed the bustle, the shouts, the quick motions, and the general air of animation which accompany an English sea-port; the Scotch are certainly a slow and phlegmatic and silent people compared with the English. I am aware, however, that business is far from being brisk at Leith just now. One Gottenburgh vessel was unloading a cargo of flax, and that was all that we saw going forward; the docks were full enough, but chiefly of Greenlandmen and coasting vessels. . . . . You can scarcely imagine my longing for familiar faces. I have met with much civility here, and some real kindness; and this dear family I shall love as long as I live; but as for the other figures that flit in such rapid succession before me, they take no hold upon my fancy or my heart—they are a gallery of portraits, nothing more, and I have had enough of them. Mrs. F. tells me that they say I am very reserved—of course some will think it pride, and others timidity. I believe it is not so much of either, as of a feeling of being out of my element, and a dread of being thought obtrusive. I find that I want ease for the great world. I believe, also, that I am too indifferent to the good opinion of strangers. I have been a close observer, however, of what was passing before me, and my knowledge of life and manners has been not a little increased.

My dear mother, farewell. This family beg their kind regards.

   Believe me ever, at home or in absence,
    Your dutiful and affectionate
        L. AIKIN.

To Dr. Aikin.

Allerton : August 28, 1814.

I had begun to think that you had all forgotten and cast me off, my dear father, and for several days past I had been deliberating whether to write and scold, or to remain *sulky* and silent—sulkiness, or rather laziness, carried it. I will now condescend to tell you a few of the agreeable circumstances of the last week or two, and none but agreeable ones have I to mention.

This day fortnight Mr. Smyth[*] arrived, and, with his gay good humour, rendered Allerton itself more gay and more animated. We had terrible battles of wits, however, all the time he was with us, for the professor was rash enough, the very first evening, to give utterance to two of his fusty college notions, which brought all us ladies out in array against him. The first was that no woman is fit to govern a kingdom; the second, that the true art of tea-making is a mystery too deep for female comprehension. I charged him boldly on the first of these heretical propositions, all the females following me, and Mr. Roscoe gallantly cheering us on, and a glorious victory we gained. As for the second, the professor contrived to brew his own essence of hyson in a little separate tea-pot to the end of his visit, and the last thing he said to me was, that he hoped whenever I happened to go to Cambridge, I would pay him a visit, when he would make me *such* a cup of tea as I never drank before. I believe I expressed rather a slighting opinion of 'Lara' in my last; but one day the professor and I turned out of the room Robert (who has written a wickedly witty parody on the said poem) and all the other scoffers, and I read it aloud to him my very best; on which he fell into such raptures with several passages, that I was

[*] The late Professor Smyth, of Cambridge.

also moved to change my opinion, and to discover that it is by no means unworthy the fame of the author.

On Tuesday last, to everybody's sorrow, the professor took his departure, and, false man, without having written the sonnet on me that he promised. The same morning, Mr. and Mrs. Roscoe and Jane went to look at the Moss, and James's new cottage, and William was obliged to go on business into Wales; so only Mary-Anne, Robert, Tom, Henry and I were left; but I cannot say we found ourselves very disconsolate. In the mornings we went mushroom gathering, visited the fruit garden, played with the puppies, and took the elegant diversion here called *shaddling*, i.e. see-sawing on a plank. At night we told ghost stories, and the rest of our time was occupied in the grand enterprise of contriving a farce something on the plan of 'Les Facheux,' to be performed by us in honour of the return of the heads of the family. The time was short, for everybody was to be back on Friday night, but we worked hard, and last night, Saturday, we performed with vast applause; the audience consisting of Mr. and Mrs. R., Jane, William, James, and three cousins. As our company was not strong in females, I was obliged to undertake two principal parts; one a Quaker preacher, (copied from the old lady who held forth to me), the other, a certain Penelope Pry, who produced much laughter. Robert had an ignoble fancy to appear in petticoats, and was very droll as a waiting-maid. I have not seen much of Liverpool or its inhabitants since I wrote, for we live here in a little world of our own. The only grand event that has occurred was the flowering of a night-blowing *Cerius* (perhaps I spell it wrong), in the hothouse. Nearly the whole family sat up till twelve to see it, and, after watching its very perceptible motions for some time, we had the satisfaction to behold the golden calyx of many divisions expanded into a beautiful fringe, surrounding a snowy flower of magnificent size and delicious fragrance. A short-lived beauty, however; though cut and carried into a dark room, it was withered by morning! . . . The same morning I had been doing duty work by calling on the ——'s. Exceedingly good hospitable folks they are—too hospitable, indeed. How to get off spending two or three days with them, and not affront Mrs. —— I know not. 'Our house is very dirty,' said the good lady (I was glad there was nobody with me to laugh), 'for we have been prevented painting this year, by Mr. ——'s having the gout; but if you will take us as we are, we shall be very happy,' &c. I thanked, and promised nothing. . . . This day were brought hither, from on board a wine-ship from Bourdeaux, a French sheep, and a beautiful little kid from the Pyrenees—the latter, which is black with two white stripes down its face, has excited great alarm among the sheep, who run from it as from a dog the moment it looks at them or begins to cut capers near them. Mr. Roscoe, as a planter of trees and shrubs, is not much delighted with this addition to his live stock, and regards with more complacency a great fat-tailed Turkish sheep, whose cumbrous appendage scarcely allows it to run at all. I wish you could see his collection of American plants, which is considerable and curious, and, O! that you could behold the rock at the Botanic Garden, with all its treasures. Mr. T. brought Mr. Roscoe the other day, from the curator of the Botanic Garden at Montpelier, a catalogue of the plants contained in it. That institution, it appears, continues to flourish greatly, and the curator hopes to establish exchanges of plants and seeds between it and the Liverpool one. A goodly thing is peace! There is a charming little gentian in flower on the common here, of which we long to send you some roots.

I think you will allow that I must now conclude. Adieu,

my dear father and mother! I hope you do not want me *very* much; I am so well and happy here. Love to all.

Your dutiful and affectionate
L. A.

To Mr. E. Aikin.

Stoke Newington: Dec. 1814.

Dear Edmund—I was tempted to write you two letters for one, meaning to send the last by Robert Roscoe, but he being gone sooner than I expected, I thought you would rather pay for it than lose it, and thus our letters crossed. I will not wait till I hear again to answer yours. . . . So much for bulletin; now to other matters. We all liked your account of yourself very much; in visiting matters you seem to be doing everything that is right and everything that is pleasant, and I have no doubt of your finding business go on briskly, especially since this happy news of peace with America, which cannot but give a fresh spirit of enterprise to the Liverpool merchants. . . . I wonder with which of our friends you ate your Christmas dinner; I guess you were not left to eat it alone at your lodgings. With us the day was very flat, I missed you sadly. . . . We had a little party in honour of Bessy, last Thursday, which went off very well; for Arthur Taylor, in consequence of a hint from me, came all armed for pantomime, bringing in his pocket a regal crown, a cap and feather, a wand and a burnt cork, and we got up several scenes with vast applause. To-day everybody is dining at my aunt Barbauld's, except me, who am kept at home by a foolish panting—snow in the air, I fancy. A few days since I had the pleasure of a letter from Henry,* dated Naples, November 24. He expresses the utmost satisfaction with his situation in every respect. After speaking with delight of various other objects of curiosity,

---

* Sir Henry Holland, Bart., M.D.

he mentions their abode at Rome, 'where,' he says, 'amid the grandeur of ancient and modern times we found a source of additional interest in the society which was around us. To explain the variety of this interest, it may be enough to mention the names of Pope Pius VII., of the King and Queen of Spain, of the Queen of Etruria, Lucien Bonaparte and his family, Louis Bonaparte, Cardinal Fesch, Canova, and many others of minor repute. I talked with the Queen of Spain about her health, with Lucien Bonaparte about poetry and statues, with his daughter about England, with Cardinal Fesch about clerical celibacy, with Canova about the progress and future attainment of his art; in short, each moment that was not occupied with the Coliseum, Pantheon, St. Peters, or Vatican, was taken up with the novelties of this strangely compounded society. Something I witnessed of what remains of the richness of catholic worship at Rome--it might inspire with a certain degree of veneration a more temperate man than Eustace. The Pope is venerable and pleasing, and I preserve with all due regard a rosary with which he presented me. I confess myself disappointed with ancient Rome. I compared it with Athens; there is no comparison: nature and art have severally done ten times as much for the latter spot, nor has the lapse of ages changed this proportion.' . . . .

'Naples is perfection in its natural scenery; its population is but a sorry compound of misery, bad institutions, and bad morals.' . . . Well! now I think I have talked about most of the other things I had to say, and may with a tolerable grace begin to talk to you about my own affairs. I am glad you like the notion of my Queen Elizabeth project. I know not how I shall succeed in the execution, but the preparation is delightful to me. I mean to call it 'a view of the court of Queen Elizabeth,' or some such thing, and intend to collect all the notices

I can of the manners of the age, the state of literature, arts, &c., which I shall interweave, as well as I am able, with the biographies of the Queen and the other eminent characters of her time, binding all together with as slender a thread of political history as will serve to keep other matters in their places. Of books I shall certainly want a great number, but the Red Cross Street library will furnish a good many—Mr. Roscoe has kindly promised me several of his—from other friends I can borrow some, and when all these are exhausted, perhaps I may contract with a bookseller to supply me. I shall want your assistance in my account of matters of art. That reign forms, I believe, an era in architecture—it was the period of the introduction of Greek and Roman models and of the utter depravation of the Gothic. Was it not then, too, that the residences of our nobility began to be transformed from castles into mansions?

The post is just going, and I have but just room for all our kind loves to you. I miss you perpetually.

Your affectionate sister,
L. A.

To Mr. E. Aikin.

Stoke Newington : May 9, 1815.

Dear Edmund—I hope you will allow that everybody loves ten times better to receive what you call a gossiping letter than to write one—judge, then, by the size of paper I have taken to fill, how welcome are your epistles to me! . . . .

Well! the beginning of last week I was, as I told you, in town. An evening party on Monday at the N——'s, rather too grave and presbyterian ; but to make amends we had an alderman, a person excellent in his way, thinner indeed than alderman beseems (but his wife atones for that), and he had a red face, hair powdered snow-white, and one of those long foolish noses that look as if they thrust themselves into everything. Then, ye gods! he is musical; summoned Miss N—— to the instrument by touching a few call-notes, and would fain have sung with her, but wicked H—— had left her duets behind, and would not patronise his proposal of taking *two-thirds* of a glee for three voices, so, to my unspeakable mortification, he had no opportunity of exhibiting. . . . Have I got thus far in my letter and said nothing of last Friday! It is a great proof of my methodical and chronological habits of writing that I did not jump to this *period of my history* in the first paragraph. Know, that on Thursday last arrived an invitation from the Carrs to my father and my aunt to dine with them the next day, to meet Walter Scott—apologies at the same time that their table would not admit us all. Well! nothing could persuade my father to go, so my aunt said she would take me instead, and I had not the grace to say no. A charming day we had. I did not indeed see much of the great lion, for we were fourteen at dinner, of whom about half were constantly talking, and neither at table nor after was I very near him; but he was delighted to see my aunt, and paid her great attention, which I was very glad of. He told her that the 'Tramp, tramp,' 'Splash, splash,' of Taylor's 'Lenora' which she had carried into Scotland to Dugald Stewart many years ago, was what made him a poet. I heard him tell a story or two with a dry kind of humour, for which he is distinguished; and though he speaks very broad Scotch, is a heavy-looking man, and has little the air of a gentleman, I was much pleased with him—he is lively, spirited, and quite above all affectation. He had with him his daughter, a girl of fifteen, the most naïve child of nature I ever saw; her little Scotch phrases charmed us all, and her Scotch songs still more. Her father is a happy minstrel to have such a lassie to sing old ballads to him, which she often does by the hour together, for he is not satisfied with a verse or two, but chooses to have *fit* the first, second, and third. He made her sing us a ditty about a border *reiver* who was to be hanged for stealing the bishop's mare, and who dies with the injunction to his comrades,

> If e'er ye find the bishop's cloak.
> Ye'll mak it shorter by the hood.

She also sung us a lullaby in Gaelic—very striking novelties both, in a polished London party. Nobody could help calling this charming girl pretty, though all allowed her features were not good, and we thought her not unlike her father's own sweet Ellen. I had the good fortune to be placed at dinner between Mr. Whishaw and Sotheby, better known by Wieland's Oberon than by his own Saul. He is a lively, pleasant, elderly man; his manners of the old school of gallantry, which we women must ever like. A lady next him asked him if he did not think we could see by Mr. Scott's countenance, if Waverley were mentioned, whether he was the author? 'I don't know,' said Mr. S——, 'we will try.' So he called out from the bottom of the table to the top, 'Mr. Scott, I have heard there is a new novel coming out by the author of Waverley, have you heard of it?' 'I have,' said the minstrel, 'and I believe it.' He answered very steadily, and everybody cried out directly, 'O, I am glad of it!' 'Yes,' said Mr. Whishaw, 'I am a great admirer of those novels;' and we began to discuss which was the best of the two, but Scott kept out of this debate, and had not the assurance to say any handsome things of the works, though *he* is not the author— O no! for he denies them.

Mr. Whishaw was lamenting that his friend Dumont is returning to Geneva; 'but he has the *maladie du pays*, like all Swiss. Talleyrand says that to a Genevois, Geneva is *la cinquième partie du monde*, and Dumont has a prospect of being Secretary of State, with a salary of 50*l.* per annum. And they do not give cabinet dinners there, but *goûters.*' 'Of what?' 'Peach tart, I suppose.' He asked me what was become of that Roscoe who was under Smyth at Cambridge some years ago? 'A pretty romantic young man, and the gods had made him poetical. There were verses to a lily by moonlight.' 'O,' said I, 'he is a steady banker now.' 'A *steady* banker?' 'Yes; there is something of the old character left, certainly, but he is more a man of the world than he was then.' 'O, of course; a banker is *of the earth, earthly.*' I greatly doubt whether *the lion* of the day uttered any roarings equal to these. But the latter part of the evening, our laughing philosopher fell in love with the little Scotch lassie, and only 'roared like any sucking dove.' . . . .

I positively must chatter no longer, I am so busy to day.

Your affectionate,

L. AIKIN.

To Mr. E. Aikin.

Stoke Newington: July 1815.

I had been longing to hear from you, my dear Edmund, for a great while, but guessed how it was that you deferred writing. At last, by some mistake at home about the time of my return, your letter was sent to Brighton just after I left it; no matter, it reached me safe at last, and I thank you very much for all its contents, particularly the letter to Warwick, of which the PS. is certainly very curious.

Well, but Brighton!—you will expect to hear about it. I, for my part, care very little if I never hear of it more; it is a most stupid disagreeable place, but has the advantage of making home quite a paradise in comparison. I saw no person whatever that I knew except Mrs. —— and her family; Mr. —— was only once there from Saturday night to Monday morning, so that we were forced to put up with petticoat parties—things which in the long run rather weary me. Nothing, however, could be more friendly than Mrs. ——'s attentions to me, and I greatly enjoyed both my rides and my bathing, for which I am also somewhat the better. The situation of Brighton is certainly far from beautiful,—a shingly shore without sands and without rock, except a bald low chalk cliff on one side—a sea without ships and land without trees; but it must be confessed that it assembles all imaginable conveniences for summer visitants, lodgings of every kind and price, horses, chaises, gigs, sociables, donkeys, and donkey-carts to hire; excellent shops, libraries, news rooms, &c. The bathing, however, is not in general very good; they do not often push the machines far enough out to treat you with deep water, and *you*, or rather *we* ladies, have only the alternative of wading in over sharp shingles, and then sitting down to be knocked over and partially wetted by a wave, or to be carried, as I saw a gawky girl, between two bathing women, head downwards, heels kicking the air, red dirty legs belonging to ditto completely exposed, and the patient shrieking and crying like a pig taken to the slaughter—a mode which had rather too much the appearance of a penal ducking to suit my fancy. Well, but no matter for this now; I am at home and found everybody well; my aunt K—— mending. Glad they were to see me again, for you may believe that without Arthur and us two, the house would seem dull enough to my father and mother. I was also glad not to miss more of Mr. W——'s company, for you know he is a great favourite of mine. . . . To our great joy in came Mr. Whishaw, and knowing that Mr. W—— wished to see him, we sent for him. Some time after, my aunt Barbauld dropped in, and a most agreeable chat we have had. Mr. Whishaw read to us an agreeable letter from Miss Edgeworth, about his life of Mungo Park, with a postscript by Mr. E——, who is very ill and seemingly beginning to doat, about the possibility of exploring Africa in balloons, which he says he knows the art of guiding—in perfectly calm air. . . . Mr. W—— says that the Duchess of Cumberland, when she comes over, will probably gain great influence with the Regent, being a very clever intriguing woman, and that the old queen will probably be soon out of her way, as she is not likely to live—a hint this for buying mourning!

Good-bye, don't let it be nearly so long before you write again. My father and mother send their kind love.

Your ever affectionate sister,
L. A.

To Mr. E. Aikin.

Stoke Newington : Nov. 1815.

My dear Edmund—I am glad of this opportunity to thank you for your letter by H. K., and to tell you how glad we all are that you have got this new job. It seems to have been by an odd sort of chance at last, though Mr. Roscoe always hoped to be able to procure it for you without difficulty. You must now have your hands quite full of business—all the better, though it removes and lessens the chance of your return hither. We have not yet seen Mr. Roscoe, who is extremely engaged, but he has promised us a visit at the end of the week. Judge how impatient I am to see him; I shall be able to give him a tolerable account of Elizabeth, with whom I converse regularly several hours in the day. I am now pretty near the end of Edward's time, and I feel myself more and more interested in my subject.

Benger has been spending part of two days with us. She is pretty well for one who will never let herself alone, and full of curious anecdote as usual.

Charles Wesley, a while ago, took a queer very fat old

Mrs. S—— to see the Queen go to the drawing-room. In the ante-chamber, in which they waited, were no seats, and the fat lady, becoming tired of standing, at last spread her handkerchief on the floor, and seated herself in a picturesque manner upon it. Charles, being a great blunderer, and somewhat wicked besides, gave the alarm several times that the Queen was coming, and as often poor Mrs. S—— made incredible efforts to get up and see her. At last, he had cried wolf so often that she did not heed him, and when the Queen came indeed, she was not able with the help of all his tugging, to rise from the ground till Her Majesty was past; and one end of her hoop was all that blessed the eyes of this loyal and painstaking subject. To complete the misfortune, she was kept waiting for her carriage, owing to Charles's stupidity, till her dinner was spoiled, and the friends she had invited to eat it were quite out of patience; and to mend all, this rare composition of wit and goose tells the whole story as a good joke, mimicking her to admiration!

Pray read when you can meet with it, a tragedy called 'Fazio,' by a very clever young Mr. Milman, whom I once saw at Allerton. The language is the best imitation of our old dramatists that I have seen; it is brilliant with poetry, and contains fine scenes and situations, though the plot is shocking and improbable. . . . If I mistake not, this is a rising star, destined to blaze far and wide. . . . . Talking of choice people, to be sure, I ought to tell you that we have had a call from Mr. Rogers, who was very agreeable and entertaining with his accounts of Italy. What a beau king Murat is! The morning Mr. Rogers was presented to him, he was standing in the middle of a large room, displaying his fine figure in a Spanish cloak, hat and feather, yellow boots, pink pantaloons, and a green waistcoat! In the evening he appears in a simpler costume, but still wearing roses on his shoes, a white plume in his hat, and his hair prodigiously curled and frizzed, with a long love-lock hanging down on each side. He does not dress above five times a day. Then, no king in Europe, probably, cuts such high capers in the dance—but for other qualifications for reigning, I hear nothing of them. Naples is beautiful, says Mr. Rogers, and the court very gay and pretty; but after all, Florence is the place one longs to live in. No city of its size has half so many fine domes and towers; then the beautiful Arno meets your eye at every turn, and beyond it the finest woods and distant mountains. His descriptions quite set me longing; such gales of myrtle, such groves of orange trees, stuck as full of fruit, he says, as the trees you see sometimes painted by a child!

To-day being Sunday, William Taylor dines with my aunt, and I suppose will call here. As my letter cannot go till to-morrow, I will leave it open, in hopes of some sayings of his. He was very agreeable the short time he stayed; with his usual calculating spirit, he said that if it was necessary to have a war with France, better now than three years hence, when two or three more conscriptions would have grown up. It was to be wished that such a balance could be re-established as would allow the ten-years peaces in Europe which there had been formerly—we could not well bear longer ones, for man was essentially a fighting animal, and a twenty years' peace would turn any republic into a monarchy. He is visiting Dr. Southey, who is thriving greatly, and about to marry again, and, to our great regret, he cannot promise us a day. We have likewise had a call from Mr. J. Taylor. Great joy to see him again in London, looking tolerably, and able to walk from Islington hither. We are all quite well here, and all send love to you.

Your affectionate sister,
L. A.

To Mr. E. Aikin.

Stoke Newington: June 1817.

Dear Edmund—Here come your cravats, which have been delayed a little, but I hope not inconveniently to you, for some of the other contents of the parcel.

Arthur's business is going on most prosperously. . . . Only two candidates are left, one a Mr. H——, who is brother to a person pretty high in the Board of Works, and supported, therefore, by some government interest; but in this Society* it seems government can do little, and on the whole the man is one whom Arthur can have no cause to fear.

The absence of members from London makes the canvass tedious, but Arthur meets, from most whom he sees, with a reception flattering both to himself and all of us. One said, 'Are you the son, sir, of the celebrated Dr. A.?— then you shall have my vote, for I am sure you must be qualified for the station.' Several others asked the same question; the Scotchmen invariably knew the literary character of the family, and were proud to support him. One man, a sword cutler, to whom he had no introduction, gave his vote to him as Mrs. Barbauld's nephew, and begged to introduce him to his family. 'Is he one of the authors of the "Chemical Dictionary"?' cried a working chemist, 'then I am sure he shall have my vote, and all my interest, for I have learnt more from it than any book I ever read!' Dr. Parsons, the civilian, was so much struck and pleased with him in a conversation of a few minutes, that he not only gave the promise of his own vote, but ran and fetched him votes in all Doctors' Commons and the Heralds' Office. Three votes have been given him by old comrades of the third regiment of

* The Society of Arts.

volunteers. One man whom Dr. Laird was canvassing for him said, 'To tell you the truth, sir, I mean to go with the gentleman who will get it; I don't choose my vote should be thrown away.' He has since voluntarily promised to Arthur. Another bird of good omen is Wilks, printer to the society, whose interest it is to make friends with the future secretary.

I have seen the Exhibition, but as everybody said, there was nothing worth looking at but the sculpture. Canova's Hebe and Terpsichore are a splendid pair of statues. I admired most the Muse, for her goddess-like air and nobleness of expression; but I believe the critics in form give the palm to the Hebe. A monument for two children by Chantrey, which represents them sleeping in each other's arms, is nature itself; and so touchingly beautiful, that it won all hearts even from the *beau idéal* of Canova.

I was not satisfied with Shee's portrait of Mr. Roscoe; the expression is vulgar—the likeness, however, is striking. There was a large picture by Fuseli, of Perseus with the Gorgon's head, which hovered, as usual, between the terrible and the grotesque, but on the whole was very striking. Your friend Dawe had a very well-painted portrait of Princess Charlotte, which I suppose will do him good. But why do I talk so much of what I do not understand?

I have been reading a book on—what do you think? I would give you twenty guesses—a book by a lady, of which I said at first, with all the superciliousness of profound ignorance, 'I shall not read it, I am sure.' But, happening to peep between two of its unopened leaves, I cast my eyes on so wise and well-written an exposé of the inconveniences of this same ignorance in which I gloried, that I found myself shamed into opening the leaves, studying it from end to end with great attention, and confessing that I found it well worth the pains—in short, I have been perusing Mrs. Marcet's 'Conversations on Political Economy.' . . . . .

I never was so busy in my life as at this present writing; for I perceive there is not an hour to be lost if I would have my book out in good time. I am, however, quite well, and pleased with my task, so let nobody pity me for meaning to stay at home and work hard all summer.

I have no time for more at present.

Believe me ever yours,
L. AIKIN.

To Mr. E. Aikin.

Stoke Newington : 1817.

Dear Edmund—My conscience tells me that I ought before now to have told you how much we were all gratified to hear that you had borne your journey so well, and were resuming your occupations with spirit. I am particularly glad of the opportunity of writing offered me by William Roscoe, having several things to say to you. . . . Mr. Whishaw and Mr. Smyth made us a call according to promise, but only of half-an-hour, alas! They were both glad and surprised at Arthur's success, not thinking, they said, that anybody on that side could get anything. Mr. Smyth wants to say something in his lectures about 'us ladies' I find; and I believe I shall have given him a clue to most of what he wants.

Miss Rogers and her two brothers dined one day with my Aunt Barbauld. My father dined there, and my mother and I went to tea, and nothing could be more agreeable. Mr. Rogers *laid himself out to be entertaining*, and gave us some very interesting anecdotes of Lord Erskine's rise in his profession, given him by himself. The first cause that he had was Captain Bayley's, in the matter of Greenwich hospital; it was decided by the twelve judges; his astonishing eloquence and energy, joined to the right on his side, gained it; and he went home that night with sixty-seven retaining fees in his pocket. Yes, talent may be buried in obscurity for a while, but it breaks out at last; think of that, and keep a good heart.

I must give you an anecdote of *lionising* which I have just heard. Mrs. Opie, who is still in London, was holding one of her usual Sunday morning levees, when up comes her footman, much ruffled, to tell her that a man in a smock frock was below, who wanted to speak to her —would take no denial—could not be got away. Down she goes to investigate the matter. The rustic advances, nothing abashed: 'I am James Hogg, the Ettrick shepherd.' The poet is had up to the drawing-room, smock frock and all, and introduced to everybody. Presently he pulls out a paper—some verses which he had written that morning, and would read, if agreeable. With a horrible Scotch accent, and charity boy twang, he got through some staves, nobody understanding a line. 'Mr. Hogg,' says Mrs. Opie, 'I think, if you will excuse me, I could do more justice to your verses than yourself;' so takes them from him, and with her charming delivery, causes them to be voted very pretty. On inquiring, it is found that the shepherd is on a visit to Lady Cork, the great patroness of lions (see the 'Twopenny Post Bag'); is exhibited; and has doubtless, since his arrival, merited this illustrious protection, by exchanging, for an habiliment so sweetly rustic, the new green coat, pink waistcoat, and fustian small clothes, in which such a worthy would naturally make a début in the great city! As for 'Lalla Rookh,' it is pretty and very pretty; tender, melodious, and adorned; but, my aunt Barbauld says, 'tis my flower dish, sweet and gay, and tastefully arranged, but the flowers do not *grow* there: they are picked up with pains here and there.

He has thrown an infinite quantity of oriental allusion into his verse, but the reader sympathises in some degree in the labour of the writer—there is no general interest, no *entrainement*—abundance of sentimental beauty, however as well as descriptive, some very manly lines on liberty, &c., in the prose some charming banter of reviewers—on the whole, I hope you will read it. My father has finished the writing of his 'Annual Register,' and is beginning his enlargement of 'England Delineated.' I cannot persuade him that he works too hard; though we are all sure that it is true.

Good-bye, good-bye; I miss you very much, and so do we all. Never forget that there are those who love and are anxious for you.

Your dearly affectionate,
L. A.

To Mr. E. Aikin.

Stoke Newington: June 1817.

Dear Edmund—I, that have a much tenderer conscience as a correspondent than some folks, have been reproaching myself ever since Tuesday se'nnight with not writing to you. For to be sure, thinks I to myself, he would be glad to hear of the annual prize distribution of the Society of Arts, and of Mr. Secretary's grand speech on the occasion, and all the grand things said to him thereon. But then several things made me busy, and I waited for a parcel which is to go, but now I am resolved to wait no longer. . . . .

Now for the meeting. It was held in that grand Freemasons' Hall which holds 1700, and was as full as it would hold, and fuller, for all the passages were crowded, and some hundreds could not even get into them. His R. H. the President made a little exordium; then came Mr. Secretary's speech or report. I was almost close to him, and should have been fluttered, but that I saw he was not so in the least, and knew that he must do himself honour. He raised that fine voice of his, from the first syllable, to such a pitch that it was distinctly heard to the farthest corner of the hall; and this without injuring at all its natural music or just modulation. After his general remarks, he gave a particular report of what had been done by the first committee; then came the candidates in that branch, to whom the Duke delivered their premiums with a little amiable compliment to each. Next came the report of the second committee, and so on. Nothing could be better than this arrangement, which was his own, and afforded respite to him, and variety to the hearers; and nothing surely more interesting than to see so many happy-looking beings coming to receive the public recompense of their talents. Some were artists, some mechanics, some girls, some boys; many of them had countenances of great talent. The whole lasted near three hours. The conclusion of Arthur's speech was followed by a thunder of applause, and when all was done, I had the proud pleasure of walking down the hall leaning on his arm, and listening with greedy ears to the compliments and congratulations of the most distinguished members.

The next night was a general meeting of the society, H.R.H. the president in the chair; when so many fine things were said, that the poor secretary was obliged to make his escape; but was soon called in again, to hear the unanimous resolution which had passed for the printing of the speech; an honour never paid by this society to speech before, and to be requested by the president to comply with the general wish, by permitting it to be done. He meant to have refused, but the Duke said 'pray' so prettily, that it was out of the question; particularly as he ended with—'In short, sir, I need only say that it was the work of an Aikin.' So printed it is to be, and you will receive a copy in a few days; and I might have saved you postage by delaying my letter till then, but whether you would have thought it well saved I do not know. I wish you had seen with what a beautiful serenity and simplicity he went through the whole—nothing about him like any of the littlenesses of an ordinary mortal. You might have heard a pin fall during the speech, so much was everybody impressed with his manner. so much for the apotheosis of Arthur. I have only to add, that he is going to give a large party next week, at which I am to preside.

I shall be very glad of your note on mixed Gothic; more especially if it should be the means of stimulating you to write some separate work on the progress of domestic and public architecture in England—a subject on which I cannot but think that a very elegant and popular book might be written, and written by you. All that I wish for you, as for Arthur, is the opportunity of showing what is in you. In part your buildings speak for you, but the opportunity of executing your designs does not always occur, and I think a work on a professional subject would be in every way a useful exertion of your talents. When habit shall in some degree have familiarised you to the effort of composition, I am convinced that you will find, as I do, pleasure and solace in the occupation. I am writing very hard—hope to have done in three or four months—printing will take as much longer, and I positively will not go to press till the last page is written—so you perceive that I shall be out, barring accidents, in spring. I shall stay at home all the summer, in spite of kind invitations, both from Harlington, and from the Haygarths, who have also most cordially invited my father and mother. Till my work is done I could not enjoy a holiday. . . . My father and mother join in kind love to you.

Ever your affectionate,

L. AIKIN.

To Mr. E. Aikin.

Stoke Newington: March 1818.

Dear Edmund—At length I can say here is my book —*our* book rather, since the appendix is yours. 'Odds tremors!' as Bob Acres would say, it is a nervous thing to face the critics of these days! I am not yet quite mercenary enough altogether to prefer solid pudding to empty praise, but solid pudding may reasonably enough surely be preferred to dry beating; therefore I may be excused for saying that, at present, the money is my most agreeable matter of anticipation. Yet the K——'s, who have had the work in sheets, assure me that they find it very entertaining, and if other people should be of the same mind, who knows but I may meet with some favour in the world? My publishers are very civil, assure me they have no doubt whatever of my success, and already try to embark me in some new scheme; but they have as yet hit on nothing which entirely pleases me. They want me to write for young people, a thing to which I have no great stomach. Of the two, I believe I had rather amuse men and women than instruct children.

The little pamphlet which I enclose with this, is a poem, attributed, as I believe truly, to Lord Byron; though not at all in his old style, it is, I think, a good deal in his old spirit. It exhibits the same bad and miserable mind through an effort at pleasantry. The piece, however, seemed to me both original and amusing, and having bought it, I thought I might as well make you a present of it. The 'antique gentleman of rhyme' is Sotheby, against whom his lordship is known to have a particular spleen. . . . My father's 'Description of England' (being the 'Delineation' enlarged) is in the press, and he gets 100*l*. for it, which we think pretty good. The book trade is at present in great activity. Within the last year a striking change has taken place; then, publishers would hardly treat for anything which was brought them; now they run about urging all their authors to be diligent. Golden days for us.

I like as little as you the cold and timid style of Dr. B——'s biographical articles. I guess you would discern 'Du Hamel' to be the work of a far other pen. I have sometimes grieved that Arthur's style should be *wasted*, as I thought, on scientific subjects, but I now perceive how much it *tells* even upon them. His glowing mind warms and enlightens all that it touches. It is curious to observe the native eloquence of Humboldt struggling with the encumbrance of all the sciences. Did ever mortal man study so many *ologies*, or travel with so many *ometers*! Yet there are magnificent passages of description in this last volume of his personal narrative. We have just been reading Bradbury with great entertainment; those tens of thousands of buffaloes are quite sublime, and the whole account of his navigation on that great river is new and very striking in its details. After my long abode among the statesmen and courtiers of Elizabeth, I feel indescribable refreshment in breathing the pure air of untamed nature in her Atlantic solitudes, and I am eager to cultivate an acquaintance with plain honest brute creatures.

Does the 'Asiatic Journal' ever fall in your way? It ought by all means to be taken in at the Athenæum,* now that the trade to India is so great an object to the town of Liverpool. It abounds with entertaining and interesting orientalisms of every kind; my father gleans from it rich pickings for the 'Annual Register,' and I eagerly explore it for hints of a hundred curious kinds of knowledge entirely new to me. The completion of my long task seems to have

---

* The Athenæum at Liverpool.

          Let fly
A captive bird into the boundless sky.

I flutter my free wings with delight, alight now upon this tree, now upon that; drink of every clear spring; taste of every tempting fruit, and enjoy a renovated youth and spring-time of existence. Charming! could it but last. . . . Mind you write to me soon again, and do not fail to tell me anything pretty that you may chance to hear of a certain book; I assure you I am not a jot wiser than other authors, or less fond of sugar-plums. The opinion, however, about which I am most anxious, is that of Mr. Roscoe, which I shall doubtless hear from himself. I can scarcely forgive myself for not dedicating to him, but even Mr. Whishaw said it must not be. Such are these times! My father and mother are both uncommonly well and send their love. Adieu.

Your ever affectionate
L. A.

To Dr. and Mrs. Aikin.

Lambridge: July 5, 1818.

My dear Father and Mother—Possibly you may begin to wish for some further tidings of your runaway. All that I have to give are good and pleasant, and since the receipt of my mother's most welcome letter, being freed from the anxiety which had before pressed upon me, I have enjoyed myself doubly. By the unwearied kindness of my friends and the convenience of a carriage at command, I have seen to great advantage the environs of this beautiful city,* in which every day has disclosed to me new charms. Yesterday we took a drive to Kelston, and though I was somewhat mortified to find that not a vestige remained of the mansion in which Queen Elizabeth was

* Bath.

entertained by Sir John Harrington, her 'saucy godson,' the rural beauties of the situation, and a certain air of antiquity thrown over the whole peaceful village, highly gratified me. One very agreeable evening we passed at Mr. Conybeare's, with whom I soon got into high chat on architecture, antiquities, history, &c., whence he digressed to mineralogy and to Arthur. I was delighted with his conversation; to a large share of knowledge on a great variety of subjects, and much taste, he adds a vein of original humour, which, united to the utmost good nature, renders him completely agreeable. He, and his beautiful and very pleasing wife, have since returned the visit and confirmed my favourable opinion of them both. . . . You may believe that I have not neglected to renew my acquaintance with my old friend, Mrs. B. After mutual calls, she invited me to a thing mightily in my line—a concert. I was gratified, however, with some of the music, and glad to find that her eldest girl is regarded as a kind of musical prodigy, to the delight of father and mother. In a corner of the room sat a little thin old lady, muffled up in a black dress, without a bit of white to be seen, with a high smart headdress, well rouged cheeks, long nose, and very lively black eyes, whose *picturesque* appearance almost instantly attracted my notice. 'Let me introduce you,' cried Mrs. B. 'to Mrs. Piozzi.' 'By all means,' exclaimed I, for a hundred associations made me long to talk with the rival of 'Bozzy;' and I went and sat by her. Her vivacity has not forsaken her, and I have been at once gratified and tantalised on our return from Bath this morning, to find her card left for me. I hope to find her at home when I return the visit. She is now seventy-nine, and seems as if she might enjoy life a long time yet. . . I do not know how I can be home before Friday. My friends are most cordially kind, and take every possible means of showing that my company is very welcome to them. Of conversation we have never had any want. The doctor* *will* talk politics with me, but we don't quarrel, partly because I let him have it pretty much his own way; but he perfectly understands my lamentations that the metropolis should have disgraced itself by the choice of so many opposition members. There is come to Bath a wild Irish apostle, himself a convert from popery, who has been the means of 40,000 of his countrymen learning to read, and of a great number forsaking their old superstition. He has called a meeting to tell his story and beg contributions, and Dr. Percival tells Miss H. and me that we must go and hear him, which I long to do, for the man, Thaddy Conolly by name, is so grotesque a creature, that even Dr. P. cannot mention him without laughing. I suppose he is a very fit instrument for his work, however, and I wish him all success. I saw yesterday the S.'s, a good specimen of Bath, for the father is literary and scientific, the mother furiously gay, and the daughter violently methodistical. With kind love to all, believe me, my dearest parents,

Ever your dutiful and affectionate

L. A.

To Mr. E. Aikin.

Adelphi: May 1, 1819.

Dear Edmund—Thank you for your second letter, which has done something towards removing our anxiety respecting you, though we shall still want to hear that your strength is returned. I wish I had you to nurse—but what signifies wishing? . . . .

The dinner at the Hollands' † was no bad thing in its way neither; one is sure to meet men there from all countries which they trade to, nearly all the civilised world. We had

---

* Dr. Haygarth.   † Mr. Swinton Holland, of the house of Barings.

the priest and the surgeon who are going out to Buonaparte; the former a reverent and innocent-looking old abbé, who has not in the least the appearance of a man to plot the escape of the prisoner; I understood his Italian tolerably well, his French less, his English least of all. The surgeon is a little sharp-looking Corsican, who has quitted a good situation at Florence for this banishment—surely from some hope of seeing his master one day reinstated. He spoke Italian with a harsh accent, very rapidly, and in a tone which rendered it almost utterly unintelligible to me. I was actually surprised into speaking a whole sentence of Italian to the abbé, greatly to my own astonishment, and little, I fear, to his edification. When the party was nearly all assembled, in strode the longest, leanest, brownest, most ungainly mortal I ever set eyes on. He had scarcely knocked his head against the lamp in the middle of the room, when I had decided upon him; 'an American,' whispered I to Mrs. H. It was even so, a senator from Carolina; I had him for my neighbour at dinner; the 'grim feature' was disposed to talk, and certainly wanted neither sense nor knowledge. There were some stories told of borough jobbing which made this republican bless himself, but he longed to witness the humours of an English election, and anxiously inquired if there was any chance of a vacancy in any popular place. I had on my other side at dinner a much more prepossessing person, Mr. Haldimand, Mrs. Marcet's brother, who is not a little proud apparently of such a sister. I suppose he is one of the ablest and most enlightened mercantile men in London, and learnedly talked he of usury laws and so forth; observing that ladies now studied political economy, on the whole I found him polished, clever, and entertaining. We had another great merchant with a Dutch name, which I dare not spell, who was a kind of dandy and picture-fancier; we had also Dr.

Holland, but he was so seized upon by the Italians that one had nothing of him.

This morning my mother and I go with Arthur to this Arctic panorama, from drawings by Lieutenant Beechy, which all the world sees and admires as something quite new and striking.

It is high time for me to stop scribbling and get ready to go out.

Ever your affectionate
L. AIKIN.

To her Niece.

Hampstead: June 15.

Dear Susan—I, like you, must make out a letter without great events; but what, though! I hope we have either of us brains enough to spin one poor sheet out of! Observe, however, that I have much the least assistance from circumstances of the two; I have no change of scene, no new acquaintances, and though I have lounging plenty, it is not, as I wish it were, 'by the resounding main,' but only among the herbs and flowers of my own garden. I am concerned to inform the younger members of the family, that my great brag of fruit is reduced to two peaches, one cherry, and three plums, with a small sprinkling of apples, and a few gooseberries and currants. The grapes, indeed, promise great things as to quantity, but let me see them ripen. What is worst of all, my two greengage trees, as they ought to have been, turn out paltry egg plums, and I am enraged. But my flower-beds begin to look quite Newingtonian.

Last Thursday, went to Mrs. Mallet's; nobody there but Mr. and Mrs. B—— and Mrs. Mulso, and we sat in a long straight line down one side of the drawing-room with our hands before us. I was next to the enchanting Mr.

B——, who discoursed on commercial distress. He was mightily puzzled with the coffee cups being handed about empty; and never found out the coffee-pot or the waiter, and would have gone without till now, had I not humanely assumed the office of Hebe. This being the only *incident* of the evening, I judged it highly worth recording. If they catch me there again—that's all!

I am cumbered with many things at present; between idle visits and idle books I have no leisure for my business. We have had the first volume of the 'Betrothed Lovers,'—that Italian novel you know. It is very interesting, both as a story and a picture of manners; and the sentiments are very sound and rational. It has had prodigious success in Italy, which is good as a sign of the liberality of sentiment now diffused there, and good also because it is highly important that they should have books which may serve to rouse the Italian women from their darling 'far niente.' Mrs. Marcet says there is no medium with them at present, between being professors of anatomy and not knowing how to read. Being ignorant, they are idle; being idle, they fall into intrigue, profligacy, and gaming. A thousand pities, for with tolerable instruction the Italian genius shows itself the brightest in Europe. At the school of mutual instruction at Florence, Mrs. Marcet was requested to examine the boys; and their quickness, and accuracy, and variety of useful knowledge, perfectly astonished her. By the way, I exceedingly longed for you when we had a delightful morning visit from Mrs. and Miss Marcet; I know no woman comparable to Mrs. Marcet in the charm of her society, and I assure you that her daughter is exceedingly agreeable also—affected! no such thing indeed. She joined in conversation with an ease, a sweetness, a modest grace which delighted me. Forgetfulness of self is the greatest charm in manner; but to young people this charm scarcely ever belongs. Their inexperience makes every appearance in society a kind of experiment to them, and they usually watch its success with too visible an anxiety. To this anxiety faults apparently the most opposite may equally be traced; bashfulness, invincible taciturnity, forward chatter, and the whole tribe of affectations have all their root in egotism. Their common cure is to be sought in the cultivation of that amiable spirit of social sympathy, which lends itself with ease to the tastes and pursuits of others, which, forgetful of self, seeks to give pleasure to all around, and secures approbation by evincing good will. From early youth this was the distinguishing charm of your most lovely mother, whom everyone loved at sight and half adored on thorough knowledge. By this charm she silenced detraction and made envy relent; her learning, and even her beauty, were forgiven by rivals, and old and young, men and women, pressed around to claim her as a friend.

Dear love to Kate, and tell her if she will write to me, I will write to her. Your father says he will write soon.

Ever, dear girl, your affectionate aunt,
L. AIKIN.

To her Niece.

Hampstead: Nov. 17.

Dear Sue—I said I would not write to you till I had dined with the king and queen at Guildhall, which might excuse me from correspondence with you for a longer time than your visit even is likely to endure; but at the heavy risk of being accounted a person lost to all sense of the obligation of vows, here I am putting pen to paper for a little chat with you. To be sure it is a great pity that I have been robbed of an occasion on which it would have been so 'easy to be eloquent,' as that grand display of festivity and loyalty; a still greater pity it is, that the splendid sleeves of net and satin which Anna had constructed for me are still unworn, and likely to be, and that my old Mansion House plume has been cleaned to no purpose: but what is the use of fretting? The day before, I think I had a greater trial of patience—I had Mrs. and Miss Hoare, Mr. Crabbe, Mrs. Mallet and your father to tea, and also Mr. Whishaw, who happened to have volunteered for the same evening, and somehow or other I had got so deaf that I could not speak to anybody; for whether you may happen to have thought of it or no, certain it is that there is no talking when one is deaf, which I take to be the great objection to it. There I sat, a stupid dummy, wishing myself in bed all the time. This deafness lasted the whole week. On the Saturday I was engaged to dine at Mr. Justice Parke's *— could not put it off—set out feeling as if I was going to execution, but stopping at James Street by the way, I got syringed, and went off in high glee, hearing as well as ever. . . .

The grand news of Hampstead is, that Mr. Webster is giving us a course of geological lectures; to-day we have the second. Said your uncle to me in the summer, 'Don't you think you could get Webster a class here?' I said, 'I will try;' and having so said, I was obliged, contrary to my habits, if not to my nature, to become an active, canvassing body in the parish—wrote letters, called on people, got the Lord Chief Justice for patron—and behold a class of about forty, with which I apprehend he is well content, and with his first lecture everybody has seemed pleased; and there was all the science and intellect of the place (at least I am afraid so). In the introductory lecture we have had both the Huttonian and Wernerian theories, and fire and water have been fighting in my brain ever since. To-day we are to proceed from theories to facts, things which please me better. When I read

* Lord Wensleydale.

theories, by which I mean such hypotheses as, even if true, could never be adequately proved, I think I hear people telling their dreams. They have, however, their use; ingenious men, by the zeal for supporting or opposing them, are urged to search into facts, and thus much real knowledge is brought to light.

I have been reading a very deep and very able book, with which I should certainly have endeavoured to task your intellect had you been with me. This is a history of ethical philosophy in England, written by Sir. J. Mackintosh for a new edition of the 'Encyclopædia Britannica.' He begins with a slight view of the system of Plato and other ancients, and of the schoolmen, of whom I believe he is the only living person who knows anything. He shows a wonderful comprehension of his subject in all its branches and bearings. The style somewhat disappointed me; his friends say it was written hastily, but there are luminous and original remarks which give great value and interest to the work. I found it never dry, though sometimes difficult; and I should like few things better than some time to go over it again with you It is peculiarly desirable for women to exercise themselves in works of reasoning; without this discipline, prejudice, and sentiment, and fancy, take such possession of them, that logic is turned quite out of doors, and then the men go and say the sex have no heads, which makes one mad. Talking of she-heads, Miss Edgeworth has come to town, bringing us a new novel, which I hope to see excellent, were it only to prove she can stand alone. Mrs. Joanna Baillie once got out of her that 'Rackrent' and 'Ennui' were all her own. 'Very well, Maria,' said she, 'that is enough, I don't want to hear any more.' To be sure it is the lion's share. Yesterday I dined with the S. Hoares, and enjoyed it much; there was no great party, but all was very kind and friendly, and we talked of the days of our youth. Mr.

Crabbe came in the evening, and we made him tell us of Johnson, whom he had met with Burke at the house of Reynolds; then we spoke of modern poets—Burns, and Montgomery, and I had the good luck to please the amiable old man by alluding to a poem of his which he said no one had ever mentioned to him before. 'I thought,' he said, 'when I wrote it, that there was something in it, but as nobody took notice of it, I supposed I was mistaken.' I told him I had known my father read it repeatedly and commend it highly. It is called 'Reflections;' I will sometime show it you, I think it excellent.

It begins to be a monstrous long time that you have been away, and some murmurs are heard amongst us from time to time; however, I am persuaded you are turning your time to good account, both for pleasure and that kind of improvement which only the intercourse of varied society can afford; therefore I shall take patience myself and recommend it to others. Let me hear from you soon, and believe me ever,

My dear girl, your affectionate aunt,
L. AIKIN.

To Mrs. Taylor.

Stoke Newington: Jan. 27, 1803.

When you were in town, my dear Mrs. Taylor, you were so kind as to express a wish of hearing from me sometimes, and Eliza's return to Norwich affords me so good an opportunity of writing that I shall no longer refuse myself that pleasure; yes, pleasure I may indeed call it, for next to seeing and hearing from a dear friend there is nothing to me so gratifying as to write to one; and I much wonder that among those who have leisure for this employment, a taste for it is not more common. But 'out of sight out of mind,' is so much the way of the world, that I believe we must content ourselves, in many cases, with a rather mortifying solution of this difficulty. . . .

I am full of plans and projects for the ensuing spring, when it arrives; sometimes I dream of another visit to the Welsh mountains—then my fancy rambles to the Highlands of Scotland—but one of the most agreeable of my anticipations, and that which is most likely to be realised, in another journey to dear old Norwich; which I need not assure you that I shall enjoy as much as the last, and more I cannot say. Yes, my dear Mrs. Taylor, the longer I live the more am I convinced that connections formed in early childhood are the strongest, the most durable, and the most delightful of all. The image of the friend of infancy is associated with a thousand endearing recollections of those days of careless, but unclouded happiness, that pass so swiftly, never to return. The friend of riper youth is ever connected in our memory with some of those cares, those passions, those severe pains and lively pleasures that give to this period a more exquisite flavour of bitter and of sweet than to the preceding, or perhaps any subsequent portion of life. When I feel my mind agitated by the too vivid ideas of scenes that have passed more recently, I think of Norfolk, and the careless days spent there among my early friends, and all is calm again; of what other place can I think with unmingled pleasure, with perfect satisfaction? But what has enticed my pen into this long strain of sentimental reflection; I fear you will not much thank me for anything so *sombre*. . . . There is a singular work lately published, of which I should much like to hear your opinion, Mary Hayes's 'Female Biography.' She is a great disciple of Mrs. Godwin, you know, and a zealous stickler for the equal rights and equal talents of our sex with the other; but, alas, though I would not so much as whisper this to the pretended lords of the creation—

> Her arguments directly tend
> Against the cause she would defend.

At the same time that she attempts to make us despise 'the frivolous rivalry of beauty and fashion,' she holds forth such tremendous examples of the excesses of more energetic characters, that one is much inclined to imitate those quiet good folks who bless God they are no geniuses. However, a general biography is something like a great London rout, everybody is there, good, bad, and indifferent, visitable and not visitable, so that a squeamish lady scarcely knows whom she may venture to speak to. Alas, alas! though Miss Hayes has wisely addressed herself to the ladies alone, I am afraid the gentlemen will get a peep at her book and repeat with tenfold energy that women have no business with anything but nursing children and mending stockings. I do not think her book is written quite in an edifying manner neither—the morals are too French for my taste.

But what are we to think of Madme. de Stael's new novel, that all Paris, all Geneva, and all London is reading? I hear Rousseau is revived in her, with all his 'virtue in words and vice in actions,' and all his dangerous eloquence. I have not read the book yet, but we voted it into a lady's book society here, and had afterwards some doubts whether it ought to be circulated. My mother wickedly proposed that all works written by ladies should be carefully examined by a committee before they are admitted into the society. And now that I have mentioned our society, which is a great hobby horse with my aunt Barbauld and me, I must beg your congratulations on our spirit in setting up an institution into which not a single man is admitted, even to keep the accounts. I must indeed whisper in your ear that it is no very easy matter to get the ladies to suspend their dissertations on new plays and new fashions to discuss the merits of books, and that sometimes it is rather difficult for the president, treasurer, and secretary, calling all at once to order, to obtain a hearing. But our meetings are not the less amusing for this.

We had the pleasure of seeing our good friend Mr. Whishaw, the only person almost who has had the charity to come and see us this dismal weather, very lately; he speaks of Norwich, and of my best friends there, with an enthusiasm that delights me. I have commissioned Eliza to remember me to all who enquire after me, and to send me word how everybody does; nevertheless I hope to hear from you when you have leisure to write, and that a very good account of dear Mr. Taylor will make a part of your very welcome despatches. To him, with yourself and all your family, our fireside circle joins in cordial remembrance with

Your very affectionate
L. AIKIN.

To Mrs. Taylor.

Stoke Newington: March 23, 1805.

How is it possible, my dear Mrs. Taylor, that I can have been so negligent and stupid as to have suffered more than two months to elapse since the receipt of a letter from you without having answered it? Indeed I know not how to give a better account of the matter than by saying that I have had much to do, and little to say. At one time my hours have been engrossed by company in the house; at another my fingers have been engaged in employments which offered little food to the mind; lastly and chiefly, I have been loth to write till spring arrived to give a *fillip* to my spirits.

I have now the pleasure and satisfaction to tell you that I have passed, on the whole, a very tolerable winter, that

I am gradually reviving with the year, and that when your Norfolk north-easterns have ceased to blow, I shall be ready to attend your first summons to come and make you idle a little. But may we not hope to see you in town for a few weeks first? Richard tells me that he has been humbly petitioning for a little of your company, and surely you cannot find in your heart to give him a denial.

What an utter pause, cessation and nonplus is the present! How miserably dull for us bookworms to hear of nothing new from day to day! I am much afraid that we shall actually be compelled to go back to the ancients of last year—if any of their immortal works may hitherto have escaped the rapacious hands of grocers, trunkmakers, and renovators of paper. I wish this rebellion had fortunately taken place before the two last volumes of Fleetwood were committed to the press, for certainly, with a little more leisure, a man of Godwin's talents could not possibly have produced so bungling, lame, and impotent a catastrophe. What a pity it is that he should have been converted by the outcries of bigots from eloquent absurdity to ponderous common sense! But we have nothing piquant now-a-days.

My poor work does not proceed with very great rapidity. I have, however, got about a hundred lines of the third epistle; and after visiting Troy, Sparta, and Athens, am just going to arrive at Rome at the very moment when the Sabine women separate the threatening armies. On the whole, I consider the Roman dames as the queens of their sex, but there are a few ugly facts against them which I do not well know what to do with. At one time they had a disagreeable habit of poisoning their husbands; but I don't think much of that, for no doubt the men gave them provocation. What think you of a heroine who has lately sprung up at Newington Green? She was a cook maid, and having long been on bad terms with the footman, resolved to give their disputes an effectual settling. For this purpose, whilst the man was waiting at table, she concealed herself behind a door with a carving knife in her hand, and on the man's passing by, started out and plunged the weapon in his body. His life was at first thought to be in danger, and our heroine was sent to Newgate; but on his getting better she was released, because, forsooth, her mistress thinks it would be a pity to send her to Botany Bay! I hope you have seen Scott's 'Lay of the last Minstrel;' I have read no other poem of last year that deserves to be compared with it. There is something in the wild and lawless manners of the old Scotch Borderers uncommonly striking. I know nothing that more irresistibly seizes the imagination than the adventures of valiant marauders. Who can refuse an ear to the tales of Robin Hood, or the history of the Buccaneers?

The Barbaulds are going next week to lodgings in town, which they have taken for a few weeks, in order to see everything and everybody with little trouble. They wish me to go and share in their gaiety; but I feel by no means equal to racketing at present, and my father shows little inclination to entrust me to the prudence of my aunt, who is at least forty years younger than I am. Is it not a most fortunate symptom of old age to have lost one's curiosity and to prefer, as I do, comfort to pleasure? Well, I think it pretty well to enjoy all the homebred satisfactions that fall to my lot. Home, to me, becomes every day more delightful, and its revered inhabitants more dear and more necessary to my happiness. Oh! how could I ever bear to be separated from those who unite in themselves all the strongest titles to my gratitude and affection! . . . .

I *have* a taste, I do assure you, for the epistles of such

girls as Susan,* and therefore I beg you will tell her, with my kindest love, that I hope she will assume the office of secretary to her mother, and give me the pleasure of a long letter very soon. As for you, my dear Mrs. T., I know too well your numerous and important occupations to expect more than the favour of a letter now and then; that highly-prized indulgence I hope you will never deny me. . . . My mother desires me to return you her thanks for some game which you were so kind as to send us.

Our fireside begs its best remembrances to yours.

Believe me, my dear Mrs. Taylor,

Most warmly yours,

L. AIKIN.

Good Mr. Roscoe has been laid up with the gout, but is now recovered. Do you not long to see that admirable being again?

To Mrs. Taylor.

Stoke Newington : Oct. 1805.

A letter of congratulation from Lucy; how formal! Will you say so, my dear Mrs. T.? No; you will give me credit for feeling what I express, and you will be sensible of the pleasure I take in expressing what I feel. I am glad the deed is done, for till that was the case I know your maternal anxiety would be at work; now all suspense is over, and has yielded the place, I hope, to pure and entire satisfaction. My father and mother beg to express to you and Mr. T. their warm sympathy on this occasion of happiness. I beg you will remember me to John in the kindest manner. . . . I trust he will not fail, on reaching this part of the world, to set apart a day for Newington—we all long to give him a hearty shake of the hand. . . . I am obliged to Susan for a very charming letter, pray tell her so, and that it shall be answered, *in course.*

* Afterwards Mrs. Reeve.

Do you ask what I have been about since I came home? I have been re-writing the beginning of Epistle the first, with some additions, and after various other alterations and corrections, I have begun to lengthen my web. Twenty or thirty new lines have conducted me from the vigour to the 'Decline and Fall' of the Roman State, from the ruins of which I am just about to make my escape, and seek an asylum among the pathless forests and impenetrable marshes of ancient Germany. In Latin, I am reading 'Cicero's Offices,' whence I gather that the improvements in moral philosophy, since his time, have been few or none; for a purer or more rational system than his, or one better adapted to the actual condition of man, and the practical regulation of life, can scarcely be imagined. In Italian, I am re-reading with increased delight 'Jerusalem Delivered,' which appears to me certainly the most sweet and interesting, though not the most sublime, of epic poems. I much question whether Boileau had ever read it when he spoke so contemptuously of 'Le clinquant de Tasse.' If he had, I would give little for his taste. I have just discovered in myself some aptness for the study of Natural Philosophy, and thinking that my profound ignorance of its various branches might some time bring me to shame, and likewise that I might glean a few new similes and metaphors from this kind of knowledge, I have resolved to apply to it in good earnest, and make it my principal *study* for the winter. But within the last few days everything has given way to 'Practical Education,' which my mother and I have been studying with great diligence for the benefit of George's little boy, who was brought to us last Tuesday. My aunt Barbauld laughs at us excessively; she says, 'I know that everybody reads works on education as pleasant books, but this is the first time that ever I heard of anybody's sitting gravely down to study them for use.' But we don't mind the laughers, and can see no reason why a child may not as well be brought up *after* 'Practical Education' as a pudding made *after* the 'Experienced English Housekeeper.' In the meantime the boy is gone to school as a day-boarder, so it is only at his hours of recreation that these fine recipes can be tried; all the rest will be managed in the usual way, as in most culinary operations a good deal is left to that golden rule, *the rule of thumb.* My time will, it is true, be a good deal encroached upon by the care of this young nestling, but you know the feelings of my *auntship*, and will believe that I do not grudge it. You have seen, I imagine, my father's memoir of poor Dr. Currie, and perhaps, likewise, a small token of my respect for his memory in the last magazine. I believe you have heard me speak of this most exalted being, and express my gratitude for the distinguished kindness with which he had treated me. You will believe that his death, which I learnt from a most affecting letter written by his son to my father, and which in my father's absence I opened, affected me deeply. A few days since, our feelings were again awakened by a visit from this son—a son worthy of his father—who speaks of him with equal grief and pride, considers his little brothers with a kind of paternal affection, and appears to be prompted in every word and action by the hovering spirit of his father. He showed us a few trembling lines, traced by his dying hand, in which he says that he shall consider his fame as safe in the hands of my father; mentions him and his 'dear friend Roscoe' with the strongest affection, implores a blessing on them and *all theirs*, and expresses the hope of a meeting in 'the regions beyond the grave.' I think you and I have spoken together of the sensation caused by the handwriting of a dead friend, but I never *felt* it in its full force before. Such a man, such a friend—I shall never forget him! But what am I doing? this is a letter of congratulation, and I have filled it up with sorrow. To 'rejoice with those that do rejoice, and weep with those that weep' are two duties which sometimes fall upon one so nearly at the same time, that it is difficult to keep them distinct, they blend like day and night producing a kind of twilight of the spirits, calm, sober, sweet, best fitted to tender thought and various musing and philosophic moralizing, on the strange medley which makes up the sum of human life ... I forgot to tell you, among my other employments, that, as literary characters must now and then descend from their altitudes, I have been several days hard at work upon parlour curtains, which are at length hung up, to the great glory and satisfaction of my mother and me. You can't think how smart we look. I am quite stout and hearty in spite of this premature winter. May every blessing wait on you and yours is the warm wish of your

LUCY.

To Mrs. Taylor.

Stoke Newington: July 1806.

... I have of late been quite stout, and resolving to enjoy the full privileges of a person in health, I went, on New Year's day, to visit my friend Mrs Carr, whom I accompanied to some London parties. The most *piquant* of these was a dinner at Hoppner's, where were, besides Hoppner himself, who has more wit than almost any man, Memory Rogers, and Anacreon Moore, otherwise 'Little,' who is an Irishman, and told us some Irish stories with infinite humour. In the afternoon came the Opies; presently Mrs. Opie and Moore sat down to the instrument. Mrs. Opie was not in voice, but Anacreon! upon my word he gave me new ideas of the power of harmony. He sung us some of his own sweet little songs, set to his own music, and rendered doubly touching by a voice the most sweet, an utterance the most articulate, and expression the most deep and varied, that I ever witnessed. No wonder this little man is a pet with duchesses! What can be better fitted for a plaything of the great than a ruddy joyous laughing young Irishman, poor but not humble, a wit, poet, and musician, who is willing to devote his charming talents to their entertainment for the sake of being admitted to their tables, and honoured with their familiarity?

As I was determined to 'exert my energies,' I readily accompanied my friends on board Mr. W. Carr's ship, whence we saw Nelson's body carried in procession up the river. The ships with their lowered flags, the dark boats of the river fencibles, the magnificent barges of His Majesty and the city companies, and above all, the mournful notes of distant music, and the deep sound of the single minute-gun, the smoke of which floated heavily along the surface of the river, conspired to form a solemn, sober, and appropriate pomp, which I found awfully affecting. It did but increase my eagerness to witness the closing scene of this great pageant exhibited the next day at St. Paul's. Richard, who was our active and attentive squire, will probably have given you an account of our adventures on this occasion, and the order of procession you would see in the papers; but perhaps you might not particularly attend to a circumstance which struck me most forcibly—the union of all ranks, from the heir-apparent to the common sailor, in doing honour to the departed hero. In fact, the royal band of brothers, with their stately figures, splendid uniforms, and sober majestic deportment, roused, even in me, a transient emotion of loyalty; but when the noble Highlanders and other regiments marched in who vanquished Buonaparte's Invincibles in Egypt, and, reversing their arms, stood hiding their faces with every mark of heartfelt sorrow, and especially when the victorious captains of Trafalgar showed their weather-beaten and undaunted fronts, following the bier in silent mournful state, and when, at length, the gallant tars appeared bearing in their hands the tattered and blood-stained colours of the 'Victory'—and I saw one of the poor fellows wiping his eyes by stealth on the end of the flag he was holding up—I cannot express to you all the proud, heroic, patriot feelings that took possession of my heart, and made tears a privilege and luxury. No, on that day an Englishman could not despair of his country! And now, after this taste of the gaieties and glories of the great city, I am returned to my snug little home, which is at present, however, less snug than usual. The Estlins of Bristol are on a visit to the Barbaulds and we meet almost daily. . . . Miss Edgeworth's 'Leonora' is full of wit, observation, and good sense: if it falls in your way it will entertain you much. I will write to Sally* at my first leisure interval, but when that will arrive, I cannot guess. Melancholy indeed is the face of public affairs; sometimes it infects me with gloom; but so much more to us is our own fireside than all the world besides, that whilst we see happy faces there, we are half inclined to say, 'Let the world wag!' When I wish to cloak indifference in philosophy, I think how good comes out of evil, and evil out of good, and on the whole how impossible it is to tell which is which. Pray remember me most kindly to the little circle respecting whom I can never be indifferent, including therein Mrs. Enfield, from whom my mother has just had a very affectionate letter, and Eliza. We were all quite well here; my aunt Barbauld hears as quick as ever. Richard tells me that we are to see his father soon, at which I rejoice not a little, for after all, what pen can convey a tenth part of what *one*, that is *I*, wish to say to my friends? For instance, I have now written almost a pamphlet, and

* Miss Sarah Taylor, afterwards Mrs. John Austin.

yet I feel as if I had but just got into chat with you. I have scarce left room to say, my best of friends, Adieu.

To Mr. Taylor.

Broad St. Buildings: August 1806.

Here I come at last, my dear sir, to have a little chat upon paper with you, and wipe off the long reproach of faithless vows and promises unperformed. My party—aye! after all *your* promises, to steal off just that very afternoon, I sha'n't forget that yet awhile, I promise you—and *such* a party! If it was not mentioned in the 'Morning Post,' it must have been by some strange negligence in their quid-nuncs. Vexed I was, to be sure, that Mr. Taylor did not grace and enliven my circle with his attic wit, his store of anecdote, &c. It was very well I did not do like Mr. —— when he gave a grand ball the other night. After supper, the good gentleman's heart being warmed, he rose to make a speech to his 'dear five hundred friends,' in which he told them he had invited several members of parliament and other people of consequence, but that unluckily the best and genteelest part of his acquaintance had all sent excuses.

I wrote Mrs. Taylor a very full and true account of all our wedding proceedings, of which, I suppose, she will communicate to you—as much as is proper. If you wish to know what we are engaged in at this present writing, let me have the honour to tell you that we are *sitting up for company*. Do you not think that we are much to be envied? This house is so changed, you certainly never would know it for the same; and the bride looks so blooming and pretty, it would do you good to take a salute of her. Suppose you come to town on purpose! Immediately on their return, the happy pair was greeted with a most elegant epistle from 'Your humble servants, the marrow bones, cleavers, and drummers of the parish of St. Botolph,' whom, as the alternative was 'pay or play,' or rather as they must be paid at any rate, there was no doubt about bribing to silence.

Saint Andrew's brave bells did so loud and so clear ring,
You'd have given five pounds to have been out of their hearing.

I think their house should be called Pic-nic Hall, for it is almost furnished by the contributions of friends. Talking on gay and pleasant subjects, pray have you seen a very facetious little book called 'The Miseries of Human Life,' in a series of dialogues between Messrs. Sensitive and Testy? It is really a most amusing performance, and shows a world of observation, for there is scarcely any class of minor calamities and daily rubs, which has not found a place, except, indeed, such as are peculiar to our unfortunate sex; for the 'Supplementary Sighs' of Mrs. Testy are miserably defective.

My father and mother were not particularly delighted with their expedition to G——'s, as far as the beauties of nature were concerned. My father heard there an anecdote which will give you an idea of the extreme barbarity of the fen country. A Cambridge physician being sent for to a patient in that part, and finding the road scarcely passable, though it was the middle of summer, enquired of his conductor, a simple country lad, what the people could possibly do for medical assistance in winter? 'O, sir,' replied the gawky, 'in winter they die a natural death!' My father has got something from his fen expedition however, namely, a descriptive letter for the Athenæum, for which Dr. Falkener has also sent a dissertation on the Elysian fields. There is a man at Acle, whose name I forget, who has written to say that if my father will accept of his service for the Athenæum, his mind will be found 'a perpetual source of poetic and prosaic strength;' he confesses, however, that there is a kind of confusion in his head, but hopes my father will be so good as to 'put him in order.' O, the Norfolk geniuses! Poor Dr. Parr! do you hear that all his flattering epistles to Lord Chedworth are printed, and that it appears in the course of the correspondence, that the pompous inscription on a silver tureen which he begged from his lordship, in which he is called 'doctissimus,' and I know not what, was composed by no other than the reverend doctor himself? As Dr. Parr was not subpœnaed, but volunteered his evidence, I think this revenge on the part of the executors is very fair, but it will chafe the lion.

I hope you are in no very great hurry to get Susan home again; there are those who have a plot to stop her in her way, I can assure you.

If my letter is full of blots and blunders, allow, I pray you, for a man who is putting up pictures in the room: he and Anne alternately perplex me—one by knocking nails, the other by asking my advice. Here come visitors—adieu, my dear sir,

Believe me, ever yours,
L. AIKIN.

To Mrs. Taylor.

Stoke Newington: April 1814.

My dear Friend—In your present deprivation of Sarah's company, I shall be particularly glad if my pen may help to amuse one of your leisure half hours; to you it is always easy and always a pleasure to me to write, and at a time like this can topics be wanting? . . . In the fate of Europe, what food for meditation! The first, the most welcome, thought that strikes me is, that for sovereigns as for private persons, for nations as for individuals, it is good to have been afflicted. Could anything less than the severe lessons they have received have taught so much political wisdom to the French people, such a magnanimous clemency to the allied sovereigns? How great and important a step must opinion have been silently making when a constitution as free as that which five-and-twenty years ago half the powers of Europe armed to prevent the French from forcing upon their late king, is offered to the acceptance of his brother under the sanction of the mightiest despot of Europe and Asia, and with the acquiescence of all the potentates who took part in the former quarrel: when the great principle that foreign nations should take no part in regulating the internal government of a country seems admitted by all, and when no partition of the territories of a long hated and feared, now vanquished and prostrate nation, is even hinted at by any of the victors!

The overthrow of the tyrant and his works, with all its details, as the release of prisoners, the restoration of their rights to the wronged, &c. sounds like the adventure of some peer of Charlemagne, or knight of fairy-land, when, having vanquished the giant in fight, he snatches the rusty keys from his side, enters the castle and unlocks all its dismal dungeons: one ceremony only has been omitted, the decapitation of said giant, and that unpicturesque omission alone will spoil the subject for future epic poets. For the philosopher and moralist it spoils nothing; that the bold bad man who has filled Europe with blood and slaughter should be permitted, and should endure to live, degraded and pensioned, is the finest and most impressive satire on the false greatness of a conqueror that history has ever read to ages. I should have grieved if the villain had extorted from us one phrase of admiration by a death generously voluntary like that of Otho. But enough on a subject on which you will have thought so much better than I can do. I will end by giving you an anecdote which will please you and which I believe authentic. Some years ago, the Emperor Alexander had the curiosity to ask an Englishman for the explanation of the terms Whig and Tory, and having received it, 'I believe,' said he, 'I am the only Whig in my dominions.' How welcome in every view is the idea of peace! among other benefits I think it will tend to the advancement of solid learning. When that intense interest which the events of the war have inspired in public affairs is at an end, the active minds of men must seek for exercise in science, and in those more solid branches of literature which appear to me at present in a rather neglected state; novels and novel-like poems will not then engross the whole conversation of reading people; deeper studies may recover a vogue which they seem to me to have lost. I shall, for my part, hail the day when the state of public feeling shall prompt me to lay aside my idle trade of tale-weaving, for the completion of that historic design which I desire to regard as the basis of my highest literary hopes. At present, however, I am endeavouring to form to my satisfaction that long-suspended history of the heart, of which I have spoken to you so often. The vision that at present flits before my eyes clothed in the fairest colours, my favourite castle in the air, exhibits to me the *good city* of Paris, and myself surveying its numberless objects of interest and curiosity, but when, or how, or whether ever this charming dream is to be realised, I know not; I only mention it as the object towards which the eyes of my mind are directed, should a favourable opportunity and eligible companions offer. I have made up my mind to believe that the profits of my little tale cannot more satisfactorily be expended, but in this case the *will* and the pecuniary means go but for little in furnishing the *way* .... There is at present a good opening for a new candidate for public favour in this branch. 'Patronage,' with all its merit, has not satisfied the expectations of the public, because they were raised to an extravagant pitch; the same may be said of 'The Wanderer,' that is, that it has disappointed high expectations, but certainly with more fault of the author, for it seems to me, at least in most points, a very indifferent work. Mrs. Inchbald, alas! suffers her enchanting pen to lie idle, and all our other writers are far inferior. Sarah is so full of engagements that we have only had a call from her as yet, but she promises us a longer visit soon; she looks remarkably well. My father and mother join in every affectionate wish to you and yours. Believe me, my best friend,

Gratefully and affectionately yours,
L. AIKIN.

To Mrs. Taylor.

Stoke Newington: August 1816.

My dearest Friend—I have been longing to converse with you by the only mode at present in our power, and nothing but an extraordinary press of interesting occupation could have held me silent to this time.

What delightful satisfaction have I had in recurring to those sacred hours which we were permitted to pass together! Who can express the cheerfulness, the vigour, the sense of inward refreshment, procured by such expansions of the heart and mind? To meet a kindred soul, whose intuitive sympathy gives the power of clothing in words thoughts which must otherwise have bloomed and died in long and joyless succession within the dark recesses of the bosom, is a boon more bright than all the fabled gifts of fairy benefactors, and one in which there seems to be as much of spell and talisman. What is the charm, my friend, by which you thread the whole labyrinth of my bosom, and find access to cells of which I myself must have forgotten the existence? How is it that every conversation with you seems an event in my life, and to be treasured among its dearest and most sacred recollections? . . . Since we parted, everything has prospered with me. First, my mother's arm is much better; she is now able to work at her needle, and in her garden as before, and I have the satisfaction of believing that my perseverance in rubbing the limb night and morning has principally contributed to this great amendment.

Now that she is able to pursue her usual occupation, I am completely restored to mine, and Elizabeth goes on with increasing facility and satisfaction. Your opinion on the advantages of this mode of writing history, is peculiarly gratifying to me. It appears to me that a historian who undertakes to narrate the events of centuries must necessarily neglect the illustration of their literature, their biography, the manners, and domestic morals; but are not these, to the great body of readers, at once the most instructive, and the most amusing branches of the knowledge of past ages? On the other hand, the mere antiquarian presents all the minuter parts of this knowledge in a detail which is often dry and disgusting; he is frequently destitute of all powers of writing, and almost always void of that philosophical spirit which combines, which generalises, and infers. Yet the writer of essays on the progress of civilisation, on manners, &c. is still worse; he is generally a Scotch or French metaphysician, who sets out with a system; if the former, he gives you facts so exaggerated, so embellished, or so distorted, that you would give the world to get clear out of your head all the error that he has put into it. All these things I see and feel, and of course I promise myself that my work shall be of a kind free from all the objections of all the others; yet thus it will not be, or if it is, it will have faults of its own as great, perhaps, as theirs. In short, perfection and man! To do our best, and estimate our efforts with humility, is all that remains, and both shall be my study. In the midst of these labours for a public which, perhaps, will neither thank nor reward me, I am devoting two or three hours of each day to a private object in which I anticipate no disappointment. We have got with us George's daughter, a girl of thirteen, to whose education we thought it right to lend a hand. A delightful disposition we all knew that L. possessed, and a little face that it was pleasure to look upon, but we were not prepared to find in her, combined with extreme diligence and perfect docility, a quickness of apprehension very uncommon, an awakened and enquiring mind, and acquisitions which showed that of moderate advantages the best had been made. All these discoveries have endeared her to us extremely; she is indeed the darling of my father and mother, and to me, at once pupil, plaything, and companion. It is impossible for me to grudge the hours which I devote to her, and which are taken, for the most part, from frivolous books and more frivolous visits. The more there is for head and heart in life, the happier we are. . . . We also expect the Carrs, with whom I spent a delightful day last Monday. Mr. Whishaw was there in his highest spirits. Oh, that you could have heard his history of Lady Cork's inviting, as a *lion*, a black agent sent hither by the Emperor of Hayti to engage schoolmasters! How the poor man's head was gradually so turned by this extraordinary honour, that at length he thought it necessary to be *at home* himself in his lodging of one room and two closets—how he petitioned his sovereign to send royal presents to the ladies who had been so kind to him—and how the sweetmeats which came in consequence, and which he had announced, were stopped for the duties, and sold 'by inch of candle at the long room of the custom house.' An excellent satire he made it on the ridiculous passion of some fashionable women for having people of every possible kind of notoriety at their routs, utterly regardless of the mischief which their selfish and foolish patronage produces. Mr. Whishaw is just set off for Holland and Flanders, whence he will doubtless return 'full of matter.' Kindest regards from all this house to the whole of your dear family. Does Mr. Taylor mean to cheat us of his London visit? I hope not.

Ever my best friend,
Most affectionately yours,
L. AIKIN.

To Mrs. Taylor.

Stoke Newington: Nov. 29, 1818.

For once, my beloved friend, it is better to be at a distance from you than near; convalescent as, I thank God, we learn you to be, you must not yet be tempted to talk; and your chamber door would be closed against me in person, whilst my letter will be admitted without scruple, for I hear that you read much, and happy I am that you find yourself able, knowing how greatly it delights you. To catch new hints for the reflections which your mind furnishes in such inexhaustible abundance is, you have often told me, the thing which you seek after with the greatest earnestness; but how difficult is it to furnish novelty to you! I wonder whether you ever happened to read the thing I was looking at last night, 'Ben Jonson's Discoveries;' remarks, or reflections, they might have been called. They leave me with a high opinion of the moral principles, no less than the mental power, of the learned old poet; and there is no difficulty in understanding how such a man, though intemperate in his habits, and probably somewhat coarse in his manners, should have been the chosen companion, nay, the 'guide, philosopher, and friend,' of the virtuous and elegant-minded

Falkland, as well as others of the most distinguished men of that age of giants, with which I am now beginning to form an intimacy. Will you go with me some evening, *incog.*, to the club at the Mitre? Raleigh founded it, and we have for members, among others, Selden, Cotton, Ben Jonson, Beaumont and Fletcher, and that pleasant fellow, who is so full of his jokes, Will Shakspeare. Donne, too, is one of us; of whom Jonson says, that his poems will perish for want of being understood, and, he might have added, for want of being poetry; yet they are full of matter, and he lashes, with a learned hand, the vices and follies of the age. And all these men were the subjects, and some of them the adulators, of that paltry king and pedant James! I wish I had a better centre figure for my picture. It must be like Barry's picture of the other world—in front, a number of separate groups of great-souled men in Elysium; in a corner, pride, licentiousness, and all the vices of courts, with the leg of a garter-knight in Tartarus. Thus, my friend, my busy mind

> Lives in former times and places,
> Holds communion with the dead;

but not, you will well believe me, to the exclusion of living worth and living friendship; no, nor to the exclusion of the glorious scene of honourable and benevolent exertion in every line, and of continual advancement in every science and every elegant or useful art, which is happily opened to the eyes of this generation. Surely the spirit of Howard beholds our Bennet, our Buxton, our excellent Mrs. Fry, and smiles. Even government seems awakened to the importance of the subject; and our prison management will not, I trust, be much longer a source of vice and wretchedness, and a national opprobrium. I begin, too, to have some idea that the exertions of the missionaries in various remote corners of the earth, will at last produce some good; they are growing wiser by the warning of past failures, and I cannot think that so much good intention and disinterested exertion will or can be thrown away.

Arthur's situation gives him opportunities of hearing of all the improvements in science and the arts; and I rejoice to learn how many laudable and interesting objects he has the power and the constant will to promote. The Marchioness of Hastings, who is every way worthy to be the honoured friend of my excellent friend Mrs. Fletcher, lately applied to Arthur to find some workman able to spin a quantity of exquisitely fine wool, brought to her from India, which no common artificer would undertake. He succeeded, and the Marchioness in return has conceived a lively interest in *his* objects, and will procure for the Society specimens, quite new to Europe, of the vegetable products of India. Dr. Leech is indefatigable in extending and perfecting and placing in scientific arrangement the zoological collection of the British Museum; in his hands, this national repository will soon become as noble a school for the naturalist as it now is for the draughtsman and sculptor.

Campbell is lecturing at the Liverpool Institution on Poetry, in a manner, E. writes to me, entirely worthy of the subject, and of his reputation. This gratifies me much. I am still a little jealous for my first love, though I myself have ceased to court her; and I have sometimes feared that science, with her rich train of *utilities*, would usurp upon the due honours of the dowerless house. You will be glad to hear that Montgomery expects soon to put to press a new volume of poems, after a four years' interval. I know not the subjects, but am inclined to hope something good.

Have I not now given you too much? I fear I may; and must I close without expressing how dear, how very dear, the life and health of my earliest, most revered, and most beloved friend must ever be to this heart, grateful as it is for all her love and all her kindness, and how agonising has been my late anxiety on her account? With my father and mother's most affectionate regards to yourself and to dear Mr. Taylor, I rest

Ever yours,
L. AIKIN.

To Mrs. Taylor.

Stoke Newington: Sept. 1819.

My dear Friend—May I congratulate you on parting with so dear a daughter, so sweet a companion and friend? Yes, for it is to the man of her heart, who deserves her by his talents, his virtues, his love, and his constancy. Fair and happy are their prospects; may they long live to enjoy their felicity, and you, my dear friend, to partake in it. I will beg of you to tell the bride, with my kind love, that I long to congratulate her in person, and that I hope we shall contrive, in spite of all the obstacles of wicked London, to meet now and then in a rational manner. Of your good and busy sons we do not see so much as, I believe, all parties could wish, but Mr. Whishaw was so good as to bring Richard to us one day last week, and we all thought him looking remarkably well—as if he was just come from enjoying a great deal of pleasure with all whom he loves at Norwich. . . . I am proceeding in my task, but slowly and anxiously. Success has made me timid; like Horace's soldier, I am fearful of risking anything audacious now I have something to lose: and it is so difficult to treat that reign of James without manifesting what the church and king party will be apt to call a factious spirit. Yet truth must and shall by me be told. I have lately had the good fortune to form an acquaintance with Mr. Butler, the mouth-piece of the English

Catholics, who, after thirty or forty years of unceasing efforts to obtain for his church the restoration of civil rights, approaches, I trust, to the accomplishment of his wishes. Perhaps you have seen some of his curious and laborious works. I have derived considerable instruction from his 'Memoirs of English Catholics since the Reformation,' and still more from some books which he has lent me. I believe few Protestants have any adequate idea of the degree of persecution which they underwent during James's reign, and which I shall not fail to state very fully.

You have read, I hope, that excellent work of Lord John Russell's. How *sound* it is! What excellent feeling, what judgment, what deep thinking! How honourable to a lord of seven-and-twenty!

I have been wishing you in London very often lately; we have had the society of the woman to whom I should most of all desire to introduce you—dear and excellent Mrs. Fletcher, of Edinburgh. She brought with her her younger son, and two younger daughters—all fair branches of so fair a stock. . . . My father was perfectly astonished and delighted at the quantity of laughter which she and I contrived to keep up between us. I think you would come to a better opinion of girls, if you were to see some that I could show you. . . . On the whole, and from various causes, I cannot help thinking that we Englishwomen have risen more in the scale of things within the last twenty years, than within the preceding two hundred; and what is become of the men's jealousy of female acquirements? I see nothing left of it—to their praise, be it spoken; and it is, I believe, not fifty years since Dr. Gregory left as a legacy to his daughters the injunction to conceal their wit, and even their good sense, because it would disgust the sex they were born to please!

My aunt Barbauld, though complaining a little occasionally, has contrived to make many visits and enjoy, I think, a great deal of pleasure this summer. My dear father and mother continue, on the whole, in very good health. They unite in kindest remembrances and sincere good wishes to you all. Pray give my kindest love to dear Susan. I should be very thankful for a letter from her, to tell me how you all find yourselves. I know too well what writing costs you.

     Ever, my best friend,
      Your most affectionate
        L. AIKIN.

To Mrs. Mallet.

Hampstead: Sept. 1827.

My dear Mrs. Mallet—I am glad to snatch this opportunity of sending you a short greeting, for it seems already a dreary length of time since you left us, and yet your absence is to last much longer. I should have sent you a message, at least, by Mr. Mallet, if I had seen him when he called; but I was in bed with one of my good-for-nothing headaches: however, I have been quite well since, and if it was the tax I was to pay for my excursion to Mymms, I ought not to complain, for it was full of a variety of entertainment and enjoyment: the Cambridge excursion itself was scarcely more successful. Lord Salisbury was obliging enough to show us himself the mementoes of Queen Elizabeth remaining at Hatfield, and exceedingly curious and interesting I found them: there is her cradle, her pedigree *from Adam*, the tower in which her sister kept her prisoner, with the spike upon it, intended, they say, for her head; there is the oak under which she was informed of her own accession. Her portrait, presented by herself to Burleigh, is also there, with Burleigh's own, that of his son Robert, and several others of great historic interest, especially a Charles and a Strafford, both Vandyke's. The house itself is wonderfully magnificent. It is well observed, I think by Price, that the *sky line* in the mansions of that time is peculiarly rich and picturesque, from the turrets, domes, and open battlements, and of this Hatfield is a fine example; at a distance you think you see a town, such is the variety of outline.

We dined at Gorhambury, which is not, alas, the old mansion of the Bacons; but it is full of their portraits, with copies of which, and many others, Lady Verulam has illustrated my Elizabeth. The Heygates themselves occupy a very noble house of the same age, so that everything contributed to assist my associations. Sir T. More had a seat in Mymms parish, and they point out his pew in the church.

I hope to hear that your visit is passing as pleasantly as mine. I already learn that Henry is well, which is a most essential condition of your enjoyment. . . . . I am just going to dine at the Baillies, with the Sothebys and a few more, and expect a pleasant party. Mrs. Greaves and I shall adjourn for an hour to the committee at Mr. Reid's—we are to vote in two new members without Mr. Mallet's sanction. Of books, I think we shall not order many, but I shall propose Montgomery's new poems.

My mother desires her kindest regards to Mr. M. and yourself, and pray believe me,

Very truly yours,
L. AIKIN.

To Mr. and Mrs. Mallet.

Hampstead: Sept. 25, 1831.

Many thanks, my dear friends, for your kind joint letter. It is delightful to receive such letters, and much more delightful to think that the occasion for any letters will soon cease.

Hampstead has been the abomination of desolation to me in your absence. I have likened myself to the old watercress woman in the 'Deserted Village.' Possibly I may have felt it the more because I was tantalized with the hope of a little excursion myself. Arthur was to have taken me to explore the beauties of Tunbridge; but, most unfortunately, he was seized with a very severe bilious attack, which disabled him during the only week it was possible for him to go—but he is quite recovered, and that is the great thing.

Some pleasure, however, I have had, which I wished you could have shared. Mr. and Mrs. Kenrick have been spending a week at Hampstead, which has given occasion to two or three pleasant enough little parties in our own little set.

I always very much enjoy Mr. Kenrick's company.* He has—what has he not to make his conversation interesting?—learning, with taste and judgment to teach it when to show and when to conceal itself; wit, of a high order; a most amiable disposition, and a sober zeal for every great interest of mankind. Last Sunday he preached here, and the excellent Rajah came to hear him, taking first a breakfast at Mr. G. K.'s, to which they were so good as to invite me. The Rajah loses nothing by a second view—quite the contrary. We drew from him a very interesting account of the lawsuit he had to maintain against his relations, who wanted to deprive him of his inheritance on account of his change of religion.

'Many,' he said, 'would have given way to them, but I, no! I withstood them, and I succeeded.' The particulars are too long to write, you shall have them when we meet. He was brought up as a Pundit, and this enabled

* The Rev. John Kenrick, of York.

him to take a valid ground of defence. The best is, that he has promised me a second visit, and I shall take care to remind him of it when you return. No one can stand better than he does the severe test of talking of oneself. He does it with a dignified simplicity which marks the real man of merit, having certainly the further advantage of being a born and bred gentleman.

This last phrase reminds me to tell you that I have had the honour of a call from Lord Eliot, who brought the additional papers he had promised, and was accompanied by a very pleasing lady, his sister. I was pleased with his conversation, and thought him intelligent, but I certainly sympathise more with his patriot ancestor than he does. . . . .

I have to brag that I am writing very diligently, partly to preserve myself from *ennui*. I even begin to build castles, and to say, 'At this rate—next spring.' But then Experience thrusts forth her ugly, wrinkled visage, and says, 'Yes, but you must not expect to go on at this rate.' We shall see, however. I am much better in health.

My dear friends, adieu; happy words till we meet!

Believe me sincerely and affectionately yours,

L. AIKIN.

To Mr. Mallet.

Jan. 1835.

Dear Sir—I hoped to have called on you and Mrs. Mallet to-day, but I do not find myself equal to it. I want to talk with you of the excellent man who is gone. From my childhood I have been in the habit of seeing him from time to time, when he used to call on my father, whom he valued both for his own sake and for the sake of my grandfather at Warrington. No one who knew him could help loving him, but what author of our day has been so much maligned. For the honour of the Whig ministry one may wish they had conferred some mark of esteem on such a man as Mr. Malthus; but what could it have added to him? He possessed a competence, and there was so much of the true philosopher about him that I should have grieved to see him a clerical sinecurist, instead of the useful and respected head of a college.

I hope the duty of setting his character as a man and an author before the public will fall into *very* good hands. In his case this is more than usually important. I did not like the tone of yesterday's notice of him in the 'Morning Chronicle.' Who is there that would be likely to do him justice? Some friend should take it up, with all his regret and his affection full upon him.

Believe me, very truly yours,

L. AIKIN.

To Mrs. Mallet.

Hampstead: Oct. 6, 1836.

No, my dear friend; at least, my lazy aversion to letter-writing has not gained such a head as to prevent my returning your kind greeting, and telling you how much I want you home again. Hampstead is almost a desert: the Eales away—Mrs. Greaves away—the Misses Baillie not expected till to-morrow.

Last week the weather was dismally wet and stormy with us; no going out, and I was three whole days without seeing a face but those of my servants and the carpenter; but for the amusement of having a book-case moved *out* of my dressing-room, and a new carpet put down *in* it, I know not how I should have survived the dullness of my solitude. You remember Miss Edgeworth makes Lord Glenthorn put off shooting himself from *ennui* till he had seen his new pig-stye built, and I am decidedly of opinion that nobody perpetrates such a deed with a carpenter in the house. Yesterday the heavens began to smile, and to-day I had my gardener—better still than the carpenter—and also took a walk: 'Il faut du mouvement,' as Mr. Whishaw says. . . . . Mr. Whishaw has not been near me yet. I wonder whether he has been out of town again, or whether he or his coachman thinks the weather not settled enough to venture to Hampstead.

* * * * * * * *

I used to receive daily a morning visit from a lady well, or, perhaps I ought rather to say, much known in London circles. She was a prodigious gossip, and always boasted of having the earliest information of everybody's movements; and sometimes I found her chit-chat amusing enough. But then she was so little select in her topics, that she would as readily give you an account of the squabbles of cabmen in the street, in their own vulgar slang, as of a horticultural breakfast, a new opera, or the fête of a duchess. She was a mighty politician, too; but she seemed to me absolutely O'Connell mad, and I could not help suspecting that she was a papist at heart, and she really gave her tongue such liberties in speaking of the Conservatives, that I was ashamed even to listen to her. At last my patience and tolerance were quite exhausted, and I fairly desired her to come no more to my house. Though a daily visitor was something of a resource to me, I hitherto find myself all the happier for being rid of a person of so very unedifying a character and conversation, and I think it very unlikely at present that *Madame* '*Morning Chronicle*' and I should make up our quarrel. I content myself at present with a weekly visit from *Miss* '*Examiner*,' a better-bred person. You will think all this mighty flimsy; but I have nothing better to offer you at present, during so dead a time, so I hope you will accept it for my sake. . . . . With best regards to Mr. Mallet and the boys, pray believe me,

Ever truly yours,
L. AIKIN.

To Mrs. Mallet.

Hampstead: Oct. 5, 1838.

My dear Mrs. Mallet—Many thanks for your kind letter. I have been wishing to hear of you, and was glad to have so good an account upon the whole, though I much commiserated your early rising and water-*swilling*, may one say ? I have no idea how any human stomach can ever contain the six glasses. I am sure you, at least, deserve a cure of all ills. . . Book-committee to-morrow night, when we shall miss Mr. Mallet, the more as Mr. K. is absent also. I know of nothing to propose, but if we can find nothing now, we may save our money till another time; better than buying, as we did last time, an account of a fellow-prisoner of Pellico, a Frenchman, whose name I forget, whose narrative is translated by Prandi, with many omissions, he says, of the sentimental passages, and attempts to bring it to sobriety and simplicity. It was little worth the labour, being in its present state duller than if it had been written by the heaviest Dutchman, and not a whit the less like a romance for that.

I have just been reading, in the way of business, Scott's 'Life of Dryden.' One anecdote of him and his bookseller pleased me. Jacob Tonson, his publisher, being himself a staunch Whig, wanted to persuade Dryden to dedicate his 'Virgil' to King William, which he foresaw would be difficult, after all the writings and actings of the poet in the former reigns. To prepare the way, he ordered the engraver employed to touch up the old prints of Ogilvy's 'Virgil' for the new translation, to aggravate the nose of pious Æneas into a manifest resemblance of the eagle's beak of his majesty. This was done, with ludicrous effect; but, after all, the poet would not dedicate, but left the nose *planté la*, without any apology. This biography does not appear to me one of Scott's better performances. It is slovenly in style, very low in moral sentiment and estimate, deeply tinged with party spirit, and by no means exquisite in literary taste and critical remark. No man does justice to the public who presumes to offer it a *post-haste* biography and criticism of such a poet as Dryden.

I have had a letter from Dr. Channing, in which, among other agreeable matters, he gives me a pleasing account of a visit which he made while in England to Mr. Wilberforce. 'I could not but respect him,' he says, 'though I saw not a sign of intellectual force. He asked me about the Unitarians of Boston, not suspecting me of the heresy; and when I told him that I was one, though some of his family did not receive the communication with the kindness which hospitality required, the good old man went on to talk with undiminished complacency. On my leaving him, he took me into his study, gave me to understand that he thought more of a man's spirit or temper than his opinions, and chose to write my name and his own on a pamphlet, which he presented to me as a memorial of our interview.'

Vexatious! I was bent upon finishing this letter yesterday, that it might be certain to reach you during Mr. Whishaw's stay, but one interruption succeeded another the whole day, and I have been obliged to keep it for another day's post. I still hope, however, that it may be in time. . . Your gardener has brought me both wall-fruit and pears, for which I am much obliged to you. Charles and I feasted upon them. I must now conclude in haste, with my best remembrances to Mr. Mallet, Mr. Whishaw, and your olive-branches.

Believe me, ever truly yours,

L. AIKIN.

To Mr. and Mrs. Mallet.

Hampstead: August 10, 1839.

A Rowland for your Oliver, my dear friends! You sent me a very agreeable account of your view of York Minster and Harrowgate, and I can now retaliate with my impressions of Windsor Castle. Last Tuesday, K. and I accompanied my brother Arthur thither by railroad, and I am proud to say that I bore the journey very well, and was well pleased with the mode of conveyance for that short distance; for a hundred miles I think I should find it dull, and wish for the old high road, with its variety of vehicles, and the amusement of passing through towns and villages. How few ideas of a country would a foreigner gain by being whisked through it on a railroad, always on a low level, and often passing between high banks!

That castle is a glorious mass, extremely picturesque, both by its forms and its position. It requires a resolute suppression of one's feelings respecting architectural antiquities to relish its modern restorations on a nearer view; and I confess that the only part which gave me much sentiment was the chapel, in which some relics of former ages are left still untouched. The two plain slabs in a retired side chapel, lying almost side by side, and bearing the simple names of Henry VI. and Edward IV., say much to the mind, and so do the banners and ancient scutcheons of the knights. I took a full survey of these objects, whilst my more vigorous companions were climbing the round tower, for its panoramic view. In the state-rooms are a few, though not very many, objects of interest, besides the old pictures, which we had not time thoroughly to examine. Some Gobelin tapestry struck me a good deal; it is in excellent preservation, as well as beautifully executed, and the air of the figures most amusingly French. How impossible it is to mistake any production of the age and country of Louis XIV.! The same misapprehension everywhere of the grand for the great. But if such a style can ever be in place, it is in court-saloons and ball-rooms, as here. We much enjoyed a row down the river, with the castle towering on one hand, Eton College 'crowning the watery glade' on the other; and it is only on the spot, by the way, that one feels the graphic propriety of that expression.

I quite agree with you, Mr. Mallet, as to the poorness of the towns on the north road. I doubt not their great inferiority to those of the continent; but I am a little disappointed that you did not distinguish Newark, with the noble Trent winding through it, and its old ragged castle. Perhaps, indeed, I am biassed by historical associations. No town was the scene of so many interesting events during the war of Charles and the Parliament. It was held out long and stoutly for the king; he was long there; it was there, also, that the Scotch sold him. I apprehend that since the centralisation produced by the increased facilities of travelling, our provincial towns have been more and more outstripped by London. Formerly, the neighbouring noblemen's and gentlemen's families were often content to occupy during the winter, a good house in York, Chester, Worcester, or Exeter—now, they all come to London. The commercial class, too, are more inclined to shun than to seek municipal honours and offices. No rich manufacturer now builds a handsome mansion in a town, in hopes of keeping his mayoralty in it; he builds a villa, washes his hands of the corporation, and cares not for the embellishment of a place in which he holds only a factory or a counting-house.

Mr. Whishaw and Mr. Smyth drank tea with me last week. Mr. Smyth brought one of Mr. Hallam's volumes, in order to read to me a most eloquent and excellent paragraph on the tragedy of 'Lear,' which I highly enjoyed. In the midst of our chat, who should come in but Mr. Duckworth. The moment he saw how snug we looked, 'I must go,' said he, 'and put up my horse,' which he did, making a most welcome accession to the party, and I indulged them all with bits of Dr. Channing's letters. Mr. Whishaw's carriage was ordered early, because Mr. Smyth was to set out for Cambridge soon in the morning, and he hurried our old friend away sooner than he was quite willing to go. I was glad to find he had enjoyed his evening.

Mr. Duckworth came to tell me that he had at length procured for me the Tonson papers. I am now in the midst of them, and, although the letters of Addison are few and of no great consequence of themselves, they are very valuable to a biographer, as throwing light on the beginning of his literary career—little known before; what is still better to me, they confirm a favourite opinion of mine on the formation of style, so I hail them as a treasure. . . . .

And pray, my dear Mrs. Mallet, how many tumblers have you reached in your *crescendo* progress? You certainly deserve a speedy and complete recovery, and I trust will find it. I hope, too, you will be able to take a good survey of the lions of Yorkshire. Mrs. Greaves and the Misses Baillie are quite well. No Hampstead news that I know of—who am the last to hear any.

Tonson says I must gossip no longer.

Ever, my dear friends,
Cordially and affectionately yours,
L. AIKIN.

To Mr. Mallet.

Hampstead: Sept. 1843.

Indeed, my dear sir, I agree with Mrs. Mallet that your grand spectacle of our gallant Queen on her own element, attended by her noble fleet, was an incident well worthy of being related. Nothing abated my pleasure in your description of it, except a little twinge of envy, which seized me involuntarily and unawares. Much would I have given for such an inspiring sight. Her reception by that fine old French gentleman was like a chapter out of 'Amadis de Gaul,' and perhaps ought to have stood alone for this year: yet, in their way, the burger festivals of Bruges and Ghent were also excellent, and carried the mind back to the days of the old counts of Flanders, England's faithful and valuable allies. The whole excursion was charming, especially for us who are old enough to recollect the bitter feelings of the long war which preceded this long blessed peace.

It is strange that people should so studiously run away from their own ripe peaches and nectarines, and leave it to their neighbours to tell them how good they are! This very day, after dinner, I shall treat Charles with some of yours. This brilliant weather is delightful to him, and does him good. For me, the nights especially are rather too sultry, and I long for a few sea-breezes. I believe, however, I shall not leave home this season, unless some special temptation should arise. Hampstead is in a state 'of solemn silence and of dread repose;' but my Sunday parties have been animated by a few forlorn males from London, forsaken of their 'womankind,' and glad to be noticed. I had a very delightful note from the Professor, lately, who does appear to be in a delightful state of health and spirits. Long may it continue! .... In fact, I have plucked up my spirits pretty well. The solemn 'Eclectic' is very civil to me, and so have some other oracles been. At present I am in a state of beatitude. Having no book to write, and no society ephemerals to read, I converse all day long with such people as Shakspeare and Bacon. Also, I am reperusing with increased admiration Guizot's 'Lectures on Civilisation in France'—Europe indeed, he says, but he generally means France, and scarcely ever refers to England, either as confirmation or exception to his views. In his system we are indeed *divisos orbe.* But he is surely a remarkable writer; clear, sagacious, original, and admirable for fairness and impartiality. We have only Hallam to place beside him. Young people, after Smyth, might read Guizot, but I doubt if any academical class could thoroughly enter into his observations, they are so perfectly mature ones. How many things are there that we never begin to understand till we are nearly past making any use of them! A dismal thought, therefore I will put an end to my prose when I have begged you to remember me very kindly to Mrs. Mallet and your sons, and believe me,

Ever very truly yours,
L. AIKIN.

To Mr. Mallet.

Albion Street: Nov. 4, 1845.

Thank you, my dear friend, for your kind note. I am reluctantly obliged to admit the force of your excuses for not making your personal appearance in Albion Street at this season, and I therefore fear it may be some time before we meet.

The inscription pleases me very much; I confess I was not prepared for such very good taste in that quarter. The only word that any one could scruple is '*Truth*'—

every sect claims it for its own champions, and refuses it, of course, to all others; but no one certainly was more devoted to what he thought the cause of truth than Channing, and those who raise the monument believe that he attained it.

I am sorry that Thiers should be a more popular writer in America than our friend; but this was to be expected, from the anti-anglican spirit which they now indulge. I hear from Dr. Holland that Thiers is delightful in society. This doctor, by the way, is just returned from a tour of eight weeks, in which he crossed and recrossed the Atlantic, and travelled three thousand miles on the Western Continent. (Sydney Smith said, the doctor might well travel fast, he never encumbered himself with more luggage than five grains of calomel and a pair of black silk stockings.) He attests the perfect accuracy of Dickens's description of the dressing accommodations on board American steamers.

Do you happen to know of such a person as a pastoral poet? If you do, I will give you a subject for him. A lady related the tale to me with much praise of the *simplicity* of the parties. A young gentleman danced one evening at Almack's with a young lady of seventeen, who was so very pretty that he 'simply' told her he should like to marry her. 'But,' said the simple nymph, 'have you got enough to maintain me?' 'Yes, if twenty-five thousand a-year is enough.' 'Ask my papa.' Papa, it should appear, thought it was; for thus Mr. Alexander Hope of Deepdene did achieve a wife. 'I think,' said Master Duckworth, 'the young lady knew a good deal for seventeen.' One might say something similar of the *state in its teens*, for which, pretty innocent, Mr. Ticknor pleads so earnestly with the professor. It knows nothing as yet, poor dear, of dollars, or bonds, or annexations! . . . I rather congratulate myself on not being in Church Row during the delightful excitement of the murder * and the inquest, which appear to have had so many charms for the million. One comfort is, that the murdered appears to have been anything but a loss to society. But I think the event will give me a kind of dislike to Belsize Lane, which I used to think the pleasantest as well as shortest way from us to you.

Yours ever very truly,
L. AIKIN.

To Mr. Mallet.

Wimbledon: July 4.

My dear Friend—Your last note made me quite melancholy, by your account of the very little enjoyment you are able to derive from your pretty garden. I cannot but hope that with the advance of summer your rheumatism will become less of an obstacle to your movements. Just now, indeed, we are all made prisoners by the rain, and I have had feeling admonitions that sitting out of doors is a piece of youthiness in which I ought not to take upon me to indulge; but the sight and scent of flowers is still a gratification, in which you, I trust, share also.

You ask me about the 'Annual Review.' It was published yearly, in a thick octavo, in double columns, and the *entire* publications of the year were noticed, each under its own class, with short prefaces summing up what had been done in each department. The work had a great sale in the colonies, and there was always a hurry to get it out for the spring fleet to India.

I may venture to say that the editor's maxim of 'fair play and no favour' was most honourably carried out. There were many and able contributors, each in his own department. Mrs. Barbauld reluctantly took part of the

* The murder of Delarue.

poetry and polite literature in one or two of the earliest volumes, and gave that critique on the 'Lay,' which the author said he had approved and admired the most. My father, who hated reviewing, could only be prevailed upon to do 'Hayley's Cowper.' I had the heartfelt pleasure of singling out for praise small pieces of Montgomery's in the 'Poetical Register;' and from the 'Poems of a Minor,' gibbeted in the 'Edinburgh,' I predicted that Byron would prove a poet.

But the chief writers in literature of a general kind were Southey and William Taylor. Some of the best writing of each is there. Southey did best in travels, where his knowledge was extensive, and his dogmatism had little scope. Taylor's great knowledge, his extreme acuteness, tending sometimes to paradox, his singularities in language—for which he could always render a reason—and his occasional eloquence, raise his articles above all the rest in interest and entertainment. Jeffrey justly observed, 'If Taylor's reviews were collected, we should all hide our diminished heads.' He anticipated in many points the greatest writers on political economy. If you see the last and preceding number of the 'Gentleman's Magazine,' you will find an article on Southey's 'Life' in the first of them, and some pretty sharp comments of mine in the second, exposing the vileness of his conduct to Mrs. Barbauld. It is impossible now to doubt that all the scurrilities of the 'Quarterly' respecting her were his. I am persuaded that he hated most literary women; and latterly, all dissenters. Respecting the 'Annual Review,' I may add, that my brother found the office of whipper-in to an ill-disciplined literary pack so intolerably harassing that he resigned it; and under an incompetent successor the work ceased to answer, and after one or two years was dropped. . . .

I dined with Lady Coltman the day before she left

town; and in my way down Piccadilly, just missed being a witness of the audacious assault upon the Queen. Little did I imagine what had drawn the crowd together. Surely they will not let off the ruffian on pretext of insanity!

I hope Mrs. Mallet would remember to tell you that I *gave* you the copy of Mrs. Barbauld's letter, having the original. Among her letters to Miss Edgeworth is one containing some excellent criticisms on Mr. E——'s practical education. Amongst other remarks, she takes notice that casual circumstances will often give a bent to the mind of a boy quite in opposition to that which his parent might have designed to impress upon it. In illustration, she mentions that a friend of hers was sure that her son received an indelible impression in favour of the law from seeing their neighbour, a barrister, return every evening carrying a great bag, which the child thought was filled with guineas. I know the person she alludes to; he is now a rich, and ultra-sharp attorney. . . .

I must really put an end to this long scribble.

Ever truly yours,
L. AIKIN.

To Mr. Mallet.

Wimbledon: Jan. 8.

My dear Friend—Thanks to Macaulay, if it were only for rousing our dear Professor * to the effort of writing such a gratifying and excellent note as you have sent me. To be reminded of those times, and of my own labours upon them, is like returning to some previous state of existence—so completely am I now separated from all such studies and discussions.

I think still with those who regard it rather as an article than a history; very clever, very dashing, with all its

* Professor Smyth, of Cambridge.

detail, but not very deep or very philosophical. Thus he says, in his off-hand way, that the great struggle of Charles's time was the change from a feudal monarchy to a modern limited monarchy. This sentence has but very little truth in it; the quarrel turned on no such matter. The long parliament in their bill of rights asked for no new privileges, only for better security to the old ones; it attacked no feudal rights of the crown. *The* truth was condensed by Lord J. Russell in one sentence of his little tract on the Constitution: the Tudors had tyrannised through the parliament; the Stuarts sought to tyrannise without a parliament. Why did James II. fail in an enterprise which had succeeded with Mary? For this very reason: the parliament abetted her return to Rome; for his its consent was never asked.

He has failed to explain why James was not warranted in his attacks on the establishment by his authority as head of the church. The statutes on religion passed in the beginning of Elizabeth's reign should have been recited, by which that authority was restricted. On the dispensing power he is very unsatisfactory. I conceive, that the illegality of those monopolies which Elizabeth and her successor were *compelled* by the parliament to cancel, consisted in their 'non obstante' clause. It never could be *lawful* for the sovereign to dispense with *laws*. Certain I am, that it was not even among the irregular things which the Tudors were tolerated in doing by proclamation.

I am much taken by Lord Melbourne's saying; it well characterises these dashing reviewers; and so does a certain coarseness of style, very striking in Macaulay when he deals with characters. He *blackguards* Jeffreys and James as if they were live authors. I am not a sufficient judge of his fairness, or unfairness, between whigs and tories; but the character I like best, as a portrait, is Halifax, the head of the Trimmers. On the whole, I much admire the book, and think its politics sound and seasonable. In our horror of the revolutions of the continent, we must not forget all that we owe to our own.

Most of this I had written some days ago; when the severity of the cold brought on my asthma, and nearly disabled me. Now I am becoming acclimated, and even enjoyed a walk yesterday in the sunshine.

Last evening I received the pretty wedding cards, and I rejoice sincerely with you all. I hope Mrs. Mallet enjoyed the day. You would enjoy it for her, snug in your hybernaculum. Neither you nor I shall be off to dig up gold in California; multitudes will though; and I suppose they will be fighting for the treasure by-and-bye. It is like nothing but a fairy tale at present—Manchester does not take it in that sense, however. Think of the wild Indians all so gay in printed calicoes and gaudy shawls! I hope some clever fellow will put it all in a novel for us. What strange scenes! . . . .

Kind love to Mrs. Mallet and your two sons at home; cordial congratulations to H—— when you write.

Ever truly yours,
L. AIKIN.

To Mr. and Mrs. Mallett.

Wimbledon: Sept. 12, 1850.

Dear Friends—By this time I trust you are again quietly settled in your own house, and all your bustles well over.

I am sure I need not tell you how great a mortification it was to me to find you quitting Hampstead just as I arrived there. I had a glimpse of you, however, and that was worth something. The change was of advantage to me; I have been a better walker ever since, and if it were not for this obstinate east wind, I should enjoy myself very much in this bright sunshine. My brother dined with me two Sundays in Hampstead, and we had great enjoyment in retracing our old paths, notwithstanding the recollections which met us at every turn of those who once trod them with us—now lost to us in this world for ever. At our age, such spectral appearances start up at every turn, and we learn to accept of them as a condition of our being—indeed we should feel life a blank without them. It is in the past chiefly that we live.

It was a great pleasure to me to see the Misses Baillie on the whole so well. Agnes seems to me quite herself still; her sister's memory certainly fails a good deal, but the heart is warm as ever, and there are still flashes of a bright mind.

Here I converse with the dead almost entirely. The fifth volume of Southey has been occupying me. The effect of the work is on the whole melancholy, notwithstanding his perpetual assertions of the buoyancy of his disposition—his gaiety even, which no one could possibly divine from the tone of his writings. With very considerable talents, and unwearying diligence, it was yet his destiny to miss almost every mark he aimed at. But a small proportion of his numerous works succeeded even moderately, and the world refused to honour his bold draughts upon it as a great historian, and a poet, 'if not first, in the very first line.'

I can remember when his friends said, 'No doubt he is arrogant, but he will mend of that, he will find his level.' There was the mistake—his was an incurable case; neither the mellowing hand of time, nor the rude shocks of disappointment, could in the least degree moderate his self-opinion. Posterity was to do him justice—his fame was to be immortal. It was a kind of monomania, and was the true source of his bigotry, religious and political, and of that virulence of abuse and invective by which he disgusted his own party almost as much as he provoked the opposite. He could not conceive that any treatment could be too harsh, any terms of contempt and hatred too strong, for those who resisted such manifest truths as were taught in the writings of the infallible Robert Southey. To differ from him was to reject a prophet. I do not think this publication will raise him in public esteem, good man as he was in all his private relations. . . . .

Your gardener supplied me abundantly with fruit and vegetables while I remained at Hampstead, for which I thank your kind thoughtfulness. Adieu, my dear friends, let me hear speedy and good accounts of you both.

Yours ever truly,
L. AIKIN.

To Mr. Mallet.

Wimbledon: Feb. 16, 1851.

Dear Friend—It begins to be very long since we had any communication, and I am anxious to hear how you and Mrs. M. bear the winter which has come upon us at last. . . . . .

We have nothing here but causes for thankfulness—all well, and the young ones thriving and learning. The pet of the house—a fine boy of fifteen months—is not spoiled as yet, though such a consummation is assuredly to be looked for in due time; meanwhile he is a great amusement to me, and I foolishly think him something more than common. But why foolishly? What would life be worth, if we had none left of these kindly illusions?

Talking of illusions, I actually made the effort of going to view that gigantic fairy illusion, as it seems, the Crystal Palace. It is indeed a wonder, and one of which no description, no representation, gives the slightest idea. The form, indeed, is quite simple, so are the materials and all the details, the whole impression depends on the size, which is quite inconceivable. It is not a sublime work, nor is it awful, nor yet strikingly beautiful. You have no associations with it to render it impressive or affecting—but wonderful it is in a supreme degree. And if you looked round you at the spectators, every face wore the same expression of gaping wonderment—'young astonishment'—like so many boys and girls watching a conjuror. I would not have missed the sight on any account—at our age what a treat is a new sensation! Whether the effect will be equally striking when it is filled I doubt. The space will be in some degree cut up.

As if I were resolved to go as far as possible out of my calm routine, I have plunged with Major Edwards into his 'Punjab Adventures.' He is a *little* boastful, but tells his tale none the worse for that; and a very curious and interesting tale it is, and makes me acquainted, as I never was before, with those Indian races, Hindu and Mahometan, whom our soldiers and politicals have to deal with. Cruel and treacherous they are, like all barbarians and all subjects of despotic sway; but there is good ground for hope that a just and firm government, such as that to which British India is now, I hope, subjected, will very much correct these vices of Sikhs and Affghans. It is at least a fine experiment on a grand scale, and one in which I have long taken a deep interest. In fact, I would rather turn my thoughts anywhere than to the continent of Europe, where despotism triumphs as the sole antagonist able to put down anarchy. I often think of Horne Tooke, and suspect that after a time even he will long to try purgatory again. In France I have lost all interest. Who can tell what a Frenchman wants or wishes?

There is some hope that we may improve in point of society here. . . . New *friends* it is too late for me to think of; all I want, are a few conversable acquaintances.

By the way, is it not a feature of the age that this word acquaintances is nearly obsolete? All are friends now after once meeting. Everybody lives so much in a crowd, that it is quite too great a trouble to make distinctions. What will it be when all Europe pours in upon us? Amongst other distinctions, I suspect that of meum and tuum will often be slipping out of memory.

You will like to hear that I am quite well, and absolutely enjoying the bright frost. My brother is well also. ... My dear *friends* of five-and-twenty years, adieu.

Ever truly yours,

L. AIKIN.

To Mr. Mallett.

Wimbledon: June 9, 1851.

Dear Friend—In all your remarks on the world's fair I entirely concur, and I rejoice that you and Mrs. Mallet should have had a glimpse of it, though little more. I have made it only one visit, and that not a very long one, and the difficulties to me are so great, that I fear I shall scarcely accomplish another.

My visit to London was so short, that to my great regret I could not accomplish a drive to Hampstead. All I did accomplish, besides the Great Exhibition, was to show my face at Mr. and Mrs. Yates's archæological party at Highgate. A very pleasant garden lounge it was, for we had fine weather, and I met half the people I know. An intended archæological lecture in Polish-English, by Count Pulski, was very judiciously *cushioned*. Poor children are always made to swallow 'instructive and amusing' at one mouthful, like bread and cheese, but I am shocked to observe, that the longer we live, and the cunninger we grow, the less we believe in medicated pleasures.

Mr. Y——'s place is called Lauderdale House, and was built by the atrocious minister of Charles II. for Scotland. It is a low white building, of no outside show, but there is a gallery 90 feet long, and several other large rooms, and a charming old garden in terraces down the slope of the hill, with fine evergreens, and especially the largest bays I ever saw, which were in full blossom. Mr. Y. has added a palm-house, being a great botanist, and having devoted his chief attention to this class. He is a man of immense acquisition in various lines, and the house is filled with his books and multifarious collections, which I had not time to inspect. His wife is the best of all his acquisitions, with her intelligence and unaffected good humour. I longed to be domesticated with them for a month.

As you say, it is in vain to invite attention at present to anything unconnected with the Crystal Palace, but there will come a time, I trust, when 'arts and industry' have had their day, and the claims of our dear friend* to monumental honours will be admitted. I am even told that the abbey would not be so difficult as I imagined. It was suggested that the Queen and Prince Albert, if applied to, would be likely to patronise the design. May these hopes be realised! I have been re-perusing many of her tragedies with renewed admiration. The high *soul* shines through them all, and they are full of poetry; fine touches of character, too, though the moral refinement is sometimes over-wrought. Would she had omitted all her comedies from her volume, and all the prose tragedies! . . . . I forget London and all its shows and splendours when I enter our pretty garden. We are now in a blaze of rhododendrons and azaleas, with China roses and other flowers coming on, and my rock, I assure you, is becoming a positive *lion*. Mrs. Marryatt has given a solemn sentence that it is the best arranged rock of her acquaintance

* Mrs. Joanna Baillie.

I only say that it is quite covered with plants, and very gay at present with flowers of all hues.

In a garden, a small one especially, it is certainly something very different from nature that we look for; and I am satisfied that the perfect artificialness of these little rocks is one of their great charms. Another recommendation with me, is the number of rather rare plants which you thus collect immediately under your eye—the greatest of all is the quantity of fid-fad occupation which the care of it supplies. Alas! I have no better employment for the hours which it wearies to spend in the equally idle occupation of reading without an object. An Arabian barrenness in the book-mart. I am looking through the letters of Walpole to Mason, but they are by no means his best: a great deal of political croaking from both correspondents; a scarcity of anecdote, and an abundance of profession, which their twelve years' quarrel shows to have been very hollow. I am at the end of my paper. My dear friends adieu.

L. AIKIN.

To Mr. and Mrs. Mallet.

Wimbledon: June 26.

How is it, my good friends, that we have not had a single word together since my pleasant glimpse of you at Hampstead? Is it, alas! with you as with me, that the days of these latter years glide on so little marked with new impressions, that they are gone before we are conscious they have arrived? 'Unfelt, uncounted.' Yet if, as I suppose, Somerset House is now given up, this must make an epoch to you, and a man at entire leisure might make the effort of telling a friend how he likes it. I know for myself, that after I determined to write no more books, I felt lost for a while without a daily task—now I feel that it would be insupportably irksome to me to resume it.

So much, however, of old habits remains, that it is a real gratification to me, or rather the satisfying of a want, to give a daily lesson of some kind to a little niece or two; and as the eldest is now a creature with whom one may read some parts of Locke with the conviction that it is understood and relished, you may believe that the interest of this occupation increases daily. On the whole, I feel more and more that it was good for me to take up my abode in a house full of children. They keep constantly awake those sensibilities without which elder life would be mere vegetation.

True it is that these are times in which the history of Europe might seem enough to keep all our thoughts and feelings alive, even without domestic interests. With me, however, this is not the case. I seem to be looking out upon chaos; and whether cold or hot, or moist or dry, gains a momentary advantage, is really a matter which I cannot bring myself to take to heart. My prevalent notion is, that the French have a new military despotism to pass through before long, during which they will again be the scourge of the earth, unless this dread visitation be averted by a prolonged state of anarchy and civil war among themselves, ending in a fresh restoration of the elder branch of the Bourbons. Of the destinies in store for Germany and Italy, who can venture to form even the slightest conjecture!

Pray tell me whether you know a French book published as long since as 1809, Barente's 'History of French Literature in the Eighteenth Century,' and what is your estimate of it. A friend has lent it to me, and I am reading it with great admiration, and esteem of its wise, virtuous, and impartial spirit, as well as of the acuteness and *finesse*, combined with what appears to me the constant soundness and judiciousness of the remarks, whether moral or critical. He observes, that any one who should undertake the history of *vanity* in France, would soon discover a great part of the causes which produced its revolution. I conceive that if this excellent author be still living, he may find in recent events more and more confirmation of this pregnant remark.

My dear brother regularly visits us on Sundays, and the sight of him in such excellent health and peaceful comfort as he continues to enjoy, is one of my chief blessings. . . . Pray let me hear of the dear professor, and when you write assure him of my kindest regards. I know not whether he is still in a state to be gratified by a note. I would write if I thought he was. Adieu, my dear friends; remember me to your sons.

Ever truly yours,
L. AIKIN.

To Jerome Murch, Esq., of Bath.

Hampstead: Dec. 20, 1841.

Dear Sir—You ask me for some recollections of Mr. William Taylor in the freshness and vigour of his powers, and the melancholy plea with which you urge your request, that there are very few now left competent to speak on the subject, insures my compliance. I feel it a duty not to withhold the little it is in my power to contribute towards the posthumous reputation of a man of merit and of genius, to whom, while he lived, the reading public was so much a niggard of its applause.

Of his youth I can only speak traditionally, but I know that high hopes were conceived of him by those who knew him in his boyhood, and especially by her whom I have heard him name with gratitude 'the mother of his mind'—Mrs. Barbauld. His talent for poetry was early discovered by her. It was deeply regretted by some of his friends that his father did not educate him for the law.

He possessed, indeed, that union of perseverance and method in study, with subtlety of discrimination, of inexhaustible fertility in the invention of arguments on all topics, with eminent skill and facility in the statement of them, which could scarcely have failed of appreciation at the bar. At the same time, that strong stamp of individuality which rendered him so much an object of curiosity and interest to those who enjoyed his society, must soon have lost its sharpness under the friction of London life and professional collision.

During his meridian, which might be loosely reckoned to comprise about ten years of the last century and fifteen or twenty of the present, Norwich contained within its walls a lettered and accomplished circle, fully capable both of appreciating and of being stimulated by his genius, and he was constantly attended by a band of admiring disciples. His conversation was inexpressibly attractive, by its richness, variety, and originality. So copious were the materials which his wide range of general knowledge, and his stores of many-languaged literature, offered to the choice of his busy constructive fancy, that not the most familiar associate could anticipate on any topic his ready information, his novel inference, his strange hypothesis, his ingenious illustration, his ironical suggestion, or his playful banter. The peculiarity of his diction, always interspersed with words of his own coinage, added to the zest of his sayings by its admirable aptness and significance.

With these rare endowments, he was no engrossing or overbearing talker, but a true *converser*. He was without vanity, and his manners, deficient in ease, were yet free from affectation. 'That unnaturalness,' said an excellent judge of men, after closely observing him, 'is natural to him.' His imperturbable calmness of temper, his perfect candour, and an urbanity which never deserted him, conciliated general esteem, and certainly were his protection from much of acrimonious dispute and social persecution. But for this, attached as he was by philosophy to the broadest principles of civil and religious liberty, and by habit to the unbounded range of discussion indulged in a German university, he could not with impunity have so constantly exerted that privilege of free utterance of opinion, which bigots, seizing for themselves, deny to others. Often, indeed, it was matter of great doubt how far he could be serious in the bold speculations which he would advance as admitted principles, and the startling paradoxes he uttered with the air of truisms. In any case, there was such an absence of all idea of offence in his demeanour, that it was scarcely possible to meet him with angry invective or rude contradiction.

He had other qualities which conspired to the same effect. In hospitality, generosity, and warmth of friendship, in probity and honour—the moral part of the gentleman—he had no superior; and the filial devotion with which he made himself eyes to an excellent mother deprived of sight, claimed for him the love and reverence of every feeling heart.

In reference to Mr. Taylor's mintage of words, it is right to observe that it was not arbitrary or capricious; they were always learnedly and analogically formed; a few of them have crept into use, and more might perhaps be adopted with advantage. Of his profound knowledge, indeed, of the English tongue, and fine tact in the employment of words, he has raised an enduring monument in his 'Synonymy,' a work which cannot be too diligently perused by the student in the art of English composition.

To what extent he was indebted for his literary stores, and for the cast of his thoughts and style, to German models, it is not for one unacquainted with that language to determine; but whatever may have been his obligations, they were assuredly not unrequited. When his acquaintance with this literature began, there was probably no English translation of any German author which had not been made through the medium of the French, and he is very likely to have been the first Englishman of letters to read Goethe, Wieland, Lessing, and Bürger in the originals. He hastened to spread the fame of his new favourites; and from this time, translations, or imitations, more or less close, from the German, formed the bulk of his writings in verse; although he has left us specimens enow to prove that the fame of an original poet of great vigour of thought and vividness of style was completely within his powers of attainment.

How far Mr. Taylor was instrumental in kindling that violent but transient passion for the lighter literature of Germany which raged among us about forty years ago, it is difficult to determine. None of the dramas which then became so celebrated or notorious were introduced to the English public by him; but some years earlier, he had begun to enrich the pages of the 'Monthly Magazine' with some of the most valuable materials afterwards included in his survey of German literature. He had likewise published in a separate volume, 'Nathan the Wise,' and that exquisitely graceful and interesting drama, 'Iphigenia in Tauris,' which he has rendered into blank verse of the most finished beauty.

A remarkable anecdote belongs to his incomparable version of Bürger's 'Lenora,' which I heard from the lips of Sir Walter Scott himself, as he was relating it to Mrs. Barbauld. After reminding her that, long before the ballad was printed, she had carried it with her to Edinburgh and read it to Mr. Dugald Stewart, 'he,' said Scott, 'repeated all he could remember of it to me, and this, madam, was what made me a poet. I had several times attempted the more regular kinds of poetry without success; but here was something that I thought I could do.' A translation capable of lighting up such a flame certainly deserves all the praise of an original; indeed no one could guess it to have been any other, so racy and idiomatic is the old English in which he has clothed it.

For very many years, Mr. Taylor was both a frequent magazine correspondent and a diligent reviewer. For this last office he possessed in large measure the leading qualifications of extensive knowledge and critical acumen, always sheathed by him in the courtesy of the gentleman, mingled with those striking peculiarities which never failed to betray his authorship to the discerning reader. His articles are thus admirably characterised by Sir James Mackintosh in one of his published letters, written from Bombay:—'I can still trace William Taylor by his Armenian dress, gliding through the crowd in Annual Reviews, Monthly Magazines, Athenæums, &c., rousing the stupid public by paradox, or correcting it by useful and seasonable truth. It is true that he does not speak the Armenian, or any other language but the Taylorian; but I am so fond of his vigour and originality, that, for his sake, I have studied and learnt his language. As the Hebrew is studied for one book, so is the Taylorian by me for one author. . . . I doubt whether he has many readers who so much understand, relish, and tolerate him.'

It does not occur to me that I have anything further to write to you; for though many more particulars of the life, writings, and opinions of my own friend, and my father's friend, together with not a few of his remarkable sayings, live freshly in my memory, they might prove neither interesting, nor even intelligent to a new generation and an altered world.

No person has ever come within the sphere of my observation, of whom I should so emphatically say,

  We ne'er shall look upon his like again.

  Believe me, dear Sir,
    Yours very sincerely,
      LUCY AIKIN.

LETTERS
TO
THE REV. DR. CHANNING.

No. 1.

Hampstead: July 9, 1826.

I FEAR, Sir, I must have appeared negligent and ungrateful in not sooner returning you my thanks for a copy of your excellent remarks on the character and writings of Milton; but since I received them, which is about a fortnight, this is my first opportunity of writing. Accept my most cordial acknowledgements of the justice and honour you have done to that great and injured character—that true servant of God, that sublime teacher of the noblest truths to man.

From my earliest youth I have been an assiduous and reverential student of his poetical works, that inestimable storehouse of instruction and delight, that fount of inspiration; lately I have reperused them with a more direct reference to the circumstances of the times, and the character and situation of the author, and I am thus enabled to give my deliberate testimony to the soundness, and at the same time the novelty and originality of your observations. In a short fragment of observations on Milton, which I found among Mrs. Barbauld's papers, was an expression of surprise that his ardent attachment to liberty so seldom breaks forth in his verse, but your remark that it was principally the freedom of the mind to which he paid homage, well explains this circumstance. He deeply felt that 'who loves that must first be wise and good,' and to make men so, he accounted the first and most important service to be rendered them. What you say of the futility of looking back to the Primitive Church for authority, is excellent, and so far as I know entirely new; the notion of a progressive Christianity is very strikingly expressed, I remember in that pamphlet of Mr. Wakefield's on public worship, which I think was considerably misconceived by my aunt, and therefore misrepresented in her answer. It is manifest that Christianity can only be permanent for the future, has only been so through past ages, by silently adapting itself to the manners and sentiments of different times and countries; even the Church of Rome is far from being now what it was in the tenth century. I was surprised on first looking into the puritanical writers, particularly Prynne, to find how much he relied on the authority of the fathers, and even of some of the early popes; and I enquired how and when it was that those writers had lost their authority with modern English theologians, even those of high church principles; an intelligent friend answered me, 'ever since Middleton gave them an incurable wound.' On this subject Milton did not advance beyond his age. You have certainly not given Johnson more reprehension than he richly deserved for his outrages against one so inestimably his superior. My dear father made many efforts to counteract the effects of his prejudice and bigotry in this and many other instances; he was once engaged in the office of re-editing Johnson's Poets with corrections and additions, and I always regretted that the failure of a bookseller interrupted this design; he published Milton, however, with some spirited remarks on his former editor. In this country where Tory and high church principles are still lamentably prevalent, it is impossible to estimate the mischief, as I should call it, which Johnson has effected, by lending the sanction of his authority to popular prejudices. I know no other example of powers so vigorous, self-devoted to the drudgery of forging chains and riveting fetters on the human mind.

The great questions on liberty and necessity, matter and spirit, have evidently much employed your thoughts, and I cannot but wish that they may employ your pen; the first especially, is a theme of vital interest, and one on which there is the strangest contrariety between the results of our reasoning, and in some degree of our experience—for we witness the apparently irresistible sway of external motives in many instances—and a certain internal conviction which ought perhaps to be of still higher authority with us. I recollect that when I had the pleasure of seeing you at Newington, we spoke of the neglect into which metaphysical science had fallen among us, and certainly very little appears to be written on these subjects; nevertheless they must always, I conceive, occupy a portion of the meditations of every inquiring mind, and I believe it will always be in the power of an original and able writer on them to attract considerable attention. The general progress of light and knowledge, too, reflects in various ways upon these pursuits, and makes it right that the standard works should at least be from time to time reexamined; it appears to me that Locke himself requires modernising in several parts of his subject. Your glimpses of the advancement of the human mind are wonderfully cheering and animating, and who shall presume even in thought to set limits to its high career in a land where you already possess that prime boon which the learned and enlightened Selden vainly sighed for, 'freedom in everything?' Here it may still be the work of ages to liberate the mind from bondage, for that great engine of civil and intellectual tyranny, a state religion, stands, and is likely to stand; but with you liberty is its birthright. It ought to be a cause of thanksgiving to every lover of man and his best interest to think that there is in the world such a temple of freedom erected—May God prosper it!

Believe me, Sir, with high esteem,
Very sincerely yours,
LUCY AIKIN.

No. 2.

Hampstead: May 1, 1827.

I have many acknowledgements to return you, Sir, for a letter so truly acceptable to me, in various respects as that with which you have favoured me. Since its date I have also received from you a dedication sermon, which I have read and reread with increasing admiration and satisfaction. Of all the products of my aunt Barbauld's fine genius, which you have commemorated in a manner most gratifying to my feelings, there is none which during my whole life I have prized so highly as her 'Hymns for Children,' by which, with the most delightful allurements of style, the infant mind is insensibly led to look up through all which it beholds, whether of animated or inanimate, physical or moral nature, to the infinitely wise and beneficent cause of all. To a spirit early and deeply imbued with this general religion particular systems have something of low and narrow, from which it recoils with a sense of disappointment or disgust, ready to ask, like Lucan's Cato at the Temple of Jupiter Ammon, whether the universal deity,

Steriles ne elegit arenas,
Ut caneret paucis, mersitque hoc pulvere verum?

But such spirits your views of Unitarianism are well calculated to conciliate, by showing it in strong and lovely contrast to those systems which you well describe as 'shut up in a few texts,' and insulated alike from all which nature teaches of a God and from all the lights which the cultivated intellect is now deriving from reason and philosophy.

Your remarks on the influence of Trinitarianism in 'shutting the mind against improving views from the universe,' open up a long train of interesting reflections, which I should be glad to see you pursue much further. It has often grieved me to observe how extensively this popular system of theology operates to degrade and distort men's moral sentiments and their views of human life. Certainly the deity of that system is not *good*, he is jealous of that love of happiness which he has himself implanted in the human bosom instinctively, and hence endless contrarieties between the language of its followers and their feelings—between their system and their intimate convictions. Men are supposed to be called upon, not in time of persecution alone, but universally, to choose between this world and another, to renounce the enjoyments of the present life, and to count sorrows and privations as the only wholesome food of souls. But this is hard doctrine, and its most obvious effect is to prompt a very offensive species of *canting* which prevails at present in this country to such a degree as to afflict and perplex all who are inclined to hope well of the progress of human improvement. To him who regards the Deity as truly *one*, and unchangeable through all ages, there is no such contrariety —this world, the present life, are parts of God's space and God's time; His goodness is here and will be everywhere for ever; and he has not written one thing on man's heart, and another in a book of laws for his guidance.

Pray go on to give us more of the products of your acute, enlightened, and pious mind, and your most eloquent and masterly pen. Bear in mind that you are writing for England as much as for America. The fifth edition of your discourse on the ordination of Mr. Sparks, printed at Liverpool, a Liverpool edition of your 'Duties of Children;' and a Bristol one of your 'Discourse on the Evidences,' all lie before me. Your remarks on Milton, and this last discourse, have also been reprinted, and so will everything be that you write; but if you would give us a *volume*, it would draw more attention and produce more effect than many tracts, because it would be noticed in reviews, circulated in book societies, and displayed on library shelves. Oh! that you would give us a system of morals according to your own views, this would be a treasure to the present and following generations. In your noble country, where all faiths stand on equal ground, you write both without the fears and without the exasperation of a sect struggling to erect itself beneath the frown of an imperious establishment, a circumstance which gives you a superiority *here* more felt than expressed. I find in it an additional reason for joining you in the wish that the intellectual intercourse of our two countries should be continually extended, and that the utmost cordiality of feeling should exist between the friends of light and knowledge in both. I rejoice to hear of all your advances, and inquire eagerly after all your literary novelties, and so do many of my friends, and now that our administration has happily ceased to be *Tory*, it will be less than it has been a fashion to undervalue your efforts. My New York correspondent is not Miss Sedgwick, but her very intelligent brother Mr. H. D. Sedgwick, but I imagine that writing to either is writing to both. Nothing will give me more gratification than to hear from you as often as your important avocations will admit. The state of America is a peculiarly interesting subject to many of my friends, and one on which it is difficult here to gain authentic information; we want to hear towards what form of religious sentiment your people most incline, and whether the absence of an establishment leaves in fact any considerable number destitute of religious worship—in short, how this great experiment turns out.

Believe me yours, with great esteem,
LUCY AIKIN.

No. 3.

Hampstead: May 28, 1828.

Dear Sir—A few days since I had the pleasure of receiving your valued and interesting letter by Mr. Sparks. I had long been your debtor for that which accompanied your admirable remarks on Napoleon, and I am now impatient to avail myself of the recovered power of writing, to assure you that I am not ungrateful. I say the recovered power, because I have been struggling for many months with a state of weak and precarious health, which by compelling me to remain in a recumbent posture, made the act of writing exceedingly troublesome and fatiguing. Though still much of an invalid, I am now considerably better, and my medical brother gives me at length assurance that I am proceeding, though slowly, towards complete recovery. This I had so little expected, that I have found some difficulty in returning to the interests of a life which I was fully prepared to quit—its cares and duties, clogged with a long arrear of neglected business, seemed to summon me almost rudely back from a state of languor which was not without its charms. In such a state, I have often repeated the line, 'Resigned to die, or resolute to live,' and thought the former much the easier part of the alternative; it must now be my endeavour to brace my mind for the latter. I have a great task before me to fulfil, and I pray God I may so fulfil it as to prove my gratitude to him for life and all its blessings.

You will not wonder after this to hear that King

Charles has been at a complete stand; yet I am not without doubts that the future work may have been gaining by an interval in which I have found opportunity for some general reading in history, and much meditation. Everything imprints more and more deeply on my mind the importance of the great historic virtue which I thank you for exhorting me to—that of impartiality. Certainly, instead of doing a service to the great cause of liberty by veiling the errors of its champions, we do it in fact the greatest injury, especially where we have failures to relate; for if the fault was not in the men, it seems a just conclusion that it must have been in the cause. On the other hand, by representing its opponents as worse men than they really were, we lighten arbitrary power itself of the reproaches justly its due, to discharge them on the vices accidentally adhering to its supporters. But certain principles have a tendency to produce certain effects, good or bad, on the minds and manners of their advocates; and the chief utility of introducing biographical details largely into works of history is, that these tendencies may be impressed and illustrated by examples; that both the rule and the exceptions to it may be fully understood, and thence just inferences may be drawn regarding principles themselves—and how can these *just* inferences, so important to virtue and happiness, be drawn from any but *true* premises?

You have done the world, I think, a great service, by your view of the character of Buonaparte, which appears to me a model of just and wise appreciation, and which has attracted with us much attention and applause. I lately recommended it to the perusal of an old lord, whose manly and rational mind seemed to me likely now to approve it, though in his youth he had visited your land in the capacity of aide-de-camp to Clinton; clearly he entertained no prejudice against the nation of the writer. I believe—I fear, that as long is there is man, so long there will be war upon the earth; and in war, as in all human things, good is mingled with evil, and sometimes we seem to see that providence has effected great and beneficial changes by its means, which no other means within our knowledge could have produced; but this is no reason why a conqueror should not be shown as what he truly is —a scourge of the earth. Your view of the character of this surprising man delighted me the more, because I found in it a very remarkable correspondence with the sentiments which my dear father was accustomed to express; he, like you, regarded him as in most respects a man of vulgar mind—a mere soldier of fortune, and he expressed the same indignation against those who, calling themselves friends of freedom, yet ranked among his partisans. With respect of the style of your piece, I am almost afraid to express to you the extent of my admiration—but with what pleasure did I hear a literary friend, a few days since, decidedly pronouncing Dr. Channing the most eloquent living writer of the English language!

I am very much *enlightened* by what you say of religious sentiment amongst you. Certainly the sovereign will be everywhere flattered and worshipped; and in these matters the sovereign people is not likely to be wiser than other sovereigns. My father used to say of the popular systems, that they *bid high* for mankind, and I believe mankind must become a good deal wiser before Unitarianism will be able to outbid them in the minds of the multitude; but certainly there is a progress in both countries; here it has lately been marked by the abolition of our test laws, and you go on founding Unitarian churches. The celebrated political economist Malthus, a clergyman, but a liberal—for he was brought up under my liberal grandfather at Warrington, and has always acted with our Whigs—slid into his pocket the other day my copy of your dedication sermon, saying, 'It is a system which every good mind must wish to be true, but I think there are considerable difficulties from some of the texts.' I have not yet had the opportunity of enquiring whether you have removed his difficulties.

I thank you much for your introduction of Mr. Sparks. I have yet seen him only for half an hour, and that was chiefly occupied by my questions and his answers respecting his objects of pursuit here. He has been illtreated at our State-paper office, through the illiberality or exclusive caution of Mr. Peel, and was hopeless of being allowed to take copies of papers which were at first promised him; but I think means may yet be found, and I have set a friend to work, but without the knowledge of Mr. Sparks. Next week I hope he will meet at my tea-table the professor of modern history from Cambridge, Mr. Smyth, a very liberal and enlightened person, who will be happy, I know, in the opportunity of giving and receiving information; and two other literary friends, who will probably be able to assist his objects both here and at Paris.

I feel that I have written you an enormous letter, yet I think you will hear of me again before long. During my illness I have just been able to amuse myself with preparing a little lesson book for children, most of which I had by me in pieces, written for my brother's young ones. Learning from Mr. Sparks that you have a little son, I shall venture to send you a copy, and with it a book for young people, which we have lately printed from a MS. of my father's.

Believe me, dear sir,
Yours, with true esteem,
L. AIKIN.

No. 4.

Hampstead: June 12, 1828.

Dear Sir— I have now the pleasure of requesting your acceptance of my father's little book and my own, which I hope may be not unwelcome to the younger members of your family. How deeply do I feel myself indebted to you for your introduction of Mr. Sparks. He is indeed a mine of information respecting everything which it is most interesting to learn of your great country; and I am proud to tell you that he did us the favour to communicate his knowledge and his sentiments with great freedom. His very looks bespeak goodness, and the more I conversed with him the more I was struck with the candour of his mind, as well as the strength of his judgment. I had the pleasure of introducing him to several literary friends, and all speak of him in terms of esteem and admiration.

He promises to visit us again on his return from the continent, and I hope by that time he will find all the obstacles surmounted which have been opposed to his consulting our state papers. It is plain that historians of the war of independence are much more likely to arise on your side of the water than on ours; and those who are anxious that more than just blame should not be called on the measures of our government, can do nothing so effectual as to promote the throwing open of all our documents to an American, inclined to relate the facts with candour, and an endeavour at least at impartiality. Mr. Sparks assured me that the effect of all that he had been permitted to inspect at the Home Office had been to soften his feelings towards the British Government; and certainly this modification of judgment is the natural result of hearing both sides. I think you would rejoice to hear of the abolition of our sacramental test. It is the more satisfactory because the measure was carried in direct contradiction to the wishes of the king, by the sole force of public opinion declaring itself through the House of Commons with an energy which ministers found it vain to oppose. Alas! that the Catholic question should not also have been gained! All thinking people must dread the effects of renewed disappointment on the minds of so formidable a body as the Irish Catholics. In granting to them the civil rights of other subjects, I confess I see neither difficulty nor danger, neither probably do most of the opponents of the measure; but they say, concede that, and they will next demand the establishment of their own hierarchy on the ruins of the Protestant Church of Ireland, on the plea that the established church ought to be that of the majority—a plea not easy to be refuted. In your country you have at least no dilemma like this to apprehend. I think I have never answered a question in one of your letters respecting the credit of Lingard's history. I have examined carefully the narrative of those reigns which I have studied, and I do not hesitate to affirm that with all its apparent candour, it abounds in artful misrepresentations; but can or dare a Catholic priest be an honest historian of events involving the interests or the reputation of his church? I greatly doubt it.

Believe me, dear sir, yours with much esteem,

LUCY AIKIN.

No. 5.

Hampstead: Aug. 12, 1828.

Dear Sir,—I hope you will have received before this reaches you my long delayed little book and a letter accompanying it; Mr. Sparks put me in the way of sending it through his London bookseller, addressed to his care, by which direction you may hear of it should it not have reached you; a poor return at best it is for the two admirable pieces with which you have last favoured me. Of the sermon I may truly say, that it was by far the noblest view of the Christian religion ever offered to my mind, and the most persuasive; it derives a novelty and originality from its sublimity, its purity and its simplicity; it is worthy of the most philosophic minds, the most enlightened ages, and I regard it as the best illustration of the idea of a *progressive Christianity* thrown out, as I remember, but not sufficiently unfolded, by that virtuous and accomplished, though not always judicious man and writer, Gilbert Wakefield. It is fitted to do incalculable good, and I am certain that in this country it will now find 'audience fit,' and by no means 'few.' The friends to whom I have communicated it are all ardent in their expressions of delight, and the forthcoming English edition is impatiently expected. Your further remarks on Napoleon are worthy of the same mind and pen; I subscribe to them with all my mind and heart, and regard them as no less enlightening on political than your other piece on religious topics. This too has been greatly admired with us, and read by those for whom ethical writings in general have no attraction. I have sincerely to thank you for the acquaintance of Mr. and Mrs. Norton; their society afforded me great pleasure and I only regretted that their stay in London was not further prolonged. Mr. Norton was so kind as to send me his 'Remarks on true and false Religion,' which convinced me how well-founded was your commendation of him as a deep and powerful thinker; his sensibility and amiable enthusiasm it was easy to discover from his manners and conversation, nor could the intelligence and animation of Mrs. Norton fail of attracting regard and interest. You put me on a great topic when you ask my sentiments of our religious reformation. A much better answer to your question than I am able to suggest you will find in Hallam's 'Constitutional History of England,' published last year, which I entreat you to read, as the most informing work on this and many other important passages of our national story which has yet appeared. The author is probably known to you already as the able historian of the Middle Ages, of the English part of which work his new one may be regarded in some measure as a continuation. This writer, it may interest you to know, was educated in the bosom of toryism and high churchism, being the son of a very courtly canon of Windsor, and brought up at Oxford. By the efforts of his own vigorous and independent mind he has liberalised his politics and come to a judgment of our Anglican church and churchmen which galls them sorely, as you may see by Southey's furious abuse of him in the 'Quarterly Review.' He *knows* the dignified clergy *thoroughly*, and out of that knowledge contemns them, as servile, beyond any other class of Englishmen. From him they cannot pardon it. Et tu Brute! You will find that he ascribes the ready acquiescence of the nation in Henry's reform in great part to the wide though secret diffusion of the doctrines of Wickliffe, respecting which you may see some curious facts in Turner's 'English History,' which I think confirm Hallam. But I confess I think that great weight must also be given to the consideration that the memory of the civil wars was still so recent and so bitter that Englishmen were then willing to yield to almost anything for a quiet life. It is also true, that the personal character of Henry, by all its qualities good and bad, was formed to assert a strong ascendency over the minds of his people, by whom he was at once more admired, esteemed and dreaded than any other English king. It must further be considered, that he innovated nothing in rites and doctrines, he hated and persecuted the Protestants; and so long as he did so, it is probable that the Catholics continued to flatter themselves that sooner or later he would return within the allegiance of the holy father. The ground of quarrel also was favourable to him; it was thought hard that he should be refused his divorce; it was visible that the Pope only refused it for fear of offending the Emperor, and the great body of English nobles had signed a threatening letter to Clement respecting it. Lastly, Henry was supported by parliament in all his measures, and I have quoted in my Elizabeth the argument urged by the attorney-general to More, founded on the omnipotence of that body: 'You allow that parliament may make kings, why not a head of the Church?' Still there ought to have been more martyrs among the clergy for their own credit; but the Romish Church had been so long triumphant, that we cannot be surprised to find it unprovided of the virtues militant. It behaved better afterwards; all Mary's bishops with one exception refused to crown her successor, and submitted patiently to deprivation. The Protestants had taught them to prefer conscience to interest. But I believe that under Elizabeth, all the laity would gradually have conformed to protestantism, but for that master-stroke of Rome, the institution of the order of Jesuits. They were a militia levied purposely to fight the battles of the Pope, and were certainly, in their way, a band of heroes. It is curious to see the efforts to revive them to meet the present dangers of the Church in France and elsewhere. My poor King Charles scarcely goes on, so very much am I impeded by ill health; but my mind still clings to the subject, and I live in hopes of being yet enabled to complete it. Have you seen the very able and accurate French work of Guizot on the 'English Revolution,' in which he includes the reign of Charles I.? I think it is the best history of the reign we yet possess. I have detected no errors and no important omissions, except with respect to the religious sects, of which he evidently knows but little.

Believe me, dear sir,
With sincere esteem and regard,
Very truly yours,
L. AIKIN.

No. 6.

Hampstead: Dec. 26, 1828.

Dear Sir—My paper bespeaks your patience for a long epistle; but I have two kind letters to acknowledge, and I perceive that the more we write to each other, the more we may write; for new topics of enquiry and discussion are constantly springing up between us, which is delightful. I have to talk to you of our old Puritans, of the present state of opinion and of morals amongst us, and of your own works; all which requires a large sheet. Your remark that fanaticism injures the moral character more than is usually supposed, has my full concurrence; and all I have learned of our old Puritans and their descendants confirms it. With fanatics, religion is rather a substitute for morality than a support to it; and I have seldom studied the character of a thorough-paced enthusiast without finding reason to believe that it contained a dash of knavery. Our old Puritans made their religion more directly instrumental to the purposes of worldly ambition than almost any other fanatics; the prediction that the saints should 'inherit the earth,' was constantly in their mouths; they declared that its accomplishment was close at hand, and they never hesitated to claim the character of saintship for themselves. I have been so fortunate as to procure a large collection of thanksgiving sermons preached before the Long Parliament, which will enable me to convict many of these holy men out of their own mouths. One example of the spirit they were of, I will give you. After a string of furious invectives and denunciations against the royalists and prelatists, the preacher turns round with a—'but it will be said that Christians are commanded to forgive and love their enemies; certainly their own enemies, but not the enemies of God, as those ungracious persons are!' As for their descendants, the Calvinistic dissenters, they had the misfortune of living in one of those middle states between direct persecution and perfect religious liberty, which sours the temper by continual petty vexations, without affording scope for great efforts or great sacrifices—which drives men to find a perverse pleasure in hating and being hated, and to seek indemnification for the contempt of the world in a double portion of spiritual pride and self-importance. 'We can prove ourselves saints,' 'being Christ's little flock everywhere spoken against,' is the plea put into the mouth of this set by Green, a poet, who was born and bred among them.

I have as much presbyterian blood in my veins as any of your New Englanders, and from the elders of our family I have picked up volumes of traditionary lore concerning the old dissenters of Bedford, who built a meeting-house for John Bunyan, and their brethren of Northampton and Leicester—still strongholds of Calvinism. From the whole, I conclude that they were usually lordly husbands, harsh parents, merciless censors of their neighbours: systematically hostile to all the amenities of life, but not less fond of money, or more scrupulous in the means of acquiring it, than the worldlings whom they reprobated. Long before my time, however, my kindred the Jennings, the Belshams, my excellent grandfather Aikin, and his friend and tutor Doddridge, had begun to break forth out of the chains and darkness of Calvinism, and their manners softened with their system. My youth was spent among the disciples or fellow-labourers of Price or Priestley, the descendants of Dr. John Taylor, the Arian, or in the society of that most amiable of men, Dr. Enfield. Amongst these there was no rigorism. Dancing, cards, the theatre, were all held lawful in moderation: in *manners* the free dissenters, as they were called, came much nearer the Church than to their own stricter brethren, yet in *doctrine* no sect departed so far from the Establishment. At the period of the French revolution, and especially after the Birmingham riots, this sect distinguished itself by the vehemence of its democratical spirit, and becoming in a manner a faction, as well as a sect, political as well as religious animosity became arrayed against it, and I now remember with disgust, not without compunction, the violent contempt and hatred in which, in common with almost all the young, and not a few of the more mature of that set, I conceived it meritorious to indulge towards the Church and the aristocrats.

The doctrines called evangelical make all the noise now, both within the Church and without. Yet I fancy that their success is at its furthest, and I should not wonder to hear of a party professedly latitudinarian, and really unitarian, beginning to show itself within the Church. Oxford partakes very little in the evangelism of Cambridge. Of these evangelicals too, one encouraging symptom is to be observed—they have gradually and almost imperceptibly quitted Calvinism for Arminianism; therefore they feel less confident of being amongst the elect, and take more pains to work out their own salvation, not only by religious observances, but by deeds of beneficence and mercy. With much of the Puritanical rigor, in such points as the observance of the Sabbath, and the avoidance of public amusements, they are certainly a better set—indefatigable superintendents of schools, munificent patrons of Bible societies and missions, and incessant visitants of the sick and poor. Of course there must be many self-intereste hypocrites among them, and not a few sour and censorious fanatics; and to a system so exclusive as theirs, some bigotry must adhere: but I think that many of them are so exemplarily good, and so sincerely pious, and act from so profound a sense of duty, that they must at length win from God the grace to think more worthily of His intentions towards the human race than they seem to do at present. I think, however, that their moral influence on the whole, and particularly amongst the lower class, is in many points unfavourable. They make religion exceedingly repulsive to the young and the cheerful, by setting themselves against all the sports and diversions of the common people, and surfeiting them with preaching, praying, and tutoring; they bewilder, and sometimes entirely overthrow, weak and timid minds by their mysterious and terrific doctrines, and they do much towards confounding moral right and wrong by the language which they hold on the efficacy of sudden conversions and death-bed repentance. The assurances of eternal bliss which they hold out to the most atrocious malefactors are often a just subject of scandal. On the whole their system has much of the debasing, and as it were vulgarising effect, which you justly ascribe to such views of religion—and is perhaps one of the great causes of that apparent want of moral progress which you remark amongst us. Other causes are cheap poison in the shape of gin; over population, which makes it hard to thousands to gain a livelihood by honest labour, and the improvident habits produced by our poor laws, and by the excess, or in many cases the injudicious application, of public and private charity. Our long wars, and the crushing weight of taxation which they have drawn upon us, are perhaps the remote source of most of these great evils.

Our state is a very strange one—unexampled activity in every kind of pursuit—excessive activity, I should be inclined to say—unexampled diffusion of knowledge, but bad institutions of many kinds, tending to crush the many, to exalt the few; abuse and corruption in every department; vast luxury and corresponding rapacity, and a great fund of stupid and illiberal prejudice, diffused through all classes. We are in the main a Tory people, and what you may well think strange, the greatest Whigs and reformers amongst us actually hail a Tory ministry like the present, because no other kind of ministry has ever strength or permanence to effect anything, being unwelcome both to the king and the people; and at a time when so much light and knowledge prevails, even Tories are influenced by public opinion, and often indeed by the necessity of the case, to favour *some* reforms (like Mr. Peel's of the criminal law) which in their hands become effective. If the Catholic claims be granted, it will be a concession which only a Tory minister could extort from our king, or carry against the clergy. The agitation of these claims, by the way, produces some of the strangest anomalies of our situation. Here are our highest churchmen abusing without mercy the Catholics, whom Horsley formerly with greater reason declared to be 'nearer and dearer' to them than any Protestant sectaries; and here are we *liberals* almost driven into a league, offensive and defensive, with old popery, whom we have been bred to scorn and hate from our cradle. And now to my last topic. Nothing can be more sincere than the admiration I have expressed of your works, and none have I more admired than your last. Your views of the relation in which the Deity stands to man, and of the light in which He is to be regarded by rational beings, seems to me developments of my own thoughts, and the spirit of the whole discourse elevates, consoles, and delights me.

God bless you, my dear and valued friend.

L. AIKIN.

No. 7.

Hampstead: June 12, 1829.

Dear Sir—Your friends Mr. and Mrs. Ware visited us last night, and I hasten to thank you most cordially for the acquaintance of these excellent people. If my letter, which is lost with the little books, had reached you safely, it would have told you how welcome were your other friends, the Nortons and Mr. Sparks; but they have returned to you, and have brought, I trust, no ill report of their reception. I know not exactly why it is, but your people always feel to me more like kindred than strangers; we are acquainted as soon as we meet. Simplicity of manners with elevation of mind and a cultivated intellect, form a union admirable anywhere, but less rare, I apprehend, in your state of society than in ours; amid the bustling crowd of luxurious London it is a refreshment to the spirit to meet with it. Continue by all means to send us these noble specimens—it must tend to break down prejudices and to strengthen the bands which ought to unite together the true friends of man in every clime. It is indeed time to throw aside the fetters of nationality already amongst us, the best men have the lead of it, and the blessed influence of peace which now renders an Englishman or an American free of the whole civilized world, emancipates the mind with the person and teaches it to scorn all littleness.

I have but a shabby account to give of Zwingle. I certainly verified nothing and do at present regard that biography as a very rhetorical prize essay, and worthy of little confidence. My translation was made in early days, long before I became a searcher into history, and, truth to say, I undertook the task merely that I might have the satisfaction of earning a journey to Scotland by my own labour, instead of going at my father's expense. Zwingle however was an excellent man, and I was pleased to find that the best of English reformers and martyrs, Latimer, Ridley, &c. were followers of his pure and simple doctrine. Many thanks for your Fenelon. I thought there was a little inconsistency between the agreement with some of his leading tenets, which you begin with professing, and the very important disagreements which you go on to explain; but your sketch of the Catholic bishop is beautiful, and calculated to do much good; and, in a very different way, I regard your remarks on self-immolation as highly valuable. I remember making several reflections cn the mischievous absurdity of that notion after reading a French selection from eminent Catholic divines for the use of young persons. The doctrine of original sin is the root of that and various other highly noxious errors in the popular systems of ethics; and though the *selfish system* has never satisfied either my reason or my heart, I think we owe great obligation to Paley and others who have set it up against its opposite. The Calvinists, by the way, stated the opposition between God and what they called self, as strongly as the Catholics. I found in some contemporary writers the cant term of *self-seeking* mentioned as a new coinage of the Scotch covenanters, and looking then into the matter, I was inclined to think that the word *selfish* was scarcely of earlier origin, at least in its present acceptation. What a dreadful idea that our Creator has planted within our bosoms a domestic foe, from whom we can never fly, and whose malice never sleeps a moment, an evil principle solely occupied in working our perdition! When will the most enlightened nations of the world take courage to banish from the midst of them superstitions far more baneful than the wildest dreams of savage ignorance? Did you ever read a life of Fenelon by Charles Butler, the Catholic? It is a curious work, and I had some curious conversation with him respecting it. He plainly regards Fenelon's submission to the condemnation of his work, which papists and courtiers united to call sublime, as something like a politic manœuvre. The whole story is an example, equally melancholy, and instructive, of the sullying influence of temporal and spiritual despotism upon characters made for sincerity and magnanimity. But this further moral it perhaps did not suit the purposes of your tract to deduce from the history of one of the best men of his class.

Believe me with the highest regard,
Most sincerely yours,
LUCY AIKIN.

No. 8.

Hampstead: Oct. 8, 1829.

Dear Sir—I too, either from temper or habit, am a great procrastinator, and therefore I sit down to reply to your most welcome letter immediately, whilst the impression is quite fresh : I shall not be 'gravelled for lack of matter.' Hallam, I was certain, would both interest and inform you, and I wish you could put your historic difficulties to the author himself, as I did some of mine a few months ago, at a party where we were glad to discuss instead of dining. Such a torrent of knowledge he poured upon me! He talks faster than any other mortal who talks wisely and who has lost his teeth, and hard task it is to follow him. But as to some of your difficulties respecting our Tories, and no-popery high-churchmen, I almost think I can give you some solutions myself. Toryism and high churchism are so closely and naturally connected that it is scarcely possible, in general, to estimate the separate influence of each; and in all our troubled times from the long parliament to the revolution, it is plain that religious and political principles were both busy in the fray, but the shares belonging to each have been very differently stated by writers: thus, Fox maintains that James II. was deposed chiefly for his tyranny, and Hallam holds that it was chiefly for his popery, and I know not which is likely to be nearest the truth. However, it is certain that the smoke of Smithfield fires and the fume of Fawkes's gunpowder have to this day an unsavoury odour in the nostrils of the people. The clergy, as a portion of the people, partake of the same sense of things; moreover, the penal laws were a formidable obstacle to apostasy from the State religion. Laud himself, though in ritual, and in some points of doctrine, he wished to return as near as possible to Rome, felt that he could not conform entirely 'till Rome were other than she is,' and said 'No,' as you remember, to the cardinal's hat. His master also seems to have been well aware at least that it could never stand safe upon the head of an Archbishop of Canterbury; moreover, he himself hated popery like his father, on account of its assuming power to depose kings, and he would not have resigned his supremacy. Now it has been a constant maxim of Rome to concede nothing to schismatics; all schemes of compromise between it and the English Church have constantly failed, and differences are sure to gain importance in the eyes of those who by experience have found them to be irreconcilable. Hence the determined alienation of some of our highest churchmen from a church which they would have met, perhaps, more than half way. James II. strove to establish one exclusive church on the ruins of another. In this extreme case the bishops must give up one of three things, honour and conscience, their mitres, or their favourite principle of passive obedience, and it is not wonderful if they judged the last the smallest sacrifice. In Dryden's 'Hind and Panther,' you may see, too, that Catholics, especially those who were converts or conformists to the king's religion, used at this crisis language sufficiently provoking and contemptuous to the Anglicans. With what intolerable point and justice too, he tells them

> But, half to take on trust, and half to try,
> It is not faith, but bungling bigotry.

After the revolution, and down to George III. with the exception for high church Anne, things were in a different position. The court was by necessity Whig. The bishops, or those who desired to be so, were therefore, by like necessity, Whigs also, and the fight against popery and arbitrary power, which always went together, was carried on by low churchmen and latitudinarians with Stillingfleet and Tillotson at their head; the country squires and country parsons meanwhile remaining in the enjoyment of their high churchism, toryism and Jacobitism. During the last reign, Jacobitism becoming extinct, *high* principles resumed their place at Court, and did their utmost to resist the spread of all freedom at home and abroad. Dissenters and democrats underwent much abuse and some persecution, and Horsley then spoke of the French emigrant priests as much 'nearer and dearer' than the sectaries at home. Since that, however, the scene has changed again. Popery in Ireland is the religion of the mob, it has acquired a deep taint of radicalism, and its claims being patronised by our liberals, were opposed by the Tories of both islands till all statesmen saw that concession was unavoidable. The clergy, as a body, had interests of their own at stake, and stood out longer. 'Give the Catholics this,' they cried, 'and you give them strength both in parliament and without. They will resist the payment of tithes, they will overthrow the Protestant church in Ireland, and then Heaven knows what they, with the dissenters to help them, may attempt against tithes and church in England.' They struggled hard, and certainly scrupled no means to work upon the prejudices of the vulgar, high and low. But the spirit of the times, joined to the necessity of the case, proved too strong for the spirit of the Church; it has sustained a signal defeat and humiliation, and I hope good will come of it.

My health is still very indifferent, in particular I am much troubled with severe headaches, which so continually interrupt my studies, that I have the mortification to see my King Charles making very little and often no progress. With occupation it is comparatively easy to keep up the spirits under almost any circumstances, but compulsory idleness I sometimes find it a hard task to bear with cheerfulness. However, I do my best, and with time and patience I still hope that my health will be restored, and my work finished. One advantage this delay brings me, it gives time for friends to take means for procuring for me family papers and other valuable documents, which one chance or other is continually bringing forth to daylight. In consequence of a base attack by Disraeli on that patriot martyr, Sir John Eliot, his descendant Lord Eliot has rummaged out a correspondence between him and Hampden, and promises to put it into my hands. Pray procure, if you can, another interesting family relic lately published, Lady Fanshaw's Memoirs. She was a royalist, and I feel proud of the women on both sides when I place her account on the same shelf as Mrs. Hutchinson's. There is much less of literary skill on the part of Lady Fanshaw, but her artless tale is full of interest and amusement.

Passing from old times to new times, I have two pieces of intelligence for you, that German metaphysics (in the train of which German theology may follow) have got into Cambridge, where youths are puzzling their brains with Kantianism; and that it is whispered—monstrum horrendum!—that Unitarianism is infecting some of the most enlightened of the clergy of Oxford. What will the world come to? Some of these clergy, and those of Cambridge, also addict themselves to the modern science of geology and other branches of natural history—this connects them with the Geological, Linnean, and other similar societies in London; at their meetings they come in contact with the men of enlightened and independent minds, and thus they rub off professional stiffness and prejudice, and learn to assert something of the birth-right freedom of the mind.

I had a glimpse and no more of the Wares on their return from their northern tour. Mr. Ware was looking better in the face, and there was less of languor in his air, but there seems to be still great room for amendment in his state. He ought to recover with such a wife to nurse him. They did well to hasten to a more genial climate; ours has this season been unusually trying to all invalids. I am afraid that Canada keeps up in your country a somewhat bitter feeling against England which *here* is not reciprocated; for when we want to hate our neighbours, the French are far more handy than you.

You may wonder that I should talk of my inability to write a volume; but a letter may be written lounging, and requires no apparatus of folios and quartos.

Pray believe me,
Very cordially yours,
LUCY AIKIN.

No. 9.

Hampstead: June 1, 1830.

Dear Sir—Many thanks for your welcome letter, which I was well able to decipher: I was the more glad to receive it as I wanted such an excuse for writing to you, having, as you will find, abundant topics. My first shall be one concerning yourself. That article in the 'Edinburgh Review,' I am charged to convey to you the regrets and indignation of a large group of your unknown friends and admirers, who are hurt at it much less from any fear that it should either disturb your mind or injure your literary reputation, than from an apprehension that your country should regard it as a mark of national enmity, the more startling as appearing in a journal usually the organ of liberal principles. It is, in fact, the ebullition of one malignant temper, and it is easy to show you the sources of his hostility. The writer is William Hazlitt, a vehement admirer of Napoleon, of whom he has written a Life, in a very different spirit from your remarks. He has also written on the English poets with an acute sense of their blemishes, and a very blunt perception of their beauties, another sin of *yours*; further he is at enmity with your commender Southey; lastly he was brought up at the feet of Priestley and Belsham, and probably retains of their system materialism and necessity, and little more. The matter was discussed amongst us at a literary dinner, and there wanted not those well disposed to make you *amende honorable*; but no one could suggest a fitting vehicle—if the attack had but come from the Quarterly, the Edinburgh would have gladly received an appeal, but as it is, I believe it must be overlooked. I must tell you, however, that Mr. Hallam was one of the most indignant, and that he charged me to convey to you his wish to be regarded amongst your warm admirers, and his pleasure at learning that you had given some approbation to his labours. You would scarcely understand the reviewer's accusation against you as a trimmer, but seemingly he supposes that those who rank with the Priestleyans in theology ought to maintain the same doctrines in metaphysics, though it would be hard to show any necessary or natural connection between them. But what an obstacle is it to the progress of truth, that a man must take or leave *all* the opinions of some party, or leader; on pain of being accounted a time-server! It is one of the privileges of a mere spectator, like myself, to be free to accept or reject as conviction prompts, and accordingly I find myself often discarding old prepossessions, and striking out to myself new lights.

Now the time may have been that I did frown on metaphysics, and 'as at present advised,' I am a Lockist and Necessarian, and yet I am beginning to wish well to the progress of intellectual philosophy, and I will tell you why. This age and the men of it are 'of the earth, earthy,' and I wish to see some upward movement. There is a pseudo science called political economy which dries up the hearts and imaginations of most who meddle with it—there is Bentham's system called the Utilitarian, which has a similar effect, there is Paley's system of morals, long the text book at Cambridge and just introduced as such, I am told, in the Scotch universities, which is another grovelling thing; and to all these, a lofty philosophy would act, I believe, as a counterpoise of great value. Metaphysical inquiries may, on many points, show only 'how little can be known;' but when conducted in a proper spirit, I have seen them work much good on the mind and character: yet, as you say, they do not always make men the better reasoners on religion, or set them above vulgar cries or vulgar prejudices. Benson, now master of the Temple, one of the most distinguished preachers and theologians in London—a Cambridge man ---once favoured me with a luminous and beautiful lecture or harangue on Kantism, yet that man has renounced acquaintance, after a very long and dear friendship, with venerable Mr. Turner of Newcastle, one of the best of human beings, on account of his Unitarianism, and has publicly preached that this faith was contrary to morals! Yet my Oxford news is true; not of any of their logical or metaphysical writers, that I know of, but of some of their geologists and other natural philosophers, who, turning the force of their minds to those branches of science in which they may speculate unshackled, whisper in corners to other men engaged in similar pursuits their contempt for the Articles they have signed. My brother Arthur hears such talk from Oxonian members of the Geological Society, when they attend its meetings.

I have heard the two works you mention spoken of with high praise by a few good judges, but I have not yet seen them; the author, I am told, is a Mr. Bailey, of Sheffield, but this is all I can learn. You cannot conceive how much the lettered aristocracy of London society disdains to know anything of provincial genius or merit, at least in any but the most popular branches of literature. Montgomery, a Sheffield poet, being also an Evangelical, is tolerably well known in London, and may, in some companies, be slightly mentioned without committing the speaker. But a Sheffield metaphysician! bold were the London diner-out who would dare not to be ignorant of him. You once observed to me that everywhere the *sovereign* is worshipped; with us, that sovereign is an idol called Gentility, and costly are the offerings laid upon the altar. Dare to make conversation in the most accomplished society something of an exercise of the mind, and not a mere dissipation, and you instantly become that thing of horror, a *Bore*.*

No. 10.

Hampstead: June 7, 1830.

Dear Sir—By the kindness of Mr. Ware, I have it at length in my power to send copies of the two little books so long since destined for your daughter; and though I have written to you at large so lately, I cannot resist the temptation of adding a letter. I hope it cannot be very

* The rest of the letter is missing.

troublesome to you to read what it is so agreeable to me to write.

Your friend Mr. Goodhue spent an hour with me one morning, and I was much pleased with his mild and amiable manners, and the information which he gave me respecting many of your institutions and societies. I wished for more of his company, and invited him for the next evening, when I expected Mrs. Joanna Baillie, Professor Smyth, and another valued friend, Mr. Whishaw, a gentleman who has written little, but whose literary opinions are heard in the most enlightened circles with a deference approaching that formerly paid to Dr. Johnson. Mr. Goodhue was unfortunately engaged, but he sent me Mr. Richmond, and the result was, one of the most animated and amusing *conversaziones*, chiefly between him and the two gentlemen I have named—for we ladies were well content to be listeners—at which it has ever been my good fortune to be present.

A more fluent talker than Mr. Richmond I think I never heard, and I doubted at first how he might suit my two old gentlemen—both of them great eulogists of good listeners—but he is very clever, and there was something so *piquant* in his remarks on what he had seen here, such a simplicity in his questions, and when he spoke of his own country, such abundant knowledge, so ably and clearly expressed, that they were content for once to take such a share of talk as they could get by hard struggling. I think the professor of modern history got matter for a new lecture on American law and politics; and he and Mr. Richmond took pains to contrive another meeting. But to me the most curious part was Mr. Richmond's wonder at having got into such high company as two or three baronets, a Scotch countess, and some lord; and his difficulty to imagine, and ours to explain to him, how our difference of ranks *works* in society. He evidently supposed a much wider separation of classes than actually takes place. I believe the structure of society with us may best be expressed by what an eminent naturalist has said of organised nature — it is not a chain of being, it more resembles a net, each mesh holds to several others on different sides. Our complicated state of society, in recompense of great evils, has at least this advantage, that it brings the rich man or the noble into relation with a multitude of individuals, with whom he finds it necessary to his objects to associate on terms of social equality, notwithstanding great disparity of birth or fortune. Those very societies of which we agree in condemning the epidemic prevalence, are useful in our country by their levelling effect. In a bible society or a missionary meeting, the zealous labourers, and still more the effective speakers, find themselves enabled to give the law to wealth and title. Scientific and literary institutions concur to the same results, and so does the cultivation in the higher ranks of letters and of arts. There is no fact, no talent, no acquirement, either useful or ornamental, no celebrity of any kind, but what serves its possessor as a ticket of admission to the company of some of his superiors. I imagine that in no country there can be less of undiscovered or unrewarded merit than in ours. Do you begin to suspect the insidious aim of these remarks? Your 'Means and Ends of a National Literature' lies before me, and I am pleading for some exception as respects England to the general truth of your observation, that in Europe 'it is for his blood, his rank, or some artificial distinction, and not for the attributes of humanity, that man holds himself in respect.' Perhaps, however, my position, that men in this country value themselves, and are valued by others, very much according to their talents, tastes, acquirements, and their power and will to serve a sect or party, may not be irreconcilable with your position that they do not respect themselves sufficiently for the attributes—the common attributes—of humanity. Here in the lower, that is the more numerous class, it is too near the truth that 'man's life is cheap as beast's.' Your estimate of our literature I think very just. I am not, however, without hope that in labouring as you say for ourselves, which the difficulties of our present situation render imperative upon us, some general truths may be elicited which may be capable of extended application, at least in the other old countries of Europe, which continue to look to us for examples of many kinds—to you they will be less available.

The oldest minister of the Scotch Church, Mr. Somerville, author of a valuable history of the reign of Queen Anne, died very lately at above ninety, but possessed of all his faculties. The venerable man uttered his 'nunc dimittis' on having witnessed Catholic emancipation; but one more triumph was in store for him in the perusal of your works—he said he rejoiced in them exceedingly; they formed an era in the progress of religion. This trait I have from his accomplished daughter-in-law, also a great admirer of yours. She is an eminent proficient in mathematical science, and now engaged in translating the works of La Place, and her countrywoman Joanna Baillie is no more modest, gentle, and full of all goodness. Rogers the poet having seen some of your pieces, told me he was going to the booksellers in search of all the rest. Merely as 'means of moral influence' you may prize these testimonies.

It was with great concern I heard from the Wares that you had sustained a severe attack of illness, though I learned at the same time of your recovery. Pray take care of yourself for many sakes besides your own, you have yet much to do for the world; and pray take it into consideration whether you ought not to winter in a milder climate—such as ours; how very much we would make of you if we had you here!

Believe me ever
Yours with the truest regard,
L. AIKIN.

No. 11.

Hampstead: Dec. 14, 1830.

I had been quite impatient, my dear sir, to hear from you, and I am almost equally impatient to answer your letter, which had a long passage, and is but two days arrived. I have volumes to say to you; but first of the last, for fear I should forget it. I was afraid W. Burns would prove a second Sheffield metaphysician, having never heard of him; but at length my friend, the Rev. George Kenrick, supplies full and satisfactory information. Twenty years since, when a Glasgow student, he often saw Mr. Burns at Professor Woodrow's. He was a very plain man, who had received the Scotch share of education, and no more, and whose style in writing was much more refined than in conversation. He had been a carpenter, but then lived without profession on a small fortune, devoted to reading and speculation. At that time he stopped short of Unitarianism, but adhered to the liberal party in the Scotch Church, and shared the odium attached to it in those evil days. He displayed a powerful and original mind, and was of high moral worth. Mr. K. thinks him to be not far short of sixty, and knows him for the author of the pieces you mention. Several corroborating circumstances persuade Mr. K. and myself that liberal principles are now rapidly advancing in Scotland. Mrs. Joanna Baillie says the reason there are so few Unitarians there *out* of the church is, that there are so many *in* it. Their ministers sign a confession at ordination, but having no liturgy, they are afterwards free to avoid all utterance of doctrine, if they please, or to teach their own. What an age have we fallen upon! Since the French revolution we have had the Belgian, the Polish insurrection, and here we are in an English revolution! I can scarcely give you an idea of our state—we do not half understand it ourselves, but I am sure you will be anxious to hear as much as I can tell you. The panic occasioned by the postponement of the royal visit to the city was at first indescribable; everybody said 'what must this danger be which frightens Wellington?' This soon subsided; it was admitted by all but a few of the highest tories, that no case had been made out—that the Duke had either given in to a false alarm, or had wilfully raised one for political purposes. This and his foolish declaration against reform, turned him out. We have now a ministry pledged to reform and retrenchment—to non-interference with foreign States. It comprises so much virtue and talent, that if sufficiently strong and sufficiently lasting, it would seem likely to secure to us important blessings. But in the meantime we seem on the brink of that complication of all horrors, a servile war. You have heard, no doubt, of our burnings, machine breakings, and mobs attacking houses, stage-coaches, and passengers, for plunder. This, you may think, is no more than we have suffered before from the proceedings of Luddites and other collections of discontented workmen. But here is the difference—those were risings of the manufacturers of some one branch alone, confined to certain districts or towns, and comparatively easy to suppress. But this is a movement of the peasantry—the whole agricultural class almost throughout the country, and the means of quelling it are not obvious. The last thing in English history like it, was the Norfolk insurrection, under Kett, in the reign of Edward VI., occasioned by the general inclosure of commons. Happily, our mobs have not collected by thousands, nor have they yet found a leader. The tories, with their heads full of the French revolution, have spread the idea that the conflagrations were the work of political agitators of a rank much above the peasants, whom they moved. But this appears an ungrounded notion. All the persons yet apprehended as ringleaders, are loose and reckless characters from the dregs of the people; and herein, I conceive, lies the safety of the upper classes. Over-population is said, and I believe truly, to be the main cause of the distress which has produced these risings; but others have concurred, such as the laying small farms into large ones, rack-renting, the absenteeism of landlords, and various abuses in the administration of the poor laws. There is a strong feeling also amongst the people against tithes, and against clerical magistrates. In general, the gentlemen have acted in these matters with a mixture of courage and humanity which does them honour. Very able judges have been sent down to try the delinquents in custody; the wages have been raised in most places, and I trust that at the price of some pecuniary sacrifices, and some correction of abuses, we may see tranquillity restored. In the meantime, both London and these villages swarm with beggars; some of them so sturdy and importunate, that there is but a shade between them and banditti. The ministry are in a situation of extreme difficulty and awful responsibility. They are pledged to some measure of parliamentary reform, for which this is certainly a very awkward season.

I am reading Jefferson's 'Correspondence' with deep interest. I wept bitter tears at the recital of British cruelties during the war. I had no idea how horribly we treated you — pray forgive and forget; Jefferson did neither, but I dare not blame him. He speaks of 'the half-reformation in religion and government,' with which

England has sat down contented, without thinking it necessary to cure her remaining prejudices.

Say not that France is outstripping us in philosophy, unless you have read the 'History of Moral Philosophy in Britain,' lately written by Sir James Mackintosh. It is a work of immense erudition, full of acute and original remark, and showing a prodigious comprehension of the subject; yet it is said to have been hastily written, and the style is not highly excellent. I am impatient for you to see it. Being written in a supplement to a new edition of the 'Encyclopædia Britannica,' it could not be bought in a separate form; the author only having a few copies for his friends, one of which was lent me. I tried to get possession of one for you but failed. He was happily called by Mr. Whishaw 'an artist of conversation.'

Brougham is our new Lord Chancellor—the Edinburgh reviewer—the radical-whig—the apostle of universal education and popular literature, whom we are astonished and delighted to behold in that highest dignity of a subject! This is the man, the only man, whose powers I contemplate with *wonder*. In society he has the artless gaiety of a good-humoured child. Never leading the conversation, never canvassing for audience (in truth he has no need), he catches the ball as it flies with a careless and unrivalled skill. His little narratives are inimitable, the touch-and-go of his remarks leaves a trail of light behind it. On the tritest subjects he is new without paradox and without effort, simply, as it seems, because nature has interdicted him from commonplace. With that tremendous power of sarcasm which he has so often put forth in public, he is the sweetest-tempered man in private life, the kindliest in its relations, the most attracting to his friends —in short, as amiable as he is great. His first great speech in the house of peers on his plan for distributing cheap justice to the people, afforded a curious exhibition of the manners of that house. I have the account from Mr. Whishaw, who accompanied the Chancellor. 'None of the cheers, none of the applauses of the House of Commons—no interest in so great and useful a subject. On the impassive ice the lightnings played.' And when he had concluded, no one rising, no one thanking him—'they sat in their curule chairs mute and motionless (however wide of them in other respects) as the Roman senate in the presence of Brennus.' No matter, England hears him. It is the news of to-day that the Prussians are rising, and Austria dreading disturbances in Italy. We shall be free—all Europe will. I cast away alarms and apprehensions as unworthy things, and surrender myself to the spirit of the age. Religious changes in this country become probable. It cannot, I think, be questioned that the Evangelical clergy have become odious to the common people by their meddling spirit, their hostility to all amusements and the gloom with which they invest the offices of religion. To recover influence the clergy must relax a good deal, if they do not a season of puritanism may again be followed by an age of utter profligacy. A well-informed friend just returned from Paris tells me, what others confirm, that with respect to religion the French mind is a 'tabula rasa.' 'They do not write against Christianity,' I remarked to one who knew Paris: 'No, they think that settled; they do not write against Jupiter.' The churches are quite deserted, even in the south of France. I am delighted at your amusing yourself with Walpole. All classes were very coarse then, they had not yet thrown off the pollution of the Court of Charles II. Lady M. W. Montague's letters tell the same tale—the whig Horace Walpole was aristocracy personified.

I hope you will again gratify me with a letter before it is very long—your letters give me much to think upon.

Ever most truly yours,
L. AIKIN.

No. 12.

Hampstead: May 1, 1831.

Very happy was I, my dear friend, to hear from you again. There was no getting any tidings about you—I could not even learn for certain where you were, and I was anxious to learn how the change of climate had answered to you and Mrs. Channing in point of health. Boston is quite an easy distance to think of in comparison of that little out-of-the-world island which I never heard of before, and could scarcely hunt out upon the map. And Emily Taylor had not written me a word about you, for which I will scold her; but I will not be jealous of her, because I love her dearly—a purer or more amiable mind I do not know; she loves a joke, too, and we are very merry whenever we meet.

I have not been travelling for health, but keeping the house for it, which is worse. It is nearly three months since I have seen London, and I have been almost entirely disabled from writing, but I am again recovering. Great public events have occurred since I wrote last; on the whole, I think our position improved. The peasant risings are completely quelled; the reform bill absorbs all political feeling. It is a noble measure, and one which, when carried, will deserve to be revered as a new magna charta. It will render parliament, indeed, the organ of the people, and put, I believe, an effectual check upon the corrupt and oppressive influence of the aristocracy. You express a natural apprehension that our aristocracy should not discern the signs of the times sufficiently to lead the people the way that they must and will go. Certainly many are even now blindly striving to resist what is inevitable; but the terrible examples of France have not been lost on the privileged orders in general, and many

individuals have shown themselves actuated by a sense of
justice and of true patriotism, which is of the best augury
for the country. But the conduct of the king is our
grand piece of good fortune, and a most unexpected one.
A patriot king! Once in a millennium such a phœnix is
seen on earth. Alfred was our last. A levity in the
manners of his majesty had caused him to be suspected
of an unsound head, but he has under this a plain good
sense, and what is better still, a real love of seeing his
people happy, which in this instance has led him admirably
right. His appeal to the people on this great
question has utterly disarmed radicalism. The mob are
ever king-worshippers, in all monarchical countries, and
ours may be led anywhere to the tune of 'our national
anthem.' Hunt and O'Connell hide their diminished
heads; against a king and a sailor-king, too, they are less
than nothing. On the higher classes also, his influence is
very considerable, and I feel almost confident that the
measure will be triumphantly carried in the new parliament.
I agree with you that the want of harmony between
ancient institutions and modern light, is the general cause
of commotion both in this country and throughout Europe,
and that the only general remedy is to be sought in a
comprehensive reform of institutions; but the particular,
or immediately exciting causes, are various; and to these
the attention of eye-witnesses is most directed, as being
those over which events, or what are unphilosophically
called accidents, have power. Thus, I should say the
general progress of society must bring us parliamentary
reform during this generation; but the accident of a George
or a William on the throne, a good or bad harvest, a
prosperous or depressed state of trade, whig or tory
ministry, may make all the difference of our obtaining it
safely and peaceably, or through revolution and civil war.
But it is in the main the cause of the many against that

of the few. I have convinced myself of this, and am become in consequence an ardent reformer. I boast of this as a self-conquest. Women are natural aristocrats, depend upon it; and many a reproach have I sustained from my father for what he called my 'Odi profanum vulgus.' The rude manners, trenchant tone, and barbarous slang of the ordinary radicals, as well as the selfish ends and gross knavery which many of them strive to conceal under professions of zeal for all the best interests of mankind, are so inexpressibly disgusting to me, that in some moods I have wished to be divided from them far as pole from pole. On the other hand, the captivating manners of the aristocracy, the splendour which surrounds them, the taste for heraldry and pedigree which I have picked up in the course of my studies, and the flattering attentions which my writings have sometimes procured me from them, are strong bribes on the side of ancient privilege; but, as I said before, I have fought and conquered; and I confess that 'the greatest good of the greatest number' is what alone is entitled to consideration, however unpoetical the phrase and the pedantic sect of which it is the watchword.

Of the integrity of the chancellor, all distrust should cease. He has resisted more temptations than any public man in the country. An intense love of glory he certainly has, but it is for glory of the true sort. He is magnanimous and philanthropic; and these two last words I cannot write without being reminded to beg you to read the life of Dr. Currie by his son. I knew the man—he was my father's friend—and the impression of the benefit and delight I received at an early age from his society, and under his roof, will be one of the very last I can ever lose. I think him to have been one of the best and noblest of mankind, and the wisest I ever conversed with. And with these great qualities there was an elegance and tenderness of mind, a spirit of poetry, and a shade of constitutional melancholy investing the whole, which rendered him interesting beyond expression. Many of his letters are given in this work, and they are the man himself. The memoir has the very rare merit from a filial hand, of being perfectly free from exaggeration—the simple truth. There are many matters in the book which will interest you. Currie was a wide as well as a deep thinker—few subjects of human speculation escaped him.

And now let me tell you how I have been attempting to fill up one of those languid pauses of existence in which one has little to do but to wait for the return of health and strength in patience, deceiving the long, and in my case lonely hours, as best one may. I have been reading metaphysics. And this was your doing: the mention which you make, I forget in which piece of yours, of the theory of Berkeley, excited my curiosity, and I have been reading him with great admiration of his ingenuity and his beautiful style, and wonder that so much is to be said for what seems at first view so chimerical. I have since been reading Priestley's 'Disquisition on Matter and Spirit,' and his correspondence with Price. And what is the result? why, that I am perplexed and confounded—utterly unable to take a side or form an opinion on subjects, which seem to me, indeed, placed beyond the scope of human knowledge—yet pleased and *proud* that the human mind should dare to entertain such thoughts—to soar to such heights, and sound such depths. Oh! the mind of man *must* be formed for progress, eternal progress, else why these thoughts beyond the measure of his frame? If the strengthening of this conviction were the sole result of pursuits like these, they were well and amply recompensed, but I have found in them other uses. They give me a more intimate sense of the all-pervading presence and agency of the *one* cause. I did not before, if I may so speak, feel how *very near* it is—how closely it encompasses us on all sides. Second causes extend no way at all; they can account for nothing, effect nothing. I always saw that there was something amiss with Hume's famous argument against miracles, but I did not well know what, now I do; and now I feel the full force of your sentence that it is 'essentially atheistical.' That imposing term, the laws of nature, may easily lead to great misconception. The correspondence of Price and Priestley is further interesting, as a very beautiful exhibition of two characters of great but different endowments. Both have great acuteness, both great extent and variety of knowledge to bring, in illustration of their topic; but the caution of Price, fertile in objections, is remarkably contrasted with the precipitation of Priestley, with whom 'once to doubt,' was 'once to be resolved.' Priestley was the more original thinker, the greater genius, but he could not feel difficulties; neither indeed on his own favourite topics could Price, whose political theories warped even his calculations. I have a vivid memory of Priestley, the friend of my father, the dearer and more intimate friend of my aunt, Mrs. Barbauld. In his manners he had all the calmness and simplicity of a true philosopher; he was cheerful, even playful, and I still see the benignant smile with which he greeted us little ones. It pleased me to find you referring to him when you mention Berkeley. I know you have disapproved him on some points, you differ on many; but you are brothers in the assertion of intellectual freedom, and the earnest search after, and unhesitating avowal of truth! O! the noble, the glorious beings whom it has been my privilege to see and know! What would life be without the commerce of superior minds? what earth without the 'salt of the earth?' And let us rely upon it that times like these will bring forth men equal to them. France is decidedly taking a higher moral station; and those gallant Poles, they *will* redeem their country. Here, too, I see much to rejoice in. Great borough owners, the Duke of Norfolk at their head, coming forward with alacrity to make the sacrifice of them to their country. Lord Grey, whose canvassing of Northumberland in former days was called Coriolanus acted to the life—the author of the great bill. Lord J. Russell doing honour to his patriot line, and to the tuition of excellent Playfair, whom I once saw him, in an Edinburgh party, pulling along by the skirt of his coat, to be introduced to a lady of quality. (A little puny man is this Lord John, with a very small voice; sound sense his leading characteristic, and his style of expression simple, energetic, and rigidly concise.) In middle life there seems to be a good deal of real patriotism. Even members of close corporations have sided with the public, and what is more, so have some of the clergy. It is observable that there is now scarcely a whisper raised of the church in danger—when its peril was less, the cry of wolf was ten times louder. The lawyers for the most part take the reforming side. I scan not their motives. Both universities patronise darkness—but I blush most for the poets. A good while ago I saw Wordsworth in anxious museful mood, talking rather to himself than the company, as is his manner, against general education, and then bursting out, 'I don't see the use of all those prayers they make the children say after their *fugleman*. Either it will give them a profane aversion to the whole thing, or make them hypocrites,' in which I mutually agreed. Now I hear he says that if the bill passes he shall fly his country. But whither, alas? Revolution may pursue him to Spain or Russia. And so ends my voluminous budget.

Believe me ever, very truly yours,

L. AIKIN.

No. 13.

Hampstead: June 28, 1831.

It is so agreeable a thing to me, my dear distant friend, to communicate to you my impressions of passing events, with the assurance, too, that I am doing what is acceptable to you, that I have felt impatient to amass materials for a second letter. But from my parlour sofa, to which I have been very much confined, I could only send you what my neighbours brought to me; within the last two or three months alone I have been enabled to go a little into society myself, and I now offer you my gleanings.

Parliamentary reform is secure—the tories may give some trouble by their factious opposition, but that is all they can do. The *people* have shown themselves much more zealous and united in the cause, than public men on either side of the question were prepared to find them. The question therefore now is—what next? According to your prediction, we seem destined to proceed in the career of reformation until *all* our institutions shall have undergone a transformation. The friends of the Church dread that its turn will come next, and there are many tokens of it. A *stinging* 'Letter to the Archbishop of York' has appeared, and the demand for it has been such as the printer could not keep pace with. The author declaims somewhat idly, on the contrast between modern and primitive bishops—then inveighs with greater force against the alliance of Church and State, and its corrupting effects on the clergy; exposes their views broadly, and indignantly exclaims that a moral and religious people can no longer away with such unfaithful shepherds; and in the end boldly announces the fall of the Irish establishment within one year, and the English within ten years.

Mr. Beverley, the author, whom I know a little, is a very elegant classic, a good writer, and a gentleman; but wild and eccentric to the brink of insanity. After many vagaries, he has just turned Methodist preacher. His pamphlet contains nothing like a reasonable plan for the settlement of religious affairs, but it is deeply imbued with the spirit of the evangelical sect. It is professedly, at least, in love and reverence to religion that he would divorce the Church from the State, and place it on the common level of sects; and the extraordinary popularity of his piece seems to show that the large and zealous party to which he belongs are beginning to perceive how much the forms and the discipline of a church constructed on the model of the Romish—that is, on the taste of the middle ages—are at variance with the spirit of the present day, and hostile to their plans of empire over the minds of the people at large. I conceive that enthusiasm will always strive to burst through the fetters of articles and liturgies. I hear just now that the unpopularity of tithes is the chief cause of the currency of this piece. Another new and startling feature begins to appear. Hitherto both the Methodists and the Church Evangelicals have been distinguished by their indifference to civil liberty, and their attachment to 'the powers that be;' lately they seem to have entered into coalition with the radicals—at least, the lower class of Methodists, consisting chiefly of journeymen mechanics, and other labourers in towns, are engaged in the *strikes* for wages which have been so frequent and formidable, and which their masters regard as the worst sign of radicalism.

The Marquis of Londonderry, a great coal owner in the North, went lately and demanded a conference with the leader of the Newcastle *turn-outs*. He was referred to a person who proved to be a Methodist preacher, and who absolutely insisted upon the Marquis joining him in prayer (an exercise to which his lordship is little addicted), before he would proceed to business.

I own I am not quite pleased with the prospect of a second reign of the saints, for their rigor and intolerance go beyond the high church themselves; but there would be hope, I think, if the Establishment were overthrown, or considerably shaken, that a liberal party in religion might rise in some strength. I believe it is already pretty numerous, but shy of showing itself.

In the intervals of politics we talk of the Christian Brahmin, Ram-Mohun-Roy. All accounts agree in representing him as a person of extraordinary merit. With very great intelligence and ability, he unites a modesty and simplicity which win all hearts. He has a very great command of the language, and seems perfectly well versed in the political state of Europe, and an ardent well-wisher to the cause of freedom and improvement everywhere. To his faith he has been more than a martyr. On his conversion to Christianity his mother cursed him, and his wife (or wives) and children all forsook him. He had grievous oppressions to endure from the Church party on turning Unitarian. This was at Calcutta; here it is determined to court him. Two bishops have noticed him, and the East India Company show him all civilities. But his heart is with his brethren in opinion, with whom chiefly he spends his time. I hear of him this remarkable saying, That the three countries in Europe which appear even less prepared than Asia for a liberal system of religion, are Spain, Portugal, and England.

You will read, I think with interest, and in part with great satisfaction, Godwin's new volume, entitled 'Thoughts on Man.' Probably, it will prove the last fruit of his mind, for he is now rather nearer eighty than seventy, and I believe declining. With all his extravagances of opinion, some of which in the early part of his career did considerable mischief and threatened more, I have always entertained a respect for some parts of his character, as well as a high admiration of his powers; and felt sincere pity for the long misfortunes in which partly his own errors, but still more the proscription of society, have involved him. I believe he justly describes himself in his new work as 'one who early said to truth, go on, whithersoever thou leadest I am prepared to follow.' And is not this of itself a noble character of a man? It was remarkable in him that the reasoning powers seemed to have been developed long before the sensitive part of his nature. Thus his system was originally constructed with a total disregard of the passions, the affections, and almost the instincts of mankind. But it was beautiful to observe him, in his own experience of the tenderest ties of life, gradually expanding his groundwork to give admission to private and partial affections, and at length doing, as it were, public penance for the slanders which he had uttered against them in his days of ignorance. Those noble and rare virtues amongst the founders and champions of systems—candour and ingenuousness, have always attended him. And they have produced to him good fruit. They have enabled him, after discarding one error after another, to work out for himself principles which, in the midst of degrading embarrassments, and even of domestic dishonour, have preserved to himself respect, philanthropy, and cheering views of the character and destination of man. This volume is a repository of thoughts on many subjects, often I think original, often just, as well as striking, and frequently expressed with great eloquence. He everywhere shows himself 'lenior et melior.' Do not almost all men grow better as they grow older? I was pleased to find poet Crabbe maintaining that they do, which from the tone of his writings I did not expect. Have you ever met with any writings of

Paul Louis Courier? If not, you will know all about him, from the very able notice of him and his works which appeared some time ago in the 'Edinburgh Review.' I have just been reading a selection of his political pamphlets, and with extraordinary admiration. His style is like that of Pascal, but still more lively and striking. A sharp thorn he must have been in the sides of the restored Bourbons, with their priest and emigrant faction—and it was this, probably, which caused his assassination. I had no knowledge till I read his pieces, how the system of the restoration had worked—but the oppression was terrible, especially in the provinces remote from the control of the public opinion of Paris. The maires and préfets, themselves slaves of the court, the ministers, or the Jesuits, were so many despots over the peasantry and middle class, and carried on a frightful persecution against the means and the principles of the revolution. I see here abundant explanation and vindication of the revolution of last July, and I judge the men who planned and achieved it to have been true benefactors to their country. Courier strongly asserts what you likewise hold, the vast improvement of the national character since 1789. Possessed of personal liberty, and a share in the soil of his country, the peasant has became industrious almost to excess, frugal, and, generally speaking, moral—he has the virtues of a labourer in exchange for the vices of a laquais, or the abjectness of a serf. It is from intimate views of private life in various ages and countries that the *moral* of political history is alone to be derived—and without this what is the value of long tales of wars and conquests, and one king deposing and succeeding another, and republics changed into monarchies, and monarchies into republics? This principle has been always in my view in writing my 'King Charles,' and will impart, I think, its chief merit to my book; that is, should health and vigour be lent me for its completion. I have hope of it now, but I have been sorely tried by repeated disappointments on this head, and sometimes I have reached the very verge of despondency, and I have wished for the termination of a suffering and useless existence—my spirit beat itself against the bars of its cage. Then again I have called to my aid all I could summon of philosophy and religion, and I have soothed my soul by prayer.

I should like to know what you take to be the origin of the almost universal belief amongst mankind of a future state—was there, think you, a revelation to our first progenitors, of which all nations preserved some tradition? Or did it result from the reasonings of man upon the moral differences between individuals of the human race, not always accompanied here by corresponding rewards and punishments? Or was the wish for reunion with departed friends father to that belief? Or is it (with Locke's pardon) an innate idea, an instinct? I think there is something mysterious—something, if I may so express myself, *sui generis*, in so strong and general a persuasion contrary to all appearances, and unsupported by any real analogies. I should like to believe it a revelation, but there are difficulties.

I must not conclude without telling you some news of yourself. A friend of mine, just returned from Geneva, met there M. Vincent, Protestant minister at Nismes, a liberal and worthy man, who deplored the ignorance and narrowness of his flock, still buried in the gloom of Calvinism. He had set up a journal, in which by mingling theology with literary criticism and general topics, he was gently insinuating into them more enlightened notions. My friend asked if he knew your writings, and finding he did not, she gave him several of them. In the first number of his journal, after his return, appeared as the leading article a translation of your sermon on the resemblance of man to his Maker. Thus the good seed is sown—you may water it if you think proper. I hear from further evidence, that in several parts of France a simple form of Protestant worship, with liberal doctrine, would be highly acceptable to the people.

Have you heard of our absurd sect of Millenarians? Some say the end of the world is to be in the year 1860, others only give us to 1836, and one gentleman has actually turned his property into an annuity for six years.

Pray let me hear particularly of your health.

Yours, with the truest esteem,

L. AIKIN.

No. 14.

Hampstead: Sept. 6, 1831.

Dear Sir—I cannot longer refrain from acknowledging your last welcome letter, although I suppose you must have received one of mine soon after you wrote. There is always topic enough, since the interests of all mankind are ours. Just now my feelings are more cosmopolite than usual; I take a personal concern in a *third* quarter of the globe, since I have seen the excellent Ram-Mohun-Roy. I rejoice in the hope that you will see him some time, as he speaks of visiting your country, and to know you would be one of his first objects. He is indeed a glorious being,—a true sage, as it appears, with the genuine humility of the character and with more fervour, more sensibility, a more engaging tenderness of heart than any *class* of character can justly claim. He came to my house, at the suggestion of Dr. Boott, who accompanied him, partly for the purpose of meeting Mrs. Joanna Baillie, and discussing with her the Arian tenets of her book. He mentions the Sanscrit as the mother language of the Greek, and said that the expressions of the New Testament most perplexing to an European, were familiar to an Oriental acquainted with this language and its derivations, and that to such a person the texts which are thought to support the doctrine for the pre-existence, bear quite another sense. She was a little alarmed at the erudition of her antagonist, and slipped out at last by telling him that his interpretations were too subtle for an unlearned person like herself. We then got him upon subjects more interesting to me—Hindoo laws, especially those affecting women. He spoke of polygamy as a crime, said it was punishable by their law, except for certain causes, by a great fine; but the Mussulmans did not enforce the fine, and their example had corrupted Hindoos; *they* were cruel to women, the Hindoos were forbidden all cruelty. Speaking of the abolition of widow-burning by Lord W. Bentinck, he fervently exclaimed, 'May God *load* him with blessings!' His feeling for women in general, still more than the admiration he expressed of the mental accomplishments of English ladies, won our hearts. He mentioned his own mother, and in terms which convinced us of the falsehood of the shocking tale that she burned herself for his apostasy. It is his business here to ask two boons for his countrymen—trial by jury, and freedom for British capitalists to colonise amongst them. Should he fail in obtaining these, he speaks of ending his days in America. The dominion we hold over India is perhaps the most striking circumstance of greatness belonging to our little island. Your acknowledgment of England for the first country in the world very much delighted me. Yes, with all its evils, all its errors, it is a land to be proud of. I have always felt with you on the calamitousness of any violent change amongst us. As long as I can remember, and through the times when French example had most influence, all the best friends of liberty and their country, at least, its wisest friends, have constantly held that our evils were not nearly great enough to risk a revolution for their removal; and now, when so many peaceable and gradual reforms are taking place, the point is so very clear that none can wish for troubled waters but those who would fish in them. You think we shall escape this danger through the moderation of the higher classes. We have a farther and perhaps a stronger security in the curious manner in which all our different ranks, classes, sects, and parties, are *dove-tailed* into each other, or, if you please, matted together, which precludes the possibility of such a clear separation of one from another, as took place between the privileged and the unprivileged orders in France. It is an inestimable advantage that we have nothing answering to *noblesse;* that with us the younger sons of the highest peers sink back into the ranks, undistinguished except by the vague boast of blood or family, which now stands for little or nothing; whilst on the other hand, the lowest birth is no obstacle to the attainment of the full honours and privileges of the peerage. Voltaire somewhere remarks, 'In England, if the king makes his banker a peer, everybody, even the highest noble, gives him his title. With us, though Bernard is a real marquis, more than hundreds who are so named, who would not laugh to think of calling him marquis?' Thus our aristocracy is in a perpetual state of flux, and no one can say in any struggle who would or would not join its standard. The tory party, again, is far from coinciding with any possible description of the aristocracy; it excludes the Dukes of Sussex, Norfolk, Bedford, &c., and includes the greater part of the London aldermen and most provincial corporations. Even the clergy are not all *serviles,* for some of them depend on whig patrons. Neither are all tories boroughmongers, nor all boroughmongers tories. The High Church indeed are nearly all Tories, and Unitarians almost unanimously reformers, but the Church Evangelicals, and all other sects of dissenters, are divided. Our debates are, I believe, ably reported, but I wonder not that they disappoint you. The house will not listen with patience to general principles, they are supposed to be taken for granted, and the ability of the debaters is often shown most in a kind of àpropos of time and person, in hints and allusions, skilful thrusts and dexterous wards, which none but the initiated can appreciate. Of late the anti-reformers talk merely to consume time, and now and then to damage the ministers in public opinion. Yes, we have many evils which lie quite out of the reach of parliamentary reform, and the extreme inequality of conditions is the one which must weigh the most heavily of all upon the humane and thinking mind. Probably it is an inseparable concomitant of commerce, manufactures, and a high state of luxurious refinement. Bad institutions and some combinations of political circumstances, however, have extremely aggravated the evil, and no doubt opposite influences may mitigate it, as I trust we may in time experience. I can trace much of the progress of pauperism to two particular sources, one of which has been but little noticed, and the other scarcely at all in public. The first was the anxiety of Mr. Pitt to keep the lower classes in good humour during the war against French principles, which led him to give to the system of legal relief its present pernicious extent, and to lay the foundation of the fatal practice of ekeing out wages by parish alms, which the landholders improvidently concurred in, from the selfish and short-sighted notion that wages once raised could not be lowered again, but that alms might be withheld when temporary causes of distress should cease. The other cause is connected with the spread and the converting spirit of the evangelicals. Ever since Hannah More published her 'Cælebs,' it has been held by a large party the indispensable duty of ladies— girls even, to spend much of their time in visiting the dwellings of the poor, inquiring into and ministering to their spiritual and temporal wants. Apparently, great good would result from these charitable offices to all parties, but you well know our national propensity to run everything to a fashion—a rage, and the result has been a great and pernicious excess. A positive *demand* for misery was created by the incessant eagerness manifested to relieve it. In many places the poor, those amongst them especially who have known how to put on a little saintliness, have been actually pampered and rendered like the indoor menials of the wealthy, lazy luxurious discontented lying and worthless. Men have been encouraged in squandering their wages in drink and dissipation, by the assurance that the good ladies would not suffer their families to want; women have slackened their efforts to provide decent clothing for their children—improvidence has become characteristic of both. These evils, however, begin to be felt pretty widely, and I expect 'the fashion of benevolence' is beginning to abate. You complain that our restlessness does not carry us to the West Indian Islands. Two things are against it, the length of voyage, and the shrinking abhorrence we all feel from the sight of slavery, but that senator would deserve praise who should defy them both in the cause of humanity. I have known these isles resorted to by consumptive invalids, and in one case within my knowledge, with complete success. I sincerely congratulate you on the benefit which Mrs. Channing has derived from her residence in the tropics, and grieve that it has not done more for yourself. Would that you would both exchange your inclement skies for our milder ones, before another fearful winter sets in. You should pass the colder months in our Montpelier—Bonchurch, in the Isle of Wight—where a friend of mine, given over in Lancashire, has been marvellously surmounting her disease; the better seasons we would enjoy your society here. Pray think of it; health is even more than country, and is not this, too, your country?

We have little or nothing doing in literature; politics absorb us wholly. The state of the continent is an object of just anxiety. I dread beyond everything the demon of military glory, which in all ages has possessed the French nation; and, combined with their treachery and love of intrigue, has always rendered them bad and dangerous neighbours. I do my best not to regard them as *natural enemies*, but it is difficult. They hate us, and with some cause too. I want to hear that your pen is again at work; we cannot afford to be deprived of its labours. You may still do much more for us, much as you have done already. As for me, I proceed in my task very, very slowly, want of health and its concomitant want of energy, the cause. Just now, however, I am in spirits, I have medical permission to make a little quiet week's tour, under the watchful care of a kind brother, and we are going to view our English vintage, the Kentish hop-picking, also to see pretty Tunbridge and make a pilgrimage to Penshurst of the Sidneys, or perhaps to Hever Castle, the birthplace of Anne Boleyn. Do you not a little envy us the historic recollections of an old country? I was present at the splendid spectacle of the opening of New London Bridge. It was covered half way over with a grand canopy, formed of the flags of all nations, under which dined His Majesty and about two thousand of his loving subjects. The river was thronged with gilded barges, and boats covered with streamers and crowded with gaily-dressed people; the shores were all alive with the multitude. In the midst of the gay show I looked down the stream upon the old deserted, half-demolished bridge, silent remembrancer of seven centuries. I thought of it fortified with a lofty gate at either end, and encumbered with a row of houses on each side. I beheld it the scene of tournaments; I saw its barrier closed against the rebel Wyatt, and wished myself a poet for its sake.

Pray believe me yours, with most sincere regard,

L. AIKIN.

No. 15.

Hampstead: Oct. 23, 1831.

My dear Friend—Your two welcome letters have reached me, both on the same day; of their various contents and of the Farrers I shall speak by-and-bye, but the urgent thing is to enter upon the discussion of Priestley to which you invite me. I have long wished to get you there. I have just been talking him over with my brother Arthur, who was his pupil at Hackney, and had both the opportunity of knowing, and the mind for appreciating him. He says that certainly in one sense Priestley was *self-satisfied*. He had emancipated himself from the yoke of Calvinism, which was little made for his sunny temper; and with such immovable, such entire conviction, he had settled it with himself that all things must at all times be working for the best, because ordained and guided by the wisest and best of beings; that neither any misfortunes of his own, nor any disappointments to those causes which he espoused, were able to make deep or lasting impressions on his spirits. He was an optimist both by disposition and system, but from *Epicurean* tranquillity no one could be further. He was the most active of men, he could not have lived inactive, and to the propagation of this, his great principle, there was nothing he was not ready to sacrifice. My aunt has said of him, with as much truth as brilliancy, that 'he followed truth as a man who hawks follows his sport—at full speed, straightforward, looking only upward, and regardless into what difficulties the chase may lead him.' This sanguine spirit prompted him to adopt the maxim, that no effort is lost; he firmly believed that all discussion must end in the advancement of truth, and here he could never perceive any mischief or danger in the fullest exposure of any doctrine which he believed. He was constitutionally incapable of doubt; what he held, he held implicitly for the time; but Arthur says he was not tenacious upon anything which did not affect his great principle of optimism— that is, of necessity. It may be considered that his system of the origin of ideas was derived from Locke and enlarged upon by Hartley, who also maintained necessity, and both these were revered names to follow. His system of materialism was more original, and more obnoxious, but his own faith in a future state being fixed on gospel promises, was quite unshaken by it; and he expected, I say not how wisely, to enhance the value of Christianity, and compel, as it were, the deist to accept of it, by proving that there was no hope of immortality without it. All these doctrines, too, were in a manner sanctified to him by the often ingenious, often powerful use which he made of them in his attacks upon what he regarded as the most mischievous corruptions of Christianity. If he had promulgated these opinions from vain glory, no doubt it would have destroyed his moral greatness; but as by the concurring judgments, I believe of all who had the best means of knowing, his motives were purely reverence to God and good-will to men, I cannot agree that anything but imprudence ought to be imputed to him by those who may most distrust their truth and tendency. His private life was radiant with goodness. He was excellent in every relation, exemplary as a pastor, particularly for the unwearied pains he took with the young, for whom he composed catechisms and delivered lectures. His Birmingham flock has never lost the character of devout zeal which he impressed upon it. His disinterested love of truth manifested itself in his scientific pursuits. The moment he made a discovery he threw it before the public; not waiting to form a perfect system which would have redounded to his own glory, but eager to set other minds on the track of investigation, and provided truth were discovered, careless by whom. In charity and forgiveness of injuries he was a perfect Christian. 'So kind was his temper,' said my father, 'that he would not have hurt his bitterest enemy.' Think, too, of his zeal for civil liberty, and the obloquy and danger which he braved for it, and make allowances for the situation of a reformer rendered more positive by often dishonest opposition. No, he had a sanguineness of temper incompatible with true judgment, and perhaps with deep feelings, but I cannot deny him moral greatness; he would certainly have laid down his life for his faith, and for mankind.

The doctrine of necessity has, no doubt, its dangers for inactive and self-indulgent tempers; and though I know not how to resist by reasoning the arguments which very long since rendered me an earnest advocate for it, I begin to *feel* against it. In affliction I have found that it rather rebuked murmuring than afforded positive comfort. I know not how any one contrives to hold it and the scriptures together; moral responsibility is surely implied in their promises and threatenings; but, in fact, some of the necessarian Christians dilute and explain them away till they come to very little. What I can least afford to part with is the idea of being approved or disapproved by a heavenly as by an earthly parent or superior; of living 'as ever in a great taskmaster's eye.' It has sometimes overwhelmed my heart with a sense of desolation unutterably oppressive, to think, that by no efforts, no sacrifices, no performance of arduous duties with cheerful patience, it would be possible, if necessity were true, to gain the *moral* approbation of the Deity, without which I could not think of God as of a *father*. Creator, I could call Him, and benefactor, but not father, that dearest and tenderest of names. Your views on these subjects are so much more congenial to my feelings, that they have, I believe, very nearly become my own without my being aware of it. I am very much pleased with your account of the origin of a belief in futurity; it accords with my previous ideas. We cannot well believe in God without expecting that He will sometimes come, as it were, to an explanation with us on all the things which so perplex us here. In appealing to an inward light thus far I think we are justified—it is rather dangerous ground, however; enthusiasm and superstition are very apt to take advantage of that inlet, as in the interesting case of Mrs. F. Of the Quakers, whom it was formerly my lot to know many rather intimately, I have always observed, that owing, I believe, to their want of professional instructors in religion and morals, either as preachers or writers, they are much more ignorant of first principles on these subjects than the members of other communities. Whenever they begin to enquire for themselves, their unpractised understandings soon get bewildered, and if they quit their own society, it is usually for Methodism, Moravianism, or some other system where reason has least to do. A vagueness of thought, with a turn for mystery, almost always adheres to them, and it is very well if, in the midst of so much confusion, they form or retain very clear notions of moral right or wrong.

The Dr. King you enquire about Mrs. Joanna Baillie knows; she says he is very upright and very benevolent, but not a man of sense. His plan, I believe, has been given up, though at first it seemed to work well. Miss Mitford I never saw, but I think her 'Village' a very pleasing picture, and quite true to nature. She lives in a cottage with an old father whom she dotes upon. I hear she is very happy in her seclusion, and her friends speak of her with much affection; in London circles she rarely appears.

I was disappointed of the little Kentish journey I mentioned in my last by the sudden illness of my brother; but when he recovered I found myself better too; and 'King Charles' is proceeding, though not the better for our political crisis, which so fills my mind that I fear its giving some tinge, or some vices to my representation of the events of a former period of revolution.

No public event ever oppressed me like this rejection of the bill, with grief and fear. Delay, for it is but delayed, must evidently increase all its dangers. It gives opportunity for the intrigues of violent and designing men on both sides. The tories are frightened now at what they have done. Many of them would never have given that vote but with the expectation of overawing the King and making ministers resign; they looked upon it as little more than a trial of strength between Grey and Wellington; they now know how the people look upon it, and how staunch the King is. The bishops are regarded as persons insane; they can never more appear on the scene. We feel ourselves standing on a volcano. With all this I love my country far too well to despair of her. I believe that the moderate party is strong enough to hold in check the two extremes, provided it *exerts* itself strenuously and skilfully for that purpose.

You have touched upon what must be the most grievous of all topics to an American who loves his country— slavery. We who praise republics, hang our heads when it is mentioned. There is nothing by which Americans are so apt to give an ill-impression of themselves here, as by unguarded expressions on this subject. The only time I saw Bishop Hobart, he said to me, in defence of creating new slave states, that 'a man must be allowed to make the best of his property.' There was a general shudder.

I turned away, and addressed him no more, and the hospitable master of the house never gave him a second invitation. Another American sometimes gave us unpleasant feelings simply by speaking of planters as his friends or acquaintances; we regard them as persons not to be mentioned without a necessity. I conceive that the greatest political difficulties and dangers which menace you are from this source: the crime will bring its own punishment.

It delights me to hear that you are writing again. Never can you put pen to paper without doing much good, and giving great delight. In a general survey of the state of the world facts will be of use to you as the grounds of reasoning; and I will take care to store up for you any I think useful. Mr. Whishaw is just returned from France, and I will keep my letter open till after to-morrow, in hopes of something worth writing.—No, he has nothing to tell me except that he found Paris so unpleasant from tumults that he left it in three days. But I have been questioning another friend, who has passed there the last year and half, on the state of religion. He says that, generally speaking, there is *no* religion at Paris. The Romish religion is considered obsolete, and very few but women attend the churches. The priests are from a low class, with a very small stipend from the state, which he believes their hearers never add to. He knows of no spread of Protestantism; some old congregations of reformed there are with Genevan ministers, who are by much the most eloquent preachers he ever heard. One congregation of English unitarians, chiefly supported by Americans. These you doubtless know of, also that they have engaged an additional minister to preach in French. I hear from others that at Dijon a Catholic congregation went over in a body to the reformed; that similar conversions have taken place at Lyons. The provinces are less irreligious than Paris. You have probably heard that the Genevan unitarians have been at length provoked to enter into controversy with the calvinists, who were carrying all before them.

I have been dining with two clergymen, who to my astonishment began a discussion upon the exclusion of bishops from the House of Lords, which they both thought impending. One said it would be a good thing, which the other did not quite deny, but thought this was *not the time* to strip the Church of honours. One of these was a reformer, the other certainly a tory; but being both, I believe, sincerely religious and honest men, they were equally ashamed of the conduct of the bishops, and sensible that temptation ought to be removed from them by the prohibition of translations and other means. There is extreme bitterness all over the country against the clergy. A gentleman who had been canvassing Liverpool for your friend Thorneley, was repeatedly told by methodists and calvinistic dissenters, 'We are willing to vote for a unitarian, because he will be reasonable about the Church.' A fearful sign for the establishment when foes league against her! In the midst of this ferment the lower classes exhibit a growing depravity which gives true patriots many a heartache. None would wish to live in an *age of transition* such as we have fallen upon, none at least but the young and ardent, or those whose faith in the high destinies of man is firm as yours. I brace my mind as I can. In the storm there is sublimity, high thoughts are stirred, and even a woman may be called upon for the exercise of high virtues.

Farewell, my dear and honoured friend,

Lucy Aikin.

No. 16.

Hampstead: Dec. 8, 1831.

I feel as if I were in some danger of becoming importunate to you by the frequency of my letters; but, to converse with my 'guide, philosopher, and friend,' has now become with me, not a mere indulgence, but a want, and I trust in your patience. It is advisedly that I have called you my guide. I daily discover more and more how much I have come under the influence of your mind, and what great things it has done, and I trust is still doing, for mine. Let me gratify the feelings of a thankful heart by entering into a few particulars on this subject. I was never duly sensible, till your writings made me so, of the transcendent beauty and sublimity of Christian morals; nor did I submit my heart and temper to their chastening and meliorating influences. In particular, the spirit of unbounded benevolence which they breathe was, I own it, a stranger to my bosom; far indeed was I from looking upon all men as my brethren. Many things prevented it. A life, for the most part, of domestic seclusion; studious pursuits, and something of the pride and fastidiousness they are apt to bring; and more than all, the atmosphere of a sect and a party, which it was my fate to breathe from childhood, narrowed my affections within strait limits. Under the notion of a generous zeal for freedom, truth, and virtue, I cherished a set of prejudices and antipathies which placed beyond the pale of my charity not the few, but the many, the mass of my compatriots. I shudder now to think how *good* a *hater* I was in the days of my youth. Time and reflection, a wider range of acquaintance, and a calmer state of the public mind, mitigated by degrees my bigotry; but I really knew not what it was to open my heart to the human race until I had drunk deeply into the spirit of your writings.

Neither was my intercourse with my Creator such as to satisfy fully the wants of the soul. I had doubts and scruples, as I have before intimated, respecting prayer, which weighed heavily on my spirit. In times of the most racking anxiety, the bitterest grief, I offered, I dared to offer, nothing but the folded arms of resignation—submission rather. So often had I heard, and from the lips of some whom I greatly respected, the axiom, as it was represented, that no evil could exist in the creation of a perfectly benevolent being, if he were also omnipotent, that my reliance on Providence was dreadfully shaken by a vague notion of a nature of things by which deity itself was limited. How you have dispossessed me of this wretched idea I do not well know—but it is gone; I feel, I feel that He can and will bless me, even by means of what seem at present evil and suffering. You have shown me clearly a Father in heaven, and for nothing earthly would I exchange the heavenly peace which this conviction brings. It is surely the highest reason to believe that our finite spirits can never think too well or hope too much of His infinity, provided only we fail not in our parts.

From the time that I first became your reader, I had a kind of anticipation that you would work considerable effects upon me; but it has been by slow degrees, and laborious processes, and hard struggles with deep-rooted prepossessions, that I have fitted my mind to give reception to so many of your views; and, but for the deep interest in them which your letters assisted to maintain, my resolution would have failed me ere the task was thus far accomplished. You have wished to interest in religion minds by which it was apt to be coldly regarded. With respect to mine, you have all that you desire; for the present I am little interested in any other subject; or at least, I view all others as connected with this, and subordinate to it. May God reward you! You have given me a new being.

All the principles that can support or elevate the soul are greatly needed with us now, to meet the tempests gathering thick and dark around us. Pestilence advances, revolution threatens. With respect to the first, I feel only the dread of surviving those I love. A medical brother pledged to go wherever called, is a great anxiety; but I will not dwell on possible evils. The poor in some European countries through which this scourge has passed, were possessed with the notion that it was purposely diffused by the higher classes to thin the numbers of the lower. I doubt not there was *talk* which showed at least profound indifference in the rich and great to this result, and unless people set a strong guard on their tongues, the same suspicions may arise here. It is felt that we have many spare hands. I have heard a good man say, that a decimation of London, if the lots fell *well*, would be no bad thing. But luckily there can be no security that the lots would so fall, if once the infection gained ground; and *therefore* we are cleansing the dwellings of the poor, and wrapping their persons in flannel; but is there not something frightful in this worthlessness of the lives of one class to another? What wonder that kings have made no spare of the blood of their subjects? I perceive more and more clearly what you first pointed out to me— the darkening effects of the spirit of aristocracy on the mind, its hardening influence on the heart. Distinct classes can never feel for each other as members of one body; and, in the want of this sympathy, all anti-social vices, oppression, arrogance, cruelty in the rich, envy, fraud, rapacity, and brutal insolence in the poor, take root and flourish. I am convinced that the deep dread with which the working classes begin here to inspire their *betters* is extremely wholesome; even such disgraceful excesses as those of Bristol have their use as warnings. Yet it is curious, though sad, to see how men drive away unwelcome thoughts, and hug again their old delusions. One day a threatened radical meeting in the suburbs puts all the magistrates and gentry on the alert; the police are arrayed, special constables sworn in, the rabble dispersed, the popular orators disappointed of audience for that time; and the next day you shall hear the aristocracy round their dinner-table confessing that some reform must take place, but assuring themselves and each other that a little will satisfy all the well disposed, and concluding that, 'if the people will not be satisfied with moderate reform (that is, something less than the bill) they must be bayonetted.' I give you the very words used to me last week by a mild, amiable, indolent young man of fortune, and one who thinks great scorn to be called a tory. I begin to fear that if, I mean *when*, a struggle comes, that *dovetailing* of the classes into one another, in which I once confided, will be apt to give way. Yet there are noble examples of rich men, and even lords, who feel for the multitude. The Catholic peers have almost all sided with the people—by virtue, I suppose, of their want of attachment to the Church. It would shock you to be initiated into the abominations springing out of Church patronage. 'What will you do with your nephew?' said a friend of mine to a great coal-owner. 'Oh, if he turns out clever we shall make him a collier; if otherwise, we must put him into the Church.' When there is a family-living, commonly the most stupid of the boys, very often the most profligate, is made to take orders. In other professions success depends in some degree on merit. For the sake of electioneering interests, there is really *no man* whom a patron will scruple to entrust with cure of souls —provided only a bishop can be induced to ordain him—

and there is always some bishop of notorious facility. I think there must, ere long, be considerable concessions to public opinion, with respect to patronage as well as tithes; and these being reformed, doctrine will next come in question, I imagine. The substitution of popular election for patronage, and the abolition of pluralities, would infallibly procure us a more diligent, more moral, more independent clergy, and one better instructed in theology, and consequently more scrupulous of teaching what they could not themselves believe. After all, these are animating times to live in; they offer hopes well worth all the fears they bring. A friend just arrived from Italy brings me some curious particulars of the state of things. The Pope has nearly lost all temporal authority out of Rome. Bologna has refused, in the most respectful manner, either to admit his troops, or to pay him any tribute. What is strange, the Roman censorship, though extremely jealous of religious heresies, takes no cognisance of political ones. You might almost publish there Paine's 'Rights of Man.' In Tuscany, on the contrary, you may print what you please on religion, but in politics you are much restricted. A tragedy on the subject of the Sicilian Vespers had been repeatedly performed at Florence with immense applause. The French ambassador applied to have it prohibited on account of the reflections it contained on the French nation. 'You need not stir,' said the Austrian ambassador to him; 'the letter is indeed directed to you, but its contents are for me.' The representation was not forbidden, but it was long before the author could obtain license to print it. At last he did, on condition that it should not be in a separate form, but stuck in a thick octavo of his other works. He contrived to take off a few separate copies, however, and gave my friend one, which I have just read. It certainly breathes a strong spirit of resistance to foreign domination; and also utters very intelligibly that earnest desire for the union of all Italy under one Government which now possesses her best patriots. Many of them, my informant says, would not object, on certain terms, to see the whole country under the dominion of Austria, which has the sense to govern Lombardy with a good deal of mildness and liberality. They hate the French.

The more I see of Rammohun Roy, the more I admire and even venerate him. Dr. Wallich of Calcutta, himself an admirable person, tells me that he stands quite alone amongst his countrymen, with neither equal nor second in talent, in integrity, and in enlargement of mind. He has provoked the bitterest enmity of the Hindoo priests by his attacks upon their gainful idolatries: but Dr. W. says that, should he return safe and well, supported by the distinguished favour of the company, and successful in his patriotic objects, a shock would be given to the whole Hindoo system, which would go near to overthrow it. He gave us this trait of the good rajah. In conversation at the house of a Scotch gentleman at Calcutta, the question happened to arise, if two persons were drowning of whom you could save only one, and one were your countryman, would you not save him in preference? 'Certainly I should,' said the Scotchman. The rajah reprobated the idea of making a choice between the lives of any two fellow-creatures, at such a moment—he would save the nearest. 'No,' he added, after a pause; 'there is a case in which I should make a choice. If one were a woman, I should rescue her.' And this from a man brought up amidst widow-burning and the exposure of female infants! I have seen a good deal of the Farrars; Mrs. F. and I are sworn friends, and I have made her tell me a vast deal about you and yours; I can now fancy your happy fireside. She says your boy and girl are perfect specimens in their kind. I shall be anxious to hear how the winter agrees with you and Mrs. Channing. With us the weather is now almost oppressively warm, to the alarm of those who are dreading cholera. Nobody knows yet what our ministers are going to do about reform; but they have declared they *will* not fail again.

Ever yours, with the truest esteem,
L. AIKIN.

No. 17.

Hampstead: Feb. 22, 1832.

My dear Friend,—I have many, many thanks to return you for those two excellent letters I have had from you since I last wrote. Nothing so much interests and delights me as the spirit in which you write of us and our concerns. Call yourself 'a foreigner,' if you must—it is a cold name, and one which we never give to Americans; but yours is a filial heart to old England still, and beats true to her in all her trials and adversities.

If you have received two letters which I have written to you since the date of your last, you will have seen that I am still far from despairing of my country. I see dangers, indeed, many and of opposite kinds, and many more there must be which are invisible to me; I see the interests of various parties, sects, and classes in society roused into fierce opposition; I see all, the high as well as the low, exposed to peril, suffering under real evils and privations, and too generally disposed, by a short-sighted selfishness, to advance unreasonable claims, and to shift as much as possible of the burden from themselves to others; I see prejudice, ignorance, obstinacy at work, and in all classes too, to perpetuate bad feelings, urge on unprofitable courses, and resist wise and salutary reforms; I see, and with deep sorrow, much depravity in the lower classes, much too in the highest, and in the middle ones a sordid, grovelling selfishness, less scandalous, but scarcely less pernicious. But I see, on the other hand, much true patriotism, and in high places too; much philanthropy, much enlightenment, active zeal, and in some bosoms fortitude and devotedness, equal to any trials we can anticipate. There is also amongst all who have anything to lose a calculating coolness, a deliberate appreciation of present good, which is likely to range them almost universally on the side of peace and order. The long discussion of reform has certainly had its advantages. You may observe that the highest tories are now brought to admit that *some* there ought to be and must be. I firmly believe, that with more or less of modification the bill will now be carried; and with a popular House of Commons, whatever partial changes of ministers shall occur, and several are talked of, it is certain that many other salutary measures, now in preparation, will be brought in, and carried too.

The political unions seem to me to have lost ground since the affair of Bristol, and I do not in the least apprehend that they will be enabled to dictate to ministers or to Parliament, or materially to disturb the public peace. We have certainly in London no class of people capable of such deeds as the barricades of Paris. Our middling orders are men of peace, never drafted off by conscriptions; and as for our mob, they are profligate indeed, but seldom atrocious. I suspect you have been horror-struck, like some persons here, by the statements and descriptions of Gibbon Wakefield, but it is not on the word of an atrocious malefactor, seeking to rise again into something like credit, and also to sell a book, that frightful stories ought to be implicitly believed. I think, in short, that the general apprehension of a revolution will save us from the reality, and that better, not worse, times are approaching.

But what must I say to the heavy charge you bring

against all the rich, the powerful, the improved, for the mass of vice, ignorance, and misery which they have suffered to accumulate about the poor of this country? I have pondered the matter over and over, for I cannot lightly dismiss from my mind such an accusation from such a quarter; and this is the best answer my lights enable me to frame. In England—I dismiss for the present unhappy Ireland—apathy towards suffering fellow-creatures is not a common fault. You have truly said, that benevolence is one of our fashions. Political causes, misgovernment, and bad legislation have had by far the greatest share in producing evils for which benevolence, often misdirected, has found no effectual remedies.

It would require a pamphlet to expose all the particulars in which the administration of Mr Pitt and the statesmen of his school tended to the increase of the curse of pauperism. During the war the enhanced price of provisions ought to have been met by a corresponding advance in the wages of agricultural labour; but this the gentlemen, from mistaken views of their own interest, opposed. Mr. Pitt legalised the payment of wages in part out of the poor rate. In the southern and some midland counties, where this practice was adopted, continually increasing misery and degradation have ensued, and of late a desperate spirit of revenge, which is likely however to compel the adoption of effective remedies for the evil, some of which are already coming into operation. The fluctuations of commerce and manufactures; the transition from war to peace; the weight of taxation; the invasion of England by swarms of miserable Irish, who underbid our own working men in the already glutted labour market; the great extension of machinery; the general inclosure of commons, and the system of large farms, are some of the many causes which have fatally conspired to the same end; and you perceive that such of these as admit of counteraction are rather in the province of politicians and statesmen than of private individuals. That our legislation has not been idle in the cause, a slight survey of the objects of the greater part of the bills brought in every session would convince you. When the great reform is effected, you will see the result. Meantime I regard all that is, and all that can be done for the poor, as palliative merely, and sometimes not that. The pauper is robbed of half his virtues as surely as the slave. He loses self-respect, the most irreparable of all losses; and neither the alleviation of his physical wants, nor even the acquirement of knowledge when the means are not earned by his own honest labour, but conferred upon him as the alms of his superiors, have any tendency to raise him in the moral scale. Neither does religious or moral instruction, so conveyed, work its proper effect. It is received as a tax upon the dole which is expected to follow. The cant of religion has been widely diffused amongst our poor by these means, but of the spirit and power of godliness little indeed.

I am convinced that an effective missionary must begin with 'Silver and gold have I none.' He should be a poor man among the poor to reach their hearts and consciences. They have an incurable distrust of those who are called their betters in these matters—having indeed often seen religion perverted into an engine of state, or an auxiliary of the police. More good, I believe, is to be done in this country at present by striving to diffuse pure and elevated and liberal views on religion and virtue amongst the higher and middling classes, through whom they may gravitate to the lower, than by attempting at once to confront degradation in its deepest caverns; though I would by no means discourage the glorious few who feel in themselves a mission for these heroic efforts of philanthropy. But the greater part of our would-be teachers of the poor stand themselves in great need of becoming learners, especially of humility and meekness. There are of course many, very many of a better stamp; and I do look with a good deal of hope on the efforts now making for the establishment of Temperance Societies. But alas! how are we to cope with the evils of an already redundant and daily increasing population? And Ireland, Ireland!

I have laid out of my account another dire calamity with which we seem doomed to contend—the cholera. Reached us it has, beyond question, and a few days will decide whether it be an infection from some single source capable of being by due care extinguished, or whether it comes as an epidemic menacing myriads. In the most favourable case much distress will arise, nay it has already arisen, from the interruption of trade, by which thousands more must be thrown out of bread. But should it assume the character of a real pestilence, who can even imagine the confusion, the misery? Methinks I see the 'grim features' of Milton's own Death exulting that his 'famine shall be filled,' and of the million and half of human creatures congregated in and near our vast metropolis! A remedy it may indeed prove for our over-population—but what a remedy!

To contemplate such horrors with perfect composure, is a height of philosophy I by no means aspire to reach; but I trust I shall not be numbered with the panic-stricken. Hitherto, I have ever found that strength is given according to the call for it, to those who are not wanting to themselves. In the lives of those dear to me I am most vulnerable, but I bow to the Divine decrees; and I have been quite enough familiarised with affliction to know what precious medicine it contains. For myself, I have never at any period within my memory viewed death as a subject of dread; on the contrary, I have usually beheld it as an object of aspiration, and with a kind of solemn joy.

I believe that at any moment of my life I should have welcomed a call to die nobly. To expose myself to infection when duty or affection bade I have never hesitated yet, and I trust I shall not now.

It rejoices me to have been able successfully to vindicate to you the character and motives of Priestley. Too true it is, that we cannot spare even one from our list of worthies. I long for a fuller development of your delightful idea of our personal interest in the high qualities of others. It is quite a new thought to me, and opens to the most inspiring views. Even in this state of being, the effects of a high principle, a grand discovery, a sublime poem, a noble action, extend quite out of sight and calculation. In other states they may reach to the whole race of man— I see nothing against it. Oh! who would bear the sight and sense of human misery—that has indeed a soul to comprehend and feel it—without the cordial of high hopes and noble aspirations! My thoughts are ever returning thither, to the invisible world, and thanks to you, they never return thence without bringing in their train deep peace.

At length I am able to send you Mackintosh's 'Essay,' and I must give you the long tale which hangs by it. I long since *begged* Mr. Whishaw to *beg* one for you of the author, which he promised; but accident prevented his doing so till Sir James had, as he believed, not one left; but he was not quite certain, for he had been moving, and his books were in confusion. To add to the chance of sending one by the Farrars I then applied to Rees, my bookseller, who said with alacrity, 'I will write to the Edinburgh publisher, and if there is one left, Dr. Channing shall have it.' He was as good as his word, and has sent one, which I see he hopes will be received in the nature of a peace-offering, from 'self and partners proprietors of the Edinburgh Review.' For the man has grace, for a bookseller, and besides he wants to stop my mouth about the odious article.

But in the meantime, the report of your admiration of his history so exceedingly gratified Sir James Mackintosh that he renewed his search, found a copy, and gave it to Mr. Whishaw to bring to me. It would have been most ungacious to refuse it, I have therefore accepted it for you; meaning very honestly to keep it myself; which will be great luck for me, since it is not to be bought separately. I should have been mortified beyond expression if I had failed to procure one for you; and I hope it will not disappoint you, but I expect it will *pose* your young readers more than once.

Have you seen the spirited sketch of the history of the Italian republics by Sismondi, in Lardner's Cyclopædia? I think it very good indeed; in a high republican strain, like all his works; and the English very good for a *foreigner* (not being an American). The author is now on a visit to Sir James Mackintosh, his brother-in-law, and I am to have the pleasure of meeting him at a neighbour's in a few days, should I be well enough; but that is a great doubt, for I am a very poor creature, and seldom able to indulge myself with going into parties. The winter, however, has been remarkably mild with us; I hope it may have been so with you likewise, and that you have been able to retain the precious power of occupying yourself for the public.

I have written you an enormous letter, and I fear a dull one; I doubt that you will think too that I look coldly upon plans for the benefit of the most numerous classes. But it is not so; I only think that the political ferment must subside a little before anything effectual can be done. Our ministers seem to be dealing vigorously with the ills of Ireland; peace and comfort there would remove many of our grievances. I will yet cling to the hoping side.

We are very loth to send you back the Farrars. They have pleased universally. Since Mr. Farrar has improved in health he has shown us that his talents are of no common order, and nothing can be more unassuming than his manners. Without any tincture of his favourite sciences, I always found that it was easy to engage him in conversation in which he appeared to take interest.

I will now at length release you.

Ever your sincere friend,
L. AIKIN.

No. 18.

Hampstead: April 7, 1832.

My excellent Friend,—Yours of Feb. 23 has just reached me. To find that the expression of my feelings respecting the effects of your writings had so gratified you, was delightful to me. But how is it that you can so underrate their power, that you can for a moment doubt the great, the inestimable good you are working on many minds in many lands? I must write to you a little more on this subject, and tell you what I think your greatest triumph, or at least that which most interests me, and it will lead me to a great topic hitherto untouched between us. The impression you have produced on the minds of *women* is one for which I bless God from the bottom of my heart. I need not tell you how precious your teaching is in the eyes of Joanna Baillie, and I have long since, I think, told you that admirable Mrs. Somerville was your zealous disciple (but make the Farrars tell you more of her). I have now to mention that you have another in Mrs. Marcet. This lady has published, but anonymously, so that her fame has been less than her merit and success—Conversations on Chemistry, on Political Economy, on Natural History, and on Botany—all elementary works of great solidity as well as elegance. She was the daughter of a wealthy Swiss merchant settled in London: her life has been almost equally divided between England and the continent; and her excellent qualities and rare powers of conversation give her great influence both here and in Geneva, which she now calls her home. She has a charming daughter married to Edward Romilly, 'Of virtuous father, virtuous son,' and from her I lately learnt that her sister, Madame Eugène De la Rive of Geneva, was engaged in translating some pieces of yours for the 'Bibliothèque Universelle,' a meritorious periodical published there. The best and most sensible women of my acquaintance are, with very few exceptions, converts to your views. Now, considering that proneness of women to the religious affections, which is so capable of being either exaggerated into fanaticism or depraved into bigotry, I regard it as a circumstance of immense public importance that such ennobling, touching, and at the same time *sober-minded* views should be so respectably patronised amongst *us*. Whilst you take thought for the human race, I concern myself chiefly with my own sex, and oh! that I could raise a prevailing voice against the manners, the maxims, the habits by which I see it fettered and debased! If I could engage you to plead in this great cause I should esteem it half won. But I am ignorant how far the same evils and defects are common to us and our Transatlantic sisters, and I want much to discuss this subject with you.

We modestly esteem ourselves the first of womankind for knowledge, for accomplishments, for purity of manners, and for all the domestic virtues. I am not sure that we are mistaken in supposing that the *union* of these recommendations is more frequent in England than elsewhere; but even granting us the whole, there is much, much to be added and to be corrected. Amid all that is put into the head, the soul, and very often the *reason*, starves.

Women are seldom taught to *think*. A prodigious majority never acquire the power of reasoning themselves or comprehending the force of arguments advanced by others. Hence their prejudices are quite invincible, their narrowness and bigotry almost inconceivable, and amidst a crowd of elegant acquirements, their thoughts are frivolous and their sentiments grovelling. Exceedingly few have any patriotism, any sympathy with public virtue. Private feelings, private interests engross them. They are even more insensible than you charge our public men with being of 'the greatness of the times in which we live.' Rammohun Roy has been justly scandalised at the want of zeal for the reform bill amongst the ladies, and I sometimes pensively ask myself whether the country could now supply many noble Lady Crokes to exhort a husband to follow his conscience in public matters, regardless of the worldly interests of herself and their children. Luxury makes great havoc with the lofty virtues, even in manly minds, and woman it quite unnerves, for the most part. You look with some jealousy on the principle of patriotism as hostile to universal philanthropy; but I am sure you will agree with me that it is better to love our country even partially and exclusively than to love nothing beyond our own firesides; and when public good and private interest interfere, to feel no generous impulse to sacrifice the less to the greater. I wish that more women were nurtured in, at least, the Latin classics, because from them they might imbibe *this* elevating sentiment, without which they can never deserve the *friendship*, whatever thay may obtain of the *love*, of noble-minded men. If you will turn to one of Mrs. Barbauld's 'Characters,' beginning—'Such were the dames of old heroic days' (it was written, by the way, for the mother of Mr. Benjamin Vaughan, a grand-looking old lady, whose figure I still can recal), you will fully understand what kind of spirit I long to inspire into my sex. Almost all my life this desire has been one of my strongest feelings. When a little girl I used to battle with boys about the Rights of Woman. Many years ago, I published 'Epistles on Women,' all to the same effect; and though I now think I dare say as ill as anybody of the *poetry* of that work, it contains many sentiments which I still cherish, and would give much to be enabled to disseminate. You may understand by this more distinctly what I meant by saying that the higher and middle classes required to be better taught themselves before they took in hand the instruction of the poor; and a great reason why I doubt of the good which women do in their visitations of cottages is, that I regard them for the most part as themselves the slaves of so many stupid and debasing prejudices. The theology of most of them is that of the thirty-nine articles, which you estimate as it deserves; and original sin and the atonement are the favourite themes of their lectures to the poor, even to children. Nay, our orthodox curate told me himself the other day that he had interfered to prevent the lady-managers of the infant school from giving the babies interpretations of prophecies, concerning the twelve tribes of Israel, to learn by heart! So undiscriminating is their reverence for all that refers to the contents of any part of the Bible! You know well, too, how the precepts of Christianity have been pressed into the service of a base submission to all established power.

I am interested in your anticipations concerning France. It is much to require me to wish her to *surpass* my own country; but I may truly say that in any real, that is, moral improvement of hers, I shall ever most cordially rejoice. This I hope I should do from a pure love of excellence, wherever it may manifest itself; but merely as a *patriot* I must wish that our next neighbours, with whom so many amongst us are inclined to cultivate the closest intimacy—from whom we derive many fashions, practices and opinions—from whom we receive (with horror I speak it) instructresses for so many of our innocent girls—should become more respectable and less a source of moral mischief to us. I own I still think extremely ill of their national character in every possible sense—they are regardless of the true, the sincere, the genuine, the natural; their vanity is odious to me, and their want of all decency, disgusting. I am far more interested in the Italians. Debased and corrupt as they are, there are noble features in their national character; if free and united, I believe that they would again rise to glory of every kind; and their literature far more delights me than that of France—*they* have poetry, and a very noble spirit breathes in the works of Alfieri and some of their living writers. There are men of great merit amongst their exiles; if they have left many equals or successors behind them, the country must and will emancipate itself before very long. But, my dear friend, is it our duty to be always fixing our eyes on the destinies of nations, on the state and character of mankind at large? May we not often permit ourselves to dismiss from our care evils beyond our cure? Or may we not lull the pain which these general views are apt to inflict with some considerations like the following? This world with all its ills, man with all his crimes and miseries, are yet such as their wise and beneficent Maker designed that they should be, foresaw that they would be. That good preponderates, we cannot doubt. All rational creatures, it is probable, find their life a boon even here— if not, how easily can futurity compensate transitory sufferings? Without falling into the Epicurean sentiment which you declare against, there surely is a sense in which we may say, 'whatever is, is right.' We ought not surely to refuse ourselves to the advances of that sweet peace 'which virtue bosoms ever,' because of sin and suffering of which we are not the cause.

Believe it, we shall some time know how and why all these things are. In the meanwhile let the sensitive and ingenuous mind combat this anxiety as its 'last infirmity,' remembering that His eyes and His love are upon all, the evil as well as the good, the destitute and wretched as well as the happy. Pardon me, pardon me, have I dared to exhort you? But no, I believe that it is the unworthy body which is in fault, when you are overpowered by human ills or unsatisfied with the amount of good which Providence has enabled you to perform. I know well how mighty that amount has been.

May you still be strengthened to go on adding to it many years! Our cholera turns out comparatively a trifle—what our reform will turn out is still in dread suspense. I feel entirely with you respecting the position of the lords. Should we, like France, be compelled, as you say, to separate ourselves from the old, there may be compensations for the inevitable evil of the parting, for posterity, scarcely for *us*; and yet the intense excitement would be worth having.

Ever most cordially yours,
L. AIKIN.

No. 19.

Hampstead: July 15, 1832.

My dear Friend—I yesterday received yours of June 7, which gave me variety of pleasure and pain: the hope of seeing you—the fear that continued ill-health might be the cause—sympathy in your sentiments towards a venerable parent, for such sentiments were my own whilst their dear object remained—all contended together; but being somewhat of an optimist, I settled it at length that *either* I should have the great delight of seeing you, *or else* the satisfaction of hoping that you were in better health at home. Ah! that health, what a blessing to those who recover it after long wanting it! I speak here experimentally. For the last few weeks I have regained a state of ease and vigour which makes my whole waking time one song of thankfulness. And opportunely has this great change come! I had been so despairing of ability to complete my work, that I had fixed to print it a fragment, stopping at the beginning of the war—a bitter disappointment in many ways; when almost suddenly I rallied, found myself able to work; and now hope to bring out my Charles *complete* next winter. This makes me very busy, and I borrow from my sleep time to write to you. By the way, I have a long *unsent* letter to you in my paper case. I wrote it on the passing of our *great bill,* when we had just recovered from imminent dread of a civil war; but at that crisis we were so whirled about by the feelings of the moment, that I felt I might give you impressions to-day which I should find all erroneous to-morrow, and therefore I kept silence. I will now say that we feel the more happy and triumphant in the victory, because the people gained it for themselves, and by means so peaceable and orderly as showed them fit and worthy to obtain it; and because there is great reason to expect that excellent men will be elected to the coming parliament. Nothing has ever given me such good hopes for my country as the conduct of the people at large on this occasion; good judges think they already perceive that the labouring classes are raised in their own esteem, and are becoming more estimable in consequence. The taste for other kinds of reading, besides political, seems rapidly to increase. The 'Penny Magazine,' set up by the Useful Knowledge Society, sells 120,000 copies; and this is only one of a multitude of cheap and wholesome productions which are eagerly bought up. To look back now upon the political state of the country, the state of knowledge, and the state of opinions within our own memory, and then to look forward is absolutely dizzying. Happy they who have been spared to behold so bright a *dawn*; the *day* I think is yet to come. It will next be seen what we can make of a church reform. The Irish resistance to tithes must lead, I believe, to vast consequences, here as much as there. A conscientious scruple of paying one's money is pretty certain to prove both obstinate and infectious.

I feel quite *enlightened* by what you say respecting the mode of acting beneficially on the poor. My own opinions, I must own, were not the result of any personal knowledge of the subject, and perhaps I was secretly swayed by a wish to believe exertions useless to which I was myself indisposed. It now strikes me that a person visiting the poor with such knowledge of their situation and such sympathy for them as the poems of Wordsworth display, could not but work much good—but, alas! to acquire such acquaintance with them is a business, a calling, and we cannot all devote ourselves like your admirable but enthusiastic friend. I will think more, however, on the subject; I have long felt an uncomfortable consciousness of deficiency in this great branch of duty.

Poor Mackintosh! You will, ere this, have learned that he is beyond the reach of your acknowledgments. He lies in the churchyard which I see from my windows. I thought there was a kind of appropriateness in the long train of *empty* coroneted carriages, with hat-band-wearing menials which followed him to his long home, and then drove back at speed without even waiting for the performance of the funeral rites.

I am not sufficiently acquainted with Hartley to give an opinion on his system, but it appeared to me in general that Mackintosh was fond of attempting to reconcile theories really incompatible with each other. And is it not rather too much of a subtilty to say that although general utility is the *test* of right actions it can never be an impelling *motive*? It is true that we cannot stop on all occasions to calculate the greatest good of the greatest number before we act, even if we possessed the necessary data; but surely we proceed upon a general idea of tendency to good in our actions; and is not the dignity of man more consulted by allowing reason that share in our determinations than by supposing them to be governed by a kind of moral instinct or appetite? But the more I think upon it the more I am struck with the complexity of human nature, and the multifariousness of the influences to which every individual is exposed; and the consequent extreme difficulty, if not impracticability, of finding out what is primitive in him. In one sense we may regard his utmost refinement as a part of his nature. We can none of us remember ourselves *unsophisticated*, if the influences and suggestions of other minds be sophistications. We have never been left to the developments of our own powers, which is the reason that we know not by intuition whether or not we have any instincts unless those of suction and deglutition. I am disposed to question the soundness of all very simple theories of man, and that of association particularly, to which I also feel a repugnance in my heart. Oh! if you do but come to England what prodigiously long conversations we shall have!—our topics will be quite inexhaustible. In writing to you I am always overwhelmed by the abundance of matter. I want you to know multitudes of English people who would be interesting to you in various ways, and yet I feel that extreme caution would be necessary to preserve you from being overwhelmed by crowds, which is the mischief and the misery to which *a name* subjects all here.

I find my historic task increase in interest as I proceed. The times are very favourable; they will allow me all the liberty of speaking I desire; and I have been fortunate in procuring unpublished documents. A volume of the correspondence of Sir. J. Eliot, the patriot-martyr, lies on my table. Hampden was his chief friend, and Eliot was worthy of all his affection. You can imagine nothing more firm, more philosophical, more truly pious, than his letters from prison. When at Christmas he was removed to a cell without fire, he writes to his friend: 'I hope you will believe that change of place makes none in my mind.' The cold was his death. A confession of guilt and a *humble* petition to the king would at any time have purchased his release; but this price he would not pay. Let me love the land which bore such heroes! 'Another family history lies before me, a folio manuscript. It is little or nothing to my purpose, but the writer was delighted to take a pretext for bringing it to me. He is such a personage as I suppose your country does not produce—a man who lives upon his pedigree. My friend is poor, for the entail was cut off and the title came to him without an acre: his father killed himself, his wife has eloped—though still young, sickness has made his once fine person a miserable wreck; he has no career, and not even an heir male, but he knows that for seven hundred years a certain castle descended from father to son in his family; he can trace his ancestry to Saxon times; he has compiled their history with infinite labour; he knows that one committed a murder, that another was tried for treason; all this is a kind of *conscious worth* to him, and he is happy. Let me, however, give him his due. The polish of his manners has a kind of fascination, and it is impossible not to confess that pride of birth has made him at least *a perfect gentleman*. What is your opinion of this principle, or sentiment? Some regard it as useful to balance the pride of purse; others look upon it merely as an arrogant assumption the more in society. I am inclined to look on it with some complacency as favourable to the graces, which certainly purse-pride is not; but I see that it often tends to political servility. A poor man of birth becomes almost unavoidably a hanger on of the court or the minister, and in one way or other subsists at the cost of the people. A rich man of birth sometimes places his dignity in defying present power and protecting the weak. In our late struggle the Howards, the Stanleys, the Russells, and the Spencers have deserved very well of their country. But here you will say that I confound the political effects of nobility with pride of blood, which is a different thing. Certainly reason cannot respect a man the more because his ancestors possessed certain manors for a succession of ages, and were sheriffs and county members in their turns. It is seldom that anything moral is connected with this kind of boast. Jesus set Himself against the claims of those who said 'We have Abraham for our father.' And yet temporal goods at least are represented to have been promised to the Jews on that very score. This strikes me as an eminent instance of what I should call His philosophical spirit, His sense of divine justice, or His enlarged philanthropy. It is somewhat in the same spirit with what you remarked of His instituting no priesthood.

I wish you would tell me whether there is any channel by which one could now and then send you a book which was likely to interest you, and which you might otherwise miss. I longed to convey to you a 'Life of Wiclif' by Le Bas. You would find in it much curious and interesting matter. There is the very noble and striking character of the reformer himself, with many instructive traits of his times—full confirmation of what I once assigned to you as the cause of the small resistance made to our reformation, namely the wide diffusion of Wiclif's principles; and there is curious proof how much an exceeding High Church-man of the present day, such as is Le Bas, falls short of the old reformer in simplifying religion. After great struggles he brings out the frightful fact that Wiclif would fain have abolished bishops and established a kind of presbyterian discipline. This volume makes the first of a set to be called the 'Theological Library,' in which the ablest pens of the High Church party are engaged. Le Bas is noted as a bitter reviewer of polemics; he is certainly an able writer, and affluent in knowledge.

My paper reminds me to release you. How eager I shall be for the next notice of your determination. Pray make health your first object.

Ever most truly yours,
L. AIKIN.

No. 20.

Hampstead: Oct. 15, 1832.

I will follow your example, by answering your letter immediately—always the time when one is most disposed to answer. I liked everything in it but the report of your susceptibility to cold so early in the season. Here we have one of the finest autumns ever known. I wish I could bag up for you the west wind which is waving his balmy wings at my open window. I still live in hopes that we shall sometime or other lure you hither, and then you will know whether I was right or not in promising or threatening that you should be a *lion*. That you would soon be weary of performing that part I can readily believe, but I am sure that we *have* minds over which you must rejoice to feel the benignant influence which you have exerted. You desire me not to use my recovered energies too freely. There is no danger. Eager as I am for the completion of my long task, I am not permitted to sit too closely at it, for I am now surrounded by a close circle of friends and neighbours who tempt me daily into delicious idleness—if I may call that social intercourse idleness in which neither head nor heart is unoccupied. It will be three or four months yet before I shall have made an end of King Charles; but I begin to ask myself, what next? With my habits of literary labour, vacation will soon become tedious, and I must look out for another task. Pray assist me. I am resolved against proceeding further with English sovereigns—Charles II. is no theme for me; it would make me contemn my species. If I could discover how my pen could do most good, to that object it should without hesitation be devoted. Profit I have no need of, and of reputation I have all I want. My mind is often burdened with the consciousness of doing little good, and an ignorance in what way to attempt doing more. If I am capable of benefiting any class, it must be one considerably removed from the lowest, of whom, whatever you may think of the confession, I have never seen enough to know at all how to address them. One *comfort* is, that there is still plenty of ignorance and noxious error to be pointed out in all classes. But the office of *censor morum* is not one which I covet; for who and what am I? I can imagine, but I know not whether I could execute, something in the way of essays, or letters, moral, literary, and miscellaneous, which might be made to serve good ends. But this is quite in the air.

Know that a great new light has arisen among English women. In the words of Lord Brougham, 'There is a deaf girl at Norwich doing more good than any man in the country.' You may have seen the name and some of the productions of Harriet Martineau in the 'Monthly Repository,' but what she is gaining glory by are 'Illustrations of Political Economy,' in a series of tales published periodically, of which nine or ten have appeared. It is impossible not to wonder at the skill with which, in the happiest of these pieces, for they are unequal, she has exemplified some of the deepest principles of her science, so as to make them plain to very ordinary capacities, and demonstrated their practical influence on the well-being, moral and physical, of the working classes first, and ultimately on the whole community. And with all this, she has given to her narratives a grace, an animation, and often a powerful pathos, rare even in works of pure amusement. Last year she called on me several times, and I was struck with marks of such an energy and resolution in her as, I thought, must command success in some line or other, though it did not then appear in what. She has a vast store of knowledge on many deep and difficult subjects; a wonderful store for a person scarcely thirty, and her observation of common things must have been extraordinarily correct as well as rapid. I believe you may dismiss your fears of too wide an extension of suffrage under the reform bill. The total number of ten-pound householders turns out less than almost anyone expected, and the 'degraded class' are almost all lodgers, and the condition of a previous paying up of rates annexed to the privilege of voting has so much further reduced them, that in many places the constituencies are manifestly still too small to be out of reach of bribery. It is impossible quite to suppress anxiety for the general result of the coming elections, but all the friends of rational liberty I talk with are full of happy auguries. It is quite true, as you say, that the tories have made, and are still making, themselves both odious and contemptible; but I do not think the public peace is threatened, because it seems pretty certain that they will be left in a decided minority in both houses, so that the people can afford to forgive them. John Bull is not of a vindictive temper, especially when a plentiful harvest has put him in good heart and good humour. You think quite as well of our bishops as they deserve. The venerable Bishop of Norwich, of whom Sydney Smith happily said, 'he should *touch* for bigotry and absurdity,' stands very much alone amongst them; however, I do not wish them hurt in the least, nor frightened further than is necessary to urge them to quit their political station. The separation of Church and State is, in my opinion, by much the most important victory which the people have still to achieve. When our bishops shall be in the state of your bishops, certainly my animosity against them will extend 'not a frown further,' but till that happens, all fair means of lessening them in the eyes of the people must be allowed. It is even marvellous to see how much the church is daily losing ground. It has no longer the reverence of the lower classes in general, and by the middling classes it begins to be regarded with the same feelings as the lay tories so generally excite. Its best friends come forward with plans of moderate reform. So long as Dissenters are compelled to pay towards the support of a church which they regard as corrupt in discipline and doctrine, and the preachers of which still thunder against the sin of schism and labour to bring sectaries into the hatred and contempt of their hearers—so long the state religion must, and will, and ought to be the object of hostility and attack to all lovers of equal justice and of the best interests of man. Such, at least, is my sense of things. I think you can scarcely imagine the tone taken by High Church people of the upper classes on these matters. A lady who belongs to the first circles, taking for granted that one must be orthodox, expressed to me lately her horror at worthy and learned old Baron Mazeres, who 'towards the end of his life not only became an unitarian, but endeavoured to propagate those doctrines.' As if a man ought to think his own opinions dangerous or pernicious to others!

Your cholera precautions are indeed admirable, and I trust they will prove effectual. Here the disease continues making considerable ravages, but we begin to grow used to it. It does sometimes, however, attack very sober and respectable people. I have personally known some victims of this class. Soon after it appeared in London, great alarm was excited by the death of a lady of quality, till it was charitably whispered that the *temperate* need not be the more apprehensive on account of this event. It is suspected that the Irish in St. Giles's and such places have perished in considerable numbers, but they disguise the cases from their violent prejudice against early burials without the accompaniment of a drunken wake. How are we to civilise these wretched people? Not by dragooning them, say you, and I agree; but this negative is more clear than anything positive respecting them. I wonder whether you have seen a small book published by Rammohun Roy containing translations of several of the Hindoo Veds? I have found a good deal of interest in this view of theology and metaphysics of a nation so remote in every respect from us and our ways of thinking. The great point which the true friend of his country and his race has had in view in his various controversies with his own countrymen, has been to show that, although some idolatrous rites are sanctioned by their sacred books, yet it has always been the doctrine of the most authentic of these, that the highest future happiness was only attainable by a pure and austere life, and the worship of the invisible, universal Spirit—that idolatry was for the gross and ignorant, rites and observances for them only. Thus he shows that eternal felicity—that is, absorption into the supreme spirit, is promised to women who after the death of their husbands lead devout and holy lives; and only a poor lease of thirty-five millions of years of happiness with their husbands to such as burn with them, after the expiration of which their souls are to transmigrate into different animals. This you will say is mighty puerile, but it is at least meeting his antagonists on their own ground. Afterwards he details the many cruelties and oppressions to which females in his country are subjected by the injustice and barbarity of the stronger sex, and pleads for pity towards them with such powerful, heartfelt eloquence as no woman, I think, can peruse without tears and fervent invocations of blessings on his head. The Rajah is now at Paris, where I doubt if he will find much gratification, as he is not well versed in the French language; he will return to us, however, soon after the meeting of parliament. I dread the effects of another English winter on his constitution; and yet it almost seems as if a life like his must be under the peculiar guardianship of Providence.

What a charming poet is your Bryant! I am just reading Mr. Irving's collection of his poems. Do you know the author? I am curious about him.

I am not acquainted with anybody in your country who would take charge of a book for me; but anything that should reach either Robert Kinder, or Dr. Boott, or Mr. P. Vaughan, would be forwarded to me.

A brimful sheet, as usual! In writing to you, my excellent friend, I never want matter. May health and every good attend you.

Yours ever truly,
L. AIKIN.

No. 21.

Hampstead: Nov. 19, 1832.

Oh, my dear friend, I was told yesterday that you had been very, very ill, and though it was added that you were now better, I have been able to think of little else since. What would I give to know how you are at this now that I am writing. This distance which separates us has something truly fearful in such circumstances. Would you had postponed all other considerations, however urgent, however affecting, to the one great object, your own health! Would you had sought our milder skies early in the autumn! I fear that, unless you should have embarked ere this, it must not be thought of till spring; but surely you will then transport yourself hither, and thus escape one of the trying seasons of your climate, which I take the early months to be. I have lately seen two or three very striking instances of the wonderfully restorative effects of our southern coasts in pulmonary cases. At this time I have a friend at Hastings reported quite well both by himself and others, who was absolutely given over last spring in London, and whom for some time in the summer, which he spent at Hampstead, I never saw within my doors without fearing it was for the last time. Another friend has been so fortified by two winters spent in the south, after the case seemed desperate, as now to be enabled to return to her native cold and wet Lancashire, where she has medical permission to winter. Well! I would not tease you with more of this; no doubt you have around you both the skilful and the kindest of the kind. My great inducement for writing was the hope that a little of this mute kind of chit-chat, which calls for no exercise of the voice in answer, might somewhat cheer your sick-room; at least you will accept it with kindness, as the only thing in which I can show my deep interest in the benefactor to whom I owe what is above all price—the sentiments which do most towards rendering us worthy of the future. Never, my friend, are you forgotten when my soul seeks communion with our common Father, and when I strive most earnestly to overcome some evil propensity, or to make some generous sacrifice, the thought of you gives me strength not my own.

I have written to you so lately, and so largely, that some of my usual topics are nearly exhausted; still we have a little of novelty. In the beginning of November term begins, and all the lawyers come to town. With their arrival commence my London dinner visits; for my most intimate friendships happen to be amongst this set, and I have already made one excursion to town, from which I gleaned a good deal. You know, of course, by reputation, our new Lord Chief Justice, Denman—the zealous defender of poor Queen Caroline, who in his excitation called our last king Nero, and our present one 'a base calumniator.' He wants caution, and is not the deepest of our lawyers; but his promotion is hailed by all congenial spirits as a triumphant example of the highest professional dignities attained by a man who never showed any other fear than that of being thought capable of sacrificing the most minute portion of truth, the nicest punctilio of honour, to any worldly interest. Glorious days in which such conduct finds such acceptance! On his taking leave of Lincoln's Inn in consequence of his promotion, a speech was made to him by his old friend the Vice-Chancellor, complimenting him on the love of liberty he had ever manifested in a strain which drew tears down the furrowed cheeks of the old benchers—practised worldlings as they must be. This glorious man—by the way, his person is made for dignity—was Mrs. Barbauld's pupil at four years old. I think it must have been chiefly for him that her 'Hymns in Prose' were written; and he cherishes her memory most religiously. In a great public entertainment where I met him last year, he came up to me and said with a look of delight, 'I dreamed of Mrs. Barbauld only last night!' He has a love and a taste for poetry and elegant literature worthy of her scholar, and I doubt not that she sowed the seed. In the move which Denman's appointment has made, another staunch friend of the people has become Solicitor-General. It is of great importance thus to recommend the laws to the many by the character of those who administer them.

I think I told you Hallam had become a conservative and alarmist; but he seems to me to have recovered his spirits since last spring, and to be relapsing into a liberal. He confesses to me that he is reading hard for a purpose, but will not yet say what. We again *croked* together over the decline of literature, and modestly concluded that it was *our* duty to write as much and as well as we could. We canvassed much the good and evil of the new Penny Magazines and Cyclopedias, which are selling by hundreds of thousands; and all we could decide was, that condemning the superficial and desultory spirit which these and other periodicals and abridgements were fitted to diffuse, it was still impossible not to rejoice that food so innocent was found for the popular mind, and was welcome to it. An indirect benefit we also acknowledged from this new literature; its having to a great extent superseded the religious tracts of the Evangelicals, which their busy zeal threatened to render the exclusive study of the working classes. Perhaps it is in this last respect that the Useful Knowledge Society has proved most beneficial; and no doubt it was a leading, though unavowed object of the founders thus to put fanaticism's nose out of joint (if you will allow such a grotesque expression).

Are we, or are we not, at war with our old friends the Dutch? This seems to be a question which nobody knows very well how to answer. For my part, I have such an opinion of the natural pugnacity of the human species, that I dread exceedingly these beginnings of strife; but poverty, the peace-preserver, still keeps watch over every European potentate, and I trust will withhold the means of mischief. There can be no doubt of the pacific dispositions of our present ministry; but they are unhappily committed in some degree by the acts of their predecessors, and there is also some danger that the obstinate King of Holland, by presuming too much on our forbearance, may render it a point of what is called national honour to forbear no longer. These are anxious considerations. No one can pretend to calculate the confusion and mischief which the expense of one campaign might cause to us in our present situation. But let us not be 'over curious to shape the fashion of uncertain evil.'

These November fogs have brought me down a little from my high boast of health, and interrupted somewhat my historic diligence. I suspect that the weakness in my chest will oblige me to keep the house in all ungenial winds this winter. But no matter, my fireside is cheery. My dear new neighbours, the Le Bretons, are an inestimable acquisition. Here I paused to welcome Harriet Martineau, with all her blushing honours thick upon her. The Chancellor has sent for her expressly to write tales illustrative of pauperism, and has supplied her for the purpose with an immense mass of documents accessible only to official persons. I believe she will do much good; her motives and principles are pure and high, and success, as I predicted, has improved, not spoiled her. Indeed, she has very extraordinary talent and merit, and a noble independence of mind. I will stop here; may this little pledge of friendship find you in a state at least of tolerable ease. I shall enquire of you from every probable source of intelligence.

May heaven preserve my precious friend.

L. AIKIN.

No. 22.

Hampstead: Feb. 10, 1833.

Many, many thanks to you, my dear friend, for your two welcome letters, and the excellent news they contain! It is, indeed, delightful to find you speaking so cheerily, both of the past, the present, and the future, and the most delightful of all is, that you still think of England. To level some at least of the mountains which, as you say, still rise between us, will be no hard task. First, the barbarous and odious practice of whipping is obsolete in nearly all our schools, except the public ones of ancient foundation, such as Eton, Westminster, &c., to which many other considerations would restrain you from sending your son. In that attached to the London University, to which my nephew goes, 230 boys are kept in order without any corporal punishment; in short, we would ensure your lad a whole skin. Then, as to your sweet girl, there would really be no more danger than everywhere arises from the little acquaintance which parents in general can have with the *individual* characters of the younger generation who are their children's contemporaries. You might easily be directed to families the most likely to afford fit associates for her. I cannot persuade myself that the very small difference of temperature between a *snug* situation in the immediate neighbourhood of London, and the southern coast, would be of moment to you—compared to the difference between the last and New England, it is nothing. Even in this village, placed as it is on a hill, very sheltered nooks may be found, and the air is eminently salubrious, and oh, if we could get you all here, how much we could do—I am confident we could—towards placing you in the midst of a small select circle where you would be appreciated, and your children would form connections such as you could not but approve! Several circumstances render society here peculiarly easy and pleasant; in many respects the place unites the advantages and escapes the evils both of London and the provincial towns. It is near enough to allow its inhabitants to partake in the society, the amusements and the accommodations of the capital as freely as even the dissipated could desire; whilst it affords pure air, lovely scenery, and retired and beautiful walks; and because everyone is supposed to have a London set of friends, neighbours do not think it necessary, as in the provinces, to force their acquaintance upon you; of local society you may have much, little, or none, as you please; and with a little, which is very good, you may associate on the easiest terms; then the summer brings an influx of Londoners who are often genteel and agreeable people, and pleasingly vary the scene. Such is Hampstead; ask Mrs. Farrar if I exaggerate. The subject threatens to run away with me; but here I leave it, for I have much to answer.

I like and can subscribe to your praise of Scott *as a writer*. Sir James Mackintosh was no doubt brought up a Calvinist; but I have seen a letter of his written from India to his old friend Robert Hall, then lately recovered from an attack of insanity, in which he warns him against dwelling on gloomy systems of religion as no one could have done who was a Calvinist; or, I should think, who believed salvation dependent on any *particular* creed. Read in the last number of the 'Edinburgh Review,' the article on Lord Mahon's history. I believe you will think the writer of it much improved since he reviewed Milton, and gave so dashing a sketch of the Puritans. This writer is Macaulay, confessedly the first *young* speaker in the House of Commons. As reviewer, as orator, as politician, he, if anyone, promises to be the successor or rival of Brougham. I have never seen him, but I hear of him as presumptuous, at least this *was* his character at the outset. He grapples boldly and ably with O'Connell in the House.

On the brink of civil war yourselves, you might well be excused for thinking little of Europe and her concerns; but we here give you credit for too much wisdom by far to proceed to that dread extremity, and I trust that by this time you are coming to some amicable compromise; if so, you may be willing to hear something of the progress of our revolution. Yes, revolution; it is no less, of this it is impossible not to be more and more sensible every day. The Reform Bill now shows itself fully in the character of means to an end—and what end? Of this different parties would give different accounts; that is, some require more, some would be content with fewer concessions of the few to the many; but all agree that numerous and important ones must and will be made. Ireland, miserable Ireland! a prey to so many evils, stained with so many crimes, and almost reduced to anarchy, what shall we do for her? To return into the right way after wide deviations, is as arduous a task in the government of nations as in the conduct of individuals; in fact, almost all the puzzling questions in public, as in private morals, arise from having set out wrong. The Protestant Church of Ireland is probably the most monstrous anomaly, the most barefaced wrong, in all ecclesiastical history; but it cannot be overthrown without some consideration for the *vested rights* enjoyed under it, and the same may be said respecting other interests there. Then, although the people are enduring many evils and oppressions, they must not be suffered to fill the land with robbery and murder; and the political *agitators*, though their views may be patriotic, and though by their efforts some wrongs have been and others will be redressed, must not be suffered to go on goading a ferocious people to fury, and an absurd people to folly and ruin. The Union must be preserved for Ireland's own sake. It is impossible to dwell upon these considerations, without alternately blaming, pitying, and dreading all parties. But how wonderful and admirable is the complication of good with evil in the whole system of things! How unexpectedly do the results of things come out! To the *Irish papists*, the objects of their bitterest, their most inveterate hatred, have the descendants of the English Puritans been indebted for their establishment of their civil rights. To the crying iniquity of the Church of Ireland, English Dissenters are likely eventually to owe emancipation from the exclusive claims of the Church of England. I view with intense interest the progress of the Church reform in which we are engaged. Take my word for it, it will go far, and end in the acknowledgment of broad principles. *Protestant* exclusiveness, when cited to the bar of reason, has nothing, absolutely nothing, to say, and this is a reasoning age. Thousands are coming to a clear perception how completely the interests of the Church and the interests of religion are different, nay, opposite things. Nor do I fear that, according to the distinction of Hume, *fanaticism* should here gain what *superstition* is likely to lose. The schoolmaster is fast emancipating the people from both, and without producing irreligion.

Eternal honour to Brougham for his Useful and Entertaining Knowledge, and his 'Penny Magazine'! They have done very much towards beating Evangelical tracts, and the *good boy* books of the High Church tories, out of the field. The whole tendency of these publications, as far as I know them, is to instil that sober morality, that pure and simple piety with which, as you would say, narrow and debasing views of God and of religion cannot coexist. And do you think *you* have done nothing towards this great work? You should see a little work published by Mr. Tagart, a London Unitarian minister, the 'Life of Captain Heywood,' to learn in what esteem your writings were held by a noble-minded, beneficent, upright naval officer. There is a chord in all such hearts which responds to your teaching. I hear of your writings, see your name mentioned on all sides; even our clergy mention it with deep respect. Oh! come to us; breathe our air, which may preserve you in vigour, not alone for your own sake, or that of your family, but for England's and mankind's!

Mr. Vaughan's ship, with your precious volume, for which I return you my best thanks by anticipation, is not yet arrived; but he says he expects it daily. I have had a glimpse, however, of the English reprint of the book; a glimpse only, for it was lent to Mr. Le Breton and to me, and in our mingled politeness and impatience, we have been sending it to each other, and then snatching it back, so that neither of us has yet had much good of it. He has been an active circulator of your works, and no one more delights in them. You must know each other some time. I lament over the unpoetical destiny of the poet Bryant; his admirers should have endeavoured to have procured for him some humble independence; but it will be long, I suspect, before you pension men of letters. We do little in this way. As to poor Spurzheim, I hear, for I never saw him, that he was much liked in society, and our anatomists much admired his mode of dissecting, or rather unravelling, the texture of the brain; but his system made few disciples amongst men of real science; and though I believe he individually was thought tolerably ingenious in it, a shade of empiricism was cast over him, which prevented his ever *taking rank* here; and his pecuniary encouragement was small. I think the spirit of philanthropy is almost a national characteristic of the frank and honest Germans; their writings, as far as I can judge of them from translations and critiques, very generally breathe it; and in the midst of their credulity and mysticism there is a deep and original vein of thinking which I should delight to explore if I possessed their language.

There is no hurry for a new scheme to succeed 'King Charles' with me. Never was I so tasked; matter grows upon my hands; to condense it sufficiently is an immense difficulty. The book will certainly disappoint you when finished, in this respect if in no other: I have been obliged, in order to keep within compass and preserve the character of court memoirs, to say little or nothing of the Puritans after the beginning of the war. When the king quits his capital so do I, and thenceforth he and his courtiers make my sole theme. I have still full three months' work to do, but I am pretty well, and work with pleasure.

What I wrote you of Miss Martineau and of the Rajah's book, I cannot now remember; but I have full confidence in your discretion, and shall be but too happy if anything I write you is capable of being made useful. Miss Martineau has been engaged by the Chancellor to write, from materials in the possession of government, a series of tales illustrative of the working of the poor laws. She says the documents are rich in pathetic interest. I believe she is doing much good. Joanna Baillie has written some very affectionate lines on Scott, which she will send you. I know not why she should have taken this opportunity to strike at Byron. No need of crying down one poet in order to cry up another; nor will all the just censures of Byron's morality sink him in his poetical capacity, in which he will still be judged to soar far above the height of Scott; whom my father used to call the chief only of ballad poets. His stories in verse are now almost forgotten in his prose narratives, but I think undeservedly. It is true indeed that it is only in his novels that he displays that power of humorous delineation of character which was one of his greatest gifts.

Farewell, my valued friend! May health attend you, but may you seek it here!

L. AIKIN.

No. 23.

Adelphi: June 13. 1833.

My dear Friend—Congratulate me! Yesterday I corrected the last sheet of 'King Charles.' My long and arduous task is ended; my time is now my own, and the first use I make of it is, as it ought to be, to return you my thanks for your excellent volume, so long unacknowledged, and to resume the thread of our correspondence. You would take for granted that some of your discourses would be less to my mind than others, and so it is; but how can I sufficiently thank you for the profit and delight of those which give an echo to my deepest convictions, my loftiest feelings, those which work out for me problems of the highest interest, on which my mind has often tasked itself in vain! The two sermons on self-denial, and that on the immortality of man, are to me inestimable; nor is there one in the volume in which I do not find much to admire, to agree with, and to profit by. I think I perceive in this volume, as compared with your former writings, traces of recent and profound study in the science of metaphysics. I have been exceedingly struck by the newness as well as the cogency of some of your reasonings, particularly those in page 238. As usual, I feel how long it must be before I can make myself entire mistress of the bearings of writings which contain so much food for thought, which seem to me new at every fresh perusal; and one of the pleasures of my leisure will be to go through them again, pencil in hand, marking my favourite passages. You are full of *maxims*; I have often wished to collect them by themselves as hints for meditation.

As soon as my book is out, which will be, I suppose, in a week, I shall consign to Mr. Vaughan's care a copy for you. It is of no use telling you all my fears and misgivings about it; you will judge for yourself, and freely communicate to me your remarks. The times are undoubtedly favourable for uttering the facts which I have been most anxious to put in a clear light; and it is not nearly so much the fear of any criticism, as the sense of having after all done very imperfect justice to my subject

—partly from the necessity of omitting a great number of matters which would have swelled the book inconveniently—that now troubles me. I am going to dissipate for a week in London, and that holiday I expect to enjoy; but domestic solitude and the habit of labour will soon be impelling me to seek a fresh pursuit, and my great care at present is to choose well and choose speedily. I certainly shall not go on to give the world a nearer view of the abominable court of Charles II., and this is all that I am certain of as yet. In other respects 'the world is all before me.' I suppose that by the time this reaches you, Mr. Roscoe's Life will be on your table. I am just beginning to devour it; to you it cannot have all the same sources of interest it has to me, but I shall be much disappointed if you do not find it one of the most delightful of biographies and collections of letters. Perhaps you will find in it a proof of what I have failed to persuade you of, that in this country the spirit of aristocracy opposes no obstacle to the progress of real talent. Mr. Roscoe was a splendid example of *rising from the ranks*. I think I have never mentioned to you James Montgomery the poet; but you probably know some at least of his poems, which would interest you from the fancy and the feeling which animate them, and from their deeply devotional spirit. He is a great master too, as I think, in the art of versification. I wish I could detail to you the particulars of his early life as he beautifully related them in letters to my father, whom he had not then seen. It is enough, however, to tell you here, that he was the son of a Moravian missionary, brought up in one of their seminaries, and that he had never seen an English verse, excepting their hymns, till he was about fourteen; when one of the masters walking in the fields with a few of his pupils, made them seat themselves on the grass, and drew from his pocket Blair's 'Grave,' which he read them. 'I seemed,' said Montgomery, 'to have found a language for sentiments born with me, but born dumb.' And from this time he became a writer of poetry. He quitted the Moravians for the Wesleyan Methodists; has suffered at times from religious melancholy, only less, I believe, than Cowper; but of late years his mind seems to be tranquillised, in part perhaps by the active exertions in which he has engaged in behalf of missions, Bible societies, and other religious objects. He retired from his business of a printer some years ago, on a competence, and, what seems to me very remarkable, has erected himself into a critic. He has given lectures on poetry at the Royal Institution, which were much admired, and lately he sent me a copy of a publication of which they form the larger and better part. I wish you could see it; there are portions, especially some remarks on the themes of poetry, and on its uses, which I know you would be pleased with. I am far from saying that I do not feel in the work the defective education of the writer in classical learning, and the prejudices rooted in his mind by the systematic fanaticism of the sect which brought him up; but still it is the work of an original and very interesting character, and the purity and tenderness of his mind and heart everywhere shine through. This fragment of a letter has travelled with me to London, and I can now tell you of some of my amusements. I dined yesterday in the company of Mr. Malthus and Miss Martineau, who are great friends and allies. Perhaps you may, and perhaps you may not, have taken the trouble to read the pro. and con. articles respecting Miss M. in the 'Quarterly' and 'Edinburgh' Reviews, of which the first is full of malice, and the second, I think, very empty of sound critical matter. She pursues her course steadily, and I hear much praise of her new tale on the Poor Laws, which I have not yet read; I fear, however, that it is the character of her mind to adopt extreme opinions on most subjects, and without much examination. She has now had a full season of London *lionising*, and it is no small praise to say that, as far as we can judge, it has done her nothing but good. She loves her neighbours the better for their good opinion of her, and I believe thinks the more humbly of herself for what she has seen of other persons of talent and merit.

My bookseller tells me that the editor of the 'Edinburgh Review' proposes now to give an article on my six volumes of Memoirs together. This annoys me not a little, and I will beg it off if I can. I have prospered pretty well under the silence of the critics, and it pleased me to have no thanks to give them. Also, I suspect I should fall into the hands of the same dull and tasteless critic, or rather gossip, who reviewed Miss Martineau; in whose prolix articles I have often stuck fast, and from whose remarks I should expect little benefit. It is likewise to be considered, that if praised in the 'Edinburgh,' I should certainly be abused in the 'Quarterly.'

Do you mark the course which our absurd conservatives are taking? Nothing could be more fortunate for ministers or more dangerous to themselves than the vote which they carried in the House of Lords. I hear the Duke of Wellington is so violent that he would gladly push the difference btween the two Houses even to civil war. What madness! Does he not perceive it would be the peers on one side and the nation on the other? And as for the bishops—No; words cannot do justice to their infatuation. Have you made this reflection on our triple legislature— that the king can free himself from an intractable House of Commons by a dissolution, that a House of Commons can compel a king to change his counsels by refusing the supplies, but that neither king nor commons, nor both united, possess any regular or obvious means of controlling the lords, consequently, that if they oppose the general will with obstinacy, they expose themselves to imminent danger of seeing their privileges curtailed or perhaps abolished. The bishops' votes especially hang by a thread.

How I long to know whether you are proposing to cross the sea to us! I cannot help thinking it would answer to you in every way. It is really a new world since you saw England. The progress in many ways has been of unexampled rapidity. You would find London embellished beyond expression. I ramble amongst the new buildings with unceasing admiration, striving in vain to recal the old state of some of the best known streets. We may now boast in the British Museum of a collection to which the world has nothing comparable, and the suite of rooms lately added is worthy of its destination. What adds a moral interest to this assemblage of the treasures of nature and art is the splendid testimony it affords to the public spirit of Englishmen. The gifts of individuals to their country preserved here are almost of inestimable value, even in a commercial view. In France, on the contrary, their museums have been entirely furnished by the purchases or the plunder of the government. Not even ostentation there moves private persons to make presents to the public. There is another pleasing circumstance. A few years since, access to the Museum was so difficult that it was scarcely visited by twenty persons in a day; now, in compliance with the spirit of the age, it is thrown open to all, and Brougham's 'Penny Magazine' has so familiarised all readers with the collection, that you see the rooms thronged by thousands, many from the humblest walks of life. I observed common soldiers and 'smirched artisans,' all quiet, orderly, attentive, and apparently surveying the objects with intelligent curiosity. Depend upon it there never was a time in which true civilisation was making such strides amongst us. You said very justly some time ago, that we were only in the beginning of a revolution; the spirit of reform has gone forth, conquering and to conquer, every day it extends its way into new provinces; but it is, it will continue to be, a peaceful sway, a bloodless conquest. The strongholds of abuse yield, one after another, upon summons. Wellington himself will not be able to bring his 'order' into conflict with the majesty of the people. I never looked with so much complacency on the state of my country. I believe her destined to a progress in all that constitutes true glory, which we of this age can but dimly figure to ourselves in the blue distance. The bulk of our people are at length well cured of the long and obstinate delusion respecting the wisdom of our ancestors, which so powerfully served the purposes of the interested opposers of improvement. Novelties are now tried upon their merits; perhaps even there is some partiality in their favour. Pray, pray, come and judge of us with your own eyes!

Believe me, ever yours most truly,

L. AIKIN.

No. 24.

Hampstead: Oct. 23, 1833.

My dear Friend—Just as I had embarked in one of my pamphlet-letters to you, comes yours of August 30th; and it makes me begin afresh, that I may first notice its contents. I am glad you have been reading the life of Roscoe, and feeling so much with me respecting it;—*how* much you may learn if you please from the forthcoming number of the 'Edinburgh Review,' where I obtained leave to be the critic. But this pray keep quite to yourself; I never before wrote an article for any review but the 'Annual,' and should be very sorry to be known in this, as it might cause me to be suspected of what I never wrote.

You ask if I received a letter from you last spring or

summer. I not only received one of May 30th, but wrote an answer, which I think you ought to have received before the one to which your last is a reply; I sent it as usual through Dr. Boott, and fear it may have been lost, perhaps delayed only. No, on recollection, I believe that letter of mine accompanied my book, which I hope you have by this time. Since that I have had your line by Dr. Tuckerman. I was in Kent when he called here, and therefore only saw him last week, but I am exceedingly struck and delighted with him, and impatient to hear him speak more of his noble exertions and designs. On Thursday next I hope he and Mr. Phillips will meet over my breakfast table my friend Mr. Le Breton and dear Joanna Baillie. You will be with us in spirit, for many associations will bring you to the minds of all of us. When I have the privilege to be present at a meeting like this, of the gifted and the excellent from the far ends of the earth, it seems to me a foretaste of the happiness reserved for the world of spirits. Alas for one who gave me this feeling beyond all others—the admirable Rammohun Roy! He has been frustrated of one of his cherished hopes, that of seeing you face to face, either in this or the other hemisphere—but you were no strangers to each other. Scarcely any description can do justice to his admirable qualities, and the charms of his society, his extended knowledge, his comprehension of mind, his universal philanthropy, his tender humanity, his genuine dignity mixed with perfect courtesy, and the most touching humility. His memory I shall cherish with affectionate reverence on many accounts, but the character in which I best love to contemplate him is that of the friend and champion of woman. It is impossible to forget his righteous zeal against polygamy, his warm approval of the freedom allowed to women in Europe, his joy and pious gratitude for the abolition of *suttee*. Considering the prejudices of birth and education with which he had to contend, his constant advocacy of the rights and interests of the weaker sex seems to me the very strongest proof of his moral and intellectual greatness.

You are very kind in what you say of your expectations from my late work and my future exertions in literature, and this encourages me to talk to you a little of myself and my affairs. I am very well satisfied with what is said of my 'Charles.' All whose opinions I have heard seem to think I have been diligent and impartial, and they praise my style for its clearness and simplicity, my remarks for justness, and particularly for their moral tone. This is the kind of commendation which I most desired, and if I could find out in what walk of literature I should be most likely to earn more of it, that walk would be my choice. But I am still quite undetermined on this head. In fact, I have had as yet little leisure for reflecting upon it, as I can show. Early in August, having printed my second edition, and seen my niece married, I set out for Sandgate, a very agreeable watering-place near Dover, where I should have enjoyed my leisure much had I found my strength equal to the fatigue of the little journey, and of the walking and riding necessary to explore the country. But I came back ill, and had scarcely done nursing myself when I was called upon to assist my poor niece in nursing her young bridegroom, who was three weeks confined in my house with a fever. I had the satisfaction, however, of sending him home well recovered, and next week I am myself proceeding for London, to take up my abode for three months with my brother Charles and his family. I go prepared to see and hear all I can, and thence to judge how I may best and most acceptably employ my pen. I sometimes think that a volume of essays might be useful addressed to my own sex, and chiefly intended to point out the particular vocation of women in these times of change and improvement. I am of opinion that few of them have yet raised their minds to the 'height of this great argument,' and that there is no small danger of their becoming despicable in the eyes of high-souled men by an anti-popular spirit, and a determined preference of trifles and triflers to everything truly great and elevated. I am far from wishing to play the censor, or to lay down the law; a few suggestions modestly thrown out, and temperately discussed, would suffice for what I mean. Bulwer Lytton in his 'England and the English,' a book which is making some noise here, falls violently upon the Englishwomen for their spirit of aristocracy, which, indeed, he considers as the prevailing spirit of the whole people; and I know you have the same idea. I want to go to the bottom of this matter, to consider what is strictly speaking a spirit of aristocracy—its causes, effects, remedies. One thing is plain, that in any country where, as in the old monarchies of our continent, noble birth should be the only passport to power, distinction, and command, the spirit of aristocracy could never be that of the nation, but only of the privileged class which profits by it. If, therefore, it pervades all classes in England, it must be because no one is excluded by birth from the hope of becoming in some mode or other a member of that large and loosely defined upper class which is supposed to comprehend all the meritorious and all the fortunate. Aristocracy in old France, in Venice, and in England, at the present day, are three things so distinct, that they ought not to bear the same name. Bulwer reproaches us ladies at our horror at associating with tradesmen, a horror which causes all young men who can possibly find the means to crowd into the professions, which are greatly overstocked. To this, perhaps, the ladies might be content to answer, that tradesmen, shopkeepers that is, are equally excluded from fashionable clubs and other resorts of gentlemen, that in truth their education and manners seldom entitle them to admission into either refined or literary society, and that individuals who deserve to be made exceptions to the rule usually are so. If ladies were equally guiltless of his other charges against them, that of flattering the follies and vices of the high-born and wealthy young men—it would be well. But the disgraceful practice of fortune-hunting, much more prevalent now among women than it ever was amongst men, renders this kind of vicious assentation very frequent, especially in the highest circles, and it deserves to be severely rebuked. There is great encouragement at present for all attempts at raising the moral tone amongst us. It fills me with joy and gratitude to contemplate the many reforms now proceeding with a reference to this end. The abomination of slavery put away from our people; poor factory children taken under the protection of humane laws; Church abuses effectually checked, and tithe compounded for; the criminal law amended; the poor laws revised; election bribery severely repressed, and the boundless corruption and jobbing of close corporations cut up by the roots. Carry all these great measures from their causes into their evident and unavoidable results, and say if ever there was in the history of mankind a revolution so morally great and glorious! But I need not boast—you generously rejoice and triumph with us, and I on my part sincerely hope that your country will not long suffer us to put her to shame with the word slavery. All fears for the working of emancipation in the colonies seem to have died away. I value commercial greatness as little on the whole as you can do, but yet I do rejoice in the present prosperity of our manufactories, because the full employment of the poor in most parts of the country will signally facilitate the meditated retrenchments of the relief granted at present by parishes to those who ought to live on the wages of their labour. To *dispauperise* the working classes must be the first step towards raising them from their degradation. After that there will be a fair field for the efforts of Dr. Tuckerman and his missionaries; at present they would have to struggle against a system of premiums for improvidence and self-indulgence, such as no other nation ever had the absurdity to institute. Miss Martineau is doing good service in crying it down.

It rejoices me to find you so full of cheering hopes respecting your own health and capacity for further usefulness. In these cases we *can* very often when or because we feel strongly the wish and the hope, and I reckon upon seeing the two heaps of materials converted within a reasonable time into so many volumes. You have great influence here, and I cannot help wishing that you would take some occasion to explain to us the advantages of the perfect equality in which all religious sects are placed amongst you. With us, people are just beginning to perceive the injustice of assessing dissenters to the Church rates; this once admitted, long consequences may be deduced. I think our universities cannot long continue to require from laymen subscription to the Church articles, since the sacramental test is in all cases abolished, and even Jews are now admissible to every civil office. Mrs. Jameson's book I have not seen, and scarcely heard of. 'Silvio Pellico' has been much read and praised, but I have not yet found time to read it. I think you would be interested in the life of that great preacher Robert Hall. There is something affecting in the evident struggle which his powerful mind and benevolent heart maintained for many years against the horrors and absurdities of the Calvinistic faith in which he had been educated, and into which he finally almost relapsed. He was also an illustrious example of the mind rising superior to dreadful bodily sufferings.

An intelligent friend of mine, lately from Paris, said to me of the Parisians, 'They are the most irreligious people of the world, but yet they have five or six new religions which they have invented.' She also said, 'Morals are so very bad there, that I think they can grow no worse, or rather, that they are beginning to mend.' She mentioned as a particular source of corruption the manner in which young girls of the higher class are married. A father says to his daughter, 'You are to be married to-morrow.' He names the gentleman, and it is one whom she has never seen. Yet she always submits without resistance or repugnance, regarding matrimony like presentation at court, simply as the customary and indispensable preliminary to coming out in the world, and being somebody. Young girls are never seen in company except at balls. The conversation in mixed society is unfit for them to listen to. Single women have there *no existence.* A great proportion of the marriages are brought about by paid brokers. Can you picture to yourself any state of things so utterly degrading to woman? It is remarkable that the French have no writers of any note at present, except in the sciences.

I have kept my letter open till I could tell you of the visit of your two friends. It was to me a most agreeable one. I was much pleased with the intelligence of Mr. Phillips, and the excellent information which he gave us in answer to our many questions respecting your country. Much of our conversation related to the state of religion and the arrangements for the conduct of religious worship amongst you, and I told them both that Americans could do nothing so useful to us as to publish these particulars in refutation of the prevailing notion here, that religion could not be supported without an establishment. Dr. Tuckerman is immersed in the study of our poor laws; very few of us, I suspect, know so much about them. I am struck with his eloquence, and should like much to witness its effects on his poor hearers. Such self-devotion must command admiration and reverence from the most depraved. I held up to him your letter in triumph. 'Let me look at his hand,' he cried, and he took it and kissed it repeatedly. What a perfect friendship is yours! Long may you live to enjoy it! Nay, death will not end it!

Ever yours with true regard,
L. AIKIN.

No. 25.

Hampstead: Feb. 2, 1834.

My dear Friend—On my return yesterday to my own house, after a sojourn of three months at my brother Charles's in London, I found your kind letter just arrived to welcome me, and I will not resist the impulse to make an immediate return to it. You gratify me much by what you say of my book; I perceive, however, that you think I a little want indulgence to Charles. This makes me regret that I forbore to sum up his character. I shrunk from the task as a difficult, and in some sense a dangerous one; for I should have made for him such allowances on account of education, and the influences generally to which his situation exposed him, that the almost unavoidable inference would have been, that all kings must be, more or less, the enemies of liberty, of public virtue, of the happiness and progress of mankind. I have come as near this inference as I well could, by showing that Charles was absolutely suckled in falsehood and dissimulation, and that *as prince* he thought himself as much above the laws of social morality as those of the land; but I believe I ought somewhere to have distinctly stated, that in his most unprincipled acts he was probably never self-condemned except in the case of Strafford. I plead guilty to *complicity*. I knew that this French word was scarcely naturalised, but it had been used; I had a vague idea that my father thought well of it; and knowing no English word of the same meaning, I ventured. May one not *now and then* do these things with good effect? I am not conscious of any other offences in this way, but it is likely enough that I may unconsciously have picked up odd words from my old authorities. Certainly, in the course of my labours, collateral subjects of remark did now and then occur to me; but I fear I have let them slip away. I do, however, feel some temptation to venture into the essay line, when, perhaps, thoughts might recur on the morals of history. At present, however, I am absolutely like poor Burns, 'Unfitted with an aim.' One friend suggests to me Memoirs of Caroline, queen of George II.; another would have me go on to Cromwell; another would send me back to Edward III., as a subject out of harm's way, involving neither theology nor politics. 'The literary class,' said the very sensible advocate of the last scheme, 'are almost all for Church and State, and your last subject is one which they do not like. They would not have much enquiry into King Charles.' This remark might lead me wide into a dissertation upon our present state of political and religious feeling; but before I enter such a field, I think it prudent to answer some passages of your letter.

I wonder not at your deep feelings on the subject of slavery. It is worthy of you so to feel, and to devote your powerful pen and all the energies you can command to that great theme. I am quite incompetent to pronounce any opinion of my own on the state of our islands, but that excellent old abolitionist William Smith seems to me highly satisfied with the working of the new system hitherto, and Dr. Lushington also. It has been said that the planters begin to judge it conducive to their own interests—a grand security for their exertions to make it answer. It seems that the protection of the black population will be secured so far as law can secure it, by depending on a reformed magistracy which, in other respects, is likely to be welcome to the planters. But I know not the particulars.

Excellent Rammohun Roy: I wish I could obtain more particulars of him to offer to you; but like all remarkable foreigners in this, and I suppose in other countries, he was beset by the enthusiastic, the ignorant, the impertinent, and often the malignant; in his case political and theological passions conspired, and he was misrepresented on all hands. That good man Dr. Carpenter has published an account of him, and I know of no better. It is now known that the title of Rajah, which some suspected him of unwarrantably assuming, was conferred on him regularly by the Great Mogul, or King of Delhi as he is now called, in the character of his ambassador. He was able in negotiation, and obtained for his master the large sums which he claimed of our government. In his demeanour there was all the dignity and gracefulness of *high caste* tempered with not only courtesy and benignity, but with a kind of humility only to be accounted for, as Dr. Boott acutely observed, by recollecting that he belonged to a conquered people, and had been compelled in India to submit to social inferiority. It was impossible, however, to charge him with servility. He sometimes evaded indiscreet questions, but the information which he gave voluntarily was so precise and satisfactory that it was impossible to question its perfect truth. His knowledge of languages was prodigious, and when he spoke of the light cast by an acquaintance with oriental literature and manners on the sense of scripture, or when he explained the laws and customs of his country, with the modifications which they had sustained from its Mussulman conquerors, you perceived that he was able to draw from all that he had learned and seen the inferences of a clear sagacious mind. But perhaps his greatest charm was the atmosphere of moral purity in which he seemed to breathe. To women this was peculiarly striking; he paid them a homage reverential as that of chivalry, without its exaggeration. Absolutely new to their society as he must have been, an innate sense of propriety revealed to him always the right thing to say and do. Persecution, calumny, injustice, public and private, only strengthened him to endure in a good cause, without either saddening or embittering his spirit. Benignity was the leading characteristic of his countenance and his expressions, his love of liberty was fervent, and nothing which concerned the welfare of his brethren of mankind was indifferent to him. May we indeed meet that pure and noble spirit where only such are admitted!

Of Godwin's domestic habits I know nothing; but it is unfortunately true that he has often been reduced to solicit pecuniary aid. The late Earl Dudley gave him a thousand pounds. The mercy of Lord Grey has rescued him from this humiliation, by conferring on him the office of a keeper of records, with 300*l*. per annum. It was his misfortune or folly to adopt, with the other debasing views of the French school, their contempt of chastity in women, and he took for his second wife a person of bad reputation: a connection which has tended, in various ways, to disgrace and embarrass him.

Bentham I did not know, and I have never heard anything respecting his religious opinions. There is no hint of atheism in his theological works, nearly all of which I have read; these are full of logical and critical acuteness. His dissection of the 'Church Catechism' in his 'Church of Englandism' would amuse you, as well as his sarcasms on 'My Lords the Bishops,' whose 'very footmen are clothed in purple.' Mr. Whishaw, I think, characterised him very happily when he called him 'a schoolman born some ages too late.' He lived latterly in a narrow circle of worshippers, reading nothing and writing incessantly; and probably did not sympathise extensively enough with other men to understand human nature profoundly. Consequently he was rather fitted to supply legislators with principles and suggestions, than to legislate himself. Brougham has very handsomely acknowledged his obligations to him for the idea of many of his reforms, particularly, I think, his legal ones. Romilly, a man of great piety, lived in strict friendship with him. Neale seems to be a slight and rather paltry person, very little qualified to measure the mind of Bentham, and probably only knew him in extreme old age. On such authority it would be unwarrantable to impute to an innocent and certainly a benevolent and public-spirited man, one of the ablest thinkers and the most skilful logician of his age, the brutish absurdity of atheism—a word, as you well know, used by ignorant or prejudiced people often without any definite meaning. The masterly lectures on jurisprudence published by my friend Mr. Austin, a very zealous promulgator of the utilitarian system founded by Bentham, are firmly based on theism, though they make no reference to Christianity, with which, however, their subject had no concern. I have just been assured, on what I think pretty good authority, that neither is Godwin an atheist.

During my stay in London, it was my great object to learn what *our* world is doing and thinking—and this is what I make out. Literature is low indeed—*swamped*, as our phrase is, by the *tract makers*, with the Useful Knowledge Society at their head. Bulwer has protested with good reason against the prevalent practice of anonymous writing. We shall at this rate soon have no such character as an author amongst us; the public will account it as idle to enquire who wrote an essay, or even a book, as who set up the types—and one artificer will become as much a mere labourer for wages as the other. But that this state of things cannot well become permanent in a civilised country, it would almost break one's heart. In the meantime, the nullity of literature leaves all the thinkers and all the talkers at leisure for a few great practical subjects, which must become the business of Parliament in the coming session. These are, Church reform, poor-law reform, and general education. On the first some things are decided as far as ministers are concerned. They will bring forward a commutation of tithe, and probably some new regulations against pluralities and non-residence. They will propose to grant the dissenters redress of their grievances in respect of marriages, burials, and birth registries, and may, perhaps, be willing to exempt them from Church-rates. But here is the danger! The orthodox, that is, the Calvinistic dissenters, or Independents and Baptists, emboldened by their great and growing numbers, and by what they view as the spirit of the times, have plainly declared that they regard the whole connection of a favoured sect with the State as an abuse and an injustice; and that they will never be satisfied till it is totally dissolved. This decision, made in defiance of the prudential remonstrances of the calmer and better informed Unitarians, is beginning, as it seems, to produce a strong reaction in favour of the Church; to which, with a small exception for Catholics, and another for Unitarians, the whole of the two Houses of Parliament and of the nation, down almost to the shop-keepers and mechanics, is at least nominally attached; and which carries with it also most of the agricultural class, and a good portion of every class. There is danger, therefore, to the most moderate claims of the dissenters, should the ministers desert their cause; to the ministers themselves, should they remain steady to it; and I dread from the whole affair a fierce renewal of religious dissensions, and of a persecuting spirit directed against all sectaries and free enquirers. It would be most unfortunate should a measure of general education be proposed and carried into effect during such an access of High Churchism, as its character would of course be narrow and exclusive, and the effect would be to fix on the children of dissenters a universal stigma. It is also certain that nothing would strengthen so much the hands of the tories as a rally for the Church. Nor would the poor-law question be uninfluenced by such a crisis. To promote a spirit of independence amongst the labouring classes would not be the aim of triumphant squires and parsons. I am obliged to state all this very crudely, but *verbum sapienti.* You will see on the whole that our state is an anxious one. I could wish that the Irish Church question were first to be dealt with. It was Catholic emancipation which repealed the English Test and Corporation Acts. You will not wonder that, with my *historic experience,* I dread beyond everything the mingling of ecclesiastical disputes with questions of civil government, especially as our people are much less advanced in religion than in politics. Fear nothing for Dr. Tuckerman. He interests us the more for his bursts of sensibility. 'He has enthusiasm,' said Mr. Le Breton happily, 'but no fanaticism.' We all love him, and his suggestions are heard with respect by persons who have both the will and the power to carry them into effect to some extent. He could not have visited us at a better time: the state of the poor has become such, that all agree *something* must be done to amend it, and everyone who can speak from experience on the subject is heard with deep attention. There is much benevolent activity amongst us, which only wants and asks to be well guided. We are all struck with his eloquence. 'He took me by the button,' said Mr. Le Breton, 'last time I saw him, and certainly preached a short sermon; but I did not wish it ended.' In fact, the oftener he is heard, the less one wishes him to end. Since I finished the last sentence, I have taken two ladies to call on him; I never heard him so interesting and eloquent in the illustration of his principles and plans. The ladies were all attention; and one of them, who lives with her brother, a country clergyman, and devotes herself with him and his daughters to the welfare of a village, found much correspondence between their modes of proceeding and his—except that they talk to the people of original sin. I admired the dexterity with which he slid over this difference. He has more tact and sagacity than I ever saw united with such ardour. You trace a beautiful outline of what essays for women ought to teach. I fear I could not fill it up; but I feel that in these days knowledge of points of debate is necessary, to prevent our quick feelings from making us fierce upon them. Ignorant partisans are always the most violent. Candour, the virtue of the wise, is that in which women are most deficient.

I fear I must at length have quite wearied you; in writing to you I know not where to stop.

I rejoice in the good account you give Dr. Tuckerman of your health. Believe me ever,

Most sincerely yours,
L. AIKIN.

No. 26.

Hampstead: May 29, 1834.

My dear Friend—In your welcome letter received about ten days since, you said it was long since you had heard from me, but I think you must very soon after have received a long one from me; at least, I wrote one and consigned it as usual to Dr. Boott. This is to go by Dr. Tuckerman, whom we are very loath to part with, for we all revere and love him, but there is some satisfaction in his assurances that he also loves us, and will do his utmost to send you to visit us. Mr. Phillips we hope to keep a little longer. He is a general favourite, and perhaps even better liked in society than his friend, whose mind is almost engrossed by one subject. It mortified me to catch only a glimpse of Mr. Dewey, his stay was so short that he was gone before I could find an opportunity to invite him. I heard great praise of his pulpit eloquence from very good judges. Send us more such visitors, they will do much to overcome prejudices on both sides. And now to reply to the questions in your letter.

'Godolphin' I have not read. I understand it was written by a Mr. Sunderland, who is genteelly connected, and was educated at Oxford; but as his extreme youth cannot have allowed him extensive opportunities of observation in any society, it would be unreasonable to put much faith in his view of manners. All novelists run into exaggeration of one kind or other, for the sake of effect. Formerly they were chiefly reproached with painting 'faultless monsters,' whose charms and graces threw all living merit into shade, and disgusted young people with the sober realities of life. But this was a splendid sin compared with that of the present fashionable school, who exaggerate nothing but vices and follies, and delight in representing as odious or contemptible those classes who will nevertheless continue to be objects of envy to most of their inferiors. In high, as in low and in middle life, there will always be many who yield to the peculiar temptations of their situation, but many also who resist, and I know no reason whatever for believing that our aristocracy are worse in any respect than in past ages; on the contrary, I know some strong reasons for thinking that in several respects they are better. No one denies that they are much less addicted to drinking, less also to gaming; for men play less, in general society at least, and women scarcely at all. I cannot say whether there is less licentiousness, but you who have read Walpole will not dispute that there is much more decorum, much more of at least outward respect for religion and virtue, and I think it is plain that even hypocrisy must put some restraint on vice. Then it is certain that the circumstances of the times keep the higher classes in a state of extraordinary mental activity; that they feel it necessary to cultivate all their talents, to inform themselves on every question of practical importance, and at the same time to preserve the graceful accomplishments which may serve to conciliate public approbation.

With respect to what you have heard of a class of fashionables who set their own pretensions above those of rank and title, there is something in it: the most fashionable persons in London are so rather by *merit*, if one may so apply the term, than by birth. A certain talent, or tact, is necessary to become an 'arbiter elegantiarum;' and although there may be not a little of presumption and conceit amongst the *exclusives*, they have at least the recommendation of daring to show great lords and great ladies that they may be looked down upon in society if they rely too much upon mere rank and pedigree. You cannot without seeing it imagine the charm which waits upon a patroness of Almack's. Perfect good breeding is a beautiful thing to behold, and no *fine art* deserves to be more studied.

I leave it to Dr. Tuckerman to describe to you the society in which he has lived, which consists chiefly of the higher part of the middle class, and is the same with which I mostly associate. I know he will give you a good account of it, and that he will especially attest the zeal prevalent in this set for the improvement of the character and condition of the poor. *Much* is doing for the ignorant and degraded, and I trust that they will not long be numbered by millions, even in Ireland. Immense things are in agitation regarding the poor and regarding the Church, and both subjects are approached by many, especially the first, in a pretty good spirit. I do not yet wish to see the establishment overthrown, because at present the fanatics would be able to seize the chief power and oppress all free enquirers; but it will do mother Church no manner of hurt to be put in mind of her end, and the Dissenters are willing enough to jog her memory on this subject. The worst is, that we must expect an increase of bitterness and animosity as these Dissenters proceed, for when was ever an ecclesiastical question settled in a Christian spirit? And in the meantime, I grieve to see literature *swamped* as it is between politics and theology. You may enquire in vain for light reading. Poetry we have none, and though we have novels not a few, I really know of none which are much praised by people of taste. We can scarcely find new works sufficient to keep our Book Society alive. The dearth is something quite strange, and hardly credible at a time when everybody affirms that there is more reading than ever in the country. I suppose people will be tired of two-penny tracts ere long, and then there will again be a demand for *books*. In France there is an equal stagnation, in Germany alone literature really flourishes, although, or perhaps *because*, literary labour scarcely brings there any pecuniary reward, on account of the impossibility of securing copyright beyond the limits of a single state. The most laborious works, I hear, are composed by professors of universities, as in some measure a part of their duty, or a means of distinction. I wish I could tell you that I am again settled into some substantial work, but I cannot yet fit myself with a subject. Two in English history have engaged my attention; that which you suggest,—the Commonwealth, and the two first Georges. But I rather dread the quantity of dry reading, especially of the polemical kind, which the first would require, and in general the *ruggedness* of the theme, on which it would scarcely be practicable to strew flowers. The second also somewhat affrights me by its magnitude, for the materials would be redundant, and it also repels me by the want of great and interesting events; in short, I am not enough pleased with either of these periods to be willing to *live* in it for years. Sometimes I meditate another kind of writing—essays, moral and literary. I seem to myself to have some thoughts which it might be useful or agreeable to put on paper; but here fears and scruples of many kinds assail me. If I were to give the rein freely to my speculations, I know not whither they would lead me— most likely into a kind of Pyrrhonism which would give great offence to this dogmatising age. I am not here referring to religious topics, on which I should never think of addressing the public; besides that, on these my mind is pretty well settled, though not in opinions which would be approved; but I have in view many points relating to morals and the conduct of life, on which I am much more convinced that error generally prevails, than prepared to pronounce what is truth or reason. I am a little disposed to envy those who can adopt a sect or party and stick by it with unfaltering allegiance. Such people know at least what to wish for, what to aim at, what to praise or blame, what and whom to love and to hate. With me it is quite the contrary. I remain suspended and neutral amid the unceasing clash of parties and principles which rages around me. I listen to both or to all sides till I can take part with none, and I fold my arms in indolence for want of knowing anything to be done which might not just as well, or better, be let alone. Can you prescribe any remedy for a state like this, which I am disposed to regard as a morbid one, because one sees that if it were to become epidemic, the whole world would go to sleep?

Events press fast upon us. Since I began this letter, a few days only ago, a split of the cabinet has been announced on the important question of the appropriation of the temporalities of the Irish Church. Mr. Stanley and two more, who insisted on preserving the whole to the Protestant establishment, go out, and we may consequently expect to see the cause of Church Reform espoused by the government. In this I do unfeignedly rejoice. It gives some reason to hope that a compromise may be effected with the *English* Dissenters also, which will divert them, for a time at least, from seeking the utter overthrow of the establishment. But much will depend on what cannot well be reckoned on, the prudence and moderation of our upper house, especially the lords spiritual. There are sinister reports concerning the sanity of our poor well-meaning king. A regency, with a tory queen at its head, might prove under present circumstances a dangerous incident. Political unions are said to be spreading over the country, or rather trades' unions, which, on the slightest cause of jealousy given by the government, would immediately become political ones. I should exceedingly dread to see more power fall into the hands of the low and ignorant, the selfish, and, on the whole, not moral classes, of whom these associations are composed; and nothing can preserve us from this peril but a wise, just, and liberal, but moderate administration. After all, though I have been murmuring at the *swamping* of literature between religion and politics, I feel that I cannot myself resist the influence of circumstances. We are in a state of revolution, it cannot be denied, and however one may wish to divert one's mind from the present and the directly practical, it will not be; and those who do not pretend to be able to instruct the public on the great questions of Church and State (and I am sure I do not) must be content, as matters stand, to hear, see, and say nothing. I am reading a long and a great work, Sismondi's 'History of the Italian Republics.' It errs somewhat on the side of minute detail, as might well be expected, considering that the author had occasion to take for his authorities the native historians—those masters of prolixity. But with this abatement the work is surely a very noble one, full of interesting circumstances, and lively, graphic descriptions, both of places from personal knowledge, and of characters and incidents. The moral tone is admirable. The author seems to me unerringly faithful to the best interests of mankind, except that he perhaps prizes a little too highly the turbulent liberty of Florence; fertile, however, it must be owned, in great men in every line. I am told that Sismondi's 'History of France' is, however, his best work; and if I do not set myself to writing, I think my next task may be to read it. History never tires me.

Pray make Dr. Tuckerman tell you a great deal about all *us*, especially ask him about my friend Mrs. Coltman, in whom he delights, and then figure to yourself how you will enjoy finding yourself surrounded by such disciples (for all this set are your disciples, and have received your friends in your name).

An unpleasant suspicion comes over me that I have been inditing a vastly dull epistle, pray excuse it if so it be. There will be better and worse in letters as in other things; there is a happiness in topics and expressions not to be commanded, and if my letter be good for nothing else, let it at least serve to assure you of my continued esteem and friendship, and my anxiety to keep up my privilege of communication with you.

Ever most truly yours,

L. AIKIN.

No. 27.

Hampstead: June 19, 1834.

Mr. Phillips offers me conveyance for a letter to you, and though rather pressed for time, I will begin: at least I may be able to thank you for your last admirable letter and to convey my sense of its contents. I am very much enlightened as well as pleased by your remarks on your own country. What very curiously corroborates their justness is, that the characteristics which you note as of presbyterian origin are, or were, almost equally observable here in the Scotch and the old English dissenters—the same coldness and reserve of manner—the same repression of enthusiasm—the same caution, and mutual superintendence, I have been struck with in them ever since I have been able largely to compare them with our episcopalians. Miss Martineau, being herself of dissenting parentage and connection, will be fully prepared to find warm hearts under cold manners, but even our sauciest travellers bear ample testimony to the hospitality they find amongst you. Do you know I am half inclined to quarrel with you for calling us *foreigners* with respect to you. I think we never call you so. Our common origin, common language, and common history down to a period not yet beyond the memory of man, forbid the use of that chilling word—pray leave it off.

I think you quite right in the main respecting our religious state. There is, however, a great deal of earnest belief amongst our Evangelicals in and out of the Church, and a good deal of unobtrusive piety amongst individuals of all communions, and I would say that the warm reception your works have found from persons in as well as out of the establishment is a strong proof that spiritual religion is congenial with many minds. In the meantime the present struggle between the Church and the dissenters must be regarded as partaking more of the nature of a civil than a religious contest. The question is, Shall the Church-monopoly be suffered longer to exist in all its rigour, or shall it be made to yield more or less to the spirit of the age, and the demands of justice? You will see that the bill for abolishing subscriptions at the universities as a condition of graduation, has been carried by a great majority in the commons, being supported by most of the Scotch and Irish members. It is probable that the lords will throw it out, but it will nevertheless be a great triumph to the dissenters to find the representatives of the people so decidedly in their favour. The question of the appropriation of tithes in Ireland particularly, will next come to be discussed; and should the two houses form opposite decisions on this question likewise, very long and very important political consequences may, *must* be the result. The establishment is by no means so willing as you have been led to believe to correct its own abuses. It is highly probable that Brougham's Church Bill will also be lost among the lords spiritual and temporal. It will, unless a salutary fear of provoking one knows not what should seize upon these noble and right reverend personages. I am surprised at daily proofs of an alienation of the minds of men from the Church, for which, as you know, I was not in the least prepared. In no one county, town, or city have the friends of the establishment ventured to call a public meeting for the purpose of raising the cry of 'The Church in danger.' The blustering of Oxford with its military chancellor has failed to excite emulation. I believe that if the Church is to stand, great concessions must be made, not only on the points of pluralities, sinecures, and non-residence, but in the matter of church patronage. The Scotch General Assembly has found it expedient to allow the parishioners at large a negative on the appointment of the patron, and I look daily for some similar claim here. Now all these may be regarded as tendencies towards what is called the 'voluntary' church system, which I have no doubt you will allow to be much more favourable to *spirituality* than an establishment dependent chiefly on the crown and the hereditary aristocracy of the country.

You will gather from all this that I conceive the popular interest to be fast gaining ground, and that I believe it must finally carry every point in contest, whether civil or ecclesiastical. I believe also that important reforms will thus be effected, and the well-being of the people at large promoted. Nevertheless, I cannot exult in the tone of national feeling. I fear we do indeed deserve to be reproached as a nation of shop-keepers—all our quarrels are money quarrels—every question in high debate may be resolved into one of £. s. d. Ask the trade-unions what they require? Higher wages. The shop-keepers? The repeal of the assessed taxes. The manufacturers? Free trade, especially in corn. The landed interest? The continuance of the corn laws, and of all others favourable to the maintenance of their rents. Now this universal worship of Mammon makes me sigh and blush for my country. In the first political struggles I can remember great and noble principles were at stake; now it is a vulgar dispute who shall pay most, or least rather, towards a long reckoning. Fox was the type of the former period, Joseph Hume of the present. But looking at the causes of this extraordinary activity of the mercenary principle amongst us, I am willing to believe that they are in great measure of a temporary nature.

The taxes have pressed with crushing weight on every class and interest by turns. It was the hope of relief from pecuniary distress principally which has brought the people into collision first with the borough-owners, now with the tithe-owners. Some burdens have been already lightened by our reformed legislature, but the court and the tories still resist retrenchment, and it is necessary that even a clamour for it should still be kept up. But let reforms in expenditure once have been carried fairly through all departments, and this extraordinary pressure removed, and the active spirits of our people will demand higher and better occupation. Then shall we find the great results of the illumination of the popular mind which has been all this time proceeding with a constantly accelerating pace; then expect from us moralists, poets, philosophers. I will tell you a little anecdote which has made me hope highly of the effects of the diffusion of literature amongst the lower classes. Dear Jane Roscoe, whose head is all benevolence, having accidentally discovered that various cruel practices prevailed amongst the market people at Liverpool, caused a committee of ladies to be sanctioned by the mayor for the prevention of these offences. It then occurred to her, that to go to the root of the evil the market people themselves should be humanised by knowledge, and she got a society instituted by ladies for supplying them with a circulation of books. Soon after, the wife of a small butcher requested of her, on the part of her husband, a second view of one of the volumes: 'He says, madam, that they say the tracts the gentlefolks give us poor people to read are books for children, but that he is sure this is a book for a man, and such a book as he never saw the like of; and never anything did delight him so much, he can talk of nothing else.' It was 'Paradise Lost.'

The Archbishop of Dublin (Whately) is doing much

good by reconciling the Catholics to the national schools, from the system of which he has banished everything offensive to their religion. 'To be sure,' said an old Oxford colleague of his to me, 'he is the very opposite of the sort of person I should have chosen for the situation; I would have had a man remarkable for mildness, patience, willing to hear and to answer all objections; but God knows better how to appoint His own instruments. I know many people who, if the archbishop were to be roasted, would go to get a bit of him, because he has yielded to the Catholics respecting giving children the whole Bible. But he goes on, and he could not care less for abuse if he were made of wood. He says of the Sabbath, "Spend if you please, or if you can, the whole day in religious exercises, but put things on the true footing; do not tell your children it was instituted by God's command to Moses to commemorate the creation, but tell them it was fixed by the Apostles to commemorate the resurrection. Give it all the sanctity you please, but not on a wrong ground." This has given great offence. So has a very learned and philosophical work in which, by tracing the origin of many Romish superstitions to the principles or the weaknesses of our common nature, he has been charged by some with extenuating them.' He added, that the archbishop had a great fondness for parables in conversation, which were often rather homely ones, and for experiments. One day at a great set dinner at the lord lieutenant's, a question arose, how long a man could live with his head under water. The archbishop quitted the room, and presently returned with a great bason full of water, which he set on the table and plunged his head in before the whole company. Having held it there an enormous length of time, he drew it out, crying, 'There! none of you could have kept your heads in so long, but I know the method of it.' Another time, also at a formal party at the Castle, he spoke of the great weight a man could support on the calf of his leg, bending it outwards. 'If your Grace of Cashel,' said he, 'will stand upon mine, as I stretch it out, I can bear your weight without the slightest difficulty.' But his Grace of Cashel would not have done so odd a thing in that company for millions. I take a fancy to a metropolitan who dares to be odd, to conciliate the Irish Catholics, and to provoke the saints, alias bigots. No, I shall not go back to Edward III., never fear. No black-letter documents for me. But I am not yet the nearer to finding work for my pen. I do want a *noble* subject, and I cannot find one in our history after exhausting Charles I. I am in a thoroughly unfixed state of mind, which begins to feel irksome to me. This whole London season I have been much in society, and I have seen so many and such various people, and have put myself in the way of hearing such various opinions, that I feel as if I had been on an excursion with the Diable Boiteux; that is, I seem a spectator of all things, inclined to be satisfied with that indolent amusement, and to take part in nothing. I suppose there is a limit to the benefit of hearing all sides. La Fontaine came at last to the two maxims that, Everything may be true, and that everybody has reason on his side. With such notions I do not see how anyone could write eloquently, or indeed give himself the trouble to write anything at all, but tales and fables to divert idle people. If my letter is to go to-day, as it ought, I must not fill up my corners as usual, but despatch this hasty scrawl, in which you will find, I believe, some things contradictory of my former views of things, an inconvenience not to be avoided when every day developes popular feelings more and more.

Believe me ever with true esteem,

Your attached friend,

LUCY AIKIN.

No. 28.

Hampstead: Oct. 19, 1834.

My dear Friend--Your welcome letter arrived as I was actually putting pen to paper to enquire after you, and petition to be written to. Thank you very much for the interest you take in the employment of my pen, and your suggestions on this subject. My own inclination is likewise to essay-writing; but I feel diffident, well knowing it to be a difficult and an exhausting kind of composition. Sometimes I have thought the form of dialogue a convenient one for exhibiting the different sides and bearings of a subject, and I have lately made one or two attempts in this kind, and shall perhaps proceed a little further. I think at least I have made up my mind not to search further for a historic subject. But I am again impeded in my pursuits by a failure in health, and am not able to apply much force of mind to any object. I read, however, much and variously, and seek to lay in ideas for more propitious seasons—should such be in store for me. It would be a great undertaking to 'teach this age to understand itself;' one ought first to be very certain of its being understood by the teacher. That spirit of aristocracy of which you speak, is of itself one of the most perplexing and, at the same time, important subjects of meditation and enquiry that I know, especially with reference to these times and this country. I have not only thought and conversed, but even made several attempts at writing on it, without being able to come at all near to the end, or the bottom of it. Is it true, I have asked, as some people say, that the English have more of this spirit than any people in Europe? Certainly not, if by the terms it is meant that the distinction of noble and plebeian families is broadest here. We have, in effect, no *noblesse* in the sense of old France or present Germany. Only the head of any family is a nobleman; the younger branches are all commoners, and do not even retain a titular distinction beyond the first generation from a peer. Yet there is some reason to assert that haughtiness of demeanour towards inferiors acknowledged as such, and still more, an extreme jealousy of rank and precedence, and an indignant rebutting of the pretensions of those a very little below themselves, are striking characteristics of our people. And why is this? I believe because there never was a country or a state of society in which men were so much the artificers, not only of their own fortunes, but of their own rank, as modern England. Every advantage, every distinction, is held forth to be struggled for. Each is striving to surpass his neighbour, and still more to be acknowledged by his neighbour himself to have surpassed him. It has been a frequent remark with our essay-writers and novelists, that persons of real rank and gentility were much less arrogant than pretenders or upstarts, which is likely enough to be true as a general rule. But in this land of merchants, manufacturers, men of science, men of letters, orators, preachers, politicans, and dandies, you may easily imagine that there are hundreds of pretenders and upstarts, or at least of men who have raised themselves, for one person of established, acknowledged hereditary rank, fortune, and consequence; and thus perhaps, in some degree, have arrogance and insolence become unfortunately almost national characteristics, at least this seems likely to be the solution of the fact, if fact it be. When you reflect upon the activity of all these various competitors for the respect or admiration of society, as well as its more tangible prizes, you will perhaps better understand the grounds of what little partiality I may feel towards the old aristocracy, the claims of which sometimes act as a useful counterbalance to other claims not better founded, and urged with more offensive self-sufficiency. But the tendency of our political state is to diminish all kinds of personal preeminence, a tendency of which, as you are aware, the associating spirit is both effect and cause. The diffusion of knowledge is in some respects to all the aristocracy of this age, what the discovery of gunpowder was to the military aristocracy of one age, and the Reformation to the ecclesiastical aristocracy of another. As for the trades' unions, I had absolutely forgotten that ever I had been afraid of them. It is now manifest that they cannot become *political* unions. They are not, as you seem to suppose, combinations generally of the poor against the rich, but of one particular class, the journeymen mechanics, against all the rest of society beneath and around, as much as above themselves. The unreasonable attempt of this class to enhance the price of *their* commodity, skilled labour, would if successful cause a general advance in the money value of all other commodities, which, by disabling our manufacturers from maintaining their ascendency in foreign markets, must bring poverty on the journeymen themselves in the first place, and then on the nation. This is so clearly perceived, that they have found no sympathy anywhere, and the delusion amongst themselves is subsiding, or will subside.

You may be right that we shall have no religious reform, but I think we must have various Church alterations before long. In Scotland, which has now first become a free country, and is likely enough to give the tone to England on several topics, the seceders have lately increased prodigiously: and it is not on doctrine that they depart from their Church, but on what they call the *voluntary* principle, that is, that the minister should be elected by those who are to attend upon him, and paid by them alone. The refusal of vestries to impose church rates, which is becoming general, proceeds on the same principle. In this trial of strength, or at least of numbers, between the Church and Dissenters, the Church, which is almost synonymous with the tory party, has been on the whole signally defeated. Even Church congregations begin to kick at patronage. Just now, a populous and respectable London parish, on losing its rector, sent a deputation to the Bishop of London, the patron, which took the novel liberty of requesting him to appoint a particular clergyman, unconnected with the parish, whom they named. The bishop replied that, in that case they, not himself, would be the patrons, which he did not intend to permit, and so sent them off malcontent. Tithe must be abolished forthwith in Ireland, and must, I conceive, be much modified here. Now, though these be in themselves secular matters, they indicate in the middle classes an hostility to ecclesiastics and their authority and interests which cannot be without its influence on religion itself, at least on the public exercise of it. The Evangelicals have not made a conquest of the whole people, far from it, as the defeat of their Sabbath Bill by the representatives of the people abundantly proves. Those, too, whom they have not subjugated they have vehemently provoked by their sourness and their spirit of dictation and exclusion, and I see great reason to believe that a large proportion of those who now unite with the *serious* party against the Church, would equally oppose giving either additional wealth or power to them.

It strikes me also as unlikely in itself, that ecclesiastics should escape being losers by that tendency to the levelling of all personal distinctions which I have already noted as belonging to this age. Their authority is more immediately dependent on public opinion than any other. It may seem an obvious remark, yet I know not that anyone has made it, and observed its bearings, that the necessity and value of oral instruction of every kind is, and must be, exceedingly diminished by the vast extension now given to the art of reading, and the circulation of books. A well-read layman, even of a humble class, will be little inclined to bow to the mere authority of a pulpit. Unless, therefore, some man of genius should arise to promulgate some new system peculiarly adapted to the tastes, the feelings, and the wants of this age and people, I prognosticate a period of religious indifference, and widespread disbelief. Even from the lighter literature of the day, one may infer the rising of a different spirit from that which, not five years ago, prompted all candidates for popular applause to mix up something of piety with every tour, every novel, every song, and every sonnet. I doubt if 'Sacred Annuals' will long continue in vogue. 'May religion,' I once heard a devout man say, 'be always in honour, and never in fashion.' Whatever has been in fashion will soon be out of fashion. Now in this land religion has been for a good while in fashion. The mode is changing. How I run on, as if I wanted to practise essay-writing upon you!

As to a history of England for your daughter, there is none for anybody's daughter. Hume is still the only very agreeable one, and his deficiencies and partialities you well know. Lingard is biassed by his profession and religion; and Turner is warped by systems and crotchets. However, they all deserve to be read, and out of them the careful reader may pick a history. What Hallam has given us both in his 'Middle Ages,' and his 'Constitutional History' is of inestimable value to the student, but too deep, and too technical for young ladies. There is a 'History of Great Britain,' by a Dr. Andrews, a Scotchman, which I read with great pleasure in my youth. It is written on the plan of giving in separate chapters the civil history of a reign, then the ecclesiastical, then the

history of commerce, of literature, of manners, &c. There is
no great merit in the style, which is flat and commonplace,
and the first chapter on manners is rendered strangely
absurd by his deriving those of the ancient Caledonians
from Macpherson's fabulous Ossian; but in spite of these
deductions, it is a valuable and agreeable work for the
early periods. It stops at either the death of Henry VIII.
or the accession of Elizabeth. I have not seen the work
for years, and later ones, Turner's especially, may have
gone deeper into the topics of manners and literature; but
I suspect it first opened my mind to those uses of history
which produced my own works in this kind, and I therefore owe it a good word.

You tell me nothing of your own plans or pursuits. I
fear you are not coming over to England for the winter,
as we had all been hoping—which is very shabby in you.
We shall but just be able to forgive you should another
report prove true, as I trust it is, that you are writing a
book. That will be some compensation, but indeed you
must not give up the dear project of coming hither, and
introducing your young people to English society. Recollect what you have sometimes written to me on the advantage of your best people coming and making themselves
known here. I shall make diligent enquiry after Bryant,
whom I long to see. Poets are rare with us. Coleridge
we have lost, and where have we his poetic equal? Of
which of his contemporaries can we say that he has written
too little?

Will you think me outrageously sentimental if I confess
to you that I have deplored even with tears the conflagration of our two Houses of Parliament, rich as they were
in historic recollections? The name of Pym was still to
be seen cut over the place which he occupied in the House
of Commons, the Armada tapestry still lined the House of
Lords. St. Stephen's chapel was built by our third

TO THE REV. DR. CHANNING. 321

Edward. In the Painted Chamber James and Charles used to lecture their sturdy houses of commons—and all are now ashes and ruins! We must be thankful that Westminster Hall itself did not share the same fate. There was great manifestation of feeling amongst the spectators of every rank. With all our faults as a nation, few of us are without a touch of filial love for old England, and pride in the memory of her glories. How absurd to call your mob *tories*! I trust your whigs will defeat them. There can be no fear of your lower classes not having power enough.

With every good wish for you and yours, and particularly that you would give us the opportunity of showing you hospitality,
Believe me, yours with true regard,
L. AIKIN.

No. 29.

Hampstead: March 10, 1835.

Avaunt! carpenters, bricklayers, gardeners, painters, and upholsterers; and let me hold converse with my dear distant friend. These people whom I exorcise are employed, be it known to you, in preparing for my reception a house to which I hope to remove very shortly; but this being Sunday, they and I enjoy a respite. It is no long flight, only to the opposite side of the street; but it will give me, besides better rooms, a delicious prospect from my windows. Thirty miles of varied and verdant country, sprinkled only with white houses, and bounded by the range of Surrey hills. This will be a new pleasure to me; I shall scarcely feel my solitude in the presence of so much of nature, and I *do* promise myself that, in the intervals of gazing through my window, my pen will exert itself to better purpose than heretofore.

Y

All that you say on the subject of dialogue I think just. The chief advantage of that form is not in conveying information, for which it has many inconveniences, but in representing discussion, and thus prompting the reader to exercise his own powers of reasoning and judging. It will serve to *hint* subjects of enquiry which it may not be convenient to treat more openly; and it may save a writer from hostile criticism, by enabling him to plead that he has represented both sides of a question without pronouncing for either. Call these paltry utilities if you please, but amongst a people where ancient prejudice is *hugged* by the million, the best friends of man's best interests may be thankful to take advantage of them. At present, however, I have scarcely made a beginning of my work; that is, I have got only one dialogue and a half, and some scraps which I think will hatch into essays. But of this enough. I have had by me for some time a message for you from a prince (but, thought I, I shan't write purely for that; the republican doctor will laugh at me). This prince, however, is a man of merit; it is the Duke of Sussex. At a dinner which he gave some time since to the Fellows of the Royal Society, of which he is President, and a few others, he beckoned to him my brother Arthur, to talk aside on the topic that he loves— religion. He spoke with delight of your sermons—said he had read every one that was printed. He had heard (would it were true!) that you were coming to England in the spring. 'I understand,' he added, 'that your sister corresponds often with him; tell her that when he comes I shall think it a great honour to be introduced to him. Will nothing tempt you to come to us? Surely, after the illness you have had, you would find travelling a restorative, and should you not like, 'antiquam exquærere matrem,' to make your own researches in Dorsetshire? Meantime I shall not lose sight of the object.

The first time I can get sight of Joseph Hunter of the Record Office, our first living topographer, one of our first genealogists, and withal a York student and Unitarian divine, I will mention the subject; and I dare say he can at least inform us how information can be gotten. It happens that I know absolutely not a person in that county. But you are Cannings, you say, and if so, I am afraid you must be content to take, along with the eminent statesman, a certain Bet Canning, who, about the middle of last century, contrived to make herself the talk of the whole kingdom by a well-invented tale of having been carried off and kept prisoner in a lone house near London, from which she made a marvellous escape. The particulars might be found in an old 'Annual Register' if you are curious; but perhaps you are not. I believe she is mentioned (either in the 'World' or 'Connoisseur') as the rival of a certain Mrs. Tofts, who professed to have brought into the world—a litter of rabbits.

Talking of pedigrees, I think I never told you that I saw, too late for my book, one of Queen Elizabeth, kept at Hatfield House, and certainly drawn under the eye of Burleigh, in which she is traced up to a personage called 'the second wife of Jupiter,' and collaterally, to no less a worthy than Cerberus himself; whence, no doubt, her habitual vigilance and occasional *doggedness*.

I quite agree with you as to the *prose* merits of our lake poets. Southey is an excellent prose man. The first circumstance which tended to redeem style from the cold regularity of the French school, and the pedantic latinism of Johnson, was the appearance of Percy's Reliques; from that time, and by the help also of the *true* elucidators of Shakespeare, Steevens, Malone, &c., old true English has been understood and written by all our writers of genius. There is no better English than that of poor Charles Lamb—a true and original genius—the delight of all who knew, still more than of all who read him, and whom none who had once seen him—my own case—could ever forget. Your praise of Artevelde I cannot quite agree in. The energetic simplicity and purity of the style, indeed, I much admire, but I cannot say that his personages do strike or interest me greatly. But I may be biassed. The detestableness of everything relating to the depraved creature whom he has made the heroine of his second part—the unspeakable coarseness and vileness of the man who is represented as running a long parallel between her and the virtuous wife whom he has loved and lost—these things we women could not bear or pass over. We have made no outcry, however, but our silent indignation has been felt. I thought his criticisms on Byron able, and to a certain degree just, but invidious. Byron's deficiencies, however great, do not prevent his having in some kinds, and in some passages, exhibited merits and beauties of the first order. Mr. Taylor is, I think, somewhat of a heretic in poetical doctrine, inasmuch as he says in company, that he holds Wordsworth for a much greater poet than Milton.

Twelve years ago I saw at Dr. Holland's a man of three-and-twenty, tall, rather well looking, with an air of talent, promptitude, and moderate self-confidence. He was the son of a clever gentleman-farmer, and just arrived from Northumberland to seek his fortune in London, bearing a letter of introduction from excellent Mr. Turner of Newcastle, his father's friend. Within three days, Wilmot Horton, then colonial secretary, said to Dr. Holland, 'These lords' sons do no good in our office, I wish you could recommend me a young man who would be willing to work.' The doctor mentioned the young Northumbrian; he was examined, approved, and immediately installed in a lucrative situation, which he still retains—and this was Henry Taylor. He printed some years ago a tragedy, which had no circulation. He was often at Coleridge's evening parties, and long ago I heard of his provoking some of the company by an *invidious* eulogium on the Koran. They were the more angry because he possessed the slight advantage in argument, of being the only person present who had read the book. I think, or hope, that he will yet write things worthy of ungrudging praise; and I much approve his manly style, as an antidote to the sentimental jargon of which we have so much; but he must cultivate moral refinement, to give pleasure where he must wish to please. Above all, he must never again make his hero exclaim, 'How little flattering is a woman's love!'

Almost two great pages without a word of politics! Not that they are not *the* object of interest at present; but what to think! what to remark or to predict! In the first place, however, I am not surprised at anything that has happened. I always thought it likely that the tories would make some effort to reinstate themselves in what they have so long regarded as their birthright—the government of the country, with all the advantages, privileges, and emoluments thereunto belonging. Something like treachery on the part of the king was also highly probable, considering the natural antagonism between royalty and whiggism. But in all this *I* see nothing alarming. With such a House of Commons as the present proves itself to be, in spite of the utmost efforts of the tories, who scrupled nothing of corruption, or intimidation either, to pack it to their minds—reforms we must and shall have, and effectual ones too. It is, I believe, not amiss, that every step of amelioration should be won with some effort and struggle. Every reform is the more valued, as well as the better understood, for being the result and reward of long agitation. We might therefore afford to have patience with the reluctance of ministers to proceed in the road which after all they must travel, were delay the only evil of the case. But I confess I feel hurt at the restoration to power of a party which I regard as essentially that of injustice and abuse—a party which in its best measures must always be open to the reproach of acting inconsistently with its own principles. Surely its reign will not be long. It is hazardous, however, to predict in circumstances unprecedented. A ministry outvoted in the Lower House, and an opposition outvoted in the Upper, is a new dilemma in the history of our mixed constitution. It is the opinion of wise men and friends of religious as well as civil liberty, that great part of all the reaction that there has been against reform has arisen from the rash declarations of certain classes of dissenters against an established church. They egregiously miscalculated their strength if they supposed that the Church could, yet at least, be outvoted, and the natural result of their vehemence has been that of rousing the clergy to tenfold fierceness against all sectaries and all liberals. There may be some chance, however, that ultimately the *sacred order* will find itself to have sustained irreparable injury, in lay opinion, by the exhibitions of its temper, and its maxims which have thus been drawn forth. I stand by my belief, that no form of religion in this country is extending, if preserving its authority over the minds of men.

You may be interested to hear that Brougham, like Cicero in his banishment, flies for support under political disappointments to the study of philosophy. He wrote the other day, to an old and respected friend of his and mine, to send him the works of Tucker, the answer printed, but not published, by Milne to Mackintosh's attack on Bentham, and several other books on ethical subjects. Will you charge yourself with my cordial thanks to Dr. Tuckerman for his ordination sermon and his pamphlet, from which I am glad to learn that his noble experiment proceeds and prospers? Your charge has very much delighted us all. One point, however, I want to discuss with you. It is the opinion given by both you and Dr. T., that, as well with you as in Europe, it is the tendency of modern improvements to increase the distance between the upper and lower classes. Now, with respect to your own country, it seems to stand to reason that it must be so; because you are beginning, and but beginning, to have a class *born* rich, and also because parts of your country are become densely peopled, and of course the wages of labour no longer there bear the same high proportion to the necessaries of life. But I doubt whether there is this tendency in *any* of the kingdoms of Europe, and here I discern more signs of an opposite one. I grant, indeed, that in some districts over-population, combined with neglect of the wholesome old law that no cottage should be built without a considerable garden attached, has depressed the condition of the agricultural labourer, but this effect is partial, and affects only the cultivators. In towns, wages were never, I believe, so high in proportion to the price of the articles of consumption; and never was education so widely diffused, never were the people so experimentally convinced of the great truth that knowledge is power. On the other hand, several circumstances have combined to bring down our aristocracy. The depressed state of agriculture has shorn down their incomes so low, that to pay the interest of their mortgages is more than most of them know how to compass. The reform bill has deprived them of the great resources in money and preferments, civil and ecclesiastical, which they used to derive from their borough interests, and places and sinecures are much diminished. In the mercantile class it is certain that much fewer great fortunes, and many more moderate ones are made by trade now than some years ago. I throw out these hints hastily, but you will know how to put them together. I must now conclude.

Ever yours most truly,
L. AIKIN.

No. 30.

London: May 13, 1835.

My dear Friend—Mr. Phillips shall not return to you without at least a few lines from me, and I take up the pen in London, and amid many distractions.

See if I was not right! The tories are out again. The will of the king put them in, the will of the House of Commons has nevertheless turned them out. Still our state is not altogether satisfactory; it is evident that severe and perhaps dangerous party struggles await us. I wanted to tell you—but when I wrote last had little heart to mention politics at all—that I think you simplify too much in your views of our state. It seems that you think we have but two parties, that of reform and that of abuse; but we have twenty, besides infinite shades of opinion, and there are pure patriots and corrupt and selfish designers in all. You will perceive that this must be so, when you consider that now, as in the days of the Stuarts, religion, or at least theology, mingles in the fray, and sects make factions. More to embroil the scene, we have persons who desire reform in the Church and not in the State—the case of numbers of the Evangelicals; others, ultra-radicals, who in new modelling the State would destroy the Church. The champions of civil liberty are compelled to fraternise with rank Irish papists, who have perhaps for their ultimate object the separation of their country from ours, and the establishment of their own church. These are but a few of the perplexing combinations of elements naturally discordant which we see taking place around us. There is much in our moral world to remind one of the old theory of the formation of the physical world by a dance of atoms and their fortuitous concourse; but as yet we have not risen out of chaos—the order and beauty are all to come. I found the other day in that most original work Tucker's 'Light of Nature,' the startling remark, that few people know what their own real opinions are; and I have since felt the truth of it, by reflecting on the *backward and forward talking* of almost all one's acquaintance—excepting those who have tangible interests involved in questions at issue. One day you find a man a decided reformer, the next day he becomes conservative, then he appears fixed in whiggism—till the next turning of the vane. Now the love of novelty, now the force of old associations, becomes predominant: Hope, Fear, and Memory play their busy part, and fixed principles are found scarcely anywhere. I speak the more feelingly on this head because the case is very much my own. The ultras of all the parties inspire me with repugnance, and perhaps fear; but there is a wide middle space which with me is land debatable, and through which I pick out an uncertain course. In theory I find it impossible to controvert the principle, that the will of the majority ought to prevail; but when I reflect on the blindness, the ignorance, the gross selfishness of that majority—that headlong multitude—I cannot but wish that it would be content to submit to the guidance of a wise and disinterested few; but then how are these few to be discovered and invested with power, and how are they to be preserved from being corrupted by it?

After all, I believe our people are improving in knowledge and in virtue under the discipline of these struggles, and this ought to reconcile our minds to the inevitable evils attending them.

Read, pray read, Wordsworth's new volume of poems.

You will there see how the dread of innovation has acted on a mind of no ordinary powers of reflection, not warped either by any immediate self-interest, but perhaps we may say, dominated by poetical associations with old castles, cathedral service, and village steeples. As a poet, I think he rather advances than declines; for though not a few of his new pieces appear to me failures, none of them have the puerility into which he used so often to fall, and there are some which I esteem of surpassing excellence. What a treasure of original thoughts, and sublime and touching imagery, and exquisite harmonies is his ode 'On the Power of Sound!'

Montgomery has likewise given us a new volume. It has some very striking narrative poems, and many fine stanzas; but how is his strain marred by his devotedness to a monstrous system of religion! I cannot easily understand how a mind so benevolent as his should have found the peace he says he has under his tremendous belief: but is it not true that there are some secret contrivances by which the worthy mind escapes from the consequences of shocking theories which it believes itself to admit, and thus secures the serenity which is virtue's right? Thanks for your sermon on war. I am not sufficiently informed of the facts of the case in your dispute with the French to be able fully to appreciate the weight of your arguments; but I trust that, after all, your President will not find it necessary to carry his threats into execution. I believe the genius of civilised nations is becoming less and less warlike.

Last night I saw Mr. Hunter, and asked how we could get any answer to your enquiries respecting your family. He said that he thought it very likely Channings were Cannings, and that the only *gentle* Cannings whom the heralds had been able to discover were seated in Oxfordshire—that George Canning's Irish family was *perhaps* a branch of it. If the Dorsetshire Channings were people of a certain consequence, some notice of them *might* be extant in Hutchins's 'History of Dorsetshire'—if not, the only course would be to make enquiries of some Cranbourne person, if the name was still known there. But I think yet I shall be able to find something out by other means.

I must here bring my epistle to a conclusion.

Ever most truly yours,
L. AIKIN.

No. 31.

Hampstead: Sept. 13, 1835.

My dear Friend—Your welcome and long expected letter arrived a few days since, just as I had begun one to enquire what had occasioned so long a suspension of our correspondence. I cannot account for the long delay of mine, unless by the supposition that it must have waited long at Dr. Boott's for an opportunity of sending it. I have certainly written you one since—by Mr. Phillips, surely—which I hope you have received. English and American will, I suppose, in process of time, become distinct languages, at least as to familiar idioms. When I told you that the workmen were preparing a *new* house for me, you understood that I was building one: an Englishman would have understood only that I was *changing* my house—which was the fact. My present dwelling would be regarded as a venerable relic of antiquity in your country. I dare say it has much more than a century on its head, though it is still strong and in good condition. Thanks to the remission of taxes since the reform bill, and of rates since the amendment of the poor laws, I have now a much better house than formerly for about the same money. Pray do not grudge yourself your healthful exhilarating only luxury. I know how deeply you both understand and feel the claims of the poor on their more prosperous brethren, the beautiful sermon you last sent me is a striking proof of it; but depend upon it you are doing more for them, and for the world at large, by keeping *yourself* in spirits and vigour, than by any amount of money you could bestow in deeds of charity. Not to mention that by giving employment to the industrious, we are often putting money to its most philanthropic use. You lament the fetters placed by custom upon the free energies of virtue, and most assuredly there *are* those whose own sense of the good and the beautiful would far excel any agency from without, both as motive and restraint. But are not those fitted, as well as 'content to dwell in decencies for ever,'—that is, the mass of mankind —the better, do you think, for the habit of submitting to restraint? If they had more free agency, would they not rather stray into absurdity, or lose themselves in recklessness, than rise to any higher notions of excellence? But in how many different forms are the questions continually recurring—When to take off the leading strings or *when* to remove the fetters? All the questions of internal policy which have been and are still shaking our state to its very foundations, may be resolved into these, and even where the restraint is one which has most manifestly originated in nothing but the prevalence of might over right, it is often held a point for grave consideration, how speedily, or how entirely it is wise to take it off. With us there are many who hold that the 'Voluntary Church System,' though best in itself, would not *yet* be best for the English people. Our tories were loth to allow that dissenters, papists, Irishmen, and negro slaves ought *yet* to be free from their wholesome restrictions, and the other day our House of Lords decided that a few links of chain ought still to remain around town councils. At the bottom of my heart I have a persuasion that the generous and especially the disinterested are the advocates of the earliest and the most complete emancipation; and my sympathies go with them; but then the alarmists and the weighers of expediency come round one with so many plausibilities, that I often, on particular points, become staggered at least, and, if not convinced, I am silenced. With respect to our country, however, I am entirely of opinion that the *when* is the only question. The popular cause has already gained victories which must lead to further and full success; unless, indeed, the reformers should offend the characteristic moderation and prudence of the nation by some strange ebullitions—hardly to be apprehended. The detection of this widely spread conspiracy to overpower a reformed ministry and liberal House of Commons, on the part of the Orange Association, headed by that disgrace to human nature, the Duke of Cumberland—shared in by many principal tory peers, and diffused widely through every rank in the army—is in every way a fortunate event. Its result must be, I think, to bring upon its knees to the people a faction which might have continued to be very formidable, had it not rendered itself detestable, and by its dark machinations brought itself within the danger of the laws. There can be no doubt that Cumberland's aim was to make himself the head of a party strong enough to place him on the throne, to the exclusion of his niece—a mad design, indeed, unless he believed the whole people to be enamoured of the character of Caligula. He has been driven from the country, never I trust to pollute its soil again, and his principal abettors will not, I suppose, choose to abide the proceedings of the attorney-general. These are strange events, and of absorbing interest to those before whose eyes they pass. You have well traced out to me the circumstances which are exerting the chief influence at present over your national character. No! with you politics cannot now be the ruling interest. Your fathers have won for you the unmolested enjoyment of the greatest inheritance upon earth; you have now to explore, improve, and enjoy it. You are destined to the good and the ill of a state of unexampled prosperity—unless the slave question be preparing a division of your federal union, with all the formidable results which would plainly be inevitable. To adjust the balance of moral good and evil in the causes which act largely on the character and manners of a nation, is probably a task beyond human power. All that the most enlightened philanthropy can perhaps wisely attempt, is to lean against the prevalent vices of the time, and cherish its virtues. At all times in all countries advanced in the arts of life, there must be abundant scope for the preacher or the philosopher to cry aloud, 'Be not conformed to the world;' be not immersed in matter; forget not the invisible, which alone is real and permanent! Long has your voice been heard, and much longer may it yet be heard, sounding these great warnings in the ears of men, and impressing on their hearts truths of the highest order. For myself, all my exertions are confined to the forming of projects, destined very probably never to be executed. During several months I have found myself in a state of languor which reminded me of the knight, in I forget what tale of chivalry, who had drunk unwittingly of the unnerving fountain, and lay stretched upon the grass, lost to all deeds or even thoughts of 'chivalrous emprize,' and unable to lift the spear or sustain the burden of his crested helm. I ascribe this listlessness partly to a very weak state of health aggravated by the unusual heat of the season, which is now happily abated, and partly to the deep impression made upon my spirits by very melancholy circumstances affecting those whom I dearly love. I think I must have mentioned before that Mr. —— was tried by severe sickness in his family. He has now two lovely daughters in confirmed declines, and one of them in the very last stage of this dreadful and hopeless disease. This last sweet creature, who has just attained the age of one-and-twenty, has one of the noblest, yet softest minds I have known—one of the finest, purest, and least earthly spirits. She long suffered her father and sisters to believe that she was ignorant of her state: at length she confessed that for months she had been fully aware of its hopelessness, and since that avowal she has at once wrung their hearts with grief, and warmed them with admiration by a bright manifestation of the treasures of her soul. 'In observing the state of her mind,' wrote her father to me, 'I rejoice with trembling; the question constantly recurring to me —Is it possible this can hold out to the end? Such firm composure—such a calm contemplation of her approaching departure—such confiding trust in the power and fatherly goodness of God—all this is more than could be anticipated even from her.' In this situation, which has now endured about three months, your writings have been her constant solace and support. Everything I had of yours which she was not before acquainted with, I have sent to her. Her father's last account, too, has this passage: 'She said yesterday she should have liked to be under the observation of Dr. Channing, and speculated upon the nature of the advice he would have pressed upon her, in her present state; whether he would not have considered her impatient under her trial—not sufficiently disposed to bear, as well as to do, the will of God.' I had written to her, that you were full of cheerful views under a dangerous illness some time since, and she begged I would send her an extract from a letter of yours, describing your feelings. This account I could not forbear giving you. Poor —— will be released, in all human probabilty, long before this letter can reach you, or I should have asked some little message for her; but perhaps you will give me a few words in your next for the heart-broken father and his other dear sufferer, also of a most angelic sweetness and goodness, and quite devoted to the service of the sister still more oppressed with illness than herself. But let me quit this melancholy subject. You have read, or you must read, 'Mackintosh's Memoirs' by his son (not the life prefixed to his historic fragment). It will certainly interest you in many ways, though I think you will agree with me that the impression on the whole is rather a painful one. Mackintosh, with all the ambition of his countrymen, had neither the frugality, nor the steady industry, by means of which a Scotchman usually climbs to fortune or to power. I am inclined also to believe, that his abilities were overrated, or at least wrongly rated, by himself and many of his friends, especially in the beginning of his career. Hence his life offers the history of little else than abortive attempts and half-executed designs. The wide range of his reading, the promptness as well as the accuracy of his memory and his power of just and sententious remark, gave so much power to his conversation—rendering it in fact so like a clever book—that the hearer involuntarily gave him credit for more than he in fact possessed of the powers of a fine writer; as a *debater* in parliament he had no talent, and even his set speeches were delivered to half-empty benches. His highest efforts, in whatever line, went just so far as to prove that he was *all but* a man of genius. He had attained self-knowledge when he said that his true vocation was that of a professor in a college; but to this his ambition and his passion for shining in London society, made him disdain to confine himself. Coleridge's 'Table-talk' is full of strange and rash opinions. I believe it to be neither an impartial nor an intelligent report of his sentiments—and yet a man with his habits might often talk wildly enough: you will find the book worth looking through, however. The second volume improves upon the first, and some of the literary remarks seem to me both fine and just. If I find myself gaining strength, and able to write without great fatigue, I will not neglect your kind request to write often and fully.

I have not yet seen the Ticknors, but am to do so on their return to London next month.

Ever believe me, with the greatest truth,
Your obliged and affectionate friend,
L. AIKIN.

No. 32.

Hampstead: Jan. 17, 1836.

My dear Friend—I will not wait for your acknowledgment of my last letter to write again, knowing by experience how long my letters, committed by Dr. Boott to private hands, have often been in reaching you, and more than suspecting by your silence respecting them, that two or three have never reached you. . . . .

In literature, by much the most considerable publication since I wrote last is Joanna Baillie's three volumes of dramas, which you will no doubt see. She tells me that her own favourite is 'Witchcraft,' and I think that it perhaps goes deeper into human nature than any of the rest. But I nevertheless prefer her tragedies in verse, and 'Henriquez,' and still more 'Separation' charms me. All these new dramas being of the domestic kind, necessarily fall short of the majesty of 'Ethelwald' and of 'Constantine,' but I think they have as much or more of pathos than her former ones, and not less of poetry; and in the arrangement of the plots and other points of dramatic skill, she has improved very considerably. To those who know her well, the value of all she writes is incalculably increased by its affording so perfect an image of her own pure, benignant, and ingenuous spirit. Her character, more, I think, than any I have ever known, deserves to be called a heavenly one; and when I think of it in conjunction with her rare genius, I can scarcely help regarding her as a being of a higher order.

Never in my life has reading been so constantly, almost so incessantly, the business of my life. My state of health confines me very much to the house; of society I have but little, yet the time very seldom indeed hangs heavy, for I can always lose myself in a book. My pen is seldom in use; I am too much cut off from opportunities of informing myself by conversation, too unable to run about in search of documents, to pursue any kind of historical enquiries, and it is but now and then that a subject for a brief essay or dialogue occurs to me. Perhaps indolence grows upon me; it is the natural companion of a monotonous and solitary life, in temperaments not irritable and not enthusiastic; and unless improving health should hereafter enable me, as I am still in hopes it may, to apply the stimulus of change of scene and company, I believe I must be content to allow myself to be numbered with those that *were,* by all but a few dear friends and relations. You will find me but a dull correspondent I fear—but a very grateful one ever for the pleasure and the benefit of your letters. I will trust mine no more to the precariousness of private hands, for I am quite sure that several proofs of my punctuality, if of nothing more valuable, have not reached you.

You have sometimes been inclined, I think, to reproach us with the miserable state of a large portion of our population, especially the congregated poor of our cities. I am happy to acquaint you that this great evil is rapidly diminishing. Never were manufactures, arts, and commerce in such a state of activity amongst us. An extraordinary impulse seems to have been given to *everything*; whence derived in the first instance, I know not. Manchester daily puffs forth fresh volumes of black smoke from more and more huge steam-engines. She invites all agricultural labourers who want work to come to her, and sets them down instantly to spin and to weave. Norwich, which I have known from my childhood as the melancholy seat of decaying manufactures and redundant population, has not now one able-bodied man on the parish books, and twice within six months the doors of her empty jail have stood wide open, for forty-eight hours each time. Our new poor-laws have happily cooperated with this state of things to raise the moral tone amongst the poor, by compelling them to rely more on their own exertions. With the outward prosperity of this class, there can be no doubt that their desire of giving school-learning to their children will go on increasing. The difficulties of establishing a national system of education I believe to be insurmountable in this country of religious divisions, but I think the object is likely to be on the whole better accomplished by the efforts of the labouring classes themselves, aided by the voluntary exertions of the benevolent and enlightened working on their own plans and within the limits of their respective religious societies. I apprehend that some kind of parish provision for the wretched poor of Ireland will be established in the coming session of parliament; but there also religious divisions formidably obstruct almost every plan for the general benefit. There is, and must be in a Protestant government, a reluctance to entrust large funds for the support of the poor to the management of the ignorant, and bigoted, and furious popish priests of Ireland; yet they are indisputably better acquainted with the necessities of the people than any other persons, and the want of a middle class, consisting of substantial farmers and decent tradesmen, in almost all the agricultural districts, seems to point them out as the only qualified dispensers of parish relief. I like to state to you such facts as these, that you may not underrate the difficulties or the efforts of our statesmen, amongst whom I believe that there is at present much wisdom and a very pure love of the public good. In a new country, or under a despotism, a general system may be laid down, and carried into effect with little or no modification; but here, hampered by ancient usages and inveterate prejudices amongst the people, compelled on all sides to respect vested rights, and yield to powers of resistance in bodies and in individuals, an administration can do no more than apply partial remedies to inconveniences, and carry plans and principles into a modified and restricted execution. There is, however, this great compensating advantage, that no changes can be made by any other power than that of public opinion, deliberately formed and strongly pronounced; and that a habit of discussion is thus formed and preserved by which one cannot but hope that much truth important to human happiness will continue to be elicited; especially as reasonings on practical questions of government and political economy are here continually made the subject of actual experiment.

We have all been sympathising with the sufferers in the conflagration at New York—one of the greatest, I should think, within memory; and we have felt for them the more, on account of the spirit and energy with which they have set themselves to repair their losses by their own exertions, which have been surely admirable, and quite in accordance with your national character.

Winter is dealing rather severely with us, and I fear with you likewise. I shall be happy to learn that you have not been a sufferer in health by it.

Pray believe me ever yours most truly,

L. AIKIN.

No. 33.

Hampstead: June 12, 1836.

This is indeed an awakener to my conscience! A second kind and delightful letter from you, whilst an answer to the first is still lying half-written in my desk, where it has remained untouched, I believe, a full month!

My only excuse is one which I rejoice that you had not to plead—an unusual severity and continuance of illness and debility, and perhaps an indolent disinclination to exert the little power which I still possess. But away with such impediments; I will make mind victorious for once over body! Your account of Harriet Martineau gives me great pleasure. I rejoice that her remarkable and fearless sincerity has been rightly appreciated among you; it sometimes made me fear for her in London, but there also what friends she made she kept. No doubt she will write a book about you, but I entirely agree with you that travellers always see imperfectly, and with a bias. Nevertheless, I should like you to look at Von Raumer's account of us. I believe him to be upright and sincere, and he gave me the idea of an industrious, and zealous, and rather able man of letters. The curious thing is, the coolness with which he takes for granted that Prussia is much further advanced than England in the science of legislation and government, as well as in the arts of music, painting, and sculpture; and the patronising tone with which he honours us on these matters, doing homage, however, to our surpassing wealth and luxury. It is true that Prussia may boast of a national system of education which imparts the rudiments of several kinds of knowledge, and of *singing and playing* to all; and that *they* have advanced so far as to put all religions on the same footing, not only with regard to civil rights, but to state endowments. Yet

I believe we shall not be brought to look up to any despotism, however mildly or prudently administered.

Germany is a country which now interests me much more than France, though I am struck with your ideas respecting the means now at work for her improvement, and I shall rejoice to see them verified; but to us Germany is of more importance. It is a school in which numbers of our young men are learning lessons, the results of which are likely, unless I mistake, strongly to influence religious *feelings*, rather perhaps than religious opinions, amongst us. One of these gentlemen, now about thirty, poured out his whole heart to me on these subjects the other day, taking me, I believe, to be the only female relation he had who could understand, or would bear with, him. He had returned some years ago from a first visit to Germany, resolute not to fulfil his destination to the English church. A second residence has only confirmed him in his abhorrence of creeds and articles, and admiration of the freedom of a German university, where all varieties of opinion are represented by one professor or another, and the students may attend whichever they please. He seemed to me devout as well as sincere. The cheap and simple life led by the inhabitants of Munich, where he has also found an agreeable circle of lettered and polished society, delighted him much. He will probably return to it, at least for a season; but, in the meantime, he is connected with a set of young Germanized Englishmen who write in a new British and Foreign Review, and are labouring to instil their free opinions into our public.

Full time it is now that I should thank you for your introduction of your nephew and his family. My illness, indeed, has prevented my seeing the mother and son more than once, when they paid me too short a visit, and your niece I have not seen, but I was very much struck and pleased with Mr. Channing. He instantly revived my recollection of you, which was in itself a great merit in him; but I can well perceive that he has much besides. His manners are such as no teaching could give, they are evidently the emanation of a noble and elegant mind. I was particularly struck with the candour he evinced in all his judgments, and the fine tact manifested in all he said and did. I congratulate you with my whole heart on possessing such a relation, and such a friend and associate as I am sure he must prove to you. I hope for one more glimpse of them before they finally quit London. Ah! why will you not come yourself?

I am all but a prisoner to my house and little garden. I am a miserable walker, and unable to bear without injury the motion of a carriage even for a short drive. I accommodate myself, however, to my circumstances better than I could have anticipated. Whilst I have books always, and the sight of friends sometimes, I find life more than bearable. The only thought which sits heavy on my mind is that of my own inutility. Alas! what important end of existence do I fulfil? To whom is it of any real consequence whether or not I continue to fill a place in the world? I hope only that involuntary uselessness will not be imputed, and that we may say, 'They also serve who only stand and wait.' The thing I find chiefly to be guarded against is indolence, or the habit of filling up time with trifling occupations which unfit the mind for any strenuous effort. I own myself guilty this way; I promise to amend—but how difficult to *make* motives for exertions! A necessarian would say, impossible. The thought of necessarians brings me back to that system of Hartley which you dislike so much. Surely it must be wrong to trace human character or human actions to any single principle, whether that of association or any other, for we cannot well help observing in ourselves the operation of a great complication of causes. But yet I suppose you would admit that there is not one of our active principles which is not strongly influenced by the power of association. How then do you limit its sway? The more I reflect upon the formation of human character, the more impracticable I feel it to reduce the facts to any general rule. It seems as if the doctrine of association had been employed by the French *philosophers* to represent that chance to which they were willing to ascribe everything. But the pious Hartley no doubt believed 'All chance direction which we cannot see.' Still I never could understand how his system was really compatible with moral responsibility—with the sense of human actions which God himself has surely implanted in our souls. I do not wonder that Mackintosh struggled so hard to find a middle way between two systems which appear each of them false and each of them true, according to the side on which they are viewed. This is all very crude, I am sensible, but I want to strike a light out of you if I may.

Pray believe me
Ever most truly yours,
L. AIKIN.

No. 34.

Hampstead: Dec. 10, 1836.

My dear Friend—Will you, or not, regard it as a palliation of my shameful deficiencies as a correspondent, that I have had in my paper-case for above two months a letter to you half-finished, which I have never found resolution to complete? The fact was, that I had there entered into some political speculations, the soundness of which I began to distrust as soon as I saw them on paper. I said to myself, 'Let them wait till I see more of the course of events in Ireland.' And thus they remained till a few days since, when I finally condemned them. Wiser people, and much more skilful politicians than I, have been as much perplexed to know what to expect, or even what to wish, for that luckless country. It seems to me that all the really puzzling questions in public morals, as in private, arise from having previously gone wrong. The straight line is generally obvious enough to those who have never quitted it, but hard to be distinguished by such as having deviated, are anxious to return to it by the nearest way. This is what one feels about the Protestant establishment in Ireland. The wrong step was to set it up whilst the majority of the people were papists; but to give to that abominable superstition the triumph of seeing it now at length pulled down again, goes very much against one's feelings, and all one's better hopes for mankind. Still worse would it be to see the reestablishment of popery, which seems to be aimed at by O'Connell and his red-hot followers. Meantime, there is unmingled satisfaction in observing the equal justice which is now administered there between men of the two religions, and the means taken to civilise their fierce manners, and to relieve their wants. Should this system be steadily pursued for some time longer, it may so mollify angry spirits as to render an equitable adjustment very feasible.

The warmest wish which my heart now forms for my country is the cessation of the vehement party struggles which have agitated us so long. To say nothing of the interruption of old friendships and of the comfort of general society which they occasion, they occupy many of the ablest heads, and most accomplished characters, to the exclusion of objects of higher, because more extensive and permanent, importance. Literature, as you well know, is in an unsatisfactory state amongst us. By writers it is too much regarded as a mere trade; by readers as one only of the contrivances for filling up the vacant spaces of life; like dancing, singing, or sight-seeing. But we may live to see a change. I have lately been paying a good deal of attention to the literature of the time of William and Anne; and it is cheering to observe what an impulse was given to it by that revolution which, like the one in which we are now living, was peaceable, and carried in favour of freedom, by appeals to the reason, the best feelings and the true interests of Englishmen.

Pray read, as I am doing, the 'Literary Remains' of Coleridge. In one passage he denounces with such indignant scorn those readers who presume to intimate that an author does not understand himself, when it is only that their stupid or ignorant minds are incapable of understanding him, that I certainly dare not intimate any such suspicion regarding him. I will only say that he has very many passages which pass my comprehension: some indeed, which are quite too deep in scholarship for me; others which I do comprehend, but which seem to me exceedingly absurd; others, again, which have more of the philosopher, and more of the poet, than we can hope from any one of our living writers with whom I am acquainted. His native proneness to the mystical seems to have received added force from his study of the German philosophy; but from that deep I often perceive that pearls are drawn up. I have frequently wished myself a diver in it. I feel, as I know you do, the 'flat, stale, and unprofitable' of our utilitarianism in everything. It rejoices my spirit when Coleridge launches a thunderbolt at that clay idol of our universities—Paley. As to his assaults upon unitarianism, I do not suppose they will much either irritate or alarm you. He is a perfect enthusiast for the Trinity, and especially for the doctrine of the fall of man. Of the last he says, that it is not only inconceivable to him *how* it should be true, but *that* it should be true; but that *it is* his conscience tells him so. As if a man should say, I know I am a beggar, and that convinces me that my great grandfather must have had a fine estate and forfeited it for treason. Next to these grand mysteries, he seems to cherish the notion that the genius of Shakspeare was actually superhuman; and he approaches an *apparently* absurd or immoral passage in his writings with full as much awe as a text of scripture—the plenary inspiration of which, by the way, he strenuously denies. Yet his lecture, on English literature, and particularly his remarks on Shakspeare, are full of deep thought, exquisite discrimination, profound sensibility, and brilliant and truly poetical illustration. It is a great pity that, as he delivered them almost entirely without notes, we have them only in the imperfect memoranda taken down by his hearers. They were perfectly *dazzling* as he delivered them. I was so fortunate as to hear two of them, almost thirty years ago.

I have not yet seen Miss Martineau, though several notes have passed between us relative to the memorial of English authors to your legislature concerning coypright. Mr. Farrar says the business would have been more likely to succeed if our government had interposed by its minister, and so I think too; doubting a little whether Harriet's interest at Washington will prove as powerful as she imagines—but the effort seems at least not likely to injure the cause, which is surely a just one. There will be, I hope, a good deal of curiosity to see our friend's book; but, unluckily, we have been inundated with books on America, and it will be difficult for her to find unpreoccupied ground. The slavery question is a rock in her way which will require wariness. Our public may think that *we* have purchased a right not to have our feelings further tortured with details of negro suffering. She will regard herself as addressing, perhaps equally, both sides of the water—for she seems to have left at least half her heart behind her—and this, I conceive, will make a difficulty. Miss Tuckerman paid me a short visit the other day, and left me desirous of seeing more of her. There is the stamp of something noble upon her, as indeed might be expected of her father's daughter.

With me time passes—as I believe it never does with you—heavily, languidly. I read and read, but can fix my mind to no pursuit, and my pen is quite idle. It might seem strange to say I am idle because I am alone, and yet I verily believe this to be the case. Under the perpetual misfortune of domestic solitude, I find it impossible to raise my spirits to the tone necessary for composition; idleness re-acts on my spirits, and unless I can make to myself, or circumstances should make for me, some kind of stimulus, this unsatisfactory state may continue to the end. Change of scene would be a grand medicine to my mind, but unfortunately travelling disagrees exceedingly with my health. Why do I trouble you with all this? I believe in excuse for a dull letter, or else from the pardonable wish of gaining a little sympathy.

Again my letter has suffered an interruption of many days. The melancholy of the last paragraph was, I believe, the gathering of a fit of illness. It is now dispersed, and I am going to enjoy myself at a friend's house in London, where much good company is to be met. I shall have the opportunity of asking Mr. Hallam when he intends to give us his history of the literature of (I think) the fourteenth and fifteenth centuries, which I am impatient to see. Just now I am reading—what indeed I have often read before, but the changes in our own sentiments often make an old book seem new to us—the great epic of Tasso. I never admired this noble work so much, and I am now wishing to see a critique worthy of it by some modern hand. The division of the poetry of Europe, since the revival of letters, into the classical and the romantic, is, I think, a good one; but it would be hard to say which school may best lay claim to Tasso; their respective shares seem balanced to a grain, reckoning, that is, by the number of lines which seem to belong to each. As to the value of the respective parts, the case is very different. From the ancients, Virgil in particular, he has servilely translated many passages and transferred some whole incidents; what is in the romantic style is full of life and interest, and, so far as I know, of originality. In one part he appears only the elegant scholar and versifier; in the other, the great poet. Had he not, from melancholy and distrust of himself, submitted his work to the tyranny and pedantry of classical critics, I cannot but think he would have given us an epic all romantic, and all worthy of his genius, which was not less fertile than graceful. How unaccountable it is that he should everywhere call the Mahomedans *pagans*, so intimately as Moors and Saracens were then known all over Italy. Did ever religious animosity so mistake the matter as when Italian papists reproached Mussulmans with idolatry! Ariosto misstates this matter as much as Tasso. I live upon the old masterpieces; lately I treated myself with the reperusal of 'Don Quixote,' which Coleridge, by the way, has very admirably and eloquently characterised. You are a great optimist; but will you give me any hopes that we shall ever see greater, or so great, works of genius again produced? The presiding power of this age is the steam-engine, and what has that to do with anything morally or spiritually great?

Pray believe me ever
Yours, with true regard,
L. AIKIN.

No. 35.

Hampstead: Feb. 12, 1837.

My dear Friend—Many thanks both for your kind letter and for your dedication sermon, in which I found much to interest me, although the general strain of sentiment is, as indeed it could not but be, very similar to what you had before expressed. I was much pleased with your biographical notice at the end of it. Here I reckon myself upon my own ground, and I entirely agree with you that 'no department of literature is so false.' Give us more of these sketches of your old worthies; this must bear to the mind of every reader the stamp of truth and resemblance, and the manner in which its subject dealt with his horrible system was very original and remarkable, and much worth recording. I formerly heard, from the lips of a large and free thinker, this problem :—Suppose that it were necessary, in order to carrying into effect the system which should produce the greatest amount of good upon the whole to the human race, that a few individuals should endure unrequited misery, such as should make existence to them a preponderance of suffering; would you say that it was inconsistent with the justice of God to adopt that system? I could find no other answer than this :—That if it were believed that there was to be even one such victim, as no man could tell that the doomed one might not be himself, it would destroy reliance upon the justness or goodness of God in every mind, and I could not believe in an unjust deity. But Dr. Hopkins would have said this was a selfish, wicked view of the subject. Somewhat a similar conclusion, though from very different premises, Mackintosh comes to in one of his speculations, where he seems to say that a man ought to be contented with believing that the *race* would go on indefinitely advancing in knowledge, virtue, and happiness, and discard the weakness of wishing or hoping that his own existence should be continued to be a witness of that advancement. But this is too sublime a height of virtue for me. After all, the origin of evil is *the* difficulty; it lies at the bottom of every system, whether of religion or philosophy, and by whom has it ever been solved? You express curiosity respecting our *visible church*, and want to hear more fully the grounds of my opinion that it is in danger, notwithstanding the stout rally apparently making in its favour. No doubt the sense of danger has called up zealous defenders, and to a small extent a coalition may have taken place between the orthodox, that is the half-Romish, and the evangelical, that is the half-puritan parties within our establishment. In fact, the ritual superstitions of one sect, and the doctrinal superstitions of the other, are not so absolutely incompatible but that interest may sometimes reconcile them, and it is from no advancement of human reason upon these points that I augur ill for the ecclesiastical fabric, but from more earthly considerations.

The spirit of our liturgy, and of our clergy, is basely, slavishly loyal. 'Fear God, and honour the King,' are injunctions which they have always coupled together as equally obligatory and sacred. Now the spirit of this age, as I need not tell you, is anything but this. Hence a wide and deep ill-will among the numerous classes towards the system, and still more towards the men. For proof of this, I cite the success which has attended all late attempts at abridging the exclusive privileges of the establishment. The new registration law, just coming into action, takes from the clergy, and without pecuniary compensation, the monopoly of performing marriages. It likewise adds a universal register of births to the registry alone of baptisms performed by the parochial clergy, and this too without compensation for probable diminution of baptismal fees.

The imposition of church rates has been so vigorously opposed by the advocates of the *voluntary system*—comprehending many churchmen, with the whole body of Dissenters—that the ministry *must* abolish them. Tithes in England have probably been saved for the present by a commutation; but High Churchmen, with some reason, regard this as placing the revenues of the church on a less independent and less secure foundation, making them stipendiaries rather than freeholders. In Ireland the tithe is certainly at its last gasp. The only claim advanced by Dissenters in which they have been as yet unsuccessful is that of admission to Oxford and Cambridge without a declaration of belonging to the establishment; but it has been found necessary to grant power of conferring degrees without that condition to an academic body in London, and probably the universities will find it their interest soon to yield.

Another awkward circumstance for the church is this. The vast increase of our population was naturally judged to require an addition to the number of places of worship. Parliament under the tories, and with many bitter speeches from the opposition, granted large sums for building churches, and by the activity of zealous persons, especially the Bishop of London, large subscriptions have since been raised for the same purpose. But how to endow the officiating ministers, and provide for current expenses, has become a greater difficulty than raising the edifices. Tithes and other church funds being already appropriated, it was necessary to have recourse to pew rents, and it appears as if the children of the establishment, accustomed to get their religion gratis, so grudge this payment, that the new churches and chapels mostly turn out failures, and starve their ministers. A person above this sordidness, but more attached perhaps to the doctrines than the forms or rites of the church, and caring more for the preaching than the prayer-book, is tempted to say however, 'If I pay, let me at least pay to a chapel, where I may hear a minister chosen by myself and the rest of the congregation, and not forced upon us by the rector or the bishop.' And thus it seems as if dissent would gain by the very measures taken to counteract its increase. To call in the voluntary principle *in part* is hazardous for an endowed church. There has also been a little civil war between a commission, chiefly bishops, appointed to attempt some gentle reforms in the church, and the deans and chapters, whom the pious prelates have defrauded of some patronage, and converted to their own benefit. Sydney Smith, that bright wit and independent politician who founded the 'Edinburgh Review,' is one of the aggrieved, and has stated their case in a keen pamphlet which unmasks that would-be Laud, the Bishop of London, and which—contrary, I believe, to the author's intentions—gives a handle to the enemies of the hierarchy altogether. These are the signs of the times on which I found my auguries; but very much of the fate of the church, as well as state, will depend on the event of the renewal of that grand conflict between our two houses of legislature which is now imminently impending. For my own part, I see indeed many dangers, many evils, on both sides of the question; but I feel my heart beating stronger and stronger towards the cause of the people; regarding that cause, however, as what would be best promoted by the preservation of our triple form of government, with some modification of the authority of the peers, and especially with the great improvement of the exclusion of the bishops from their house.

I do not wonder that you regard the kind of religion now prevailing here as little fitted to elevate the mind, and useful only as a restraint. In fact the *currency*, whether stamped with the effigies of prelate or heresiarch, is of base alloy; but our *cabinets* contain thousands of pure gold medals. The present concern should be to cry down the base coin, afterwards we may raise the standard. You will see my meaning if you will examine an article in the 'Edinburgh Review' on Evangelical preaching. I know not who is the author, but I think him on the right track. It would break my heart to believe that superstition and hypocrisy were to hold in perpetual bondage my dear and noble country. They must not—will not—shall not !

Since I began this letter I have had the pleasure of a visit from your friend Mr. Gannett. We seemed acquainted at once, and had a long and animated conversation, partly on the topics of this letter. I am much pleased with him. It is impossible to mistake his sincere devotion to the highest and best objects. I hope we shall return him to you well recruited for future exertions. In literature I have seen nothing lately of much interest, for I have not yet seen Mr. Hallam's new work. There is a life of Goldsmith, prolix, and in every respect meanly written; the account of his early days, however, is worth reading, as a picture of Irish manners about a century ago. Nothing is more remarkable than the loose notions of property among persons of some education. Those who wanted, however much it was their own fault, asked as a matter of course, and what is more, received as a matter of course, relief from persons whom the same carelessness might reduce to beggary to-morrow. It seems that the description in the 'Deserted Village' of the exemplary clergyman who so freely received all beggars and vagabonds for his guests and companions, was a true draught from Irish life, such as the poet saw it in his own father's house. According to our Irish poor commissioners the same amalgamation seems still to subsist between the begging and the farming population, and I apprehend it had its root in the old Brehon law, which gave the property of land to the whole *Sept* in common, and merely temporary occupation to individuals. One might say that the Irish have never owned anything but land, and in that, or its profits, all have regarded themselves as entitled to some share. In this there seems to be some natural justice, but how incompatible with civilised English notions. Poor Goldsmith, with his boundless sympathy and good-nature, and thus brought up, became in London a constant prey to rapacity and imposture, and when brought to distress, he preyed on others by running in debt to them. His habits of life were far from right and correct; but still he had 'a spirit finely touched,' he always served virtue with his pen, and his delightful works seem no nearer oblivion than when they first appeared. I am glad to see him brought again before the public.

I have heard no more since my last writing concerning our German students; in fact, we are too busy at present with practical matters concerning our church and state to have much leisure for the speculations of philosophy in which the Germans may freely indulge. I wish we also found ourselves too busy to dip into the infamous and corrupting novels now so prominent a part of the literature of France. You may see that our reviews, under colour of reprehending, are exciting curiosity respecting them, and I fear they are fast gliding into a half secret circulation.

Our whole country has been saddened by a severe epidemic, under the name of influenza, of which many, chiefly of the aged and the weakly, have died. It is abating now. With me it dealt lightly, and I am now in usual health.

I rejoice to hear good accounts of your recovered strength.

Believe me ever truly yours,
LUCY AIKIN.

No. 36.

Hampstead: April 23, 1837.

My dear Friend—The very great kindness of your last, which I received lately, impels me to answer it speedily, though I think you will ere now have had one of mine, written in much better spirits than that which so much excited your concern for me. Yes, body is to blame, I believe, whenever my spirits are depressed without any evident cause, for they are usually victorious over all minor miseries, and they, like my health, are now recruited. It appears that thousands have been attacked, during our long visitation of influenza, with this dejection of mind; that in many cases it has formed the leading symptom of the epidemic—so mysteriously do mind and body act and react upon each other! This extraordinarily prolonged winter has aggravated all our evils, and we are but just beginning to feel a milder air breathing upon us. The face of nature is still wintry and dark. Fortunate may those account themselves who, like myself, have not been called to mourn for any very near and dear; the mortality has been appalling. The weakly, and particularly the aged, have been mown down in heaps. Since the plague of London, so large a proportion of its population has never fallen in a single season.

Do you enquire what our public is now occupied with? We have forgotten our epidemic, we have waived politics for a space, and have been supping full with the horrors of a bloody murder. Not that we care so very much for the simple circumstance of a man's killing a woman whom he pretended to be on the point of marrying; but to have cut off her head and limbs afterwards, that is what has shocked us above measure. I believe, however, the general feeling is in this instance right, and that, even of the persons capable of a cold-blooded mercenary murder, but few could bring themselves to attempt such a mode of disposing of the remains. I should be sorry to see our populace cured of all reverence for the shell which has once contained a human spirit. In this case, the police were obliged to fight hard with the mob, to prevent them from tearing to pieces the murderer, and a woman, his accomplice.

Are you aware that the humanity of our rabble is one topic of our national boasting. Unlike the French, mobs with us never shed the blood of any whom they regard as their own political enemies. I am not aware that they have massacred since the days of Jack Cade. Then they always take the part of the weaker. A man could scarcely do anything so dangerous as to treat a child with cruelty in the streets of London. Formerly they were unfeeling towards the brute creation; but owing, I think, to two circumstances—the diffusion of the taste for natural history by Penny Magazines and by the Zoological Gardens, and the enactment of penal laws against cruelty to animals—a great and admirable change has taken place; insomuch that it is now a protection to cattle to be driven to market through the great thoroughfares of the city. I am inclined to think that no evil propensity is so generally counteracted by the influence of education as that to cruelty—the vice, peculiarly, of the unthinking and the uncivilised. In this point, at least, the connection between knowledge and virtue is perfectly clear. Would it were equally so in many others.

A strange thing, good sir, that you should have been preaching here in Hampstead church, fifty yards from my door, without letting me know a word of the matter! It must have been you no doubt, for I am credibly informed that a stranger delivered in that pulpit, a few Sundays ago, one of Dr. Channing's most admired discourses, changing nothing whatever but the text. Yours is a wide cure seemingly! This brings me to what you say of the value of a *great idea*, which gives 'unity to our inward being.' You have a great right to speak of what you know so well from happy personal experience. I will add that I regard it as the highest privilege of your profession, when embraced from pure motives and strong convictions, that it connects by so close a bond the inward and the outward life. It is the single care of the good pastor to put his most intimate thoughts into all his judgments upon the practice of others. From this concentration of his whole being, he derives that mighty power which enables him to wield the minds of men almost at his pleasure. No other class is thus privileged. A physician, for example, may overflow with devout feeling in his closet, but when he quits it he must take up studies and occupations quite unconnected with religion, which he cannot even introduce into his discourse but at the risk of giving offence, or of incurring suspicions. He must not take upon him to be weighing the actions and characters of other men in the scales of the sanctuary; if he makes them his own standard, he cannot very gracefully proclaim that he does so. Hence a kind of complexity in the scheme of life, and especially a separation between inward and outward, unfavourable to ardour and to strong moral effects. The same may be said of persons engaged in every other walk of active life; but the contemplative and the literary, if they are willing at least to live almost out of the world, may in good measure *enact their own ideal*. The ancient philosophers appear often to have done so, and they also were able to form schools of disciples, as were Godwin and Bentham in our own times. But for this, a spirit of dogmatism is requisite, with which many neither are nor would wish to be inspired. Certainly a *great idea* is like the faith which could remove mountains, but to think we have found a *great*, and at the same time a *new* idea, that is the difficulty. I own I have as much hope of finding the philosopher's stone. Continual reading, if desultory and without a definite object, favours indolence, unsettles opinions, and of course enfeebles the mental and moral energies. Writing, on the contrary, concentrates the thoughts and gives strength to convictions. I feel that since I have disused it my mind has become, if I may say so, of a thinner consistency. When by chance I turn to some passages of my James, or Charles, I am apt to say to myself: Surely I was a *man* when I wrote that, who am now a mere old woman. This is lamentable enough. I wish I dare promise to find a remedy; perhaps I may, however, for since my health is amended, I feel an appetite for labour to which I had long been a stranger.

As to public affairs, we are all *at gaze*. Must the whigs go out? Dare the tories come in? Will the commons pass this bill? Will the lords throw out that? These are the questions which everybody asks, and nobody can answer. The king will not let the parliament be dissolved, that seems certain; and parties are so nearly balanced in the legislature at present, that neither seems able to do more than obstruct the measures of the other. It is like a great stoppage of carriages in the street; the people who sit fretting in their coaches think it will never be over; but sooner or later some broad-wheeled waggon or brewer's dray will move out of the way, and people will proceed on their various errands as usual. We are waiting for some accident or incident. Meantime all parties are much out of humour, in particular the *odium theologicum* is in high venom.

Poor Lord Melbourne is half distracted whenever a bishop dies, because there is such a difficulty to find whig parsons out of whom to make a new one—that is, such as are old and seasoned; plenty may be had made up in haste, on the spur of the occasion, but those are liable to warp by change of seasons. The last who died, Bathurst of Norwich, still more venerable by his virtues than his ninety-three years, was a true patriot, a fine scholar, a finished gentleman, and what might be called the Christian of every church. *Because* he believed his own church the truest and the best, he was anxious to remove all such bulwarks from about her as tests and subscriptions; *because* he was a really pious and exemplary man, he disdained affected rigour and evangelical sourness. I once heard him deliver a charge to his clergy, which was the best adapted to inspire at once veneration and filial affection that could be conceived, and the gracefulness of composition and delivery was inimitable. On being introduced to him, I almost wished to beg his blessing. Norwich is one of the poorer sees; and, highly endowed and highly connected as Bathurst was, he might have insured a speedy translation on the usual terms. But having opposed a tory ministry on an important question he said, on returning from the House of Lords, 'I have lost Winchester, but I have satisfied my conscience.' If you look into Lockhart's 'Life and Correspondence of Scott,' of which one volume has appeared, and as many more will appear as the public will submit to pay for, you will find an amusing fragment of an autobiography, comprising enough of the early years of this extraordinary man to show distinctly the circumstances by which the turn was given to his tastes, sentiments, and pursuits. Much of his sickly childhood was passed at a farm-house, where his chief companions were cattle, and the peasants who tended them. His predominant inclination being to hear stories in order to tell them, he soon made himself master of all the epics of that border country, and hence his heroes are always of the moss-trooping order, and his machinery consists of brownies, kelpies, and fairies. Hence, too, his unquenchable animosity against the *Southrons*. Observe how seldom he draws an Englishman but as a coward or a fool. His vivid fancy, his animal spirits, his good humour and habitual kindliness, and his perfect freedom from affectation, must be liked, and might be envied; but the furniture of his mind was really made up of trumpery. Elevation of sentiment he had certainly none, and philosophy was far from him as the antipodes. Mr. Whishaw said once, of Bentham, that he was a schoolman born some ages too late: Scott was a stark moss-trooper in the same predicament, and a jacobite.

Since I began this letter I have been making a *reviving* visit in London, in the midst of kind old friends, liberals, and literati. One tone I find pervading all the men of deep and sound learning in whatever department, and it is what you will not like to hear of. It expresses a full conviction that the attempt to diffuse knowledge by means of society tracts and mechanics' institutes began in enthusiasm and proceeds in quackery; and they deprecate it, not in the spirit of aristocracy, but in the name of good letters, which they see to be sustaining severe injury by the attempt, on every subject, to write *down* to the dull or ignorant. It used to be said of learning in Scotland, that 'all had a mouthful, and none a full meal,' and it is to be feared that something like this will be the case here; at least so say the croakers. I hold out the consolation that the multitude will throw down their books when nobody is watching and take up some pastime which suits them better; and then the old distinction of learned and unlearned will return. But there is a strange tendency to fly from one extreme to another. I perceive that young ladies, fatigued with lectures and languages, have fairly returned to the stupid cross-stitch works of their great grandmothers; and who knows but they may resume the laudable practices of spelling at random, and writing from corner to corner. My present occupation is reading history; that of the Romans occupies me at present. I have purposes in this course of study, but no formed plan as yet.

Believe me ever very truly yours,
L. AIKIN.

The Duke of Sussex desires I will lend him your last sermon. He has been ill, and loves religious reading.

No. 37.

Hampstead: Oct. 14, 1837.

My dear Friend—Your welcome letter, yesterday received, contains matters which will not suffer me to leave it a day longer unanswered. Well might you be sorry at the tidings that I sympathised in Miss M.'s ideas of the sphere of woman; but if she is in the habit of advancing her opinions on no stronger foundations than she has for this, small must be the proportion of truth in them. The facts are these. I saw her a few days after her book came out, when I had only looked in it for half an hour, and was even ignorant that she had said anything on the subjects of marriage and divorce, on which I hold her doctrine to be as ignorant, presumptuous, and pernicious as possible. With regard to her notions of the political rights of women, I certainly hold, and it appears to me self-evident that, on the principle that there should never be taxation without representation, women who possess independent property *ought* to vote; but this is more the American than the English principle. Here it is, or was rather, the doctrine that the elective franchise is a trust given to some for the good of the whole, and on that ground I think the claim of women might be dubious. Yet the reform bill, by affixing the elective franchise only, and in all cases, to the possession of land, or occupancy of houses of a certain value, tends to suggest the idea that a single woman possessing such property as unrestrictedly as a man, subject to the same taxes, liable even to some burdensome, though eligible to no honourable or profitable, parish offices, ought in equity to have, and might have without harm or danger, a suffrage to give. I vote for guardians of the poor of this parish by merely signing a paper, why might I not vote thus for members of parliament? As to the scheme of opening to women professions and trades, now exercised only by men, I am totally against it, for more reasons than I have time to give.

But there is more. In a very merry little female circle, at the time I mentioned, and I have never seen her since, we hailed Harriet as our champion, between joke and earnest, and she then told us of the scheme of a periodical devoted to the good of the sex, of which she was to be the editor. The chief points she then dwelt upon were, the sufferings of the *most unhappy* class of women, and the necessity of taking more pains to explain to poor girls at school the snares which encompassed them, and the utter ruin to which one false step exposed them. In this I zealously concurred. . . . So far, and only so far, do I agree in any opinions peculiarly hers . . . . I impute to her no designed misrepresentations, but she is a visionary who, in more senses than one, turns a deaf ear to all objections and remonstrances; takes silence for concurrence, and imagines that all who show some friendly interest in her must of necessity be her *disciples* in all the force of the term. I, like you, heed little either the praise or the censure she gives young people; but indeed, indeed, it is somewhat hard that on her eulogy of American good-temper you should found a charge against us of ill-temper. Poor stupid John Bull has generally been reckoned good-natured at least. But what presumption in any individual to speak of the tempers of a whole nation! What false judgment do we often form of those of our familiar acquaintances!

I have no doubt your packet would be exceedingly welcome to his Royal Highness the Duke of Sussex, notwithstanding any republican plainness in the address—I conclude you do not direct to Mr. Augustus Guelph. You say you do not care enough for our aristocracy to learn their titles, and at this I do not wonder. The history of nobility in England is, however, a curious subject, on which an essay might be written, and I rather wonder such an one has not been written, capable of throwing much light on our history, and of explaining that attachment to the peerage which now perplexes you. It is because the nobility formed a *caste* in France, but has never done so in England, that the order is viewed with such opposite feelings in the two countries. In France all the descendants of the noble were *noblesse,* and enjoyed immunities given to the detriment of the people at large, and which no *bourgeois* or his children could hope to share. Here the children of the highest peer are, all but the eldest, and that after his father's death, commoners in the eye of the law. They enjoy no immunities, and the humblest man in society is not always without a chance of seeing his son a peer, spiritual or temporal. The father of Lord Nelson was an obscure country clergyman; the father of Lord Lyndhurst an American painter; of Bishop Blomfield, a parish-clerk. Lord Ashburton was himself a merchant. And these are the circumstances which attach the middle class to the lords: they are their own flesh and blood, and even in their haughtiness they take a natural kind of pride. To this you must add the respect which an Englishman can scarcely help feeling for the ancient families, sprung from those barons who wrung Magna Charta from a mean-souled tyrant, and who at many other trying periods of our history bought with their blood our laws, our liberties, and our glory. Think how many lords stood for the people against Charles! Almost all the parliament's first

generals were peers. And it was by a few whig lords that
the revolution of 1688 was planned and brought to effect.
Long live the principle and practice of religious dissent!
As a mass, zealous churchmen of every rank are tories at
heart. The principle of passive obedience, the worship
of the powers that be, is almost inextricably interwoven
with our establishment—certainly the most systematically
servile in Christendom. Of the present reaction, as far
as it exists, several causes may be assigned, of which I
take the strenuous efforts of the clergy trembling for
many things—their surplice fees among the rest—to be
one of the chief. There has certainly been much bribery,
and still more intimidation, on the part of the tories, and a
very unjust cry raised against ministers on account of the
new poor law, in favour of which none of them were more
warm or decided than Wellington and Peel. But several
of these obstacles to the popular cause are temporary in
their nature, none of them absolutely invincible; and if
our young queen should continue her confidence to Lord
Melbourne, whom at present she delights to honour, and
who has had the wit to surround her with whig ladies of
the household, I see not but that the small ministerial
majority may suffice to keep the whigs in office. At any
rate, I strongly confide that all really useful reforms will
sooner or later be carried, even without invading the constitution of the House of Lords. The fact is, that the
sovereign, if sincerely bent upon it, has always means
sufficient, by the application of certain court rewards and
punishments, of commanding a majority in the upper
house; and the commons, by their command over the
purse, can *compel* the sovereign to use this power in
conformity with their will. Thus the result of all is, that
a majority of the lower house can always make itself obeyed
in the long run. The house, like the nation, is at present
nearly equally divided; but with the spread of light and

knowledge I believe that the party of liberty is also diffusing itself—and think what victories it has already achieved. Rash or unjust measures on either side may temporarily depress, by disgracing, one or the other party, but I do not greatly fear the ultimate event. This great nation *will have* what appears to itself a good government. Indeed, to say the truth, we have not now a bad one, though, like all human institutions, it might be improved. I wish I could see the people better. But the crying sin equally of our nation, and of yours, and of all commercial nations the 'auri sacra fames,' goes on augmenting with the growth of trade, of manufactures, of mechanical inventions, and even, I fear, with the diffusion of the elements of knowledge. To give men new wants is indeed the way to make them industrious, but it is also the way to make them rapacious, dishonest, gambling speculators, and in public life corrupt.

Reverting to what you say of the imputations cast on H. Martineau in your country, I think it due to her to state, that I have never heard of anything against her personal morality, and large allowances must be made for the hatred which she has meritoriously drawn upon herself from your slaveowners, and their base abettors. . . . . . There are no new books much worth mentioning to you; indeed this is not the publishing season. I hope Hallam's volume will soon appear. I hear he is now able to employ himself, though still very sorrowful for the loss of a lovely, lovely daughter, who was his worthy pupil and delightful companion.

Adieu, and believe me
Ever truly yours,
L. AIKIN.

No. 38.

Hampstead: April 18, 1838.

Ah, how kind! You write and thank me for a letter of I know not how old a date, when my conscience has been reproaching me, I know not how long, for leaving your last but one unanswered. But how could I write with any comfort so long as that sad Canada business remained unsettled? Whilst I could not tell whether violent spirits might not even make us *foes*—as far as national hostilities could render us so? Happily, most happily, these fears are all at an end. We have all possible reason to praise and thank your government for its conduct towards us, and it has taken away our common notion, that your central force wanted strength to control the self-will of your borderers. Democracy has done itself great honour by you. For a while, I knew not what to say for it, to myself or to anybody else.

It is very difficult for our two nations to understand each other, yet I assure you I have long given your people credit for that 'fire under snow' which some Frenchwoman ascribes to Englishmen. With regard to our *boxing*-matches * I have only to say that they are not a *popular* amusement; being totally illegal, they are never held in cities, but only in by-places, and are frequented by few except those called, in *slang* phrase, 'the Fancy'— that is, an assemblage of gamblers, sharpers, ruffians, and profligates of every degree, from the duke to the chimney-sweeper. Respectable men, even of the lower classes, never need witness them, and seldom do. I think I mentioned mercy to animals as rather a *new* feature of our national character, brought out by laws and education.

* Since this was written the United States have sent us their Heenan, to meet our Tom Sayers.

The same causes have produced a striking amendment in respect of profane swearing; I am told that no member of a mechanics' institute ever utters an oath, and even coachmen and cabmen shock the ears less than formerly. Your rector who said the English whipped their wives, I take to have been regardless of truth; at least, in my whole life, I never either read or heard of one single instance of that infliction; though of many, alas! of husbands injuring, or even killing, their wives by kicks and blows of the fist. In ninety-nine cases out of the hundred, intoxication—either of the man, the woman, or both—is the occasion of these brutalities. If, or let us say *when*, we grow more temperate, we shall mend in this point. Our law does what it can for beaten wives, by binding husbands over, on complaint, to keep the peace; and I am told that the merest clown feels deeply the disgrace of this, and seldom offends again. *Paddy* is a much more frequent offender, by pugnacity of every kind, than cooler *John Bull* or *Sandy*.

No!—born champion of my sex as I may almost call myself—I say deliberately, on good knowledge and careful consideration, that there are only two points in which it seems to me that our laws bear hard on women. The first is, in the want of a stricter hand against the inveiglers of girls for wicked purposes; the second, in the full power which the father is still allowed to retain over his children when *his* offences have compelled an innocent wife to obtain a divorce from him. It is surely most monstrous that a woman should be restrained from separating herself, under circumstances of the most aggravated offence, from a brutal and unfaithful husband, by his inhuman threats of never letting her see her children more—of placing her daughters under the very care of his mistress—a menace which I know to have been uttered!

On carefully comparing the Code Napoleon with ours,

I am convinced that we have the advantage of French women. Yet, understand me, not as admitting that we have nothing to complain of. Society wrongs us where the laws do not. The *life* of a woman is esteemed of less value than that of a man. Juries of men are very reluctant to punish the slayer of his wife as a murderer. Her *testimony* is undervalued; men-juries often discredit her evidence against a worse than murderer. She is wounded by the privileged insolence of masculine discourse. 'Woman and fool,' says spiteful Pope, and dunces echo him. Any feeble-minded man is an 'old woman;' fathers cry out to their boys in petticoats not to care what their elder sisters say to them. These and the like insults, when my blood was hotter than now it is, have cost me many a *bitten lip*. One of our legal exemptions signally offends me. It is that which grants impunity even for felony committed by a wife in presence and under control of her husband. Has a married woman, then, no moral freedom? Must her vow of obedience include even crime? Surely this disgraceful exemption ought now, at least, to be withdrawn, when that immoral vow is no longer an essential of the marriage rite. On the whole, however, I think the present age is more favourable to our sex than any former one. Women are now, with us at least, free of the whole circle of arts and sciences; they have neither ridicule nor obloquy to encounter in devoting themselves to almost any department of knowledge. All men of merit are forward in cheering them on; they are more free than ever. Alas! I speak of women, but you may say I only mean gentlewomen. In truth, I *can* speak of none else with personal knowledge—the miserable drudges, the beaten and half-famished wives, and a class still more miserable, are never seen, never heard of by me in my tranquil home. I know not whether it ought to humble me—perhaps not, all things considered; but the fact is, that I know scarcely more by actual survey of the dwellings, the manners, the characters of the most numerous class in England, or even in Hampstead, than of the inhabitants of Pekin. As to the attachment of women to priests, it is curious to observe how little there was of it in England a century ago. Recollect how bitterly Swift complains of their contempt for divines and exclusive preference of *beaux* and the military. *Ladies* are, no doubt, much superior now in education, tastes, and manners, to that generation: then they played quadrille; now they read theology, and attend lectures, and gather pence for missions and bible societies. In this country we are subject to *rages*, and these things are, or have been, the rage amongst us. But the influence of the clergy over women is so natural that the wonder is to find that it was ever suspended. They seize the female soul both by its strong and its weak sides, its spirituality, its thirst after perfection, its docility, its hopes, its fears, its melancholy, its lively and often ill-regulated imagination, and its general averseness, or incapacity for close reasoning. And this last defect, little is done by modern systems of culture to correct. I see numbers of men, and a still greater proportion of women, full of acquirement and accomplishment, but mere children in reason—absolutely destitute of the first elements of philosophy, and willing to give up their souls to the guidance of the first who will take the charge. Many times of late it has been a project with me to write something or other respecting us Englishwomen; but alas! I have lost all energy, and my projects come to nothing. If you were to lay your commands upon me to write you some letters on this subject, perhaps— for think what I have just said of clerical influence over *us*—and I declare that if any reverend gentleman has power over me, it is you.

Carlyle *does* offend my classical taste; but the worst of it is that I have been absolutely riveted to his first volume, which I have this minute finished, and that I am hungering for the next. A very extraordinary writer certainly, and though somewhat, I must think, of a jargonist, and too wordy and full of repetition, yet sagacious, if not profound, and wonderfully candid. I think, too, that he shows an exactness and extent of knowledge of his subject which very advantageously distinguishes him from poetical historians in general. I assure you he is not without enthusiastic admirers here; his lectures on German literature last year were a good deal talked of; and I see he has announced a new course on general literature, which I must enquire about. I am ready to hail almost any striking phenomenon in literature; we have had little but mediocrity lately. Of your two books, 'Miller' and 'Alison,' no notice whatever has come to my ears. I have just heard that 'Alison' is praised in 'Blackwood,' therefore ultra-tory. If they be new works, as I suppose, the first cannot be written by Professor M. of Glasgow, nor the second by Alison (of Taste), who is now very old and quite infirm; I believe it is his son.

Pray read Guizot's 'Histoire de la Civilisation en Europe,' a small book which will give you much matter of thought.

No, our pattern speakers do not confound hōly and whŏlly; to the short vowel in the last word they give a sound between o and u, if you can imagine it. Trent-north, a grand boundary of dialect, the provincials say *woley* or *wooley*, and in Norfolk they say hully; but stick you to whŏlly if you would pass for a member of your much-respected the English aristocracy.

I really am totally unable to understand your faith in the coming of a time when all men will be regarded by all as equals. Such a time can plainly not come without community of goods, and to that I see no tendency; nor can it arrive whilst any division of labour exists. As long as one man works only with his hands, and another with his head, there will be inequality between them of the least conventional kind; inequality in knowledge, in the objects of thought, in the estimate of existence, and of all that makes it desirable. Among the rudest savages there has always been inequality, produced by that nature itself which gives to one man more strength and more understanding than another; and all the refinements of social life open fresh sources of inequality. Even in a herd of wild cattle there is inequality produced by differences of age, and sex, and size, and what imaginable power or process can ever bring human creatures to a parity? As little can I see how such a state would be the practical assertion of the preference due to the 'inward over the outward,' to 'humanity over its accidents.' Are not many of these sources of inequality really inward? Are not these accidents inseparable from humanity? The things which elevate man above his fellows are all *powers* of one kind or other: wealth is a power, since it can purchase gratifications and services; birth is a power, where the laws have made it the condition of enjoying privileges or authority: where they have not done so, it speedily sinks into contempt. Genius is a power; weight of moral character is a power; beauty is a power; knowledge is a power. The possessor of any of these goes with his talent to the market of life, and obtains with it or for it what others think it worth their while to give—some more, some less. Can or ought this to be otherwise? The precious gifts of nature must be valued so long as humanity is what it is; the results of application, of exertion, mental, bodily, cannot cease to bear their price without deadening all the active principles in man. I see, indeed, a tendency in high civilisation to break down in some degree the ancient barriers between class and class, by opening new roads to wealth, to fame, and to social distinction. Watt and Davy, Reynolds and Flaxman, could not safely be treated with disdain either by Howards and Mowbrays, or by the 'millionaires' of commerce; but this does not assist those who have nothing to rest upon but mere human nature itself. These may be equal to their more privileged brethren before God; they may and ought to be equal in the eye of the law, but socially equal—I do not see the possibility. You approve the aristocracy of wealth so far as it tends to break in upon that of rank, and to mix all classes—but how far would you carry this mixture? Shall I begin tea-drinkings with my maudlin washerwoman? Will you invite to your table the bow-legged snip who made your coat? How soon, alas! at this rate would the rivulet of refinement be swallowed up in the ocean of vulgarity! What models would remain of manners, of language, of taste in literature or the arts! What a mere worky-day world would this become! The coarse themselves would grow coarser, and in the end sensuality would rise victorious over all. The opinions in which all could agree must be absurd and extravagant ones, for, as Locke observes, 'truth and reason did never yet carry it by the majority anywhere.' The talk in which all can join is seldom such as anyone is much the better for hearing. If it be true that 'there is no man of merit but hath a touch of singularity, and scorns something,' surely merit must always be allowed to scorn ignorance, or grossness incapable of estimating it; and this cannot but include a kind of disdain of the society of the lower classes. Pray answer me all this, for I think I must have misapprehended your idea.

Not yet have I thanked you for your two kind presents of your 'Temperance' and your 'Texas.' I admire the first particularly for its discrimination, by speaking of the Temperance Societies as symptoms, rather than causes;

you have explained what I before thought a puzzling phenomenon. I could, if my paper allowed, cavil at your opinions on public amusements; but another time. 'Texas' seems to me your greatest effort yet. May success reward the patriotic virtue which inspired it!

   Ever believe me, my respected friend,
    Yours most truly,
      L. AIKIN.

No. 39.

Hampstead: July 16, 1838.

My dear Friend—There are two urgent reasons why I must make Mr. Gannet the bearer of a letter to you; first, because it is always a pleasure to me to send you a friendly greeting; and secondly, because I wish, whilst the impression is still fresh, to express the gratification I have felt in his society, and to thank you for the introduction. On his first arrival here, the lamentable state of his health and spirits, obscured, though they could not quite conceal, his admirable talents and qualities; but they now shine forth, and we all find him an exceedingly interesting companion. Of his powers as a preacher I have not enabled myself to judge, but I can bear strong testimony to the perfect modesty and simplicity with which he receives tokens of a success which would be sufficient to turn most heads. Mrs. Joanna Baillie told him truly, that he had been talked of at a time when we had scarcely leisure to talk of anyone—so full were all heads with our grand coronation; and I never saw anything more beautiful than the unaffected modest dignity with which he received the compliment—it would have delighted you to witness. He carries back with him the esteem and good wishes of all whose testimony is worth having, in spite of very industrious efforts to injure him—I believe you know from what quarter.

And what have you thought of the fever-fit of loyalty which has seized 'universal England,' on occasion of setting the crown on the head of our young queen? Perchance you may have viewed it somewhat in the spirit of the laughing philosopher; but if you had been an eye-witness of what passed, I think you would have sympathised in our emotions more deeply than you now believe possible. This young creature has thus far conducted herself most admirably. Her behaviour at her first council was described to me by an excellent judge who was present, as combining the highest degrees both of self-possession and of sensibility compatible each with the other, and such has been the complexion of all her conduct since. Her steadfast adherence to a reforming ministry has been of inestimable value to the cause of liberality and improvement; her perseverance in the same course is what we have most to wish, and to let her see the popular attachment which it has already gained for her seemed the most likely means of securing this great object. The people have to support her against the aristocracy, and I have heard it said, I believe with as much truth as point, that the ministry is kept in place by the queen and the shopkeepers. In the meantime, it seems to me that we are going on well; reforms proceeding slow and sure, and decidedly the tone of at least a large portion of society becoming constantly more liberal, both in religion and politics—the natural effect of the continuance of a whig and low-church administration. I perceive signs also of a revival of literature, which now again is able to hold up its head in the presence of science, by which it was for some time in apparent danger of being totally overshadowed. In particular it pleases me to perceive that historical literature is cultivated with great activity, for which there are two obvious causes: a state of public feeling which allows history to be written freely without incurring persecution either from the government or the mob; and, with respect to our own country, a great accession of new information from the printing of the public records.

These favouring circumstances, I think, will enable even me to conquer my long desponding indolence, and attempt a new design. My plan is not yet matured, but it is only *entre nous* that I give any hint of it; but I am turning my thoughts towards something like a view of letters and social life in England during the first sixty years of the last century, i. e. the reigns of Anne and the two first Georges. This will differ from my former works in excluding civil history entirely, for which I could not now undertake the labour of collecting materials, and my chief doubt at present is, how far the work can be rendered sufficiently interesting without it. I must intersperse biography largely; and I propose entering deeply into the subject of female manners and acquirements. At present I am only collecting materials, but that is no disagreeable or uninteresting part of the business. You may infer from my entertaining so bold a design that my health is stronger than it was, and I expect to find it still further benefited by plunging into business which will alleviate the constant weight upon the spirits of domestic solitude.

I wonder whether you have ever been a great student of the works of Addison, especially of his periodical papers. It seems to me that justice has not even yet been done, or at least is not done in this generation to his unrivalled merits. To women he was the greatest of benefactors. By his arch ridicule and gentle reprehension of their follies, especially of their idleness and their ignorance, he worked a wide reformation. By teaching them to observe the respect of the other sex he enabled them to secure it. No systematic advocate of the rights of woman, especially none who is herself a woman, will ever, we may safely predict, do them half so much service. I have a good many remarks to make on this topic, which I believe will be new, and I hope may be useful.

Did I not say to you in my last letter, that a gay young, play-going queen would make a formidable counteraction to the progress of the evangelicals? I will now add that they have been receiving a great injury from the hands of their own adherents—the sons and biogaphers of Mr. Wilberforce. The book is luckily so tiresome as well as so sour and so narrow that it meets with general abuse, in spite of the efforts of the Edinburgh reviewer, a nephew of Mr. Wilberforce. Everybody sticks fast in the perusal, and it has damaged the subject of the book scarcely less than its authors. It is plain that whatever other merits Mr. Wilberforce might have, he was by no means a man of strong understanding; and the curious disclosure of his practice of wearing pebbles in his shoes by way of penance is little likely to do him honour with the English of the nineteenth century. The life of Hannah More was a much more readable book than this, because she both wrote and received many agreeable letters *before* her conversion; but even that made no great noise out of her own set, and I believe did no good to her cause. Our rigorists of the establishment seem now to be swinging towards that kind of high-churchism which is but just to be distinguished from popery; which will do less harm, because less likely to be taken up with enthusiasm by the common people than the high Calvinism of the evangelicals. The intolerance and the pharisaical arrogance of the two systems is much alike.

One trait of popular sentiment which I observed in watching the coronation procession may interest you. There was vast applause of the queen, great applause of her mother and of your friend the Duke of Sussex, and a kind recognition of the other members of the royal family; there was generous applause of Soult, because we had formerly beaten him, but not the slightest notice of any other foreigner. The ambassadors extraordinary might display as much pomp as they would, and certainly such splendour of equipages had never before been exhibited in the streets of London; still honest John remained obstinately mute, or contented himself with whispering, 'Depend upon it those coaches are English built, and the horses bought here.' Whence I infer, that national pride was the leading principle in the popular mind; such part of the show as each man might tell himself he had helped to pay for delighted him; the rest rather provoked his surliness, and he was little disposed to thank foreign kings for all their civilities.

I trust your pen is not idle; you must go on writing, if it were only for the sake of your public here, which becomes a wider one with every new piece you give us. Texas we most of us consider as your best effort.

Pray believe me ever
Yours, with the truest regard,
L. AIKIN.

No. 40.

Hampstead: Nov. 16, 1838.

My dear Friend—You like overflowing letters, you say, and I have no great difficulty in finding materials for such in writing to you; the worst is, that I grow tired, throw aside the half-filled sheet, and leave it in my writing-desk till it is too stale to send. This is what has happened now. I have just condemned a fragment to the flames, and whether this present attempt will have better success remains to be seen. You enquired if I had read Prescott's 'Ferdinand and Isabella;' and hearing much of the work, particularly that so excellent a judge as Lord Holland called it the best history written in English since Gibbon, I was unwilling to write till I had at least seen something of it. I have now finished the first volume and entered upon the second, with very great satisfaction. The spirit and sentiment of the work is admirable; there is enough of reflection, and not too much; the narrative is lively and flowing; and great judgment is shown in the proportions assigned to the various topics on which it treats. It is entertaining, with every mark of strict adherence to truth, and instructive without deep philosophy indeed, or sententiousness of remark; but by means of a pervading spirit of candour, good sense, and liberality, the interest of the subject hurries one on, at first reading too fast, I believe, for the credit of the writer; and I have little doubt that a second perusal would disclose many fresh merits of detail. As for the style—the diction rather —*it is pretty good for an American.* 'Civil!' cry you; but like our members of parliament, I disclaim 'any personal application.' In fact, it is not in a style like yours, which neither is, nor ought to be, a colloquial one, that any difference from that of an Englishman can be detected. Neither, indeed, is Mr. Prescott chargeable with using words or phrases peculiar to your country. If it were possible in these days of steamers and railroads to imagine an Englishman possessed of the knowledge and literary talent of this writer, who should never have mingled with the good society of London, he might be expected to compose in the same style, that is to say, provided he had never made a study of his own language. He, like Mr. Prescott, might employ the Scotch term 'a border *foray*;' he might call artisans *operatives*, the slang word of Glasgow weavers; he might transplant from the newspapers, French, military, and other terms, he might perhaps want the tact to exclude from the style of history several mere colloquialisms, as well as corrupt uses of words which might be enumerated. Considering this work as one which will attain a permanent station in English literature, I cannot but regret these blemishes, and wish to see them removed in another edition. But there is a special reason why I mention them to you, which is this. You tell me you can see no use in our aristocracy. This is a use—to establish a standard of taste and refinement in language as in manners; to rebuke pedantry; to set a mark upon ignorance, provincialism, and vulgarity; to preserve the native tongue in equal purity and vigour. No one without having frequented those London circles, where lettered men and women of rank associate with lettered men and women without rank, can form a just conception of the grace and beauty of which our language is susceptible in its colloquial forms. No one without this advantage can attain finished elegance in any style of composition, except the most grave and dignified—that of the pulpit and the schools; at least, such attainment is so rare, that when we meet with it, as in the works of that *low Irishman* Goldsmith, it fills us with surprise as much as admiration. No Scotchman has ever accomplished a perfect English style. Blair and Robertson escaped faults by rejecting all idiom from their composition; but at the expense of all originality and charm. Hume supplied his want of English idiom and disdain of Scotch, by seizing upon French phrases. Burns, in prose, wrote no language at all; and Walter Scott is full of provincialisms and barbarisms, some of which, through his popularity, threaten to naturalise themselves amongst us. Charles Lamb, a Londoner, gained a pure and very racy English by study of our old writers, especially the dramatists, but he acquired at the same time a quaintness which only the best society could have taught him to discard. Dryden, Cowley, and Addison, our three great masters in the middle style of composition, all lived first with scholars, as they were themselves, and afterwards with courtiers, nobles, statesmen, great lawyers, and great ladies. A sound classical education, with assiduous study of our best writers, might indeed suffice to forming a pure and correct style, provided their effects were not counteracted by hearing vulgar speech and reading the bad writers of the day; but in general all people read the current trash more or less, and those who have no access to elegant speakers will scarcely escape the infection derived from coarse ones. An upper class, a metropolis, and a court, can alone preserve the language of an extensive empire. Therefore, woe unto you, Americans! It amuses me to think that I, who have all my life belonged to the democratic party, and have earned the lasting enmity of the admirers of King Charles and his cavaliers, should, with you, take the part of a champion of monarchy and aristocracy. You may place it, if you will, to the account of that spirit which the lords of creation affirm to be so prevalent in our much-libelled sex. But when you profess that 'the reasons for an aristocracy are beyond your comprehension,' I own I wonder a little. Allowing that I may be too much inclined, as Bacon said of James I., 'to take counsel of times past,' I still must hold that a philosophical thinker ought not to shut his eyes to the large fact that, until the establishment of your states, the whole world, as far as it is known to us by history, had never seen a nation, barbarous or civilised, destitute of some kind of hereditary nobility or aristocracy, excepting those eastern monarchies where all were equal, because all were nothing, beneath the rod of the despot. A counterbalance to the absolute power, whether of a king or a people, has the most obvious utility, and I offer it for your consideration, whether that very propensity to form associations, which you have found it necessary to rebuke in your own country, is not the consequence of the want of one. In a land where 'the right divine of *mobs* to govern wrong' is consecrated as a first principle, how can any sect or any party propose to itself another mode of carrying its points, than persuading or compelling the adherence of a numerical majority? Where the cooperation of king, nobles, and people is required to every public measure, all interests must be consulted; that even of the few must not be absolutely sacrificed to the many; reason, justice, fairness, must be allowed their plea; above all, full liberty of speech is secured. In a despotism, whether of one, of the few, or of the many 'sic volo, sic jubeo,' is sufficient. With regard to our nobility, every impartial person who will study thoroughly the history of its political conduct, must own this: that it gained Magna Charta; that it opposed effectual resistance to the despotism of the Church and its head, and the introduction of the slavish maxims of the civil law; that it controlled in many important instances the encroachments of our kings; that in the great struggle of Charles and his parliament it endeavoured, however vainly, to hold the balance; that it gave many confessors to the cause of liberty, several distinguished generals to the people, and that the abolition of its constitutional powers was one of the most guilty acts of the military usurper; that it gave us our glorious and bloodless revolution, and by its resistance to a Tory House of Commons, Tory squires, and Tory clergy, saved us from the return of the tyrannical and bigoted Stuarts; that even at the present day, a majority of the high and old aristocracy, which owes not its honours to the trade-pampering policy of Pitt, adheres to Whig principles, though it repudiates Radicalism, that is, the supremacy of the rude and selfish and ignorant many. With such past claims to our gratitude, and in my opinion so much of advantage to be hoped from it for the future, I say to the illustrious order, with all its faults, its errors, sometimes its provoking obstinacy—'Esto perpetua!' Were you more intimately acquainted with the feelings of our people, I believe you would soon renounce the opinion that the existence of the aristocracy endangers property. One proof of the contrary is, that those notable public meetings in which the working men take care to show our optimists how very little their notions have advanced since the days of Jack Cade, all take place in manufacturing towns— the very places in which the aristocracy do not reside and exercise no influence. Even in London, where the influence of the aristocracy is rather that of the class than of individuals, the ultra-Radicals could make no hand of it; indeed, I believe they are everywhere pining away under the contempt of their superiors and the neglect of the attorney-general. Ignorance is weakness. Ignorant, I believe, the bulk of our spinners and weavers must in the nature of things always remain. In your young and unexhausted country, with land cheap and labour dear, all is different. May you be able to realise the beautiful idea of a nation self-governed with wisdom and justice. With us, the old distinction of governors and governed must still subsist; but we may indulge the hope that public opinion, which in all classes above the very lowest has made, and is daily making a real progress in light and liberality, will irresistibly urge upon rulers a constant attention to the interests of those who know not what is truly good for themselves. Thus only can we hope to see them preserve that 'national feeling' which, cheap as you may hold it, Mr. Burke truly entitled 'the cheap defence of nations.' Since beginning this letter I have been proceeding with 'Ferdinand and Isabella' with still increasing interest and approbation, and I beg that when you write you will give me any particulars you think proper of the author, as I cannot help feeling great desire to know something of his personal history. What think you of our new Oxford set of *Laudists* or semi-Romanists? They at least serve as counterbalance to our evangelicals. I must now conclude, having an immediate opportunity of sending my letter to London.

Ever truly yours,
L. AIKIN.

No. 41.

Hampstead: March 23, 1839.

Months ago did I say to myself, 'My Boston friend will be making enquiries about these Puseyites before long, and I must take care to be provided for him.' At the same time I do not think them of much consequence or likely to be so; and although the sect seems to have its fanatics, it is no new illumination, but mere Laudism—an extreme of high-churchism which cannot prosper without much more countenance from the magistrate than it appears that it has any chance of receiving. Dr. Pusey was some time ago the ringleader in a plot for depriving Dr. Hampden of his divinity professorship, on account, or on pretext of an explanation given by him of the doctrine of the Trinity, which Pusey and his followers called heretical. But their zeal or malice, having impelled them to go beyond the authority given by the statutes of the university, they were called to order by the government; and Dr. Hampden, after making a sort of recantation, obtained preferment, *although* he had openly pleaded for the admission of dissenters to the universities his worst heresy. As for the origin of the sect, some say Cambridge having had her Simeon, Oxford must have her Pusey.

But the root lies a little deeper than this. Our church, as you know, is a Janus; having one face towards Geneva, the other towards the city upon the Seven Hills. Of the sour Geneva face, as exhibited by the modern evangelicals, our gentlemanly clergy began to grow very sick, and to fancy they should prefer the other, which at least becomes a mitre far better.

For the purpose of inclining the minds of the people in the same direction, this party have for several years past been publishing panegyrics in reviews and sermons, and panegyrical biographies of our elder divines, with cheap editions of their works; endeavouring quietly and gradually to bring into fashion again that edging on toward the Roman creed, that exceeding, almost scriptural tenderness for the divines of the fourth, fifth, and sixth centuries, which distinguishes the Church of England dignitaries from Elizabeth inclusively to our revolution in 1688 from other Protestants; concerning which edging Coleridge in his *latter* mind says, 'I scarcely know whether to be pleased or grieved with it.' Yet in an earlier passage of his 'Literary Remains,' we find him confessing that there was a strange lingering of childish credulity in the divines of the episcopal church down to the time of James II., when the Popish controversy 'made a great clearance.' But this, by the bye. Besides the increased reverence for priesthood by episcopal ordination derived from apostolical succession, and the notion of *authority* in the church to make orders for externals, and decide questions of faith which the study of these writers was fitted to instil, an important advantage may have been calculated upon in a great controversy. It begins to be clear to all parties, that the doctrine of the Trinity cannot be defended by Scripture, so many of the texts formerly relied upon having yielded under the assaults of modern criticism; but *make Scripture* of the fathers of the four first centuries, and you have all the authority for it that you can possibly desire. The atonement also might be much strengthened by making an apostle of Augustine; but this perhaps is rather the affair of another party. Now, although this scheme had something plausible, I doubt its solidity. Of all attempts, the least promising is that of restoring things gone by. *I*, indeed, believe folly to be immortal, but individual follies certainly live out their day and die. Much as it would redound to the glory and profit of the clergy 'to lift again the crozier,' it cannot be done without the concurrence of the state, without the restoration to the church of coercive powers long since lost, without an authoritative quashing of controversy, without a commanded exterior reverence to things fallen into general contempt; such, for example, as the keeping of Lent, so scouted in the House of Commons the other day. Therefore, depend upon it, one Pusey will not make a Laudian church. I should not wonder to see a part of the real fanatics of this sect turn Papists ('go the whole hog,' as *you* say): the others will cool down into proud stiff high-church people—nothing more. The best is, that they thwart the evangelicals, and thus divide the house against itself, for which it will not stand the faster.

With respect to the bishops who subscribed to the sermons of my venerable friend, a little allowance must be made for them. Men who are governers in a church with such creeds and such articles, cannot very consistently appear as patrons of Unitarian sermons; the Bishop of Durham,* accordingly, had stipulated to have his name suppressed, and might justly be a little vexed at the breach of this condition;—the more, as he was baptised and bred among the Unitarians, and has always been of very suspected orthodoxy. The other bishop I take to be a timid Liberal. On the whole, I think what you would call rational religion is silently working its way in

* Dr. Maltby,

society. It is remarkable that the Unitarian sect, confessedly one of the very smallest in the country, has more members of parliament in proportion belonging to it than any other denomination whatever,—a strong presumption, as it appears to me, that many more favour and secretly entertain these opinions than think proper as yet openly to avow them. The orthodox dissenters, who have not a single member, are enraged at this circumstance, and I have no doubt it sets an edge on the polemical zeal of the clergy. An Unitarian has also been made a baronet, one of the best of men. The present ministry are constantly upbraided by their opponents as enemies to the church, and not entirely without reason; yet they are supported by majorities, though small ones.

Pray observe that it was chiefly as a school of taste that I commended the society in which rank and talent meet. I am sensible that some who frequent it too much, lose that earnestness on which you justly set a much higher moral value. But I see also those who, with manners rendered adroit by the intercourse and example of the great, know how, in more select and private circles, where they meet equals, to maintain excellent opinions on the highest subjects—to maintain them with the more effect, for never losing command of themselves, or a just deference to the claims of others. These indeed are the *élite*; as to either commonplace or merely worldly people, they certainly are rendered less displeasing by polished manners, and neither more insipid nor more hollow.

One word more as to aristocracy. In this country it cannot be said to have accomplished its vocation of keeping the peace so long as we have such frightful inequality of property—that is, so long as our population continues (and what should prevent its continuing?) so excessive in proportion to the means of support. Eight shillings a week is the present pay in many parts of the country of an agricultural labourer, and hope of ever mending his condition in the common course of things he has none. Dare you trust such a man with a vote? Political power in such hands would soon conduct us to universal confusion. There must be with us strong buttresses to counterbalance the thrust which would bring all to ruin. O Malthus, Malthus! you saw the source of mischief—who sees the remedy?

I thank you much for your address to the Franklin society. It has many very valuable remarks and suggestions, but I thought there was some vagueness, for want of more divisions of the subject. Ought not moral and intellectual culture to have been considered separately? In one place you observe that books are not necessary to culture; in another you eloquently expatiate on their value. Now this I regard as no real inconsistency, but I wanted some distinctions to take away the appearance of it. You in your country of easy circumstances may look to universal school education; here I neither expect, nor indeed desire, at present to see it attempted. What a mockery to offer learning to the English labourer at eight shillings a week, or to the Irish peasant with his insufficient quantity of the worst kind of potato! Will the spirit of the age, from which you expect such great things, bring any mitigation to the sufferings of our mass? I fear not much; but it is still a duty to do all that is possible; and in as much as a government practises rigid economy, promotes legal reforms, and renders justice accessible to the poor by its cheapness, and by a spirit of real impartiality in the ministers of it—in as much as it trims the balance skilfully between the conflicting claims of different classes and interests, it will discharge its highest duties. You will not dispute, I conceive, that *these* views of political measures involve moral, and if moral, religious considerations of the utmost importance. Therefore you may find even our political events matters fit for your concern. The more, as it cannot be disputed that, in the main, the Whig is the party of reformation of all kinds, the Tory that of corruption and abuse.

A project of which I am much more in dread than the attempts of the Laudians, is one of which our busy Bishop of London * is the head. He has founded a society for the purpose of bringing education under ecclesiastical control. This body are visiting all the London schools; they enquire of the masters (I know not whether they yet take cognisance of school-mistresses) whether they will adopt the methods of the society; especially whether they will engage to teach Church of England catechism, and whether they will submit to be examined by the society as to their competence in learning. If they consent, they are patronised; if not, an opposition school is founded close by, and all means are adopted to ruin their business. The only comfort is, that this association being maintained solely by private subscriptions will perhaps die away by degrees for want of funds, and also that it savours too much of an inquisition to suit the feelings of the English public. The German divines are a thorn in the flesh of our university clergy. They dare not pretend to despise their learning; and how to prevent their heresies from spreading amongst the students of theology? Depend upon it, the hypocrisy is to the orthodoxy in our church as 99 to 1 at the least. But can we rejoice in this? I cannot, unless it is to lead to some greater good than I can conceive. A learned but heretical Cambridge divine tells me, 'this generation of us *think*, the next will *speak.*'

You cannot, I am sure, complain of this letter for want of length. I hope and think it has answered all your questions. I have *made* time to write it, for indeed I am very busily engaged in collecting materials for my 'Addison.' The writing of the work I have not begun, excepting

* Bishop Blomfield.

in detached notes, therefore I cannot yet judge what kind of figure it will make. I am in pretty good spirits about it, however—chiefly, perhaps, because my bodily health being stronger, my mind is more alert and more inclined to look on the bright side, at least of things depending on myself. I must now bid you farewell.

Ever yours very sincerely,
LUCY AIKIN.

No. 42.

Hampstead: June 19, 1839.

My dear Friend—Your very kind letter has just reached me, and I cannot be easy without sitting down immediately to thank you for it most cordially, and to give you a few particulars of myself, which I know you will read with some interest. I have indeed been long a very poor feeble creature, and during our long winter and chilly spring (the very opposite of yours, for it has been unusually backward) I was almost a complete prisoner: and a solitary one; for the unhealthy season similarly affected many of my best friends, and kept them from visiting me. My spirits were severely tried in consequence. At length April arrived, and I was looking to better times, when I *caught*, I believe, the influenza, which speedily increased from a feverish cold to an inflammation of the throat and lungs, which brought my life into imminent peril. For my own part, I had not the slightest expectation, nor, I may add, wish of recovery. The love of life, as I may have mentioned to you, has always been feeble in me. Under the influence of sickness and dejection it was at this time quite extinguished, and I was not only calm, but happy, in the prospect of a speedy solution of that mystery of existence which had often weighed heavily indeed upon my spirit. I called to mind all things and persons interesting to me, whether near or distant, and did not omit to direct a long message of friendship to be conveyed to you. But the Great Disposer had not decreed my immediate release. I am still here, speculating and reasoning; and the affectionate expressions of my friends, joined to the natural influence of returning strength, now dispose me to receive less ungraciously the boon of lengthened life —useless creature as I feel myself to be, or useful only as affording an object to the kind affections of relations and a few frends. I *live* in my sad domestic solitude and inutility, and I have the grief to see the young and amiable wife of one of my nephews sinking under a mortal disease to leave behind her a heart-broken husband and motherless babe! Mystery, all mystery!

Much have I to say to you, besides returning you my thanks for your two pieces on ' War ' and on ' Slavery.' The last I hold to be the very best work that you have yet given us. I agree with you throughout, or very nearly so, and I much admire the manner in which you have treated the exceedingly delicate topic of the abolitionists. You have dealt out exemplary justice between them and their persecutors. Your commemoration of Darwin's slave gave me a thrill of delight. From the days of my childhood, when I was among the abstainers from sugar till now, that kneeling figure has been the type of his race to my imagination. Let me add, that in this piece your style is more than ever to my taste. It is your true epistolary style, which I may well love best of all.

The lecture on War gives more hold to remark, and perhaps controversy. Yet there is very much in which I cordially concur. The preliminary observations, and more especially the remarks on the causes of the present long peace, and the summary of those which may again stir up war, the warning of the little reliance to be placed on commerce and prosperity as pacific, on account of the selfish and evil passions engendered by both, appeared to me not only just, but profound, and often original, and worthy to be widely diffused and deeply pondered. Your discussion, too, of the right in governments to declare war has much powerful argument, and irresistible appeals to the heart and to the conscience. But your exhortations to Christians to submit to martyrdom rather than obey their governments in cases of unjust war, will, I conceive, be a good deal disapproved, both in your pure democracy, where 'vox populi' stands pretty generally, I suppose, for 'vox Dei;' and in our mixed constitution, which freely admits of public meetings, petitions to the crown or the legislature, and instructions to representatives. It may be thought, perhaps justly, to tend to anarchy, and thus to war itself—civil war. You take new, and I think strong ground, in holding out a just acknowledgment of the rights of man as the firmest bulwark against war, that thousand-headed monster of wrong; this idea of the claims of man as such, you derive from the New Testament, which certainly does inculcate that equality among mankind on which rights are based. Yet, on other points, are there not considerable difficulties attending the religious view of the subject? Our old puritans found it hard to reconcile the spirit of Christianity with the armed assertion of civil liberty, and discovered no other means of accomplishing it than by giving more authority to the maxims and examples of the Old Testament than the precepts of the New. In fact, although wars of revenge and ambition are crushed in the germ by the Gospel denunciations against the passions themselves, it does so happen that even these are not so *directly* prohibited as self-defence—as any thought of resistance to tyranny, violence, and wrong, exercised against ourselves. I do not see how any Christian can stop short of quakerism on this point, without allowing himself to regard these non-resisting principles as local or temporary in their intention. You, I suppose, take this view, as you permit self-defence.

But in many cases this is permitting all. Practically, the line dividing offence from defence is very often evanescent. Once allow war not to be utterly unlawful, and we may listen to considerations of state expediency, utility. 'Necessity, the tyrant's plea,' comes in; and I own I see not on what other ground—certainly not that of justice—you yourself hold it *right* that your free states should be bound to supply troops to put down slave insurrections in the south. Thus each case of hostilities comes to be discussed on its own merits or demerits, and the applicability of the religious scruple comes to be matter of opinion. In the end, the decision is left to the moral feelings or moral principles of men—antagonists how unequal to their passions, prejudices, and interests! No cause, however, can be more worthy of the zealous efforts of good men than that of peace. Your lecture is eminently adapted to awaken conscience and reflection to the enormous guilt of war, and it will be reckoned to you amongst your best services to the interests of human nature. Meantime, let us be thankful that our two governments have shown too much wisdom, whether of the best kind or not, to make enemies of two kindred nations. The Borderers may go on jangling, but there is evidently nothing else to fear.

You who do not love our utilitarian philosophy, will rejoice, I suppose, to learn that no less men than Messrs. Whewell and Sedgwick are doing their utmost to get the works of Paley put out of the course of reading for Cambridge undergraduates; but I fear this step is not taken in favour of the beautiful mysteries of your Platonists, but of others more gainful to our state-church. Our clergy are desperately active at present, and proportionally mischievous. They will not allow us to have a normal school on terms of anything like fairness to dissenters, and they everywhere talk very big of 'the authority committed unto them' as the successors of the apostles. I have even heard of attempts amongst them to remind people of a monstrous old law, made against Popish recusants, and still unrepealed, by which persons are liable to heavy penalties for not regularly attending their parish church. I apprehend, however, that this applies now only to church people, the toleration act sheltering dissenters. They have 'all the plea' at present; the press seems as much their own as if they had an inquisition at their command. But let them beware of what is gathering in silence. Men *think* very freely now and whisper; presently they will speak out and act, I trust. If you take up a list of new publications, it seems as if nothing scarcely was written or read amongst us except theology, and of the narrowest kind; but so it is, that a person might live in the midst of the best and most literary society for a year together, and never hear the slightest mention of any one new book on these subjects. I know not exactly who are the readers, but I suspect scarcely any laymen of the smallest note. The clergy often write *at* the bishop or the patron, not the public, and there are a number of women who write theology for little children, which some mammas encourage. The Tory party are in strict alliance with the Church; but I suspect they look more to the increase of their political power through this union than to any objects of a religious nature. You may perhaps have read in our debates, on what pretexts these high allies have defeated, for the present at least, the ministerial project in favour of a normal school, in which the Church would not have been permitted to impose her own dogmas on the children of dissenters; and I think you will scarcely give such a man as Lord Stanley credit for honest bigotry on the occasion. I suppose that good is to come out of these conflicts between freedom and mental thraldom in the end, but the immediate effect is miserably depressing and irritating. One can scarcely witness with composure even the temporary success of arrogant priestly claims, supported by fashion, self-interest, or narrow-mindedness. You speak of Luther: have you read a selection from his 'Table Talk,' translated into English, which appeared about ten years since? It is very entertaining, and helps one to understand him. I respect him much.

Mr. Rogers pointed out a passage in your 'Texas' beginning, 'England is a privileged country,' as one of the finest in our language.

Have I not given you full measure this time? and yet I feel as if I had more to say.

Ever most sincerely yours,
L. AIKIN.

No. 43.

Hampstead: March 2, 1840.

You think, my good friend, supposing you have given yourself the trouble of thinking on the subject, that it is an unconscionable length of time since I have written to you—in which you are much mistaken. I wrote you a long letter very lately, and it was safely conveyed to the post; but by the egregious blundering of the Hampstead post-mistress (I have a great opinion of my sex, and certainly think a woman fit to govern a kingdom, but defend me from she-governors of post-offices!)—by her egregious blundering in our new postage law my unfortunate epistle got to the dead-letter office, whence it was returned to me, opened, creased, dirty, and unfit to send you. Ah! you will never know what a loss you had there. Such a letter! And poor I must be at the trouble to write another. Well, I submit with a good grace to any temporary inconvenience by this new law, which reduces our heavy postage to a single penny from one extremity of our island to the other. The moral tendency of the measure seems to me of greater value than figures can express. In the humbler classes it restores parents and children, brothers and sisters, to one another, who had grown strangers by long discontinuance of all intercourse; it will give a stronger impetus to national education than all the arguments yet advanced, and will 'redeem many an hour from idleness or worse, for the usually innocent, often amiable and useful, employment of letter-writing. In Scotland, where families are often so widely scattered by the impulse of necessity or ambition, which carries their active youth to the farthest ends of the earth, family attachments are nevertheless kept up with remarkable zeal and constancy; with us, I am sorry to confess that this is not the case, at least in the lower classes. A boy or girl coming to London from a remote county to seek service, seems often to forget entirely the native village and the parent's roof, and with them all the moral restraints imposed by such ties. How stands this case, I should like to hear, with your New Englanders who rush into the wilds of the *far West*? With them communication must often be difficult and tedious.

You expressed to me in your last an anxiety lest our clergy should be permitted to exert the control over national education which they have ventured to claim by right of their office. Never fear; it will not be submitted to. Notwithstanding the bluster of the Church party, nothing would so much surprise me as to see the establishment winning, or winning back, a single inch of ground. That spirit of power, the genius of the nineteenth century, says *No*. I daily more and more perceive the sagacity of those who applied to the epoch of the passing of the Reform Bill Talleyrand's expression, 'Le commencement de la fin.' We have been striding on towards essential democracy and religious equality ever since; and nothing seems to me capable of arresting this progress, unless some such absurd and furious movements of a chartist mob as might cause in the better classes the reaction of alarm. In spite of my *aristocratic letter*—written when I, too, was suffering something of a reaction from deep disgust at the interference of your border states in behalf of our Canada rebels, and their insolent and ignorant defiance of the laws of nations—in spite of feelings which the better behaviour of your executive has since mitigated—I view our domestic state with hope, and much though not unmingled satisfaction. The pacification of Ireland is a moral triumph which warms my heart with admiration, reverence, and gratitude towards the true statesmen who have compassed it; and after this achievement I know not what task of reformation can be found too difficult.

No; we *will* not quarrel for a petty boundary question—it is not to be thought of. 'What is that between me and thee?' May our rulers on both sides treat it as friend with friend, brother with brother. Believe me the tie *is* felt on our side as strongly as it well can be on yours. By all the liberal party, at least, it is strongly felt; and I cannot but regard it as the most favourable of all circumstances that this question should fall to be decided under a Whig ministry on our side.

You have, I hope, found time to read Professor Smyth's 'Lectures on Modern History,' and if you have, I feel sure of your finding in them much to approve and admire. The writer, a *young* and lively man of seventy-six, is an old and dear friend of mine; he is also an admirer of yours, and he was just sending me a copy of his work to send to you when he learned that Mr. Rathbone had anticipated him: but I said I would let you know his intentions. The merit of the counsels of peace, of tolerance, of mild government with which they abound can only be appreciated by recollecting that these lectures were delivered by a

Regius professor to the sons for the most part of aristocratic, tory, and churchly families, in those evil days when Cambridge had nearly lost all memory of her former honourable distinction as the whig university. The ruling powers always regarded them with jealousy, and, as far as they decently could, discouraged the young men from attending them. They found however, large, and attentive and gratified audiences. The style appears to me a model for the purpose—lively, easy, extremely colloquial, but rising to eloquence and brilliancy where the subject prompts; and there is over all that charm of perfect sincerity and simplicity of heart, which I think must be felt even by those who know not how much it is the characteristic of the man. You will own that he has done thorough justice to the merits of all parties in your War of Independence, and that he knows how to estimate Washington.

It warmed and cheered my heart to read your *confessions* of happiness; few have such to make. For myself, I think life has become dearer to me since I was last in danger of losing it; and this, strange to tell, in the face of a grievous anxiety, which is even now preying upon my heart. The health of my brother Charles, than whom I have no nearer and no dearer object of affection in the world, has long been in a very precarious state. His sufferings at this very time are exceedingly severe—and I tremble to think what may be the result. So dearly do I love him—so much has his life-long affection become a part of my very self—that I can think of one circumstance only which could render it tolerable to me to live after him—the prospect of being in some manner useful to his dear children.

Your friends the Farrars are just at present my neighbours. I fear he is still a great sufferer by sleeplessness, and the train of miserable ideas which attend it. A severe trial for his excellent wife, but in which there is no fear of her failing. I was glad to see her look in bodily health and vigour.

I am not now in spirits to add more.

Yours truly, ever,
L. AIKIN.

No. 44.

Hampstead: May 16, 1840.

My dear Friend—Accept my cordial thanks for your two new pieces, both of which I have read with deep interest and high approbation. That on the 'Elevation of the Working Classes' embodies much that I have often felt and thought, without being able to bring it out; in fact, it applies to all classes; and when I have seen, as I often have, families of young persons, diligent, docile, willing and able to acquire rudiments of many sciences, many languages, considerably skilled in various accomplishments, but without one original thought, one lofty sentiment, I have murmured to myself in sorrow—to what avail? Hannah More had the merit of raising her voice against mere 'finger accomplishments,' in female education; and I regard her as the setter of the fashion of domiciliary visits of ladies to the poor—a fashion which can only be followed to advantage by such among them as are capable of elevating the minds, not merely administering to the desire of temporal goods, in those with whom they converse. The kind of elevation you describe is certainly very rare at present, and perhaps will always be so, but it is nevertheless the point to be aimed at, and I rejoice that you have taken up the cause.

I was much struck and touched with your sermon, and I agree very much with your views on the great and dark question of the origin of evil; but there is one passage in which, as I feel it a duty to inform you, you have laid yourself open to severe, and, I fear I must say, just censure. 'They never can be fair,' exclaimed a candid and excellent friend of mine, and your great admirer in general, on finishing your sermon—'They never can be fair, these divines—not even Dr. Channing. Here is a passage which is an absolute slander—an aspersion which he had no right to make, and which is not true;' and he read the passage: 'Such scepticism is a moral disease, the growth of some open or lurking depravity.' 'What business,' he continued, 'has any one to impute such motives? What has the view which a mind takes of arguments on a difficult subject to do with depravity? The spirit of this judgment is precisely the same with that of a Catholic priest, who says "you must be very wicked if you do not believe transubstantiation."' I sat petrified with amazement at this burst of indignation, and I endeavoured to mitigate my friend—one of the mildest of men on common occasions; but it was to no purpose. I could only plead that the offensive passage had probably escaped you by inadvertence. 'But,' I said, 'I will mention it to him, and we shall hear what he says.' 'Pray do,' exclaimed my friend; 'he ought to be told of it.' I have now kept my word. I own that, for my own part, I cannot comprehend a doubt of the goodness of the Deity. We all feel that He has bestowed on us much *intentional* good: to believe that He has also inflicted upon us *designed*, that is, *purposeless*, evil, would be to conceive of him as a being weak, inconsistent, infirm of purpose, more than any wise and good man —an idea at which reason revolts. At the same time, all that I have known of the characters of men who speculate freely, boldly, and, of course, sometimes absurdly, on these abstruse questions, convinces me that moral character stands quite apart from theories of this nature. If divines were admitted to know the real sentiments of men of cultivated and reflecting minds on religious topics, they would often be surprised, and even shocked, to find how many, and what kind of persons, they stab in the dark. By general reflections of this nature—they might even be alarmed at the deep, silent hatred of their whole order, which these insults cause to rankle in the bosoms of a class possessed of so much real, though usually latent power. This particular doubt of the goodness of Providence I have often heard discussed among wise and excellent men; and the conclusion has usually been that, perfect wisdom and goodness, combined with that absolutely unlimited power for which divines contend, are inconsistent with the evil which we see in the world—that you must limit one, at least, of the attributes; and that power was, on the whole, that which seemed most susceptible of such limitation. To me, neither this nor any other solution of the problem appears entirely satisfactory. I believe it to be one which we have not at present the means of solving; but I believe that it will be solved, so as entirely to 'vindicate the ways of God to man.' At the same time, I know those who take a darker view of the subject, to whom you, if you knew them, would be as far as anyone from imputing depravity, however secret.

Enough, however, of this. You will, I know, rejoice with me, that the anxiety respecting the health of my brother Charles, which tormented me when I last wrote, has now subsided. He is now very nearly restored to health, and I have great pleasure in knowing that his frequent visits to me at Hampstead have been a principal means of his recovery. The breezes of this fresh hill-top are often the best of cordials to the dwellers in our over grown metropolis. This great and busy hive is at present in its busiest and fullest season—in full hum—but I know not that there is any great object of general attention much deserving your notice. One book, indeed, there is, which would interest you by the character of the writer, although many of the topics treated in it are probably too exclusively English for you to enter into. This is the 'Life of Sir Samuel Romilly,' published by his sons, and composed of his own diaries and letters. A more pure and perfectly disinterested public character has never been recorded; in these qualities he might be compared with your own Washington. No man in memory had so much personal weight in the House of Commons; and it was this alone which enabled him, in those bad times, when the very name of reform was hooted down by a corrupt administration and its sycophants, to force upon the legislature some of those mitigations of our sanguinary penal code, which opened the way for the extensive improvements which have since been demanded by public opinion, and carried through by our best and ablest statesmen. In many other causes, also, he stood forth, the undaunted, and also the skilful, champion of humanity, justice, and sound policy. His private life was that of the most virtuous, tender, and amiable of men. If the book comes into your hands, read at least his own brief memoir of his early days. You will find it one of the most beautiful pieces of autobiography imaginable. It is remarkable that poetry should have been his first love, the object of his earliest aspirations—a grand confirmation of what I have always suspected; that the heights of virtue will scarcely be reached but by those who behold them clothed in 'hues unbounded of the sun'—hues lent them by a warm and bright imagination!

The Puseyites, or Newmaniacs, as I believe they are more generally called, are certainly making progress. We have clergy who refuse to dine out on Wednesdays and Fridays, being the fasts ordained by the English Church. The other day a curate published a manifesto against a Bible Society, headed by two clergymen, for presuming to meet and to distribute the Scriptures in his parish. He declares it to be *heresy* for anyone to give away bibles, excepting the person deputed by the bishop to do so— namely, the officiating parish priest. A bold step towards Popery! What is far more extraordinary, there are two laymen, members of the House of Commons, who think fit to scourge themselves! It is in vain to talk of the illumination of the age—at all times there have been, and I believe at all times there will be, *born* fanatics, whose destiny is to make, if they do not find, absurdities to believe and to propagate. I see no more probability that this distortion of understanding should become obsolete than that squinting eyes or hump-backs should cease to be found. At the same time, I think that this exaggerated notion of Church power is less likely than any form of superstition, to find favour in the sight of the English people at large. There is a constant and natural hostility between High Churchism, and Whig, still more radical, principles in government. Under our present liberal administration, nothing is done by the state to strengthen the hands of the Church. The chief justice has just pronounced an important decision (that parish vestries cannot by law be *compelled* to vote money for church-rates), which is likely ultimately to liberate dissenters from this unjust burden; and which strikes also at the pride and assumption of the establishment a blow which will be deeply felt.

And so the French have set their hearts on having back the relics of their Emperor from his prison-isle, that they may make them the object of a grand show and ceremony. It was right, I think, in our government to grant the request, since they regard it as an obligation, but I think it a mournful sign of the temper and spirit of that people. Military glory, it seems, is still their idol. To their restless temper, peace is insipid, freedom is indifferent, they must have *excitement*, and *that* nothing can yield so largely as war. I tremble for the results. To their king, this worship of the memory of Bonaparte must be exceedingly offensive. Nothing, certainly, but fear of the consequences of refusal, can have induced him to concur in their wish, and the same fear may soon compel him to seize some pretext for going to war with one or other of his neighbours; and so the flame would be rekindled throughout Europe. Horrible anticipation! The mind cannot entertain it without shuddering. What, alas! in such a case, would become of all our hopes for the improvement of man and his destiny!

Our rumours of war seem blowing over. The King of Naples is wise enough to submit. We shall settle our dispute amicably with you. China, indeed, we shall apparently be obliged to take some hostile measures with —but we still hope matters may soon admit of arrangement.

At home, I think we are going on well in almost all respects. The Tories seem further from power than ever, and many quiet reforms, which do much unostentatious good, are in progress. I know of nothing in our political state to excite apprehension, except it be the perpetual turbulence and restlessness of O'Connell, urging on his countrymen to arrogant claims and absurd enterprises, and the violence and folly of our own radicals. These absurd people may go on to produce some reaction in favour of toryism—but that is all, I think, that is to be feared. Even with these men, I hope that a wise and liberal government will know how to deal.

Believe me ever
Yours, with true regard,
L. AIKIN.

No. 45.

Hampstead : Oct. 11, 1840.

My dear Friend—Your last letter was very peculiarly welcome to me on many accounts. I felt that in giving you the '*ipsissima verba*' of my vehement friend, I had put your forbearance to a severe trial; but it has stood it, as I thought it would, nobly; and my friend begs to apologise for the word 'slander,' and is quite satisfied that he was more slanderous in imputing to you a priestly spirit. In short, your candour has quite turned his heart, and it is a heart worth turning. You are quite right in saying that my language on the subject was 'too cold' and measured; it was indeed purposely kept down, for I wished to see the argument taken up by you alone, and was only desirous to show that *I* was not one of those touched by your censure. In fact, the goodness of God is what I have never doubted, amid all my doubts, more than just enough to make me look into the proofs. I believe, rather I feel it, just as I feel my own existence; I have, like you, a difficulty in conceiving the horror and the absurdity of an opposite opinion; and far rather would I endure any possible earthly misery, than lose my trust in Him who is *all*. Could there ever have been a good man without a Maker of man infinitely superior in goodness? One of Hume's Essays, in which he affirms that we might infer from the world around us, an intelligent, but not a moral cause, struck me, on re-reading it a few years since, as so utterly illogical, so truly absurd, that I could only account for it, from a writer of his acuteness, by supposing that he thought it prudent to throw this cloak over his atheism. Yet it is, indeed, worse than atheism—as bad as ultra-Calvinism. You ask if Carlyle makes any progress amongst us. Not with the thoroughly-read or the thorough thinkers,

the intellectual leaders of society; but he finds audiences, and
some readers and admirers (I can scarcely say disciples, for
I believe nobody pretends to make out his system), amongst
the half-read and half-thinkers. You will not admit,
with me, that some men are born fanatics, but perhaps
you will allow to Coleridge that some are born Platonists,
and others Aristotelians—in other words, that some minds
have a bent towards the mystical, others towards the experimental, in philosophy—that this difference is innate,
and is ever reproducing itself under different shapes and
names. In this country the experimental has long borne
sway, with Locke for its leader; of late there has been
somewhat of a spirit of revolt; transcendentalism has
some considerable advocates, and I think I can perceive
that the general tone on these subjects is, in degree, modified.
The high church dearly love a system which draws a
distinction between the reason and the understanding, and
affirms that doctrines which appear to the latter a contradiction in terms, may be all the more conformable to the
dictates of the former—the higher and nobler faculty—
this, you may know, is the language held by Coleridge
concerning the Trinity. I think, with you, that some
great truths may lie at the root of these speculations, but
many processes are to be gone through before they can be
brought into daylight and fitted for use. In the meantime, I both dislike and distrust the jargon—the cant of
of which Carlyle has such a quantity. You would see in
the 'Edinburgh Review,' an article on his history, which
appears to me to be an able exposure of his quackery, and
at the same time a candid estimate of his merits and
talents. The article is by a friend of mine, a man of
immense reading for his age, and a paragon among reviewers for downright honesty and impartiality—the rarest
of all qualities when the writer lies screened under the
irresponsible *we*.

The grand field for activity amongst us at this time is that of general education. A prodigious impulse has been given by the apparently insignificant grant which our liberal government has extorted from the public purse, in spite of tory opposition. The established priesthood having been baffled, and by the ministry also, in its attempt to assume the control of public instruction, and force its own creeds and catechisms on the children of dissenters, we may now hope that a free, large, and truly national system of instruction will be adopted. Little as I am disposed to sanguine views of human improvement, I own I do look with ardent hope to a general amelioration of manners and principles as the ultimate result of this exorcism of ignorance and brutality.

I trust we are in no present danger of the return of the Tories to power. This ministry has been well compared to the logging-stone, which one right arm can set shaking, but a hundred could not throw down. It seems to gain strength by the tempests which it weathers. There is great dissension, too, in the tory camp, and some important desertions have taken place. But, oh! where will be all our hopes, should we see ourselves again plunged in the misery and wickedness of war? There is no wish for it, but, on the contrary, the greatest horror of it, as I sincerely believe, both in the government and the nation at large; but I fear that the spirit of the French people is the very reverse. They long to revenge themselves on their conquerors, to gain territory, plunder, and glory—they abound in turbulent spirits, for whom peace offers no prospects, no career. I believe, indeed, that their king and all their best statesmen are pacifically disposed, but the awful doubt is whether they may not be compelled to yield to the torrent. Perhaps, after all, the heavy national debt of both countries is the best security for their peaceful behaviour. You enquire about Isabella of Castile, and her relation to the inquisition, and I conclude, from what you say, that you have not read Prescott's life of her. He is her decided eulogist, and insists on our thinking her one of the most amiable of women; at the same time, he distinctly states that she directly violated the laws of her country in instituting that new tribunal—that no provocation whatever had been given her by the unhappy Moors, or the Jews, the joint objects of her relentless and atrocious tyranny. In short, her persecutions appear to be amongst the most completely wicked—the most utterly inexcusable on record. She had not even the apology of bad example, her inquisition was an absolute novelty in the world. It is true that it was the invention and suggestion of an execrable monk, her father-confessor; but neither had Isabella the excuse of a weak and pliant character; she effectually withstood, on many occasions, the influence of a husband whom she is said to have loved, and I do not believe that she would have complied with her confessor in this matter, had she not expected to strengthen her royal authority by the destruction or banishment of her misbelieving subjects. Her bigotry, like that of Louis XIV., was little else than the spirit of despotism in disguise. The persecutions of our bloody Mary were venial, compared with those of her grandmother. *She* had great provocations.

Have you read Ranke's 'History of the Popes of the Sixteenth and Seventeenth Centuries,' translated by Mrs. Austin? If not, think that you have a treasure laid up in store. The writer has collected and studied his authorities with true German industry, and has poured a flood of new light on the most important period of modern history; and I, for one, feel it a real misfortune to have groped through a large part of that period without his guiding lamp. The history of the Papacy is so closely intertwined with that of every European nation, that no one, in future, must presume to write of Tudors, or Stuarts, or Bourbons, without consulting Ranke, and to possess a true history of this wonderful line of monarch-priests, is a greater gain to philosophy than it is possible to estimate.

But why do I speak of books to read, to you who are so much better employed in writing? I cordially congratulate both you and the public on your task, and particularly on the ardent spirit with which you are pursuing it. I long to know *what* your work is to be, but, be it what it may, I am strongly persuaded that it will prove to be something that the world 'will not easily let die.' What you have been meditating half your life cannot but be something of importance, and worthy of general attention. You did well to 'bide your time,' and to wait till you were sure of having the ear of the public in right of your former publications. May health and strength be given you to complete all that is in your heart!

In my little, quiet way, I am jogging on comfortably enough. My spirits have lately had a *fillip*, in the shape of a journey. Thanks to the railroad, I was able to convey myself, with little fatigue, to Southampton, where I found a kind friend in waiting to convey me eight miles further, to a beautiful mansion on the skirts of the New Forest. This is the largest sylvan tract remaining in England, and I was surprised to find how primitive a character it still preserves. A stone marks the spot where Rufus fell, his stirrup is kept as a relic at the royal hunting lodge, where the forest courts are held; and, on the whole, it seemed to me that his name was quite as current in the mouths of men as that of George III., the last monarch who hunted here. The cottagers are devotedly attached to their native soil; they have continued on the same spot from father to son, many of them from the Norman times, in fact; they enjoy many advantages from the neighbourhood of the forest, besides that delightful sense of liberty which waits upon the roamer of 'the good green wood,' and which he who has once tasted would scarcely exchange for a palace. The wood consists chiefly of noble oaks and stately beeches, and the undulations of the surface open a thousand picturesque glimpses of hill and vale, open glade and tangled wood, sprinkled with cottages embowered in flower-garden and orchard, and mansions standing proudly on their emerald lawns. From the higher eminences you command the Isle of Wight, with its bays and headlands, and the soft yet fresh sea air breathes the very spirit of health. I was in a state of enchantment during my whole visit difficult to describe. Since I began this letter, I have been reading an article on all Carlyle's works in the 'Quarterly Review.' This author, who sets himself so vehemently against all 'forms,' ought to feel himself rebuked by the praise which he has extorted from the ultra-High-Church reviewer, by his mystical use of the word *faith*, from which it is easy for such a reviewer to extract arguments favourable to ecclesiastical authority. Woe unto us, if our philosophers are to be as hostile to the employment of reason in the investigation of truth, as our high priests!

I must at length put a period to my long letter. I must answer some other correspondents far more briefly.

Ever yours with true respect and friendship,
L. AIKIN.

No. 46.

Hampstead: June 12, 1841.

My dear Friend—You cannot thank me more sincerely for my letters than I thank you for yours. They are a true refreshment to my spirit, which often suffers a famine from the extreme and increasing scarcity in this country of such liberal and enlightened sentiment as forms the only food on which it can exist. I allow, freely allow, that some useful truths—practical ones—have been powerfully argued—successfully promulgated among us, of late years. The cause of free trade, which I, like you, believe to be that of true and just and virtuous policy, has gained and is gaining. Our corn-laws are at the last gasp, and in timber and sugar, I believe, we are going right. But, alas! what avails all this, if free speculation is taxed to prohibition—if religious liberty lies oppressed, stifled, down-trodden—if no man dares to say, in the face of the world, that all opinions have equal rights—that no one ought to believe himself entitled to put another to silence because his doctrines are not those of the majority, those that the state has endowed? We have in this country many evils—what country is without? What a sign of the times is it, that so eminent a natural philosopher as Whewell, in his 'Life of Galileo,' labours to defend the proceedings of the Inquisition against him—calls them lenient—seems to suppose that the *Church* has a right to stop the promulgation of any truth which it regards as dangerous! Oh! I am sick at heart when I think upon these things.

You will see that we are threatened, too, with a tory administration, but this is yet uncertain; it will depend on the new parliament. Some think we shall see the fulfilment of the Duke of Wellington's prediction—that, if the Reform Bill were carried, parties would be so balanced, that it would be impossible to carry on any government at all. In France this seems to be almost the case.

I apprehend that the prodigious increase of zeal and activity, consequently of rancour, on the part of the Established Church, is mainly the result of Catholic emancipation, and the strength and courage it has lent to the Romanists, which Protestanism feels itself called upon to

resist with all its might and by all its m
being one. Such unlooked-for, and often (
flow from great public measures. The :
spent their lives in bringing them about of
in vain their own success. A consideration
to several others, convinces me that *fluc*
more than *progress*, is the great law of
But this you will be loth to admit.

I was struck with your idea of agricul
great civiliser of recent man, and I think t
so in some climates—but how this great a
acts upon every other element of human l
—how it *complicates* this whole subjec
nothing but the Book of Genesis which can
favour of the notion that the whole race
single pair. Probably there were many
adapted to different portions of the earth.
on guessing where we cannot know?' Wh
are guessing and speculating animals! I
lating and guessing, because my mind is
body idle. This whole winter and sprin
nearly a prisoner to the house; latterly I h
ill, but matters seem now mending with
grieve that you should have been so m
Perhaps we both feel that it is drawing t
with us. Well, so be it.

As for my book, it is still among the futu
I am no longer the diligent labourer I or
task proceeds, I hope. Great or small, it
kind of books that we want, the offspring
of mere reading. Original writers, I beli
benefactors towards mankind, either then
answerers are sure to bring out some new tru
old ones in a stronger light. Whether Car
all to be put in the list of original thinker

doubt; to me he still appears little more than a jargonist. He makes his way a little in society however, ay, and very genteel and very correct society, notwithstanding the tone of his work on the French Revolution, which is surely radicalism, combined with the most odious and mischievous moral fatalism. According to him, all crimes and enormities are 'by divine putting on.' You do not love the doctrines of necessity in any shape; but surely you will admit that, between the vulgar fatalist and the philosophic necessarian there is this essential difference, that the first talks as if *any* man may be destined to commit a crime, as any man may be destined to die of a fever; the second firmly holds that none but a *bad* man can ever be destined to commit a crime, since no man can do anything but what he *wills* to do; his will, indeed, is actuated by motives, but in the mind of a virtuous man those which prompt to crime will never gain the preponderance. In fact, do we not *feel* that there are many actions which it is impossible, so long as we possess our senses, that we should ever find any temptation to commit; so fixed is our conviction that nothing could ever make it worth our while. Fatalism is certainly not original in Carlyle, nor in the French school of writers from whom he borrowed it, but I fear they may have done something towards rendering it popular. There is a circumstance respecting the French people at this time which I think remarkable, and am in doubt how to interpret. During their revolution, never was there such contempt for human life; blood was poured out like water; a man was crushed with as little regard as a beetle; now the feeling is so changed that they can scarcely bear the idea of capital punishment; their juries find 'extenuating circumstances' even in the horrid act of a parricide, in order to save him from death. I should like to ascribe this scruple to none but good motives or causes; but when I consider how strong is the

sentiment of moral indignation in every pure and virtuous
and noble breast; how uniformly all nations, where morals
have been strict, and manners unsophisticated, have marked
their horror of great crimes by taking away the offender
from the midst of them, and compare this with the
acknowledged profligacy and wickedness of Paris, and the
assertion of those who know its society best, that the only
inexpiable fault there is evil-speaking, I hesitate. My
father has somewhere observed, that universal indulgence
is near akin to universal profligacy, and I confess that I
do not see with satisfaction the anxiety manifested in France,
and in some degree here also, to abolish capital punishments, while crimes are rather on the increase. The
'godly watch' set upon one another by your puritans
was one extreme, and an odious one; but the total disregard of the conduct of others, where it does not immediately affect ourselves, so inculcated at Paris, and perhaps
in high life generally, is still more fatal to all the lofty
sentiments and heroic virtues, and certainly favourable to
all the vices.

The completion of this long letter has been accidentally
delayed for a few days. In the meantime our good
ministry has been out-voted. All now depends upon the
spirit of the people. If they please they can return a
majority against the Tories—but *will* they? since it cannot be done without risk to the worldly interests of many.
The crisis may be called awful, when Ireland is taken into
the account. I incline, however, to the hoping side, so
far as this, let who will be in power, public opinion must
be respected, and, sooner or later, all really salutary
measures must be carried; the question is one of this year
or next with regard to several of the more important.
But no such calm language as this will be held on the
hustings, and the evils of party virulence will abound.
Alas for those who speak or write as the servants of truth

and posterity in the midst of party discord! You, I trust, are safe from its influence. May you only be favoured with health and strength for the completion of your work! I long to see it.

>Pray believe me ever
>Your affectionate friend,
>LUCY AIKIN.

No. 47.

Hampstead: June 30, 1841.

My dear Friend—Many thanks for your 'Memoirs of Dr. Tuckerman' and the accompanying Journal. I believe they will cause me to send you almost a pamphlet in return; but you who enjoin me sometimes to write fearlessly what I think will not, perhaps, be impatient under this result. Your character of your friend appears to me exceedingly candid and discriminating, as well as affectionate. It is unfortunately true, that with all his heroism of benevolence, he did not make an agreeable impression here in general society. This was partly because, like all men of one idea, especially such as are eloquent, he could neither speak, nor suffer others to speak, of anything else in his presence—which wore out the patience even of the best disposed; partly because, for want of knowledge either of the state of the poor with us, or of the plans adopted for their benefit, he, in the words of a very benevolent friend of mine to whom I introduced him, 'recommended as novelties the very things we had all been practising for thirty years.'

It might well have been supposed, even by those ignorant of the fact, that in an old and densely-peopled land like ours, where great inequality of conditions had always prevailed, and where, as we are apt to flatter ourselves, humanity had always been a striking feature of the national character, many schemes must have been put to the proof for the relief of such destitution, physical and moral, as our great system of parish support could not reach. But well might Dr. Tuckerman have failed to be led by this consideration to acquaint himself fully with the facts, when an unworthy Englishman goes so far in ignorance or ill will, as to calumniate his country on this very head. I refer to the very offensive speech of one Mr. Giles, of Liverpool, reported in the Journal you have sent me. It has pleased this person, after *judiciously* pointing out the efforts of pastor Oberlin as a kind of compensation for the horrors of the French Revolution, to advert generally to the exertions making in favour of the poor and indigent young, 'through the diffusion of an education adapted to raise the soul more and more from earth, and point it heavenward.' He professes, however, to speak on this subject 'with horror and shame,' as a native of England, the only country 'wanting in her duty' on this head. While 'the proud despotism of Prussia,' as he says, 'trains up her youth from the cradle to manhood, in a knowledge of themselves and the world around them, freeborn England casts them off as orphans.' And he goes on to represent our agricultural and our manufacturing population as alike existing in a state of sordid, almost savage ignorance, and the last, as abandoned to all the excesses of the worst passions of mankind, utterly 'neglected by those whose wealth and power they secure.'

In England, misrepresentation like this would not deserve refutation; but it may not be labour lost, to offer to you and to your fellow-philanthropists beyond the Atlantic, a slight sketch capable of showing both what has actually been done here in this great cause, and the circumstances which have rendered it impracticable to do more, or more speedily, or in a different manner.

After the establishment and wide diffusion of Sunday

schools, the first comprehensive scheme for popular instruction was that of Joseph Lancaster, schools on whose system forthwith arose by hundreds on every side. It is indeed true that the clergy, and other enemies to the diffusion of education among the lower classes, especially if independent of the control of the Church, opposed the poor Quaker with disgraceful virulence, and nothing could have upheld him but the protecting hand of George III., and the energy of his pious wish 'that every poor child in his dominions should be enabled to read its bible.' A kind of compromise at length took place; Dr. Bell and the Church Catechism were introduced into the system, and, under the name of national schools, we have still all over the country multitudes of establishments, supported by voluntary subscription, which afford to thousands the rudiments of common knowledge, and some acquaintance, it is to be presumed, with their duties to God and man.

A system of national education at the public expense was next projected and moved in the House of Commons by Mr. Brougham. It was rejected—and why? Because the necessity of neutralising the hostility of the clergy had compelled him, by the provisions of his bill, to subject the whole to their superintendence and authority. All classes of dissenters rose as one man against such stipulations, and by their wise jealousy, or just indignation, the measure was thrown out. In a country enjoying less either of civil or religious liberty this could not have occurred— not, for example, in 'the proud despotism of Prussia.' Without the command of the sovereign no such project could there have been brought forward; and had he commanded, it must have been carried into execution, whoever was jealous or indignant. This attempt, however, drew great attention to the subject, and was by no means unproductive of good. 'Let us alone,' exclaimed the '*free-born*' English, 'and we will do it ourselves.' Infant

schools, perhaps the most effective of all
adopted for the prevention of early corrupt
were devised, and, with the rapidity of an e
spread the whole face of the land. An
between the sects on one hand, and the Chu
now found it needful to buckle in earnest
come task, on the other, effectually prevent
either part from flagging. The small aid f
purse since obtained by a Whig ministry
equitable as the bench of bishops would a
a fresh stimulus, by the conditions annexed
to the exertions of voluntary subscribers.
has been to find fit teachers in sufficient nu
tutions, however, have been founded for the
demand, and should the prosperity of the p
with their generous ardour, the English pe
contemplate their own plans for popular e
glow of satisfaction, to which the Prussian v
'drill obligation' and 'school obligation'
same ground of compulsion, guarded by
penalties, must for ever remain a stranger.

All that a free government could properl
enactment it has done. It is now com
owners of factories, on the managers of v
superintendents of prisons and penitentiari
of ships of war, to provide for the child
under their charge the means or opport
school learning and religious instruction
little? If after all it must be confessed th
a great and lamentable deficiency in the m
civilisation, by which I understand a just
sense of the true interests of human n
out our vast population, it would be eq
to weigh more deliberately than some cer
have done the magnitude of the task, and

schools, the first comprehensive scheme for popular instruction was that of Joseph Lancaster, schools on whose system forthwith arose by hundreds on every side. It is indeed true that the clergy, and other enemies to the diffusion of education among the lower classes, especially if independent of the control of the Church, opposed the poor Quaker with disgraceful virulence, and nothing could have upheld him but the protecting hand of George III., and the energy of his pious wish 'that every poor child in his dominions should be enabled to read its bible.' A kind of compromise at length took place; Dr. Bell and the Church Catechism were introduced into the system, and, under the name of national schools, we have still all over the country multitudes of establishments, supported by voluntary subscription, which afford to thousands the rudiments of common knowledge, and some acquaintance, it is to be presumed, with their duties to God and man.

A system of national education at the public expense was next projected and moved in the House of Commons by Mr. Brougham. It was rejected—and why? Because the necessity of neutralising the hostility of the clergy had compelled him, by the provisions of his bill, to subject the whole to their superintendence and authority. All classes of dissenters rose as one man against such stipulations, and by their wise jealousy, or just indignation, the measure was thrown out. In a country enjoying less either of civil or religious liberty this could not have occurred—not, for example, in 'the proud despotism of Prussia.' Without the command of the sovereign no such project could there have been brought forward; and had he commanded, it must have been carried into execution, whoever was jealous or indignant. This attempt, however, drew great attention to the subject, and was by no means unproductive of good. 'Let us alone,' exclaimed the '*freeborn*' English, 'and we will do it ourselves.' Infant

schools, perhaps the most effective of all
adopted for the prevention of early corrupt
were devised, and, with the rapidity of an e
spread the whole face of the land. An
between the sects on one hand, and the Chu
now found it needful to buckle in earnest
come task, on the other, effectually prevent
either part from flagging. The small aid f
purse since obtained by a Whig ministry
equitable as the bench of bishops would a!
a fresh stimulus, by the conditions annexed
to the exertions of voluntary subscribers.
has been to find fit teachers in sufficient nu
tutions, however, have been founded for the
demand, and should the prosperity of the pe
with their generous ardour, the English pe
contemplate their own plans for popular ee
glow of satisfaction, to which the Prussian v
'drill obligation' and 'school obligation'
same ground of compulsion, guarded by
penalties, must for ever remain a stranger.

All that a free government could properly
enactment it has done. It is now com
owners of factories, on the managers of v
superintendents of prisons and penitentiari
of ships of war, to provide for the child
under their charge the means or opport
school learning and religious instruction
little? If after all it must be confessed tl
a great and lamentable deficiency in the me
civilisation, by which I understand a just
sense of the true interests of human n
out our vast population, it would be eq
to weigh more deliberately than some cel
have done the magnitude of the task, and

to be surmounted in its execution. Clusters of factories, mills, and warehouses, rise among us like exhalations; much within the memory of man, our principal seats of manufacture have swelled from moderate country towns, sometimes from nameless hamlets, into aggregates of human dwellings, exceeding in population most of the capital cities of Europe. What provision could exist in these places for gratuitous education, or who was there to supply the want? What orphan schools, almshouses, hospitals, established charities of any kind, could be looked for? All was to be created, and by whom? The few older families fled, one after another, from the din and smoke of machinery, and the elbowing of the newly rich, to calmer retreats. The master manufacturers, men for the most part of scanty, often of no education, narrow therefore in their views, and frequently sordid, were slow in learning the claims of those whom they regarded chiefly as a part of the apparatus employed in producing their wealth. This was to be expected: and when it is considered that the periods of greatest distress to the workmen were precisely those of difficulty and failure to themselves, from temporary obstruction of demand, it will be confessed that much destitution, physical and moral, was inevitable.

By degrees, public opinion began to bear on this mighty mass of evil, and the eyes and hearts of men to open both to the claims of these lower classes, and to the frightful dangers of disregarding them; but even then the efforts of benevolence were encountered among many obstacles, by one in particular, which there were no obvious means of overcoming. This was the wholesale employment of children, almost infants, in various branches of manufacture, particularly in that vast one of cotton twist. To attempt to give instruction to these little victims would have been absurd, and even inhuman. Not a moment could be spared from their too short hours of rest for any other purpose; and by necessity they were left to grow up to the stature of human maturity with scarcely any other evidences of humanity about them. But has no remedy been sought or applied to this giant mischief? What are all those long deliberations of parliament which matured at length the Factory Law, but the most touching evidence of the parental care of the state over those who had no one else to care for them? Under this law, the hours of working are strictly limited, and by its provisions the children will receive education—as far as it consists in giving the rudiments of literature. Those moral influences, which are indeed of infinitely more value, the state cannot give, or can give but very imperfectly. If parents be without all sense of their own duties, who can avert the dreadful consequences from their unfortunate offspring? Besides their setting to their children examples which too frequently counteract all the influence of the precepts of religion and virtue, it has been found in all parts of our country much less difficult to raise funds for the maintenance of schools, than to persuade parents to enforce the regular attendance of the pupils. Ignorance too gross to form any estimate of the value of what was rejected—false indulgence—but far more frequently a selfish reluctance to give up during school hours any profit, or convenience derived from the labour of the child, have largely operated in counteraction of all plans of this nature. The case is the same, I perceive, with you. Three-fifths appear from the Journal to be the highest average attendance on the schools of the Home Mission. In like manner church-building, the progress of which among us exceeds anything ever dreamt of by our ancestors, but yet perhaps no more than equal pace with the increase of our population, is often found easier to accomplish than church attendance. And do not your own ministers at large in effect confess a failure, when they broadly state that it is an error to suppose that their services are attended by the lowest class? Either there will always remain at the bottom of society a sediment which will refuse to be incorporated with the clearer liquor, or at least it can be but very slowly and gradually taken up. Establish, either in our country or yours, a Prussian compulsion, drive the children to school, and all ages to church, by the terror of fine and imprisonment, and what will be gained to compensate the loss of that spirit of independence, which has probably been the most important element of all in the greatness and progress both of England and her noblest offspring? No valuable end can be attained but by means of a congenial character, therefore, not the diffusion of moral feeling and virtuous conduct, or of devotion, by arbitrary force. Better a slow, better a partial progress, than one which, under the show of universality, is delusive, and must fail in the full trial.

With regard to that visiting of the poor at their own houses, to which the agency of Dr. Tuckerman was at first confined, there is little reason to impute negligence to our middle and higher classes, whatever faults may often be found in their manner of performing the office. It had always been the practice of the better kind of country ladies to distribute benefactions among the cottagers, and often to carry, as well as to send them, aids in sickness. In towns of moderate size the same things were done; but Hannah More, in her 'Cœlebs,' by representing her *pattern* young lady as regularly devoting two evenings in a week to making her rounds among the village poor, unfortunately made it a fashion and a rage. I say unfortunately, because nothing is ever done well and wisely which is taken up in this manner. Judicious people saw that it was neither an expedient, nor indeed a safe employment, for the inexperienced girls who undertook it. They objected that young ladies would be exposed to injury, both in temper and taste, by the quantity of vulgar and interested flattery, and vulgar and spiteful gossip which would be forced upon them; that their ears would continually be assailed by grossness of expression, and their minds either sullied or saddened by too close and unveiled a view of human vices in their coarsest forms. While we guarded them with unceasing solicitude against the approach of even doubtful society of their own class, it seemed strangely inconsistent to permit them to come into habitual contact with what was positively bad in a lower class.

I have no doubt that these and other objections urged in the beginning were found to be just, to a certain extent. The impulse was given, however, and nothing could stop it. It acted at first chiefly within the evangelical party; but that party became, at length, great enough to give the tone to society at large; and the practice of thus superintending the poor has become so general, that I know no one circumstance by which the manners, studies, and occupations of Englishwomen have been so extensively modified, or so strikingly contradistinguished from those of a former generation. By these female missionaries numberless experiments have been made and projects started. Some have addressed themselves to the bodies of the poor, others to their souls, and there has been much quackery in both departments. Some have distributed Calvinistic tracts, others bread and soup tickets. Some have applied themselves to clothing the children, others to teaching them, others to reading to the sick and infirm. One of the results of this system, and which will not have your entire approbation, has been the formation of a prodigious number of associations for the accomplishment of objects to which the efforts of single persons were unequal. Women in this country have seldom enough of habits of business, and especially of that habit of the world which enables men, by conciliation and compromise, to pursue their objects with almost any associates, to be good members of committees. I fear theirs are not always schools of forbearance or good manners; but practice may improve them. It is a decided advantage that the new accession of zeal among the clergy has urged them to take almost entirely out of the hands of the ladies the theological department, in which their bitterest dissensions had of course occurred.

Good and evil have arisen out of this great movement, as out of all others. The good I need not particularise. It is enough to say that much aid, much comfort, much instruction of many kinds, and, it may be hoped, some improvement in decorum, in piety, and in morals generally, may have been effected. On the other hand, I think that it has given rise among the ladies to much spiritual pride and self-inflation; much of an imperious, pragmatical, meddling habit, which has rendered many both odious to the poor, to whom they took credit for being the greatest of benefactresses, and troublesome and unamiable to their equals. It has diverted the minds of numbers, not from dissipation only, but from literature, from the arts, from all the graces and amenities of polished life, and rendered many a home intolerable to husbands, fathers, and brothers, thereby causing more moral mischief than all their exertions could eradicate among the poor. But the wise and the foolish, the gentle and the ungentle, will ever throw their own characters into all their occupations and pursuits. With regard to the poor, the benefits they have derived have been counterbalanced by a vast increase among them of hypocrisy, and a disgusting cant of piety, assumed to flatter the ladies; of fraud and imposture generally, and of a fawning, dependent, servile spirit, unworthy of freemen. Idleness and helplessness have, in many wealthy and *well-visited* neighbourhoods, become more profitable than activity and a manly resistance of the evils of life. Intemperance has been fostered among the men, by an assurance that if *they* did not provide necessaries for their families, the ladies would.

I apprehend that more good, and certainly fewer evils, have attended the exertions of some excellent men who among us have followed in the footsteps of Dr. Tuckerman; they alone ought to attempt indiscriminate visiting of the lowest of the low in great and vicious cities. Ladies might act more usefully under their directions.

I fear I must have wearied you by this long account; but I wished, besides refuting a most injurious imputation on my own country, to make you acquainted with the results of our experience in attempts to benefit the poor, the ignorant, and the vicious. Your country is still young in the arts of dealing with human misery on a great scale. The essential differences between an aristocratic and a democratic social system which penetrate into every part, must vary the working of every plan and modify every result: but, after all, it is common human nature which is to be dealt with, and the great principles must be the same.

You naturally wish that the increase of your city should not proceed, if it is to be followed by the moral evils which have accompanied, in all times and countries, a similar aggregation of men and dwellings. In vain! gregarious man will ever go on joining house to house, and street to street, and vice and misery will ever find abodes among them. But will not virtue dwell there also, and domestic happiness—warm hearts and enlightened minds? Will there not be there, as everywhere, more good than evil, more enjoyment than suffering? There will; for all is in His hands who loves the creatures He has made. This, after all, is the true balm for the wounded bosom of philanthropy, when, after many trials and much experience,

she discovers how hard a task it is to do even a little good —unalloyed, how impracticable! I will now release you.
Believe me ever most sincerely yours,
LUCY AIKIN.

No. 48.

Hampstead: Aug. 6, 1841.

My dear Friend—It delights me to think how far our correspondence is from languishing. I trust you have ere now received a long letter from me, occasioned by your Home Mission Report, and I yesterday was gratified by your letter on our Church. I answer it while fresh in my mind. I am not able to say whether methodism, meaning strictly the sect founded by Wesley, and that division of it which followed Whitfield, has been injurious to dissent or not. I believe the converts were chiefly either members of the establishment, or persons who had previously known nothing or cared nothing for religion in any shape. It seems as if the spread of the evangelical spirit in the Church had checked in some degree that of methodism, which scarcely, I think, keeps up its proportion to the population. But when I lamented the decline of dissent, I had in my mind that of Presbyterianism chiefly—that is, of the only sect which could boast of learned ministers, and which once included in its bosom a very considerable body of wealthy and well educated and enlightened families.

As for the other old denominations, the Independents and the Baptists, they are by no means declining in numbers. Formerly their congregations were seldom found but in towns, and among the trading classes, but I am now told that there is scarcely a rural village throughout the country in which either they or the Methodists, under some of their subdivisions, have not some humble place of worship.

They reckon, I believe, by hundreds of thousands. But in this aristocratic country, as you truly call it, numbers *alone* stand for little or nothing. These dissenters have no political power or weight whatever, as their ministers have confessed or complained. They have not even a single member of parliament belonging to them, while the little Unitarian aristocracy has about fifteen. Their opinions are, I believe, Calvinistic to a high degree, and it is only as persons asserting practically the right of private judgment in religion, that it is possible to prefer them to the members of the establishment. I know not at all what their political bent may be: this only we may rely on, that any administration which should strongly favour the Church would be certain of their enmity—a consideration which may come to be worth the attention of Sir Robert Peel. At periods of crisis every right aim tells. The church-rate question has served in very many parishes throughout England as a muster-roll of the rated householders, and in a majority, I think, of these, the dissidents altogether have carried it against mother-church. Observe that rating, i.e. to the poor, goes lower than the elective franchise, at least comprises much greater numbers. It may a little illustrate this matter to you, if I mention that full half the maid-servants I have had were either some kind of methodists or regular dissenters; and I believe this to be general. You see from this, that there is no apparent tendency to what you would call pure Christianity in our lower classes—except, indeed, that among the Baptists there are, or were, some Unitarians. The sect of socialists, the growth of which seems connected or coincident with that of chartism, is not a Christian sect, it seems, but a deistic one, which has exposed itself to just disgrace by condemning the institution of marriage. I know not at all to what extent it has spread, or whether it still increases. The public at large scarcely know it but through the invectives of the Bishop of Exeter in the House of Lords, in which there is probably both exaggeration and misrepresentation. Still I have heard, apparently on good authority, that there is scarcely a town in England without a socialist congregation—an ugly fact, if it be one. A comparison of the religious state of our country now, and a hundred years ago, will not, I conceive, support your theory of the progress of mankind. Then we had Low Church principles in the establishment; the dissenters learned, respected, and steady; the deists, what there were of them, learned also, moral, and too prudent to promulgate their opinions among the vulgar.

No; I cannot go all the length you have done in your late address, though I admire it very much, and cordially thank you for it; and if it be an exact delineation of the *present* state of opinion with you, especially of the tolerant, rather the enlarged enlightened state of Christian feeling, I must say that we might take a lesson from you with great advantage. But I have often wished to ask you on what special ground you fix your confidence in the constant progress of the race. You reckon much, I know, on the influences of Christianity; but in this there is nothing new, and why should this power over the human heart be continually augmenting? If the world could be considered as an individual, we might readily suppose it a design of Providence that all its experiences of every kind should be tending to increase its knowledge and improve its virtue. But when two things remain always the same—the nature of God and the nature of man—when every human creature is born into the world with the same ignorance, and what is more, with the same appetites and passions, as his earliest and rudest progenitors—when the necessity for the existence of evil, whatever may make that necessity, cannot be supposed likely to cease—can we reasonably expect more, than that in some countries the progress of the arts of life may redress some outward inconveniences, and obtain for a portion of society some outward comforts and luxuries, and that great crimes of violence may become more rare, and vice in the higher classes less gross? Men may grow more skilful in adapting means to ends, but may we hope that their ends will be wiser or better? The very diffusion of knowledge may prove little more than the beating out of the ingot into gold leaf. In this country, at least, literature in its higher sense is certainly not advancing; books must be made so rapidly, that even industry, labour, cannot be bestowed on the manufacture. For the interests of good taste, and the effectual cultivation of the mind, it would be far better if we had not above one-tenth of the new books that are published; and so in science, the sciolists may amuse themselves, but assuredly they do nothing for the advance of any branch of study.

Your new people may be making progress, and I hope they are; but in these old countries population increases upon us so frightfully, that it will be very well indeed if in any respect we can hold our own. Such are my more gloomy speculations; but it is impossible to concur more entirely than I do in what you point out as the *improvement* to be made of the present state and tendencies of society, or in the warnings which you think required.

No more will I add at present. I doubt if you will thank me for so much on the discouraging side. But you seek the truth, and it should be told you.

Ever most sincerely yours,
LUCY AIKIN.

No. 49.

Hampstead: Jan. 10, 1842.

My dear Friend—It grieves me much to find that illness was the cause of that long silence which I had been wondering at and lamenting. This cause did not suggest itself to me, because I had received from you a sermon delivered far from your home, and, as I thought recently, which certainly bore no marks of feebleness. This, I think, is almost all I shall say to you about it, for a good reason— that I know nothing of the subject. Your discourse goes entirely on the ground of religion being a social, an uniting principle; and such indeed I know it to be usually. To me, however, it has never been so; on the contrary, I have always felt it as a matter more strictly personal than any other; and the very last office I could bear to commit to any human being would be that of speaking to my Maker for me, or in my name. I mention this only as what is, not what ought to be: at least it is a matter in which everyone must do as suits best with his temper and circumstances. I can imagine that if it had ever been my fortune in youth to attend upon any minister who could either have satisfied my judgment, or moved my heart, I too might have known devotion as a bond of friendship, a social pleasure. Your charity is very large, and certainly no man ever had less of the *priest*.

I am glad my mention of it led you to read Milman's work; and I made him very happy two days since, by telling him that he had cheered your convalescence. It was very many years since we had met before, and that but once, yet we had each a strong remembrance of the other, and met like friends. I found him cheerful, animated, quite without pomp or pretension, and full of agreeable conversation. I agree with you, however, that his style in writing is by no means so easy or simple. His close study of Gibbon seems to have injured him in this point. There is no writer whose faults are more infectious than Gibbon's —condemn them as you will, you cannot contemplate them long without a strange propensity to repeat them. In fact, though certainly faults, they are seldom gratuitous ones. Most of his ambiguities prove, on examination, devices to comprise much matter in few words: this is seldom the case with those of his imitators. You ask if our church has many Milmans. Very few, I conceive; and the clergy are so far from being proud of his learned and courageous work, that they and their reviews have preserved a studied silence respecting it. I know not which way mother-church is setting her face. Oxford, indeed, casts a longing eye towards Rome, but with the powerful evangelical anti-Popery party to watch her, she durst not what she would. Then Scotland is almost in a flame on the old ground of the superiority of the Church authorities to the civil power and the laws of the land. In that country the Sabbatarian fanaticism burns still fiercer than among our evangelicals. What think you of a provincial presbytery's excommunicating a man and his wife also for burying their child on the Sunday—the general custom here, at least with the working classes? I fear indeed *we* grow no wiser.

How far, I wonder, have I brought down my own small particular story in my letters to you? I doubt if I have told you that I went, in the middle of September, to that deserted seat of fashion and gaiety, Bath. The railroad brought the journey within my strength, and I had the reward of my effort by leaving in those warm waters a very troublesome gouty affection, which had kept me long in a state of suffering and languor. Since my return I have been labouring upon Addison with vigour, and am not quite without hope of bringing it out before the end of our London spring, lasting till August. Mr. Hallam says it is time the public should be put in mind of him, for we have had no such writer since, and I find the same is the faith of all our high literati. One thing strikes me as quite unique in him. He was a great reformer of manners, yet never drew upon him the anger either of the high or the low—he improved mankind, and they did not persecute him. But perhaps I say wrongly *mankind*. His chief aim was to improve *womankind*, as the first step to amending society, and *we* were so good and so docile as to thank him even when he took the liberty of laughing at us. Had he begun with *you*——

Pray, had your Miss Sedgewick the like benevolent design in all the elaborate disparagement that she bestows on the outsides and insides of us unhappy women of England, with our Queen at our head? The hardest morsel is her choosing to record, and thus to sanction, the sentence of one of the girls of her party, that a woman gentle and lovely *could not* be an Englishwoman. Such stuff is not worth talking about, but American women visiting England will certainly be sufferers by these demonstrations of national hatred. Your niece did not look like a hater: I should be glad to be remembered to her.

You and I have our own private treaty of amity, but this slave-trading is likely, I fear, to make ill-blood between our governments.

I have been lately led to think of one of the greatest differences between education among us now and half a century ago—consisting in the introduction of German literature. The study of this language is now become so nearly universal in good society, that twenty years hence young people will be saying with wonder, ' I do really suspect that neither that old Mr. Suchaone nor his wife know German.' Just as *we* used to say of some of our elders regarding French. I have made some young people stare by telling them that, in my childhood, Mr. William Taylor of Norwich, whose translation of Bürger's Leonora was the spark which fired the muse of Scott, was quite as much wondered at for knowing German, as a person would now be for a profound acquaintance with Russ. What are to be the effects of this new ingredient on the flavour of our lighter literature, I cannot clearly perceive; certainly, if Carlyle be made the example of its influence on taste and style, nothing can be fancied more detestable. Mrs. Austin, on the contrary, is able to render a vast variety of German styles all into pure and flowing English, preserving at the same time something quite foreign in the subject-matter and turn of thought. There seems to be something more profoundly sentimental—more cordially affectionate in the expressions of the Germans than is the tone with us, and all our travellers hold their demonstrations to be sincere and trustworthy. On this account we certainly love them better than any other foreign people (it is to be considered that we have no national rivalries with them); yet a want of polish, tact, refinement, is remarked, which often gives a tinge of burlesque both to their sublime and pathetic. Mr. Taylor has somewhere said that 'there is a *too-muchness* in almost all German writers.' It seems as if the lightness of touch and perfection of taste of a Voltaire were gifts denied to their national mind. In one study their writers show a quite original spirit, combined with their well-known laboriousness—that of biblical criticism; and it is in this that I apprehend they are producing the strongest effects on other nations. Their most startling paradoxes seem to have found a welcome among your divines, and they certainly have not been universally rejected here. At our universities, 'German Theology' is a word of fear and reproach, but those who, like Milman, would dive into Christian antiquities, well know that their main reliance must be on the guidance of German *down-*

diggers. Are they destined once more to produce a revolution in religion? Will new blood be poured into the old churches of Christendom from their veins? Alas! neither of us can expect to live long enough to see these questions solved by the event. How I long sometimes to peep into the yet unopened leaves of the book of fate, to read the destinies of nations in their moral relations! It is not the doom of dynasties that I would learn.

We have nothing new in literature, and in politics we are mutely awaiting the meeting of the new ministry's new parliament. The grand trials of strength will be on the corn-laws and protective duties—momentous questions, no doubt; but on which, if all who are unqualified to judge would be silent, there could be no popular cry. Every year there is more or less of distress in our manufacturing towns, because such are the productive powers of our gigantic machinery, that every year some markets are overstocked, and the mill-owners are obliged to hold their hands. But this simple explanation never satisfies the sufferers, false or partial causes are sought out: it is now the fault of your banking system, now of our own. Once it was the decrees of Bonaparte; now it is our corn-laws. All Europe seems to be over-peopled, and the wages and condition of the working-classes sink in consequence—sink without help or hope of restoration. Sad truths, which in your new country you will know nothing of for many ages. Our magnificent colonies afford us, indeed, considerable relief, and I cannot repress some swellings of national pride, as I spread before me the map of the world, and realise it to myself, that the British Empire is the widest ever known to history. It is a proud feeling to dismiss an English MS. to the press, and think in how many zones and regions your thoughts will be read—the more reason they should be worthy and noble ones.

I must not spare more time from my Addison, even to

chat with you, but I could not bear to let your last lie a day longer unacknowledged. I grieve that you have been so long a sufferer, and shall be very anxious to hear that your strength returns completely. Be not too impatient to resume your literary labours, notwithstanding our impatience for the work you have in preparation. It is in vain to urge, while the body refuses to second the eagerness of the mind. I now feel that a week of the application of health performs more than months of languor. Do you recollect Mrs. Carter's pretty dialogue in verse between Body and Soul, and their mutual reproaches? I always thought poor Body was the ill-used party.

Adieu. May all good attend you.

Ever your sincere friend,
LUCY AIKIN.

No. 50.

Hampstead: Aug. 9, 1842.

My dear Friend—It grieves me to learn that illness has been the cause of your long silence; but it is past, I hope, and if your summer be bright and balmy like ours, it will give you strength to support the rigours of the coming winter. But O that you would come to recruit in our milder climate! We should then soon exorcise that strange phantom of a petticoated man which your imagination has conjured up during your illness, and some demon has whispered you to call an Englishwoman. I am well persuaded that you could have formed no such notion of us when you were here, although I believe you then saw but little society, and that of an inferior kind.

As to the very delicate subject of comparative beauty, our travellers attest that you have many very pretty girls; so have we, and even Miss Sedgewick pronounces that 'the Englishwoman is magnificent from twenty to five-and-forty.' We are satisfied; so let it rest.

With respect to our *step*, or *stride*, as you say, I have a little history to give you. Down to five-and-forty or fifty years ago, our ladies, tight-laced and 'propped on French heels,' had a short mincing step, pinched figures, pale faces, weak nerves, much affectation, a delicate helplessness, and miserable health. Physicians prescribed exercise, but to little purpose. Then came that event which is the beginning or end of everything—the French Revolution. The Parisian women, amongst other restraints, salutary or the contrary, emancipated themselves from their stays, and kicked off their *petits talons*. We followed the example, and, by way of improving upon it, learned to march of the drill-sergeant, mounted boots, and bid defiance to dirt and foul weather. We have now well-developed figures, blooming cheeks, active habits, firm nerves, natural and easy manners, a scorn of affectation, and vigorous constitutions. If your fair daughters would also learn to *step out*, their bloom would be less transient, and fewer would fill untimely graves. I admit, indeed, *some* unnecessary inelegance in the step of our pedestrian fair ones; but this does not extend to ladies of quality, or *real* gentlewomen, who take the air chiefly in carriages, or on horseback. They walk with the same quiet grace that pervades all their deportment, and to which you have seen nothing similar or comparable. When you mention our 'stronger gestures,' I know not what you mean. All Europe declares that we have *no* gesture. Madame de Staël ridiculed us as mere pieces of still life; and of *untravelled* gentlewomen this is certainly true in general. All governesses proscribe it. Where it exists, it arises from personal character. I have seen it engaging when the offspring of a lively imagination and warm feelings, repulsive when the result of a keen temper or dictatorial assumption. Again, your charge of want of delicacy I cannot understand. The women of every other European nation charge us with prudery, and I really cannot conceive of a human being more unassailable by just reproach on this head than a well-conducted Englishwoman. We have indeed heard some whimsical stories of American damsels who would not for the world speak of the *leg* even of a table, or the *back* even of a chair; and I do confess that we are not delicate or indelicate to this point. But if you mean to allude to the enormities of Frances Wright, or even to some of the discussions of —— ——, I can only answer, we blush too. Be pleased to consider that you have yet seen in your country none of our ladies of high rank; and few of your people, excepting diplomatic characters, have had more than very transient glimpses of them here, while we have had the heads of your society with us. Now I must frankly tell you, in reference to your very unexpected claim for your countrywomen of superior refinement, that although I have seen several of them whose manners were too quiet and retiring to give the least offence, I have neither seen nor heard of any who, even in the society of our middle classes, were thought entitled to more than this negative commendation — any who have become prominent without betraying gross ignorance of more than conventional good breeding. The very tone of voice, the accent and the choice of phrase, give us the impression of extreme inelegance. Patriot and staunch republican as you are, I think you must admit the à priori probability that the metropolis of the British empire, the first city in the world for size, for opulence, for diffusion of the comforts, accommodations, and luxuries of life, as well as for all the appliances of science, literature, and taste—the seat of a court unexcelled in splendour, and of an aristocracy absolutely unrivalled in wealth, in substantial power and dignity, and especially in mental cultivation of the most solid and most elegant kind—

would afford such a standard of graceful and finished manners as your state capitals can have no chance of coming up to. Further: it has been most truly observed that in every country it is the *mothers* who give the tone both to morals and manners; but with you the mothers are by your own account the *toilers*. Oppressed with the cares of house and children, they either retire from society into the bosom of their family, or leave at least the active and prominent parts in it to mere girls: and can you suppose that the *art and science* of good breeding, for such it is, will be likely to advance towards perfection when all who have attained such proficiency as experience can give resign the sway to giddy novices? With us it is quite different. Young ladies do not *come out* till eighteen, and then their part is a very subordinate one. It is the matron who does the honours of her house, and supports conversation; and her daughters pay their visits beneath her wing. Under wholesome restraint like this, the young best learn self-government. 'Sir,' said Dr. Parr, when provoked by the ill manners of a rich man who had been a spoiled child, 'it is discipline that makes the scholar, discipline that makes the gentleman, and it is the want of discipline that makes you what you are.'

One of your young women showed her taste and breeding by asking an English lady if she had seen 'Victoria;' and I must mention that Miss Sedgewick has thought proper to describe the first and *greatest lady in the world* as 'a plain little *body*,' adding, 'ordinary is the word for her.' It was no woman luckily, but your Mr. D——, who had the superlative conceit and impertinence to express his *surprise* to a friend of mine at finding so much good society *in London*. Now I think I have given you enough for one letter.

Let me thank you very gratefully for your 'Duty of the Free States.' We ought all to be grateful to you as one of the most earnest and powerful pleaders for peace between our two countries. I trust there is now good hope of the settlement of all our disputes. But your man-owners may as well give up all hope of our lending our hands to the recovery of their chattels; we shall go to war sooner, I can tell them. Your piece gave me much new information respecting the obligations of the free states in connection with slavery; they are more onerous than I thought. You *must* carry your point as to the district of Columbia at *all* risks, and I apprehend you will do so as soon as your people can be brought earnestly to *will* it—a state of public feeling which seems to be advancing. After our victory over slave-trade and slavery, no good cause is ever to be despaired of, not even although many of its champions may show themselves rash, uncharitable, violent. Reason, justice, and humanity must condescend to own that they need the service of the passions to lead the forlorn hope in their holiest crusades. Your lively delineations of the Southerns and the Northerns struck me very forcibly. The contrast is just what we should draw between English and Irish. Difference of climate may in great degree account for this in your case, but it can have no part in ours. We should ascribe it to difference of race, had not the original English settlers in Ireland grown into such a likeness of the old Celtic stock. Nothing more inscrutable than the causes of national character. Climate certainly modifies the original type. Thus the picture which you draw of American women in your letter bore much resemblance, I thought, to the creoles of our islands. But surely the same character cannot apply to the women of both North and South any more than to the men, for, independently of all other causes, the presence or absence of domestic slaves must modify every detail of domestic, and of course of feminine, life.

We have a new book which, if it fall in your way, will surely interest you. It is the 'Life of Oliver Heywood;' composed chiefly from his own journals by the Rev. Joseph Hunter. He was one of the two thousand ejected Presbyterian ministers of Charles II.'s time. After he was *silenced*, so far from holding his tongue, he passed the rest of his life, more than thirty years, in assiduous, almost incessant preaching, as a kind of missionary. His sphere of action was the wild mountainous tract along the borders of Lancashire and the West Riding of Yorkshire, then thinly sprinkled with pastoral villages, small towns engaged in woollen manufacture, and seats of rustic gentry —now a region of factories and steam-engines, mostly deserted by its hereditary gentry, but swarming with population. Oliver Heywood founded many congregations, and was indeed one of the chief fathers of Protestant dissent in all that country; it was a productive soil, and the seed sown by him has brought forth abundantly. The wealthy descendants of the poor and rude people whom he penetrated with his own profound sense of practical religion, his own stern hostility to the claims of *power* in the concerns of conscience, and his defiance, his scorn of persecution, have not yet quite lost the spirit of their forefathers, although they have mitigated their gloomy austerity and Calvinistic faith. Many of them are at this time the zealous and liberal supporters of the Unitarian congregations in Bolton, Manchester, Leeds, Halifax, &c. The picture of manners is very striking. I doubt if anything has been published which brings so close those rigid men whose lives might be called one long religious service —with whom to fast and pray appeared the great *ends* for which mankind were created. The intensity of their bigotry was frightful, and it was chiefly exerted against their brother sectaries. When they are themselves under persecution, one is disposed to respect and admire them;

but yet it is impossible to forget that they are quite ready to do as much, and more also, to all who differ from them if ever their own turn should come round again. You must see the book. I will try to beg you a copy of my friend James Heywood, one of two wealthy and most worthy brothers, at whose desire and cost this life of their ancient kinsman has been written. Mr. Hunter is in every part thorough master of his subject, and his own portion is full of curious and valuable matter.

This reminds me of *your* Mr. Savage, with whom I had an interesting conference. The spirit of 'Old Mortality' seems to have migrated into his form. There is something in what Carlyle keeps repeating about *real* men, *earnest* men. It is they alone who stamp their image into coming ages. *They!* I should have said *you*.

My 'Addison,' a theme on which there is no room for anything very *earnest*, though I am *real* as far as I go, proceeds at a very leisurely pace, but I hope to be ready for the next book season. I have been fortunate in obtaining much new matter, especially some very agreeable unpublished letters from the lineal representative of his executor Tickell.

Ever your sincere friend,
LUCY AIKIN.

www.ingramcontent.com/pod-product-compliance
Lightning Source LLC
Chambersburg PA
CBHW022111300426
44117CB00007B/671